THE
VOTES
THAT
COUNTED

★ ★ ★

THE
VOTES
THAT
COUNTED

★ ★ ★

HOW THE COURT DECIDED THE
2000 PRESIDENTIAL ELECTION

★ ★ ★

HOWARD GILLMAN

THE UNIVERSITY OF CHICAGO PRESS

CHICAGO & LONDON

HOWARD GILLMAN is associate professor of political
science at the University of Southern California. He is the
author of *The Constitution Besieged,* winner of the Pritchett
Award for best book in public law, and the editor (with
Cornell Clayton) of *Supreme Court Decision-Making,* also
published by the University of Chicago Press.

The University of Chicago Press, Chicago 60637
The University of Chicago Press, Ltd., London
© 2001 by The University of Chicago
All rights reserved. Published 2001
Printed in the United States of America
10 09 08 07 06 05 04 03 02 01   1 2 3 4 5
ISBN: 0-226-29407-2 (CLOTH)

Library of Congress Cataloging-in-Publication Data

Gillman, Howard.
    The votes that counted: how the court decided the
2000 presidential election / Howard Gillman.
        p.   cm.
Includes bibliographical references (p.) and index.
ISBN 0-226-29407-2 (cloth: alk. paper)
1. Contested elections – United States – History.
2. Trials – United States. 3. Contested elections –
Florida – History 4. Trials – Florida. 5. Presidents –
United States – Election – 2000. I. Title.
KF5074.2 .G55 2001
324.973'0929—dc21   2001003077

To Ellen, Arielle, and Danny

Politics in our decision-making process does not exist. By politics, I mean Republicans versus Democrats, is this a popular action or not, will it help certain individuals be elected? . . . Personal ideology or philosophy is a different matter. . . . Judges appointed by different presidents of different political parties may have different views about the interpretation of the law and its relation to the world. . . . I think the Constitution foresees such differences, and results that reflect such differences are perfectly proper.

U.S. Supreme Court Justice Stephen J. Breyer,

"The Work of the Supreme Court" (1998)

CONTENTS

PREFACE

For weeks following election 2000 the world was gripped by the struggles between supporters of Texas governor George W. Bush and Vice President Al Gore over who would become the forty-third president of the United States. It had been many generations since Americans experienced the distinctive drama of a postelection political fight for the presidency; it was also the first time that the events could be witnessed live by the nation twenty-four hours a day. The presidential dispute thus will stand as one of this generation's most memorable political moments. However, what made this saga unique in U.S. history was not the lingering question of who would be the next president. Rather, the election 2000 dispute was different because the outcome was fundamentally shaped, if not completely determined, by judges.

This book is an account of the central and controversial role played by courts in determining the outcome of this extraordinary event. Because litigation and judicial decisions were at the heart of this political struggle and moved it forward step by step until its ultimate resolution in the U.S. Supreme Court, this focus permits a fairly comprehensive narrative of these tumultuous days. More than that, though, I offer an explanation of the behavior of these judges that takes into account the influences of law, partisan preference, judicial ideology, and political context.

Assessing these influences is complicated by the fact that most partisans were divided in their beliefs about many of the topics I will be addressing. For example, many liberals thought that most judges on the Florida Supreme Court acted lawfully (and heroically) and that most judges on the U.S. Supreme Court acted lawlessly (and disgracefully), while conservatives thought precisely the opposite. Throughout my discussion I try to let both sides make their best case for their positions; I also try to clarify those places where the record is clear and those times when judgments are more speculative or questionable.

In the end, though, this analysis serves as a legal and political critique of the actions of the U.S. Supreme Court. This critique is based on some distinctions I will offer between acceptable forms of judicial politics and the illegitimate influence of partisan favoritism. Those who think that all judging is nothing but politics might think this distinction too fastidious, but I hope

I can convince these readers that there was something different about the Supreme Court's actions and that it is possible to recognize this difference while also appreciating the many other ways in which politics routinely influences courts. Others might agree with this distinction in principle but think that I have misidentified the culprit in this case. I hope it is clear that I am mindful of these arguments, and even if there is no agreement in the end I hope that my discussion contributes to a better understanding of this important issue. Others may already suspect that the Supreme Court engaged in partisan decision-making but simply not care since the intervention ended a lingering crisis. I have tried to make it clear to these readers why this came at too high a price for the country and the Court.

While I believe that election 2000 provides a compelling case study of the nature of our judicial institutions, I make no claims that these issues are the most important parts of the story of election 2000. The lack of concern among election officials nationwide about ensuring that votes will count, particularly those cast in poor and minority communities, is the outrage that represents the point of departure for my book, which is about what happened after voters (and others) went to court.

Readers should note that the cutoff date for researching this book was March 12, 2001, exactly three months after the U.S. Supreme Court determined the outcome of this presidential election with their decision in *Bush v. Gore*. Even though it is inevitable that our understanding and perspective will change – both under the pressure of new information and under the pressure of new political contexts – there is, I hope, something useful about establishing a record of our current thinking while memories are fresh and before later commentators begin the inevitable process of reinterpreting our experiences for their own purposes.

ACKNOWLEDGMENTS

One accumulates many debts of gratitude when working alongside so many wonderful friends and colleagues on such an exciting topic in such a compressed period of time.

First, I would like to thank my editor at the University of Chicago Press, John Tryneski. From the beginning (which was the day after the U.S. Supreme Court issued its stay of the final recount), he was an enthusiastic advocate for this book. A great editor has to be smart, patient, encouraging, prodding, and flexible, and John has been all these and more. I am also very grateful for the intelligent and supportive comments offered by the reviewers and for Maia Rigas's expert copyediting.

In seeking a more worldwide perspective of these events I turned to some of the top scholars of comparative judicial politics. While not enough of their responses made it into the final manuscript, I did benefit from advice and information offered by Ran Hirschl, Don Jackson, and Lisa Hilbink.

I had a chance to share some of the book's themes with students and faculty at Mesa State College, and I want to thank Michael Gizzi and his colleagues for the invitation to visit beautiful Grand Junction, Colorado. Fortuitously, around the time I was completing the manuscript, I had a chance to participate in a terrific conference sponsored by the Supreme Court Historical Society on teaching undergraduate constitutional history. The conference gave me a chance to discuss these issues with a very impressive collection of scholars, including Kermit Hall, Les Benedict, Howard Schweber, Herb Johnson, Patricia Minter, Doug Reed, Cornell Clayton, and Wayne Moore. On the final day we had wonderful discussion of *Bush v. Gore,* and the remarks of all the participants gave me a useful, last-minute perspective on how these events were being interpreted by a broader community of historians and social scientists.

As the election 2000 dispute unfolded I benefited enormously from the thoughtful and passionate commentaries shared by scholars around the world on two e-mail discussion lists: the Discussion List for Constitutional Law Professors, known as "conlawprof" and moderated by the tireless Eugene Volokh at UCLA, and "lawcourts-l," which I moderate for the Law and Courts Section of the American Political Science Association. These listservs were a source of first-rate information and analysis as well as a forum for faculty and graduate students who felt the need to engage these events with their colleagues around the country. Admittedly, these discussions made it clear from the beginning that law professors and social scientists were as likely as anyone to react in a partisan way to these developments. But it is also worth noting how frequently norms of collegiality and professionalism allowed for discussions that were more fair-minded, temperate, and probing than what one could find in the mainstream media.

Many scholars were extremely generous about sharing drafts of work in progress and otherwise responding to my requests for feedback or perspective. I am especially grateful to Jack Balkin, Lief Carter, Frank Cross, Don Crowley, Mary Dudziak, Charles Epp, Dennis Hutchinson, Pam Karlan, Mike Klarman, Sandy Levinson, Michael McCann, Julie Novkov, Richard Pildes, Judge Richard A. Posner, Robert Post, Rogers Smith, Jim Stoner, Dalia Tsuk, Mark Tushnet, and Keith Whittington. Their comments helped me work through rough drafts, appreciate new lines of inquiry, provide more appropriate balance, and avoid the embarrassment of overlooked blunders. A few deserve even more effusive thanks. Greg Sisk went above and beyond the call of collegiality by quickly reading and responding to a first draft of the core narrative. Mark Graber read the whole thing and did me the enormous favor of pushing hard on the argument and presentation to make it work better. Kim Scheppele was just a lifesaver down the stretch, sharing her enthusiasm and extensive knowledge of the dispute and going through the manuscript word for word with her usual wit, wisdom, and verve. In exchange for the assistance of all these good folks I gratefully relieve them of any unintended association with the arguments set forth herein or with the errors of fact or judgment that they did their best to eliminate.

I also appreciate the enthusiasm with which my three hundred undergraduate students in my fall 2000 general education course on law and politics were willing to jettison part of our scheduled work so that we could jump into the election controversy. Little did we know when we started that class what a historic opportunity we would have to apply our lessons in judicial politics and the rule of law to the so-called real world.

Many friends and neighbors outside the academic community provided encouragement during the relatively intense and concentrated period of writing this book, and I appreciate their support and understanding when I became temporarily (and I hope uncharacteristically) unavailable to enjoy their good company. I am also grateful to my friends who were eager to kill most of an evening arguing about the election 2000 dispute during a dads-

and-daughters Big Bear weekend. A special thanks to Rob for letting me borrow his laptop computer.

Finally, and most importantly, I must acknowledge my cherished family: my wife Ellen and our beautiful children Arielle and Danny. They understood the importance of the topic and my reasons for writing about it. They sacrificed the most to make it possible, and did it with love, grace, good humor, and just enough patience to let me know that they also wanted me back.

CHRONOLOGY OF EVENTS

November–December 2000

SU	M	T	W	TH	F	SA
5	6	7	8	9	10	11
12	13	14	15	16	17	18
19	20	21	22	23	24	25
26	27	28	29	30	1	2
3	4	5	6	7	8	9
10	11	12	13	14	15	16
17	18	19	20	21	22	23

NOVEMBER 7: Election Day, with George W. Bush (R), governor of Texas, and Al Gore (D), vice president of the United States, as the major party candidates seeking the presidency. Relying on flawed exit polls and early returns, the Associated Press and the television networks declare that Gore has narrowly won the key Electoral College state of Florida. Later that night the media retract their projections, saying that results in Florida are too close to call.

NOVEMBER 8: Early in the morning (EST) the networks project that Bush has won the state of Florida, thus giving him more than the necessary 270 Electoral College votes to become the forty-third president of the United States. This projection is later withdrawn. Later that morning the Bush total in the Florida vote is put at 1,784 votes. Under state law a mandatory machine recount of the state begins. Democratic lawyers in Florida claim that a ballot used in Palm Beach County, known as a "butterfly ballot," is illegal and led thousands of voters who intended to vote for Al Gore inadvertently to vote for conservative Reform Party candidate Pat Buchanan. Lawsuits are filed on behalf of Democratic voters; they are eventually consolidated into the case *Fladell v. Palm Beach County Canvassing Board.*

NOVEMBER 9: Gore seeks hand recounts of the ballots cast in Broward, Miami-Dade, Palm Beach, and Volusia Counties. Florida secretary of state Katherine Harris (R), who campaigned for Bush during the election, announces that counties are forced to report all results no later than one week after an election. Volusia County files a lawsuit requesting a court order that prevents the secretary of state from ignoring results that are completed after that deadline; the case is *McDermott v. Harris.*

NOVEMBER 10: AP reports that, as a result of the mandatory machine re-count, Bush's lead over Gore has dropped to 229 votes.

NOVEMBER 11: The first lawsuit from one of the two campaigns is filed by Bush lawyers in U.S. district court. They request an emergency injunc-tion to halt manual recounts on the grounds that they violate the due process and equal protection clauses of the Fourteenth Amendment. It is the beginning of the case *Siegel v. LePore;* the issues will later be com-bined with the case *Touchston v. McDermott.*

NOVEMBER 12: At 2:00 A.M. the Palm Beach Canvassing Board votes 2 to 1 to authorize a full manual recount of the county. A manual recount con-tinues in Volusia County.

NOVEMBER 13: U.S. District Court Judge Donald Middlebrooks (D) re-fuses to block the ongoing recounts. Secretary of State Harris reminds counties that all counting must be completed and reported by the next day or the results will not be included in the official certification of the election. The Florida Division of Elections issues an advisory opinion to Palm Beach indicating that their authority to conduct manual recounts to correct "errors in vote tabulation" applies only when there is a ma-chine malfunction. Broward County ends its plan for a recount. Miami-Dade has not yet decided whether to conduct one. Judge Terry Lewis (D) holds a hearing in the case *McDermott v. Harris* on whether to allow the secretary of state to ignore late-filed results from counties engaged in recounts.

NOVEMBER 14: State Attorney General Robert A. Butterworth (D), a Gore supporter during the campaign, issues an advisory opinion indicating that recounts are legal if designed to identify voters' choices that may not have been read by a properly functioning vote-counting machine. In re-sponse, Broward reauthorizes its recount. Palm Beach County joins the Volusia lawsuit designed to prevent the secretary of state from ignoring their recount results. Judge Lewis rules that counties must abide by the seven-day deadline but that Secretary of State Harris must use reasonable discretion in deciding whether to reject late-filed returns and cannot merely ignore them. Volusia completes its recount, showing a net gain of ninety-eight votes for Gore. Secretary of State Harris certifies the existing

Bush lead at three hundred, excluding absentee ballots. In light of Judge Lewis's decision she also requests explanations for counties seeking to amend their returns. Miami-Dade decides against proceeding with a full recount.

NOVEMBER 15: Judge Jorge Labarga (R) rules that Palm Beach election officials must review punch-card ballots with merely dimpled chads and consider whether they reveal an intent to vote. Broward, Miami-Dade, and Palm Beach submit explanations to Secretary of State Harris for why they may need to amend their certified returns. The Florida Supreme Court agrees to hear Palm Beach's request for clarification of the dispute between the secretary of state and the attorney general on the legality of recounts; the case is *Palm Beach County Canvassing Board v. Harris*. Bush rejects Gore's offer to end all litigation in exchange for a hand recount of all sixty-seven Florida counties. Harris announces she has reviewed and rejected county requests for more time to turn in the results of manual recounts.

NOVEMBER 16: The Florida Supreme Court refuses to halt recounts in Broward and Palm Beach and also stays Secretary of State Harris's ability to certify the election. Gore lawyers seek an emergency ruling from Judge Lewis to find Harris in contempt of his order on the grounds that her decision to ignore late returns was an abuse of her discretion.

NOVEMBER 17: Judge Lewis upholds Harris's authority to ignore late recount results. The Eleventh Circuit denies the Bush request for an emergency injunction to halt the recounts. The Florida Supreme Court agrees to hear the Gore appeal of Judge Lewis's decision in the case of *Palm Beach County Canvassing Board v. Harris*. Miami-Dade reverses its earlier decision and authorizes a manual recount.

NOVEMBER 18: Secretary of State Harris announces that with the absentee ballots now counted Bush's lead has increased to 930 votes. Republican officials complain that Democrats are attempting to disqualify absentee military ballots. Local Democrats prepare a lawsuit against Seminole County Canvassing Board alleging that election officials unlawfully allowed Republican Party officials to add missing voter information to Republican absentee ballot applications. It is the beginning of the case *Jacobs v. Seminole County Canvassing Board*.

NOVEMBER 19: Gore running mate Senator Joe Lieberman says that absentee military ballots should be given every benefit of the doubt. Republicans intensify complaints that recounts are standardless and arbitrary; Democrats complain that Republicans are stalling and disrupting recount efforts.

NOVEMBER 20: Oral arguments before the Florida Supreme Court are televised. Judge Jorge Labarga rules in *Fladell* that he lacks the authority to order a new election in Palm Beach County.

NOVEMBER 21: The Florida justices rule unanimously in *Palm Beach County Canvassing Board v. Harris* that Secretary of State Harris abused her discretion by not accepting late returns from legally authorized recounts. They extend the deadline for submission of returns to November 26 at 5:00 P.M.

NOVEMBER 22: Bush running mate Dick Cheney is admitted to the hospital with chest pains; it is later admitted to have been a mild heart attack. Soon after an encounter with Republican protestors Miami-Dade cancels its recount, saying it cannot meet the Florida Supreme Court's new deadline. Bush appeals the Florida high court's decision to the U.S. Supreme Court. Judge Labarga refuses to force Palm Beach election officials to treat dimpled chads as votes, saying that it was within their discretion to consider whether the voter's intention could be discerned. Republican leaders of the Florida legislature begin considering a special legislative session to appoint their own electors in the event that Gore is certified the winner as a result of the extended deadline.

NOVEMBER 23: Thanksgiving Day. In *Gore v. Miami-Dade County Canvassing Board* the Florida Supreme Court refuses to compel Miami-Dade to restart its recount.

NOVEMBER 24: The U.S. Supreme Court agrees to hear the Bush appeal of the Florida high court decision, creating the newly named case *Bush v. Palm Beach County Canvassing Board*. Democrats complain that Palm Beach election officials are ignoring too many ballots that reveal an intent to vote for Gore.

NOVEMBER 26: Broward County finishes its recount before the 5:00 P.M. deadline, finding an additional 567 votes for Gore. Palm Beach finishes ninety minutes too late; the extra 215 votes it finds for Gore are not accepted by state election officials. The Florida Elections Canvassing Commission officially certifies that Bush is the victor in the presidential election by 537 votes. Governor Jeb Bush submits to the National Archives a certificate of ascertainment indicating that the state's twenty-five votes in the Electoral College will go to Bush electors.

NOVEMBER 27: Gore contests the certified election results in the courtroom of Judge N. Sanders Sauls (R), initiating the case of *Gore v. Harris*. Gore claims that the official results ignored legal votes in Miami-Dade (160 extra Gore votes identified in abandoned partial recounts plus more than 10,000 undervotes that were never manually reviewed) and Palm Beach (215 votes found by election officials but not reported until after the deadline, plus almost 900 contested ballots that Gore lawyers claimed were inappropriately ruled no votes); it was also alleged that Nassau County illegally removed 51 Gore votes from its initial results. In another courtroom the official complaint is filed in the case *Jacobs v. Seminole County Canvassing Board;* the case is assigned to Judge Nikki Clark (D).

NOVEMBER 28: Judge Sauls announces that the Gore contest trial will not begin until December 2.

NOVEMBER 29: A committee of the Florida legislature recommends a special legislative session to appoint a new slate of Bush electors. Judge Sauls refuses a Gore request to begin recounting disputed ballots even before the trial begins.

NOVEMBER 30: Palm Beach ballots are delivered by truck to Judge Sauls's courthouse.

DECEMBER 1: The U.S. Supreme Court hears oral arguments in *Bush v. Palm Beach County Canvassing Board;* for the first time in history recordings of the arguments are immediately released and broadcast nationwide. The Florida Supreme Court upholds Judge Labarga's decision in *Fladell,* ending the butterfly ballot case, and refuses a Gore request to force Judge Sauls to order an immediate recount of disputed ballots. Local Democrats file a lawsuit accusing Martin County election officials of mishandling Republican absentee ballot applications; the case, *Taylor v. Martin County Canvassing Board,* is almost identical to the already filed *Jacobs* case. It is assigned to Judge Terry Lewis.

DECEMBER 2–3: Testimony and arguments are heard by Judge Sauls in the Gore election contest.

DECEMBER 4: In a unanimous decision in *Bush v. Palm Beach County Canvassing Board* the U.S. Supreme Court vacates the Florida Supreme Court decision extending the certification deadline and remands the case back to the state justices. Expressing concerns about Article II, Section 1 of the Constitution, which authorizes state legislatures to choose the manner of appointing presidential electors, and 3 U.S.C. § 5, which instructs states to resolve election disputes in accordance with the laws that were in place before Election Day, the Washington justices asked the state justices to clarify whether their decision was based exclusively on the Florida statutes or whether it might also be based on elements of Florida law that were not passed by the legislature, such as the Florida

Constitution or the court's own "equitable" powers. Back in Florida, Judge Sauls rules against Gore on all elements of his election contest, and the case is immediately appealed to the Florida Supreme Court.

DECEMBER 5: The Eleventh Circuit Court of Appeals in Atlanta hears Bush's request to stop further manual recounts.

DECEMBER 6: In an 8 to 4 vote in the cases *Siegel v. LePore* and *Touchston v. McDermott*, a bipartisan majority of the Eleventh Circuit rejects Bush's claim that manual recounts in Florida violate the due process and equal protection clauses of the Constitution. Back in Florida, trials begin in the courtrooms of Judges Lewis and Clark in the *Jacobs* and *Taylor* cases, respectively, on the question of whether 25,000 absentee ballots should be disqualified. Republican leaders of the Florida legislature call for a special session on December 8.

DECEMBER 7: *Gore v. Harris* oral arguments before the Florida Supreme Court are televised.

DECEMBER 8: Judges Lewis and Clark rule in the *Jacobs* and *Taylor* cases that the improprieties in the Republican treatment of absentee ballot applications do not justify the disqualification of absentee ballots in Seminole and Martin Counties. Soon thereafter, the Florida Supreme Court, in a 4 to 3 vote, rules in favor of Gore in *Gore v. Harris* and orders an immediate commencement of a statewide recount of all previously uninspected undervotes; the court also orders an adjustment in the certified election results, giving Gore an additional 383 votes (215 from Palm Beach and 168 that Miami-Dade had previously identified for Gore in an unfinished recount), thus cutting the Bush lead to 154 votes. Bush lawyers immediately appeal to the Eleventh Circuit and the U.S. Supreme Court. That evening, Judge Lewis holds hearing on the process that will be used in completing the statewide recount.

DECEMBER 9: Recounts begin in the morning. The Eleventh Circuit denies Bush's appeal. In a 5 to 4 vote, the U.S. Supreme Court issues an emergency injunction halting the recounts, with Justice Antonin Scalia explaining in a concurring opinion in *Bush v. Gore* that Bush might suffer irreparable harm if flawed recounts were allowed to continue. U.S. District Court Judge Maurice Paul (R) rules in the case *Harris v. Florida Elections Canvassing Commission* that it was not a violation of Article II, Section 1 for Florida to accept absentee ballots after Election Day even though Florida statutes impose this deadline.

DECEMBER 11: The Supreme Court hears oral arguments in the case *Bush v. Gore* and again releases audio recordings. In response to the earlier remand from the U.S. Supreme Court, the Florida Supreme Court issues its second opinion in *Palm Beach County Canvassing Board v. Harris;* over the dissent of Chief Justice Wells, the state justices reiterate that their decision was based on their interpretation of the Florida election statutes. A three-judge panel of the Eleventh Circuit Court of Appeals (all Republican) upholds Judge Paul's decision in *Harris v. Florida Elections Canvassing Commission.*

DECEMBER 12: The Florida House of Representatives approves a resolution to appoint twenty-five Bush electors; the state senate prepares to pass similar legislation the follow day. The Florida Supreme Court upholds the decisions of Judges Lewis and Clark in *Jacobs* and *Taylor.* At 10:00 P.M. the U.S. Supreme Court distributes its decision in *Bush v. Gore.* In a 5 to 4 vote the Court rules that the manual recounts authorized by the Florida Supreme Court violate the equal protection clause of the Constitution because the standard for reviewing ballots, which focused on discerning "the intent of the voter," allowed for too much variation in the way that identical ballots might be evaluated. While this problem was potentially correctable with a clearer standard, the majority rules that Florida seemed to want to take advantage of the "safe harbor" provision of 3 U.S.C. § 5 by resolving all election disputes before the end of the day on December 12, and this meant that insufficient time remained for a proper recount. The case is remanded back to the Florida Supreme Court. Three judges in the majority write separately to argue that the Florida Supreme Court has misread Florida law in violation of Article II, Section 1 of the U.S. Constitution. The four dissenters argue that the U.S. Supreme Court should never have intervened in a dispute that was more properly resolved in the state and by the U.S. Congress.

DECEMBER 13: Al Gore concedes the election to George W. Bush. Governor Jeb Bush informs the National Archives that the contest over the Florida electors had been "finally determined in favor of Governor George W. Bush" by the U.S. Supreme Court and that the state should thus obtain the benefit of the "safe harbor" provision of 3 U.S.C. § 5.

POSTSCRIPT

DECEMBER 14: The Florida Supreme Court dismisses the case that the U.S. Supreme Court had remanded back to them, ruling in *Gore v. Harris* that the existing State of Florida law did not provide the elements necessary to resolve the disputed issues. A final opinion is handed down eight days later.

DECEMBER 18: The Electoral College meets. Bush receives 271 votes; Gore, 266.

JANUARY 6, 2001: A joint session of Congress, presided over by Vice President Al Gore, counts the Electoral College votes. Objections to Florida's votes by members of the Congressional Black Caucus do not attract the necessary support from a senator and are set aside by the presiding officer. At 2:50 P.M., Vice President Gore officially announces that the Texas governor has received a majority of the votes of the Electoral College.

JANUARY 20, 2001: Governor George W. Bush of Texas takes the oath of office as the forty-third president of the United States.

INTRODUCTION

COURTS AND THE POLITICAL
CHALLENGE OF ELECTION 2000

*None are more conscious of the vital limits on judicial authority
than are the members of this Court, and none stand more in admiration of
the Constitution's design to leave the selection of the President to the people,
through their legislatures, and to the political sphere. When contending
parties invoke the process of the courts, however, it becomes our unsought
responsibility to resolve the federal and constitutional issues the
judicial system has been forced to confront.*

Bush v. Gore (2000), per curiam opinion

*Although we may never know with complete certainty
the identity of the winner of this year's Presidential election,
the identity of the loser is perfectly clear. It is the Nation's confidence
in the judge as an impartial guardian of the rule of law.*

Bush v. Gore (2000), Justice John Paul Stevens, dissenting

U.S. courts have been at the center of many high-stakes political disputes. But even seasoned court-watchers were transfixed at the end of 2000 when the outcome of a presidential election was thrown into one courtroom after another.

The postelection struggle between Republican governor George W. Bush of Texas and Democratic vice president Al Gore of Tennessee to become president of the United States unfolded like a ridiculously implausible hypothetical question on a college examination designed to test our faith in courts. The outcome in the key Electoral College battleground state of Florida was unbelievably close – initially a matter of a few thousand votes, and then a few hundred – and there were apparent problems with confusing ballots, error-prone vote-counting machines, and untallied votes. Claims were made that some of these problems violated Florida election law, and lawsuits were filed in state courts. Efforts were also made to have certain ballots manually recounted, and lawsuits were filed in federal courts to stop that from happening. Additional lawsuits were filed in state courts when state election officials attempted to certify the Florida election results without including the results of recounts. And this was only the beginning.

In this book, I offer an explanation and an assessment of how courts responded to the legal and political challenges associated with this historic presidential election dispute. The explanation requires attention not only to the law but also to judicial politics – the various ways in which judicial ideologies, partisan preferences, public opinion, and larger political and historical contexts shape how judges view the law and decide cases. Much of this introduction reviews some of what we know about judicial politics in ordinary circumstances. This should set the stage for an extended review of how the courts responded to these extraordinary circumstances, when the political pressures to act injudiciously were as enormous as the countervailing expectations for good faith judging.

As I will argue in my final chapter, most of the courts involved in the election 2000 dispute resisted the pressures and met our expectations. The decisions of these judges on important questions about election law and (by extension) the workings of American democracy are historic case studies of the legal and political elements that create something that looks like the rule of law. However, even more compelling and, perhaps, more important to discuss, are those examples in which judges appeared to risk their reputations, and maybe even the authority of their institutions, by giving in to the pressures for partisan justice. Election 2000 provides a few suspects, but the most notorious are, of course, the justices of the Florida and U.S. Supreme Courts.

It would be easy to treat these battling supreme courts as equivalent examples of the influence of political preference on judicial decision-making. After all, the Florida Supreme Court, controlled by Democrats, handed down some decisions that proved helpful to Al Gore, and the Republican-controlled U.S. Supreme Court handed down decisions that protected Bush's lead and then ensured his victory. But before reaching this conclusion, and before embracing the irredeemable view of judicial politics implied by it, we should review more carefully the records of these courts and the legal and political justifications offered for their decisions. This book lays out this record. In the end, I will argue that the behavior of these high courts is not equivalent, and that there is only one court that acted in ways that were uniquely partisan and outside what should be considered the acceptable boundaries of judicial power. It was the court that decided the outcome of the 2000 presidential election.

It is not that unusual for judges to become involved in election disputes when results are very close and questions are raised about the legality of the process.[1] But presidential elections have been a different matter. The United States has held such elections for 212 years, and not one was ever previously resolved by a court.[2] This made perfect sense under our constitutional design, which gave states the responsibility to appoint electors to the Electoral College – either by direct action of the state legislature or, if they so chose, in an election that would be run in accordance with state election laws – and Congress the authority to count the electors' votes and announce the result. If a problem arose, it was generally assumed that Congress would resolve it, for better or worse, often by facilitating overt political bargains among competing political factions.[3]

Prior to election 2000, the most conspicuous attempt at a "judicious" resolution of a disputed presidential election was the 1876 contest between Rutherford B. Hayes, the Republican governor of Ohio, and Democrat Samuel J. Tilden, the Democratic governor of New York. Eerie parallels exist between that controversy and the 2000 dispute. In the 1876 presidential election, the Electoral College vote was so close that problems with the outcomes in a few key states were enough to hold up the final result.[4] The Democratic candidate had reason to believe that he had won the national popular vote as well as the votes in the states he needed in order to win the Electoral College. However, the Republic candidate used political operatives in key states, including Florida, to have needed electors delivered to him without regard to alleged voting irregularities. Democrats insisted that the election results announced by Republican operatives were simply wrong – an attempt to steal the election by refusing to count all legitimate ballots – and so they arranged for the appointment of their own slate of Tilden electors.[5] The votes of two competing slates of electors were sent to the Congress. As in 2000, different political parties controlled the House of Representative and the Senate.[6]

Rather than hand this dispute over to the judiciary – which would have struck most officeholders back then as absurd and even unconstitutional – congressional leaders established a bipartisan electoral commission to determine which slates of electors Congress should count. Five members of the commission were appointed by the Democratic House of Representatives (three Democrats and two Republicans), five were appointed by the Republican Senate (three Republicans and two Democrats), and then five U.S. Supreme Court justices were asked to participate – two Democrats (Nathan Clifford and Stephen Field), two Republicans (Samuel Miller and William Strong), and a fifth justice to be chosen by the other four justices (Justice Joseph Bradley, a Republican).

There was some hope that the members of this commission might be able to transcend their partisan divisions, but in the end they decided on a strict party-line vote (8 to 7) to give all the disputed electoral votes to Hayes – despite the fact that state judges in Florida had ruled in favor of the Democratic candidate.[7] These nineteen votes gave Hayes a bare majority in the Electoral College. Congressional Democrats eventually agreed to accept a Hayes presidency after Republicans agreed to stop further efforts at so-called Reconstruction, which essentially meant ending the federal government's short-lived post–Civil War commitment to black civil rights.[8]

In the wake of the Hayes-Tilden election, Congress spent several years debating how to create a more regular process for handling these sorts of controversies. Before long they passed the Electoral Count Act of 1887. It made no provision for the participation of an electoral commission or any other national tribunal. Instead, state governments were encouraged to resolve controversies on their own. The promise was that if the states could clean up all disputes within six days of the scheduled Electoral College vote – "by judicial or other methods or procedures" that were based on "laws enacted prior to the day fixed for the appointment of the electors" – then Congress would not challenge their electoral votes.[9] If there was still a controversy, and more than one slate of electors ended up in Congress, then the slate of electors that was "certified by the executive of the State" would be counted, unless both houses of Congress decided differently.[10] If for some reason this did not provide a clear standard for resolving the election (perhaps because controversy remained over which slate of electors was properly certified by the chief executive of the state) then the dispute would presumably stay in the two houses of Congress until a decision could be reached.

Thus, our common experiences, combined with the history of presidential election disputes and the processes laid out in existing federal law, gave us good reasons to assume that judges, particularly federal judges, were unlikely ever to play a significant role in the election of a president – at least not without an explicit, bipartisan invitation from Congress for assistance in the performance of its constitutional responsibilities.[11]

It was against this backdrop that the country reacted to the courtroom battles surrounding the 2000 presidential election. Because of the razor-thin margin of difference in the vote totals any court decision that would result in the recounting of a few more votes or the disqualification of a handful of votes could mean the difference between President Bush and President Gore. Thus, courts became the eye of a political storm as well as the objects of an extensive and divisive debate on the idea of "the judge as an impartial guardian of the rule of law." This theme was articulated by U.S. Supreme Court Justice John Paul Stevens during the culminating event of this dispute, when an ideologically divided Supreme Court handed down its decision in the aptly named case *Bush v. Gore.* In that decision, the five most conservative justices, ending what would have otherwise been an ongoing political dispute, used a number of unprecedented constitutional arguments as a basis for issuing a ruling that effectively handed the presidency to Bush. This was done over the objections of the four less conservative justices, who insisted that the Court had no business interfering in a ballot recount that may have shown that Gore had actually won the popular vote in Florida and had thus earned the presidency.

While the decision brought some relief to an increasingly weary public, the outcome was dispiriting to those who were hopeful that the justices could avoid a result that appeared so overtly political. Many commentators predicted that the decision would have a devastating effect on the Court's reputation and authority. At the same time, there were those who rushed to defend the Court's integrity by claiming, not just that the majority's legal arguments were sound, but that they acted appropriately to stop a politically biased state supreme court from stealing an election for its favorite candidate. In other words, the very act that critics claimed was an example of illegitimate judicial activism was seen by supporters as a statesmanlike effort to put an end to illegitimate judicial activism.

As everyone knew at the time, the question of whether judicial power reflected partisan considerations is an obvious starting point for any discussion of the role of courts in the election 2000 dispute. Still, this question is only the beginning of an analysis of the judicial politics surrounding this event. As a way of getting some perspective on whether these judges were merely coping as best they could with an "unsought responsibility" or were corrupted by the special pressures of this high-stakes struggle, it may useful to review what we know about judicial politics in more ordinary circumstances.

JUDICIAL POLITICS, VALUE VOTING, AND EXPECTATIONS OF GOOD FAITH JUSTICE

We need not begin this examination with a mock naiveté about judges, so that we can later declare, in the spirit of Claude Rains's Captain Louis Renault, to be shocked, shocked when we discover that courts are affected by politics.[12] There may have been a time in U.S. history when some judges and law professors asserted that courts did little more than mechanically apply the law.[13] But it has always been hard to find people who have accepted such inflated claims. It is no surprise, then, that the political inclinations of judges and the policy significance of judicial decisions have been a routine part of political debate and even presidential elections.[14] In the 2000 presidential election, candidate Al Gore tried to mobilize Democratic voters by reminding them of George W. Bush's promise to appoint judges in the mold of conservative U.S. Supreme Court Justice Antonin Scalia. Candidates make such promises (and issue such warnings) because their constituents recognize that judging is inevitably shaped by the decision-maker's values, personal experiences, and political ideology. Most people would not be surprised by the results of an extensive social science literature that conclusively demonstrates that judges who take liberal or conservative positions in some cases also tend to take liberal or conservative positions in other cases that raise issues over which ideologues disagree.[15]

Moreover, most people would not be surprised to learn that the general pattern of judicial decisions tends to reflect the background political consensus – and political conflict – that exist in the political system at any given time. It was common during the election crisis for scholars to refer to the famous early-twentieth-century quip of Finley Peter Dunne's fictional Chicago bartender Mr. Dooley – that "th' supreme coort follows th' iliction returns" – to ask whether we had reached a point where the election returns would follow the Supreme Court. But in toying with this quip we should not lose sight of its homespun lesson. Judges tend to reflect the evolving views and disagreements of the communities they govern and, in particular, the views and disagreements of those responsible for their election or appointment.[16] In other words, "value-voting" by judges "is not merely the arbitrary expression of a justice's idiosyncratic views [but rather] is the expression and vindication of those political views deliberately 'planted' on" courts by voters or policy-conscious legislators, governors, and presidents.[17] Even if the professional socialization of judges may give them a distinct perspective on how they should do their job, this training does not come with special filters that immunize them from their political context.

Still, to say that judging is influenced by certain kinds of political considerations is not to say that we expect judges to act like conventional politicians.[18] Even though we know that judges are often appointed or recruited because they are partisan activists and sometimes remain involved in politics even after they reach the bench,[19] there is still a realistic expectation that judges will not decide cases based on the political affiliation of the litigants who come before them. Even political scientists who have devoted their careers to proving that judges are not neutral interpreters of law emphasize that judicial politics, when it shows up, is typically a form of relatively consistent ideological policymaking rather than mere partisan favoritism – a form of "high" politics rather than "low" politics, if you will. This distinction is important, because ideological influences on judicial decisions are properly considered an inevitable and legitimate aspect of "good faith" judging while mere partisan favoritism is treated as illegitimate and worthy of broad condemnation (or worse).[20] When researchers have examined whether judges demonstrate partisan preferences in cases that present explicitly partisan issues, such as the approval of reapportionment plans, they have found that the effects are not strong and do not undermine the more general portrait of an institution that generally avoids overtly partisan decision-making.[21] There are activities unrelated to adjudication in which we can see judges thinking about the interests of a preferred party; for example, federal judges frequently retire at a time when the presidency is controlled by a member of their political party.[22] But partisanship in the resolution of cases, unrelated to a principle or policy that a judge would be willing to defend on its own terms (that is, apart from specific litigants of a given case), is not part of anyone's list of everyday occurrences or acceptable judicial practices. Politicians and voters plant certain judges on the bench because they expect them to vote their values, not because they expect them to vote the party line.[23]

Of course, judges sometimes face political pressures to act as loyal party members (rather than as judges) and toe that line. However, setting aside what are supposed to be a judge's ethical obligations, there is at least one good political reason to think that judges will typically resist those pressures, and it has to do with their presumptive self-interest in protecting their own authority and legitimacy. In the words of one leading scholar of judicial politics, if courts are to effectively perform their distinctive political responsibilities they "need to persuade the parties that judges and laws they have not chosen nonetheless constitute a genuine, neutral third.[party]."[24] A recent study of the creation of constitutional courts in post-Communist Europe concludes that if these young courts "are to survive and if their actions are to command respect and obedience, they must somehow persuade their respective society . . . that their decisions are based not on partisan political considerations but on neutral, objective law, even when the issue in dispute obviously has very contentious political origins and consequences."[25] Closer to home, in the early years of the American Republic, the power and authority of the Supreme Court were placed at risk when the Court was perceived to have been too closely associated with the interests of a favored political party. What allowed the Court to survive these threats (associated in particular with the Jeffersonian-led impeachment trial of the highly partisan Federalist justice Samuel Chase) were a series of reassuring decisions that convinced worried partisans that the Court would not become an extension of any particular partisan interest.[26] When the Court does take its cue from larger partisan agendas or from the preferences of "the dominant national alliance,"[27] its typical practice is to transform these preferences into *law* – as with the Rehnquist Court's innovative federalism jurisprudence, which constitutionalized the preferences of many post-Reagan conservatives for more limited national government. It has not been the Court's typical practice to win political support by aligning itself with one party and then engaging in useful ad hoc decision-making.

Moreover, one of the characteristics of law or "the rule of law" – either as an accurate description of how a political system actually works or as a myth designed to make a system seem more legitimate – is the promise that power will be exercised impersonally in accordance with general standards. Even critical legal scholars who are skeptical of law's ability ever to be neutral or apolitical understand that if "the law is evidently partial and unjust, then it will mask nothing, legitimize nothing" since "the essential precondition for the effectiveness of law, in its function as ideology, is that it shall display an independence from gross manipulation."[28] In general, "while people express skepticism about the fairness of legal institutions, they appear to be committed to both the desirability and possibility of realizing legal ideals of equal and fair treatment,"[29] and they view their legal systems as legitimate when they think decision-makers are generally fair, impartial, and trustworthy.[30] Almost all judges work under rules that require them to disqualify themselves "in any proceeding in which [their] impartiality might reasonably be questioned."[31] In legal iconography this promise is represented by depicting the figure of Justice as blindfolded; the idea is also engraved above the entrance to the Supreme Court with the words "equal justice under law."

This is not to say that judges never engage in overtly political decision-making; we can find plenty such examples, even in the history of the Supreme Court.[32] The point is that it is part of the conventional political calculations of judges, including Supreme Court justices, to take into account the reputation or public perception of their institution. As the Supreme Court political historian Robert McCloskey once noted,

> The Court's claim on the American mind derives from the myth of an impartial, judicious tribunal whose duty it is to preserve our sense of continuity with the fundamental law. . . . [T]hough the judges do enter this realm of policy-making, they enter with their robes on, and they can never (or at any rate seldom) take them off; they are both empowered and restricted by their "courtly" attributes. . . . The judges have usually known what students have sometimes not known – that their tribunal must be a court, as well as seem one, if it is to retain its power. The idea of fundamental law as a force in its own right, distinguishable from today's popular will, can only be maintained by a pattern of Court behavior that emphasizes the separation.[33]

In general, because the justices' actions typically do not challenge public expectations about good faith judging, the views of the general public about the Court reflect a general "reservoir of good will," and this reservoir is deeper than those for other political institutions.[34] As former justice (later chief justice) Charles Evans Hughes wrote in 1928, the Court's high standing in public confidence is due "to the impartial manner in which the Court addresses itself to its never-ending task" and to its "freedom from political entanglements."[35] A more recent statement came from Justices Sandra Day O'Connor, Anthony Kennedy, and David Souter in the course of explaining their decision in *Planned Parenthood of Southeastern Pennsylvania v. Casey* to uphold the legality of abortion, despite pressures on these Republican appointees to overturn *Roe v. Wade*: in their judgment, the Court maintains its public support by "making legally principled decisions under circumstances in which their principled character is sufficiently plausible to be accepted by the Nation."

This reservoir of good will is sometimes referred to as the judiciary's "political capital." This, of course, implies that there may be times when judges choose to tap into some of that good will and invest in a decision that may seem inconsistent with people's expectations about appropriate judicial decision-making. Courts that are in the early stages of establishing their authority may be quite constrained in their ability to engage in this course of conduct; however, judges on more established courts (such as the U.S. Supreme Court), with presumably larger capital reserves, may feel as though they can afford to expend some of their legitimacy if they are sufficiently motivated. If this happens, and a court "becomes politicized or perceived as such, it risks cutting itself off from its natural reservoir of goodwill and may become reliant for basic institutional support on those who profit from its policies. This is a risky position for any institution to adopt."[36]

THE CHALLENGE FACING COURTS
IN THE ELECTION 2000 DISPUTES

Given that courts are fully integrated into larger structures of power, judicial decision-making can be never be considered apolitical or truly impartial. Still, the activity of judging does not normally "become politicized" in the sense in a way that threatens the judiciary's "natural reservoir of goodwill." A brief review of the reasons for this in routine cases may provide a useful perspective on the special challenges associated with the election 2000 dispute.

At the trial court level, virtually all cases are eventually resolved through an agreement reached by the contending parties – via plea bargaining in criminal cases and settlements in civil cases – and so concerns about an improper political resolution by a judge do not even come up.[37] Most cases are fairly routine (to the courtroom professionals if not to the parties) and give judges little reason to even consider political manipulation.[38] Even if there are worries about judicial bias, many lawyers who are part of close-knit courthouse "work groups" are not in a position to question the integrity of the judges they will be facing on a regular basis.[39] Maybe most important, the general public usually pays no attention, and so there is little public scrutiny of the question of bias. There is also some evidence that when cases draw special public attention judges often discard a more casual demeanor in favor of styles and practices that seem more formal and legalistic.[40] This is not always true; sometimes judges play to the mob, as happened throughout much of the twentieth century in most criminal trials in Southern courtrooms involving black defendants or victims. But more often than not, when people are watching, judges start acting as they think people expect them to act.[41]

As with most trial court cases, most decisions by appellate judges do not raise issues that divide partisans or ideologues, and so it is typically easy for these judges to insist that political calculations had nothing to do with the result.[42] As a result, in a substantial majority of cases decided by intermediate courts of appeal either there is no dissent or the patterns of dissent do not always follow predictable political divisions.[43] Even in the U.S. Supreme Court, where ideological voting is most obvious, it is not that common for issues to divide the justices into neat political camps. For example, throughout the 1990s, around 40 percent of Court opinions were unanimous, while around 15 percent ended up with the justices divided down the middle by one vote.[44] The justices also have a history in politically sensitive cases of working hard to "marshal" a near-unanimous Court. For example, from 1954 through 1970, the justices successfully maintained a united front in cases involving desegregation;[45] this same self-conscious effort to transcend political differences was evident in the Watergate tapes case.[46] When the Rehnquist Court in *Clinton v. Jones* (1997) addressed the politically sensitive question of whether standing presidents should be immune from civil lawsuits, the justices voted unanimously to allow the Paula Jones lawsuit to continue. Finally, even in the few cases in which the justices do divide into opposing political camps, it is still generally accepted that this reflects different ideological views of the Constitution rather than illegitimate political calculations.

If these practices and circumstances help us see how judges typically avoid accusations of improper favoritism and maintain reputations for impartiality, then it should be clear why the judges in the election 2000 dispute faced special challenges.

As it turned out, the specific legal questions that arose in the state courts were unprecedented, and so there was no established procedure to which judges could refer to as neutral justification for a decision. There were written laws addressing some of these questions, but many of them were ambiguous, poorly written, or even contradictory; in any event, the meaning of these statutes was a matter of continuing controversy. Even when there seemed to be very clear precedents – for example, the precedents for federal courts that balloting and vote-counting procedures were matters to be handled by the states without federal interference or that disputes over presidential elections would be resolved by the Congress – the lawyers had enormous incentives to proffer innovative lines of argument, and their stature, and the stature of their clients, allowed interested judges to take these arguments more seriously than would normally be the case when lawyers try to get fancy with judges.

Also, at various times during this process, representatives of both campaigns, but in particular those of George W. Bush,[47] were willing publicly to question the good faith of judges who handed down adverse decisions. These accusations had more resonance than they might in other cases because it was almost always plausible to claim that a judge was motivated by an illegitimate political bias and not merely by a disagreeable ideology.[48] Moreover, given assumptions about the importance of fast-approaching deadlines, these judges often faced enormous time constraints in reaching decisions, and this may have undermined opportunities for deliberation and judicial bargaining across partisan lines. For example, *Bush v. Gore* was the fastest modern U.S. Supreme Court decision handed down on the merits of an argued case, coming only three days after the justices agreed to hear it.[49] By contrast, Chief Justice Earl Warren lobbied Justice Stanley Reed for months to talk him out of issuing a dissent in *Brown v. Board of Education.*

Finally, the U.S. Supreme Court was up against one political challenge that was not faced by other courts. Of all the judges involved in the election dispute, these justices were the only ones who had not only an abstract political bias in favor of one candidate but also a direct personal stake in the outcome. After all, the president that the Court might help choose would, in turn, choose future justices. At a personal level this affected the well-being of justices who might have been waiting for the election of a Republican president so that they could retire from the Court without giving their seat to a Democratic appointee. More generally, the justices also understood that the election outcome could have a dramatic impact on the direction of the Court's decision-making and its future role in the political system, especially in light of the range of important legal issues on which this particular Court was closely divided along ideological lines. In other words, election 2000 would most likely determine which wing of the Court would control its policy-making for years or even decades to come.

THE PLAN OF THE BOOK

The five chapters that follow provide a chronological account of the days following Election Day 2000 through the aftermath of the court decision that brought an end to the dispute over the Florida electors. The narrative focuses on all the noteworthy litigation and key decisions – from the state and federal trial courts through the courts of appeal to the dueling high courts.

Chapter 1 sets the stage by examining how the presidential election ended up in courts during the first ten days after the election. I review how the use of courts by each of the campaigns was part of a strategic assessment of the larger political context in Florida and Washington, including the presumed party loyalties of other key decision-makers. I review how the political interests of each campaign were translated into a set of specific legal questions that became the basis for the court battles. These legal questions, while forged by the campaigns in their self-interested pursuit of the presidency, also raise interesting and sometimes disturbing questions about the structure of U.S. elections and the workings of the American democracy. The general reader will be happy to know that these legal debates are surprisingly accessible, which is important given that our assessment of these judges will at times depend on our own sense of whether they took legally plausible positions when they decided these cases. However, the election 2000 dispute cannot be understood simply with reference to the law. If it is true that, "in a nutshell, judges' decisions are a function of what they prefer to do, tempered by what they think they ought to do, but constrained by what they perceive is feasible to do,"[50] then an ongoing sensitivity to changing political pressures and contexts during these thirty-six days also provides an insight into the behavior of these judges. Thus, throughout the book I also highlight the actions of other decisions-makers and the views expressed by the campaigns, the press, and legal commentators. Keeping track of the views of this latter group also helps protect us against misleading attempts after the fact to "normalize" arguments that, at the time, were considered unimpressive (or even ridiculed).

In chapter 2, I focus on developments over the next week, as the Florida Supreme Court addressed the question of whether to allow continued recounts even after the secretary of state insisted that the deadline for reporting results had passed. Careful attention is given to the arguments put forward by the campaigns in legal briefs and oral arguments before the justices. Putting this material into the record helps us remember how fluid and strategic these legal debates were, which is a perspective that might otherwise get lost if we focus merely on the presentation of the issues found in final court opinions. However, surrounding these legal debates were ongoing political debates over the accuracy of recounts, the importance of deadlines, and the fairness of judges. Moreover, this phase of the conflict was a time when the strategic setting would rapidly change in unexpected ways, as local canvassing boards reacted to conflicting legal advice, changing deadlines, and stepped-up demonstrations by partisans seeking to influence their decisions. The chapter ends with the Florida court's controversial decision allowing recounts under an extended deadline and the political firestorm that was ignited by that decision.

Chapter 3 picks up the story from November 24 through December 4, starting with the U.S. Supreme Court's surprising intervention into this state election dispute and ending with its decision in *Bush v. Palm Beach County Canvassing Board.* The innovative legal arguments in support of this decision are carefully reviewed through an analysis of the briefs and an overview of the reactions of legal experts. Given the Court's eventual decision in this case, a close look at the dramatic oral arguments is also essential to understanding the different ways in which the justices were evaluating these arguments. However, while the justices worked toward their compromise unanimous ruling, developments in Florida threatened to make this historic decision irrelevant, as Bush was certified the official winner, Gore initiated his "contest" to those official results, and new lawsuits posed serious new threats to Bush's nominal victory.

Chapter 4 starts with Gore's loss in the trial court and his final appeal to the Florida Supreme Court. As those justices prepared to address a new set of legal issues, other courts made extremely important decisions in unrelated cases. The decision of the Republican-controlled federal court of appeals on the Bush campaign's equal protection challenge to the Florida recount was especially important in light of the eventual role that this claim would play in the ultimate resolution of this dispute. At the same time, two Democratic trial judges in Tallahassee held the American presidency in their hands as they presided over trials on the question of whether to throw out thousands of mostly Republican absentee ballots. The chapter ends with the surprising decision by a deeply divided Florida Supreme Court to start a last-minute statewide recount. Chapter 5 starts on December 9 with the U.S. Supreme Court's decision to immediately halt that recount, looks carefully at another dramatic oral argument before the Washington justices, reviews the efforts of other courts to clear the stage for a final resolution of the election dispute, and continues through to the aftermath of the Supreme Court's astonishing decision in *Bush v. Gore.*

In the final chapter, I review the overall record of these courts, starting with the question of whether the pressures of the election controversy led judges to offer partisan justice. It turns out that the record is more mixed than one might expect if one assumed that judging was merely a disguised form of conventional politics; this is one of the more interesting and promising aspects of this event, and it is a useful starting point for the rest of the analysis. However, special attention is given to the battling supreme courts, given that their actions prompted the most serious accusations from those decrying partisan justice.

While I have tried to make the narrative and analysis comprehensive and balanced, there is almost no point in reviewing this event unless one is willing to engage the ultimate question of whether these judges did justice to our expectations of how courts should act.[51] Thus, the book builds toward a critique of the Supreme Court's intervention, which I argue should be considered an unacceptable partisan short-circuiting of a messy but established constitutional process for resolving disputes over presidential elections. I say this knowing full well that the law is an arena of political contest, that normal Supreme Court decision-making is also a form of politics (which is sometimes even more outrageous than what occurred here), that Supreme Court justices sometimes have more to worry about than the banalities of legal interpretation, that there are political explanations as to why the majority would conclude that it could take this unprecedented step, and that there are important legal and political defenses offered on behalf of the Court by people of good will. Those points will be reviewed and addressed.

But before we are in a position to begin that assessment we have quite a story to review.

★ ★ ★

1

WHO WON?

THE ELECTION GOES TO COURT

Stay with us, we're about to take you on an exciting and bumpy ride.
NBC News anchor Tom Brokaw,
election night, Nov. 7, 2000[1]

Everyone knew it was going to be close. For weeks the two major-party candidates for president, Republican governor George W. Bush of Texas and Democratic vice president Al Gore, had been running neck and neck in national polls. Most showed Bush ahead by a few percentage points; two polls had Gore ahead; all were within the statistical margin of error. The cover of *Newsweek* magazine's pre-election special issue featured a single-word headline: "Cliffhanger."[2] More important than these national opinion polls, however, were polls showing how close the vote would be in the Electoral College. The candidates had comfortable leads in many states, but too many states were just too close to call, and neither candidate had a predictable majority of these crucial votes. During the weekend before the election most press accounts assumed that the presidency would be decided in what some called a "trifecta" of "battleground" states – Pennsylvania, Michigan, and Florida. Most commentators agreed that if Gore could win these states he would most likely win the election.[3]

The fact that Florida made the list at all was a bit of a surprise and a slight embarrassment to the Republicans. The governor of Florida was Jeb Bush, the younger brother of the presidential candidate. During the election season he had promised that he would "deliver Florida" for his brother, but a number of Republicans quietly complained that he did not campaign hard enough. Still, the state did not go neglected by the Gore and Bush campaigns. They spent more than $20 million in paid television advertising in that state alone, and in the closing days of the election both campaigns made sure that they made Florida feel special. George W. Bush visited Tampa and West Palm Beach the Sunday before the election. Al Gore made Florida the culminating stop of his campaign. At 1:00 A.M. on Election Day he was cajoling thousands of people at a celebrity-filled rally in Miami's South Beach; at 4:00 A.M. he was sitting with nurses at a cancer center in Tampa; and less than two hours later he was exhorting a Cuban American crowd in Tampa to turn out for him. It was the end of thirty-three nonstop hours of campaigning. Gore was fighting for every vote.[4]

The standard media ritual on presidential election day is for the broadcast networks to portray the election results as an unfolding drama, a race to the magic number of 270 Electoral College votes. A key feature of the ritual is for networks to wait until the polls closed in a given time zone and then make a determination whether or not they had enough data from exit polls and early returns to project a winner of those states' Electoral College votes. Most years the unfolding drama is a contrivance; news organizations and campaigns typically know who won the election early in the day. On Election Day 2000, however, the drama was real. No one knew in advance who was going to win. For once, the candidates and the nation might actually have to wait until the votes were counted.

At 7:50 P.M., after the polls had closed throughout most of Florida but while polls were still open in the western portion of the state's panhandle (which is in the central time zone), the Associated Press and the television networks declared that Gore was the projected winner of the state. It was the first sign that the vice president might actually pull off a victory. At the time this announcement was made, Justice Sandra Day O'Connor of the U.S. Supreme Court was at a party in Arizona. Upon hearing the news she reportedly said, "This is terrible." O'Connor was interested in retiring, but like most justices she wanted to wait until her replacement could be selected by a president of her political party. She was hoping for a Bush victory, and Gore's win in Florida signaled that she might have to wait another four years.[5]

After the media projected Gore the winner in Michigan and Pennsylvania, all signs seemed to suggest that he was heading for the White House. However, the news media's projections in Florida were based on a series of errors made by the organization that was hired by the networks to collect data on Election Day.[6] Governor Jeb Bush of Florida was spending election night with his brother in Austin, Texas, and he was receiving reports from his own state election officials that indicated the networks had no legitimate basis for their projection. The vote was too close. Worried that an early projection of a Gore victory might depress the Bush turnout in the western part of the country, where the polls were still open, candidate Bush let it be known that he thought the media's projections were inaccurate. "I'm going to wait until they count all the votes," he told reporters. "I think Americans ought to wait until they count all the votes."[7]

Not long after that news conference, at around 10:00 P.M. in the evening, the media took the unprecedented step of withdrawing their earlier projection of a Gore victory in Florida. That state was now considered "too close to call." Over the next few hours reports from almost every other state came in, yet neither candidate had a majority of votes in the Electoral College. While there was still some question about the results in some states (notably Oregon, New Mexico, and Iowa), it was assumed most of the evening that Florida's twenty-five votes would determine the outcome of the election. Finally, with the whole country waiting on the results from that state, the networks made another fateful decision at around 2:16 A.M.: one after the other they projected George W. Bush the winner of the popular vote in Florida. This time, along with the projection, came a declaration that the governor of Texas had become the forty-third president of the United States.[8]

Upon hearing the news many voters who had been staying up late to watch the returns turned off their televisions and went to sleep.[9] The idea had been planted: Gore lost, Bush was president. In Austin, Texas, the celebrations began at the governor's mansion. In Nashville, Tennessee, the Gore campaign prepared to call it quits. Forty-five minutes after the networks declared Bush the winner the vice president called the governor and offered his concession. He then gathered his family and entered a limousine for a drive to a campaign rally at the War Memorial Plaza, where he would make his concession public.

He never made it. While the Gore motorcade was en route to the rally Michael Wouley, a top Gore strategist who was monitoring the Web site of the Florida secretary of state, reached Gore adviser Michael Feldman by cell phone and reported that Gore was down by less than six thousand votes in Florida – a precipitous drop from the margin that was the basis for the network projections – and thousands of votes were still to be tallied. Gore's campaign manager, William M. Daley, received the message when the vice president's car was pulling into a basement garage near the rally site; the concession speech was already loaded into the TelePrompTer. "Whatever you do," he shouted into a cell phone, "do not go out on the stage."[10]

Less than an hour after he called Bush to concede, Al Gore called him back. The concession was withdrawn. The networks had jumped the gun again. The outcome in Florida was still too close. State law required an automatic recount of the ballots, and Gore was going to wait it out.[11]

Much of the country expected to wake up to hear more from President-elect Bush. But starting around 4:00 A.M. the networks once again took back what they had given, with Tom Brokaw acknowledging, "We don't just have egg on our face – we have an omelet all over our suits."[12] By the morning of Wednesday, November 8, the country still did not know who had been elected president of the United States. What was known was that Gore had apparently won the popular vote, with initial reports putting that margin of victory at over 100,000 votes – a number that would continue to rise for weeks as final tallies came in across the country, until it finally reached over half a million.[13] Under normal circumstances the possible discrepancy between the Electoral College result and the popular vote would have dominated the national conversation. But there was too much else going on.

That same morning, the Electoral College projection indicated that Gore was leading Bush 255 to 246 electoral votes, with results still unclear in three states: Oregon (with seven electoral votes), New Mexico (five), and the decisive state of Florida (twenty-five). After repeatedly projecting Florida for one candidate after another, the networks finally decided to wait for the actual results. When they came in the numbers were stunningly close: Out of almost six million votes cast in Florida Bush was leading Gore by a mere 1,784 votes. By late Wednesday, as the results of the automatic recount were reported, Bush's lead had shrunk to 1,278 votes. By Thursday morning the lead was less than a thousand. By Friday, with sixty-six out of sixty-seven counties reporting, the lead had shrunk to an unbelievable 229 votes.[14]

The lead might have been dwindling, but Bush was still winning. In fact, the position of the Bush campaign was that the election was over. The votes had been counted once, and counted again, and both times the Texas governor had won. On Wednesday morning Bush announced that "this morning brings news from Florida that the final vote count there shows that Secretary Cheney and I have carried the State of Florida. And if that result is confirmed in an automatic recount, as we expect it to be, then we have won the election." As the networks had declared the night before (for a time), Bush was the next president. In light of this, the Bush camp argued that it was time for Gore to do the honorable thing and concede the election. In the event that Gore did not take this advice, Governor Jeb Bush's acting general counsel began calling Florida's top law firms in the hope of preventing the Gore forces from mobilizing the Florida's best election law lawyers.[15] More publicly, Bush was dispatching to Florida his campaign's counsel and election law specialist, Ben Ginsberg, as well as his father's former secretary of state, James A. Baker III, "to make sure that the outcome is finalized as quickly as possible and in a calm and thoughtful manner."[16]

The Gore campaign assessed the situation differently. There had been many times during the previous hours that people had jumped to conclusions without waiting until all the votes were counted. It was true that Florida had gone through a mandatory recount of the ballots and that Bush was still ahead. But there were still many votes not counted at all. In fact, the official certification of the state election could not even take place until ten days after the election, when absentee ballots were due to arrive and be counted. In his public announcement Gore said that "[w]hat is at stake here is the fundamental fairness of the process as a whole. Because of what is at stake, this matter must be resolved expeditiously but deliberately and without any rush to judgment. . . . The consent of the governed given freely in an election process whose integrity is beyond question is the living heart of our democracy."[17] To protect these interests the Gore campaign sent a team of more than seventy advisers and lawyers into Florida; their declared mission was to ensure that "every ballot is counted."[18] Gore lawyer Ron Klain oversaw the legal team, and overseeing the entire effort was another former secretary of state, Warren Christopher.

It was becoming clear that this was not going to be over with the automatic recount. In anticipation of a contested result Florida governor Jeb Bush recused himself from the state canvassing board, which would have the ultimate responsibility of certifying the final election results after the county canvassing boards completed their counts.[19]

THE BUTTERFLY BALLOT

In recent history, when we think of voting problems that have come to the attention of the nation – and the nation's courts – what comes to mind most readily are civil rights violations based on practices that have the purpose or effect of discriminating against certain voters on the basis of some suspect classification, such as race. While the federal government has never attempted to standardize or rationalize voting practices, it has demonstrated a commitment over the past few decades to prevent discrimination and the denial of voting rights.[20] Concerns such as these were raised in the early days of the Florida election controversy. The National Association for the Advancement of Colored People issued a statement the day after the election alleging "voter intimidation and irregularities" affecting black voters in several precincts.[21]

However, it seems safe to assume that the Gore campaign was concerned about the political consequences of turning the election dispute into an issue of black civil rights. Despite the campaign's successful courting of the black vote, the theme of voting rights discrimination, heroic for a generation of U.S. politicians, now sadly seemed (in the eyes of these leaders) to pose too many political risks. This calculation revealed the sense of many Democrats that Gore could not simply take for granted support from among his Democratic base or his majority in the national popular vote; the campaign needed to find issues that would capture the concerns of a broader coalition. Thus, the complaints of the NAACP and its allies would not become the central themes of Gore's struggle.[22] Instead, the campaign complained about how the existing tallies from the machine tabulations did not reflect the actual choice that had been made by Florida's voters. The day after the election, this theme was made concrete when public attention turned to some apparent problems with a special kind of ballot used in heavily Democratic Palm Beach County – a ballot that had a lot of people fighting mad.

Palm Beach's ballot was like no other ballot used in Florida. Known as a "butterfly ballot," it listed candidates for the presidency across two face-to-face pages (the two wings of the butterfly) and included a row of holes down the middle of the two pages (the butterfly's body, if you will). As a general rule election officials think it is best to have the names of all candidates for an office on one page, so that voters do not overlook names on other pages.[23] But this unusual ballot design had been approved by the elected Democratic head of Palm Beach County's Canvassing Commission, Theresa LePore. Recent reforms in Florida election law had resulted in an expansion in the number of presidential candidates who had to be listed on the ballot; LePore knew that listing all the candidates on one side of the page would require the names to be printed in very small type, and she worried this might make it difficult for elderly Palm Beach voters to read the ballot.

How did this cause problems? Voters were directed to insert an IBM "punch card" ballot into the voting machine (invented in 1962 and known as a Votomatic) and then to use a small metal stylus to punch through the hole that corresponded to the candidate's name. On the Palm Beach ballot, the names of the two major-party candidates were on the left side of the page, with the Republican ticket of George W. Bush and Dick Cheney listed first and the Democratic ticket of Al Gore and Joe Lieberman listed second. Some voters who read the ballot starting at the top of the left page assumed that to vote for Gore/Lieberman they needed to punch the second hole down from the top, since those names were listed second on that page. But this was wrong. The second hole was reserved for the first candidate listed on the right-hand side of the page – conservative Reform Party candidate Patrick J. Buchanan. In fact, if a voter started looking at the candidates' names from the top of the left page down, and then starting again on the right side, Buchanan's name was actually the seventh candidate listed, after representatives from the Republican, Democratic, Libertarian, Green, Socialist Workers, and Natural Law parties.

The day after the election, many Gore voters complained that the design of the ballot led them either to mistakenly voted for Buchanan or to disqualify their vote by voting twice – first punching the Buchanan hole then, after noticing Buchanan's name on the right-hand page, going back and punching the correct hole for Gore. Marking two candidates for an office creates an "overvote" ballot that results in a vote for no candidate.

There is no question that the vast majority of those who voted in Palm Beach were able to follow the arrows and punch the hole that corresponded to the candidate they preferred. But very early on evidence circulated that the number of confused voters was quite high. In fact, by mid-afternoon on Election Day, LePore was concerned enough about reports of voter confusion that she issued a directive to all polling workers telling them to remind voters to punch only one hole for a candidate and to make sure that they were punching the correct hole.[24] At around 4:00 P.M. the Democratic National Committee was so concerned about the emergent problem that it hired a Texas-based telemarketing firm to call thousands of Palm Beach voters to alert them to the complications on the ballot; a company spokesperson later said that almost half the people contacted thought that they might have made a mistake when they voted.[25] The day after the election hard evidence of voter confusion quickly circulated. Buchanan received 3,704 votes in staunchly Democratic Palm Beach County, nearly 2,700 more than he received in any of Florida's other sixty-six counties. The county administrator also reported that approximately 19,000 ballots included two or more votes for president, many of which were punched for Gore and Buchanan.[26]

All of this led many Democrats to believe that Gore had properly won the election in Florida. It also did not take long for local Democratic lawyers to give the faithful a reason to think that their salvation may lie in the courtroom. Their claim was that the butterfly ballot was not just confusing but actually illegal under Florida law. Florida election law required that ballots list the candidates from the governor's party first (in this case Bush/Cheney), followed by the party that received the next highest votes in the previous gubernatorial election (Gore/Lieberman).[27] The complaint was that the Palm Beach ballot illegally put Buchanan in the second position, and that this was disguised by the design of the ballot, thus misleading voters who had an expectation that the Democratic candidate would be the second one listed. This claim became the basis for the first lawsuit of the election, *Fladell v. Palm Beach County Canvassing Board.* Late in the afternoon on Wednesday, November 8, three Palm Beach County residents who said they mistakenly voted for Buchanan when they intended to vote for Gore filed a complaint in state circuit court in West Palm Beach, challenging the legality of the Palm Beach election and demanding a new election for the county.[28] On Thursday at least four more complaints were filed.[29] The election was in court.[30]

Bush supporters knew that either an adjusted vote or a revote in Palm Beach would likely give Gore the few extra votes he needed to win, and so they vigorously objected to the claim that this situation demanded a legal remedy. They noted that the laws governing the design of punch card ballots did not require that they precisely follow the requirements for paper ballots; the order in which the candidates' names should be arranged had to be the same "as far as practicable," which meant that differences were legally permitted. Moreover, the disputed ballot was approved by an elected Democratic official in a process that was designed to catch these problems before an election, precisely because it was too difficult to address these concerns after the ballots had been cast. Historian Alan Brinkley provided a prescient summary of the situation two days after the election when he noted that "the idea has become enough planted in the media and in the minds of Democrats that [Gore] has been cheated out of the presidency" and added that, "on the other hand, a successful court challenge would leave the Republicans feeling they were cheated out of the presidency. . . . [I]n the short term, I don't see any happy solution."[31]

The debate over the legal merits of this argument would continue for weeks. Eventually, it would be overshadowed by other issues. But in the days after the election it was the story that dominated press coverage and public attention.[32] The controversy also led state circuit judge Kathleen Kroll to issue an order barring local officials from certifying Palm Beach's ballots until a hearing could be held. Stuart Taylor, Jr., of *Newsweek* speculated that this "may have been the first court order in history freezing the results of a presidential election." He also pointed out that Democratic lawyers had first filed their case in federal court, "where they were assigned a Reagan-appointed judge, Kenneth Ryskamp. The lawyers soon dropped the case there and refiled in state circuit court, where they drew Kroll – a liberal Democrat married to a Clinton-appointed Labor Department official."[33] Over the next few weeks there would be many discussions about whether favorable judicial outcomes depended more on the plausibility of the legal arguments or on the sympathies of the judge.[34]

RECOUNTS

Gore campaign manager Daley opened his press conference on Thursday, November 9, by noting that "it appears that more than 20,000 voters in Palm Beach County, who in all likelihood thought they were voting for Al Gore, had their votes counted for Pat Buchanan or not counted at all. Because this disenfranchisement of these Floridians is so much larger than the reported gap between Governor Bush and Vice President Gore, we believe this requires the full attention of the courts in Florida and concerned citizens all around the country."[35] This talk suggested that the Gore campaign was actively preparing to take the election into the courts.

But this was misleading. Top officials and lawyers for the campaign decided almost immediately that "the butterfly was a red herring." They believed that a new election was not feasible and "there was no way to disentangle the unintended Buchanan vote from those cast in earnest."[36] This was, essentially, a judgment on the legal merits of the case. While the dispute had short-term public relations benefits, in the long run it was not an argument that was likely to be successful in the Florida courts, even assuming that could be raised before sympathetic judges. While work continued on the issue for at least two weeks, the option was considered a "last resort," the so-called "nuclear button" if other strategies did not pan out.[37]

Much more promising, both as matters of law and politics, was what became known as the search for "undervotes." Undervotes referred to ballots in which a machine did not register a vote for any candidate for a particular office. One reason for this result would be that the voter chose not to express a preference for a particular office; but it was also possible that a voter attempted to convey a preference but did not have that preference registered because of some feature, limitation, or error associated with the vote-counting machines. When a machine failed to register a vote that someone attempted to cast, then that result might be more properly thought of as "undercounting" rather than undervoting; at least this was the emergent view within the Gore campaign.

This emergent view also had relevance for Palm Beach – not so much in the design of the butterfly ballot as in the operation of those Votomatic machines. With this machine an intention to vote is registered by using a stylus to punch a hole in an IBM punch card in the hope of dislodging what is now famously known as a "chad" – the tiny, pre-perforated rectangular piece of the card that covers a hole and is held on by four attachments at its corners. When these chads are completely punched through they reveal a hole that allows a vote-counting machine to pass light through the card and thus register a vote for the corresponding candidate.

The problem with this system is that voters will sometimes punch through the card without completely dislodging the chad. The stylus may punch all the way through but hit the chad at one side or at a corner rather than smack in the middle, which could result in a chad that is hanging on to the card by one, two, or three corners. In addition to the problem of "hanging" chads is the problem caused when a voter attempts to push the stylus through the card but is not successful, perhaps because there is so much chad debris under the card that a completed punch becomes difficult, or because the voter incorrectly placed the card on top of the machine rather than in the slot where there is an opening behind the card. These situations may result in a ballot that includes "dimpled" or "pregnant" chads, which are not hanging at all but have some sort of poke in the middle that reflects the force of the stylus. While some dimpled or pregnant chads may be due to voters who have an abrupt change of heart at the very moment they are attempting to cast their vote (and thus "check their swing," to use a baseball metaphor), they could also reflect an earnest desire to cast a vote – especially when the entire ballot shows dimples for many offices, which suggests a general problem with the voter's ability to punch through the card and not merely an extraordinary last-minute change of heart.[38]

There was evidence very early on that this undercount problem was plaguing a number of counties that used punch card systems. Throughout Florida, three of every 1,000 optically scanned ballots recorded no presidential vote, while 15 of every 1,000 punch card ballots were recorded as showing no vote. In Palm Beach the machines did not detect votes on 10,582 ballots; in Broward, the figure was around 6,700.[39] Unlike the butterfly ballot, the transformation of these undervote ballots into merely undercounted real votes did not necessarily involve any alleged (and hard-to-prove) confusion

★ WHO WON?

on the part of voters. Moreover, the search for these votes did not require extraordinary measures such as a revote of a county or a judicially imposed statistical adjustment in the official tally.

In fact, Florida law seemed to make the search for undercounted votes relatively straightforward. Under the Florida law that allowed for "protests of election returns" – section 102.166 of the election law – candidates had seventy-two hours after midnight the day of the election to decide whether to request a hand recount of specific counties. Florida had no obvious procedure for requesting a statewide hand recount; instead, candidates were required to identify particular counties in which one could claim that there were irregularities that called into question the initial vote count. Those requests, along with the reasons justifying the request, would have to be presented to the three-person "canvassing commission" of the particular county. Upon reviewing these requests the county canvassing commissions "may authorize a manual recount" of 1 percent of the ballots, and if that preliminary count revealed "an error in vote tabulation which could effect the outcome of the election," then the law said that canvassing boards "shall" correct the problem in one of these ways, including "manually recount all ballots."[40]

This statute laid a road map for the Gore team's preferred route: convince canvassing boards to authorize full manual recounts in the hope that they would find enough legally cast votes that had not been registered by the machines. This allowed the Gore campaign to focus on counting votes rather than mounting legal challenges. In fact, as long as the canvassing commissions cooperated, then presumably no lawsuits would have to be filed. Ironically, while the Bush campaign had been first to warn against an election fought in the courtroom, the Gore strategy could place them in the position of having to be the first ones to run into court, if they chose to fight any effort at recounting the ballots.[41] The only other issues to decide were whether to focus on several or many counties and whether to complain just about undervotes or also about overvotes. In a fateful decision that reflected the judgment of his senior political advisors rather than of his recount specialists (who knew that the standard practice was to review as many votes as possible), Gore decided to focus only on alleged undervote problems in a small number of Democratic counties. Thus, on Thursday, November 9, Gore campaign chairman Daley announced that "the appropriate Florida Democratic officials will be requesting a hand count of ballots in Palm Beach County as well as three other counties: Volusia, Dade, and Broward. . . . All we are seeking is [that] the candidate who the voters preferred become our president. . . . Let the legal system run its course, let the true and accurate will of the people prevail."[42]

This reference to "the will of the people" was more than mere political rhetoric, however. By Thursday, the Gore team knew that in 1998 the Florida Supreme Court decided a case entitled *Beckstrom v. Volusia County Canvassing Board,* which held that a state court "should not frustrate the will of the voters if . . . the will of the voters can be determined."[43] This seemed to be part of a longer tradition in the Florida Supreme Court's case law; for example, in its 1975 decision in *Boardman v. Esteva,* the court emphasized that "the real parties in interest here, not in the legal sense but in realistic terms, are the voters" who have "the right to be heard," and courts must not risk "the unnecessary and unjustified muting of the public voice." These cases would be interpreted and reinterpreted for competing purposes over the next few weeks, but the Gore campaign was going to treat them as standing for the proposition that the principal purpose of elections and election law is to accurately capture the intention of the voters. The Palm Beach experience and the preliminary undervote data from Democratic counties convinced the campaign that it would do well in Florida as long as that remained the prevailing legal standard.

The Bush campaign also had to make some quick legal decisions within the first seventy-two hours after the election. While exploring their own recounts elsewhere was a theoretical option, it made little sense to Bush strategists and lawyers. After all, Bush was in the lead; if Gore could be stopped Bush did not need any additional votes. Moreover, unlike the other side, the Republicans had no evidence that Bush voters had any difficulty voting for their candidate.[44] Thus, in the words of Bush lawyer Ben Ginsberg, their primary strategy was "to validate the results of the election" and fight all further searches for votes. As Jim Baker put it more publicly, "For the good of the country, and for the sake of our standing in the world, the campaigning should end and the business of an orderly transition should begin." To underscore the strategy, Governor Bush met with his transition team two days after the election, explaining that "I'm in the process of planning in a responsible way a potential administration."[45]

The Gore emphasis on undervotes rather than litigation was also reassuring to commentators who were beginning to face up to the possibility that election 2000 may be decided in court. An editorial in the *New York Times* suggested that "Neither the prospect of legal warfare nor Mr. Bush's rush to put together a transition team is helpful at this point. . . . Both Mr. Gore and Mr. Bush need to be asking themselves whether a scorched-earth legal strategy meets that standard."[46] Similarly, the Detroit *Free Press* expressed support for Gore's efforts to get "definitive numbers from Florida," but they warned that "if Gore opts for court, he invites Republicans to do the same, alleging equally egregious problems and irregularities across the country."[47] However, the Gore campaign also knew that the Florida courts might be important allies at some point, and so they started laying the groundwork for public acceptance of that contingency. In an opinion piece for the *New York Times*, entitled "Let the Courts Decide," Harvard law professor Laurence H. Tribe (identified as an adviser to the Gore campaign) argued that "our democracy is constitutionally grounded in the rule of law" and "it is not for any of us" to "jump the gun and short-circuit the Florida judicial process if we are as committed to the rule of law as we claim. . . . [T]he price of premature closure – of not giving the courts of Florida a chance to apply their law to the present uncertainty – might be a cloud of illegitimacy we would long regret."[48] This groundwork was necessary because the concerns were real, and increasingly were being expressed. Senator Robert Torricelli, Democrat of New Jersey, put the point most directly: "ultimately the presidency of the United States should not be decided by a judge."[49]

THE STRATEGIC SETTING

Even with these concerns it was clear from the first phase of this struggle that law was central to the strategic decisions being made by each campaign. This was most obvious in the Gore campaign's decision to focus on manual recounts in selected counties rather than litigation to overturn or adjust the results in Palm Beach. The law also short-circuited some early brainstorming by Florida governor Jeb Bush's staff about how they might stop any recounting, including the automatic recount.[50] At the same time, everyone assumed that success or failure depended on much more than the law. Each campaign knew that they also had certain conventional political advantages, mostly having to do with whether key decision-making institutions were likely to be sympathetic to one side or the other. Like all good litigants searching for the most favorable forum, the campaigns quickly focused on the importance of directing the dispute into those institutions that (they thought) could be relied on the most. In theory, of course, all institutions were equally bound to act in accordance with the same rules and legal processes; however, in practice, none of the participants assumed that their favored arguments would have the same force everywhere. It seemed a safe bet that a favorable decision-maker was at least as important as a favorable law.

In analyzing this strategic setting the Gore campaign pinned its hopes on laws and institutions that supported more vote counting. It seemed to be a major advantage that Florida's recount statute seemed to direct this dispute toward two groups of decision-makers who might be particularly favorable to the campaign's position: the county canvassing commissions and the Florida Supreme Court. Democrats controlled the boards in Broward and Palm Beach Counties; the Miami-Dade board consisted of one Democrat and two independents.[51] Not only did state law give these commissions the authority to decide whether to do a recount; it also gave them the ultimate authority to determine the intent of the voter if there was ever a disagreement over how to interpret a ballot.[52] If there were questions about this process, it might also help that the state's attorney general, Robert A. Butterworth, was Gore's campaign chairman in Florida.[53] While the state's trial court judges were not uniformly Democratic, there were enough to make it reasonable to assume that this was an advantageous forum.

Still, the real trump card was the Florida Supreme Court, which had handed down seemingly favorable decisions in the past and was currently considered (by friends and foes alike) a bastion of Democratic decision-making in a state government that was otherwise controlled by the Republican Party. The seven members of the court, who serve six-year terms before facing retention elections, had all been nominated by one of Florida's previous two Democratic governors, Bob Graham and Lawton Chiles.[54] While the court had a fairly moderate reputation on a number of issues, including capital punishment (the justices upheld the use of the balky electric chair known as "Old Sparky" in a pair of 4 to 3 decisions), it had also had some run-ins with the Republican Party's newly acquired control of the state legislature, including decisions to declare unconstitutional new legislation on speeding up appeals in capital cases, strike down Jeb Bush's school voucher program, and void a law requiring parental notification for girls seeking abortions. Months before the election 2000 dispute, several Republican legislators responded to these decisions by endorsing a plan to pack the court with appointees of Jeb Bush and tilt it rightward by expanding the number of seats on the bench. Others supported a bill to pack the judicial nominating commission by increasing Bush's appointments to the commission and decreasing the seats of the state bar association. These plans both died amid a storm of protest from bar groups and newspaper editorials, but the efforts were illustrative of interinstitutional politics in Florida.[55]

Finally, the Gore campaign had reason to hope that they could avoid the intervention of federal courts in this process. The Constitution of the United States left most issues involving elections (including presidential elections) to be resolved by the states under state law. This was especially true of the nuts and bolts of election practices, such as ballot design and vote-counting procedures. The long-standing diversity in election procedures in the United States was ample evidence that the federal role was understood to be extremely limited. Moreover, federal courts had been especially careful not to read some of the broad language of the Constitution – such as the equal protection clause of the Fourteenth Amendment – as a basis for intervening in the details of state election systems, precisely out of fear that the result would be to turn the U.S. Constitution "into a detailed election code for state elections,"[56] a code the provisions of which would be constantly supervised and rewritten by federal judges rather than local officials. Paradoxically, this deference to state practices seemed especially strong in elections involving the selection of president of the United States. The Electoral College was specifically design to be a state-based institution, and federal law made it clear that if controversies governing the appointment of electors received a "final determination" by "judicial or other methods" based on the state laws existing at the time of the election then that state resolution "shall be conclusive" on the Congress.[57]

Still, despite these apparent advantages in state and federal law and among the canvassing commissions and state courts, the Gore campaign was not holding all the best cards in this contest. The Bush campaign also emphasized those laws and institutions that would give them an advantage in the contest. This meant searching for any rules or legal principles that privileged deadlines and the certainty of the initial returns over the prolonged (and potentially subjective) manual scrutiny of ballots. In the early hours of the dispute it was not obvious what laws these might be (especially since the manual scrutiny of ballots had obviously been a part of U.S. elections from the beginning of the republic), although it would not be long before Florida statutes on deadlines for reporting vote tallies would move to the center of the election 2000 dispute.

As for favorable institutional support, the Florida governor was obviously a sympathetic (albeit publicly hamstrung) ally. More important, the Florida official in charge of overseeing elections, Secretary of State Katherine Harris, had also been candidate Bush's co–campaign chairperson for Florida, and actively campaigned for Bush in the early days of the New Hampshire primary.[58] In addition, in 1998 Republicans took over both houses of the legislature and thus controlled the state legislative and executive branches for the first time since Reconstruction. In 2000, they held a 77 to 43 majority in the state House and a 25 to 15 advantage in the Senate.

As they looked beyond the confines of state government the Bush team also had reason to be hopeful about the federal courts, particularly the Eleventh Circuit Court of Appeals. The judges on that court – seven of whom had been appointed by Republican presidents – had a fairly conservative reputation.[59] For example, the judges had recently reiterated their support for student-led prayers in high school despite having been directed by the U.S. Supreme Court to reconsider an earlier decision. In April the court blocked the Clinton administration from allowing six-year-old Elian Gonzalez (a Cuban boy who spent months in Miami after his mother died while trying to raft to Florida) to return to Cuba with his father. Then again, the flip side of their presumptive political sympathies was that many of these conservatives were on the record for believing in states rights and judicial restraint, particularly when it came to federal judicial supervision of state election processes. One of the leading conservatives on the court, Judge Edmondson, wrote in a case five years earlier that "federal courts are not the bosses in state election disputes unless extraordinary circumstances affecting the integrity of the state's election process are clearly present in a high degree."[60]

This same potential tension between a judge's presumptive political sympathies and their prior positions on the law also applied to the U.S. Supreme Court, which was narrowly controlled by five conservative justices: Chief Justice William H. Rehnquist (initially appointed by President Nixon and appointed as chief by Ronald Reagan) and Justices Sandra Day O'Connor (Reagan), Antonin Scalia (Reagan), Anthony M. Kennedy (Reagan), and Clarence Thomas (Bush). Two other justices had been appointed by Republican presidents, John Paul Stevens (Ford) and David Souter (Bush), but their voting record in the 1990s placed them firmly in the camp of the more moderate Clinton appointees, Ruth Bader Ginsburg and Stephen J. Breyer.[61] While the political ideology of the conservatives was undoubtedly closer to that held by Bush, these same conservatives were also on the record for having very strong views about federal-state relations, in particular, on the issue of the extent to which states should be free to operate without the interference of the federal government – including the U.S. Supreme Court – when it came to matters of traditional state responsibility. During the 1990s the five conservatives had initiated an innovative and controversial jurisprudence, reminiscent of the activist conservative Court of the late nineteenth and early twentieth centuries, which imposed new limits on the scope of

Congress's authority and new barriers to federal regulation of state government.[62] They told the federal government that it could not pass laws regulating the possession of firearms near schools because this subject matter was traditionally a matter for local regulation.[63] The Court also prohibited the federal government from telling state legislatures that they had to take possession of hazardous waste sites and from using local sheriffs to help enforce the Brady Bill.[64] Most recently the five conservatives had gone so far as to extend to the states a special immunity from having to defend themselves in court if they were accused of violating the Constitution or federal law – an immunity that went well beyond the limited protections offered by the Eleventh Amendment (granting states immunity from being unwilling defendants in federal courts when sued by people from other states) to encompass a more general theory of state sovereignty.[65] Within the previous year the conservatives turned their attention to elements of federal civil rights law, arguing that the federal government had no lawful authority to require state governments to abide by the Violence against Women Act or the Age Discrimination in Employment Act.[66]

It would be misleading to characterize these conservatives as completely unwilling to intervene in state affairs. Most notably, they were willing to challenge state action when states set up affirmative action programs or drew political boundaries with an eye on the racial composition of those districts.[67] Still, it was not clear what principle of law might lead the conservatives to treat the issues percolating in Florida as the sort of activity that required careful federal supervision. In particular, it did not involve the sort of race-conscious policymaking that drove the conservatives to intervene in these other areas. Obviously, because the fate of the presidency hung in the balance, the Florida dispute was attracting everyone's attention, and there was every reason to think that these justices were as mindful of these developments as anyone. However, if one focused merely on the legal issues without attention to the parties who were involved in this controversy, it would have been hard to find anyone before Election Day 2000 who would have predicted that the routine and traditional activity of counting votes – even hand counting votes – was an activity that would be of any interest at all to the Supreme Court.

Despite this pattern of decision-making, the Bush team felt confident that the Washington justices would be a friendly forum. They came to this conclusion even before it was clear what specific legal issues would emerge from the controversy. Their faith in the Supreme Court was not premised on the assumption that the justices would be sympathetic to a specific legal argument; it was their political sympathies that they were relying on. While the comment needs to be taken with a grain of salt (as it was offered after the conclusion of the dispute), it was still the position of Bush lawyer Irv Terrell that, from the beginning, "The whole Bush strategy was to build a record in state court and then get the Supreme Court of the United States to reverse it."[68]

STOP THE COUNT

By Friday, November 10, three days after the election, the Gore strategy seemed to have some momentum. While there was talk of litigation and while some Palm Beach voters had already gone to court, the focus for the Gore team had turned toward recounts. The same day that Daley requested manual recounts, canvassing commissions in Volusia and Palm Beach Counties agreed to start their 1 percent test recounts.[69]

Despite being officially behind in the vote count by 229 votes, things were looking promising for Gore. A CNN/*USA Today*/Gallup Poll showed that 55 percent of Americans supported a hand recount. A *Newsweek* survey conducted Thursday and Friday reported that by a 72 to 25 percent margin Americans said it was more important to make certain the presidential count was fair and accurate than to resolve the matter as quickly as possible.[70] By the weekend, many commentators suggested that Gore was in a promising political position, with Bush supporters worrying about hand recounts done under the supervision of Democratic canvassing boards.[71] To publicly symbolize this momentum a relaxed and seemingly confident Al Gore even allowed himself to be photographed playing a Kennedyesque game of touch football with his family and friends on the lawn of the vice president's residence.[72]

Understandably, the Bush forces were doing all they could to trip up the Gore campaign. For example, Secretary of State Harris announced that it was the position of her office that the controversial Palm Beach ballot "fully conforms to Florida law." More important, she began to warn those who were becoming hopeful about recounts that state law required counties to submit their returns no later than one week after the election.[73] Anticipating this situation two days after the election, the Volusia County Canvassing Board filed a complaint in state circuit court for Leon County. The case, *McDermott v. Harris*, asked a court to declare that "the Florida Elections Code permits the Canvassing Board to certify the results of the Presidential

Election after completion of the manual recount, . . . without regard to the deadline of 5:00 P.M. November 14, 2000," and to issue an injunction against the secretary of state preventing her "from ignoring results certified by the Canvassing Board after" that deadline.[74] At the time, this case received little attention; before long, though, it would become the focal point for the first dramatic court battles of the 2000 election dispute.

In the meantime, another court action was attracting attention. On Saturday, November 11, the Bush team became the first of the two campaigns to go to court. That morning Bush's lawyers filed a complaint before U.S. District Judge Donald M. Middlebrooks, a Democrat appointed by Clinton in 1997 (with strong support from the state's two U.S. senators, Republican Connie Mack and Democrat Bob Graham), asking the judge to issue an emergency injunction to stop the manual recounts that had just begun in the four counties.[75] The case, which would become known as *Siegel v. Le-Pore,* was brought (in the words of the complaint) "to preserve the integrity, consistency, equality, and finality of the most important civic action that Americans take: their votes in an election for the President of the United States." Written primarily by Florida lawyer Barry Richard and Washington attorneys Theodore B. Olson and Ben Ginsberg, the complaint argued that the court had to act quickly to "prevent a standardless patchwork of ad hoc decision-making from undermining the integrity of the electoral process and public confidence in election results." In particular, they alleged that under Florida law there were no standards to govern whether a recount should be held or how ballots should be counted, and they insisted that this was inconsistent with Fourteenth Amendment requirements of equal protection and due process. "Simply stated, under Florida's scheme, *identical* ballots in two different counties will be treated differently," particularly if the ballot at issue is a partially punched card. Allowing this to go forward would cause "irreparable harm" – the legal standard that had to be met to get an emergency injunction – because a "tainted result will be broadcast to the nation" and this would cause "serious damage to the legitimacy of the election" as well as "interfere with the orderly transition of constitutional government."[76]

When the Bush lawyers were debating how to bring this dispute into federal court, they kicked around many ideas about what possible federal statutory or constitutional issues were implicated by what appeared to be a routine manual recount – the sort of activity that took place all over the country in close elections. When the equal protection argument was first raised, a number of lawyers thought it was "extremely weak," even "lame."

When word reached some Washington legal circles that they were considering an equal protection attack, angry conservatives started telling Republicans lawyers that it was a terrible argument, and "Bush lawyers had to call and say cut it out, they were doing the best they could."[77]

Reflecting the internal deliberations of the Bush lawyers, a number of liberal and conservative scholars suggested that this request for emergency federal intervention was far-fetched. Stanford law professor Pamela Karlan noted that under the Bush claim of irreparable harm "there would be irreparable injuries all the time from the media projecting election results." The equal protection argument also seemed like a stretch. After all, if voters had a right to have their votes certified "in a uniform and even-handed manner" it would seem as though the original election itself would be unconstitutional, given the various ways in which Florida counties designed ballots and counted votes. In the words of Pepperdine law professor Douglas Kmiec, who ran the Office of Legal Counsel in the Reagan Justice Department, the basis for the claim was that "your vote is diluted by recounting," and he opined: "That seems unlikely given all the recounting there has been in the past" in Florida and around the country. Karlan added, "I don't see how a voter whose vote has been counted can be denied equal protection of the law just because someone else's vote is counted."[78]

Not surprisingly, the Democratic response brief, written in part by Harvard professor Laurence Tribe, insisted that "the state's method of appointing its presidential electors is indisputably and fundamentally a state law issue. . . . Maintaining the integrity of the state electoral system and assuring that the votes of all voters are properly counted, is the most fundamental imaginable state interest." The only argument offered in favor of such an extraordinary federal intervention is based on insubstantial "speculations that humans are inherently inferior to machines in the matter of counting votes" – an assumption that was inconsistent with "an electoral practice" that exists "throughout the country since the nation's founding."[79] This argument initiated a pattern of claims and counterclaims that would become increasingly commonplace during the ensuing few weeks: the Bush forces would characterize recounts as chaotic and untrustworthy, and the Gore team would insist that they were a traditional and widely accepted means of verifying the outcomes of close elections.

As Judge Middlebrooks contemplated his decision, Volusia County began its hand recount of more than 184,000 votes. The Palm Beach County Canvassing Board spent Saturday completing its 1 percent recount (about 4,600 ballots). If people watched this "sober" and "orderly" event live on cable news programs they would have seen the three-member canvassing commission holding up "high-tech computer cards to subject them to a decidedly low-tech 'sunshine test': If light gleamed through a pinhole, a vote had been cast." Later in the day, though, after experience with around four hundred ballots, the board decided to scrap the "sunshine test" in favor of a more strict "three-corner rule," which would count a vote when the chad was hanging on by only one of its four points of attachment.[80] Democratic observers objected to this new rule, claiming that the board was putting too many potential Gore votes into the "undervote" pile, but the rush to count continued.[81]

At around 2:00 A.M. Sunday morning, November 12, before a waiting crowd, the Palm Beach Canvassing Board announced that their test recount revealed that they had found an additional thirty-three votes for Gore and fourteen for Bush, a net gain of nineteen Gore votes. If the rate of "recovery" of undervotes was the same when the other 99 percent of votes were counted this would mean an additional 1,900 votes for the vice president – more than enough to overcome Bush's razor-thin lead. Given this result, canvassing board members Carol Roberts, a county commissioner, and Theresa LePore voted in favor of a motion to authorize a full manual recount of the county. Board chairman and Palm Beach County Judge Charles E. Burton voted against the motion, claiming that he wanted a legal opinion from state authorities on whether it was lawful to do a recount under these circumstances. Burton was a nominal Democrat, but he had been appointed to the court by Jeb Bush, and Democratic observers worried about his loyalties. Bush spokesman Dan Bartlett decried the Palm Beach decision, declaring that the just finished 1 percent sample count was "mass confusion" and "subjectivity that bordered on the ridiculous."[82]

On the Sunday morning network talk shows, Bush overseer Jim Baker continued with this theme of attacking the very idea of hand recounts by arguing that "Voting machines are not Republican and are not Democratic, and are not subject to conscious or unconscious bias." He also extended what he called a "compromise offer" to the Gore campaign: Gore should accept the results of the full automatic recount plus the results of the absentee balloting; in exchange, "we will withdraw our lawsuit." If Gore did not accept that offer, then "[w]e will vigorously contest the efforts for a manual recount in Florida." Later that day Gore overseer Warren Christopher responded by saying that "this is the procedure called for by Florida law. The law calls for the opportunity for hand counts to check machine counts . . . to make sure it was accurate." He added that candidate Bush had signed a

1997 law in Texas that made hand counting preferable to a mechanical re-count in election disputes.[83]

The weight of mainstream editorial opinion was still in favor of a more careful review of the ballots. The *Washington Post* editorial page called the Bush federal court challenge "flimsy" and suggested that "given the un-precedented closeness of this election and the very sizable stakes, the state should count as many legitimate, decipherable ballots as it can find. . . . People can identify legitimate votes that machines overlook. If there is an equal protection problem here, then the answer is to count more votes, not fewer."[84] The "news analysis" offered by the *Los Angeles Times*'s Doyle Mc-Manus noticed that until Saturday, "the Bush campaign had argued that Vice President Al Gore was doing the nation a disservice by supporting law-suits. . . . But now, faced with the possibility that the hand recount in heav-ily Democratic areas could erase Bush's tiny margin in Florida, the Republi-can's campaign has changed its mind: The courts have a legitimate role to play, after all."[85] Writing in the *Washington Post,* columnist E. J. Dionne, Jr., noted that "the Bush spin before Baker's move was very anti-lawyer. . . . [Now,] if stopping the recount requires lawyers, bring em in."[86] Jim Pinker-ton, a GOP strategist and former White House aid to the first President Bush, said that "[t]he Bush people win if they're fighting against a new elec-tion" (in Palm Beach, for example) but "they lose if they're fighting against a recount. . . . No one can argue against a fair recount of the election you al-ready had."[87] Still, some GOP supporters argued that Bush had no choice. Scott Reed, who was former senator Bob Dole's presidential campaign man-ager in 1996, said that the legal action was "the right, logical next step" be-cause "Republicans cannot just stand by and let this thing get stolen in Florida."[88] Besides, as other analysts pointed out, "the federal appeals court that has jurisdiction over Florida cases is dominated by Republican ap-pointees. By contrast, the state courts that would hear the case in Florida are predominantly Democratic."[89]

DEADLINES AND INJUNCTIONS

On Monday, November 13, Judge Middlebrooks, saying that he took "great comfort" in know that he was not "the final word on this," ruled against Bush request that he stop the recounts.[90] He explained that "under the Constitution of the United States, the responsibility for selection of electors for the office of President rests primarily with the people of Florida, its election officials and, if necessary, its courts." Moreover, "Florida's manual recount provision is a 'generally applicable and evenhanded' electoral scheme designed to 'protect the integrity and reliability of the election process itself' – the type of state electoral law often upheld in federal legal challenges. . . . [T]he manual recount provision . . . strives to strengthen rather than dilute the right to vote by securing, as nearly as humanly possible, an accurate and true reflection of the will of the electorate." The judge noted that granting the injunction would "run the risk" of federal courts "being 'thrust into the details of virtually every election, tinkering with the states' election machinery, reviewing petitions, registration cards, vote tallies, and certificates of election for all manner of error and insufficiency under state and federal law.'" Even if there was some variation in vote counting from county to county, it was "unavoidable given the inherent decentralization involved in state electoral and state recount procedures. . . . Unless and until each electoral county in the United States uses the exact same automatic tabulation . . . there will be tabulating discrepancies depending on the method of tabulation."[91] Bush's lawyers appealed this ruling to the Eleventh Circuit in Atlanta; on Wednesday, November 15, those judges agreed to hear the case. The development led one commentator boldly to suggest that these issues might ultimately be resolved by "the justices of the U.S. Supreme Court, whose votes could be the last ones counted."[92]

In the meantime, in response to an inquiry by the chairman of the Republican Party of Florida, the Republican director of the Division of Elections, L. Clayton Roberts, released an advisory opinion arguing that counties were only allowed to do recounts if there were problems with the voting machines themselves and that a machine's inability to read an improperly marked or punched ballot (like one with a hanging chad) was not an "error in the vote tabulation" that county commissions had to correct.[93] The following day, in response to this opinion, the state's Democratic attorney general, Robert A. Butterworth, declared Roberts's analysis to be "clearly at variance with the existing Florida statutes and case law." In his view a correctable "error might also result from the failure of a properly functioning mechanical system to discern the choices of the voters as revealed by the ballots." He ended his opinion by advising that "where a ballot is marked so as to plainly indicate the voter's choice and intent, it should be counted as marked unless some positive provision of law would be violated."[94] This advice convinced Judge Robert W. Lee of the Broward County Canvassing Board to switch his earlier position and finally vote to authorize a recount in that county.

However, it was looking increasingly likely that this decision would be for naught. The same day that Roberts tried to talk counties into foregoing their recounts, Secretary of State Harris made a forceful public statement indicating that she had no choice but to strictly enforce the seven-day deadline for county reporting of election results. In her statement she relied on language on the Florida statutes that said that "if the county returns are not received by the Department of State by 5:00 P.M. of the seventh day following an election, all missing counties shall be ignored, and the results shown by the returns on file shall be certified."[95] This led her to say that "I anticipate the presidential election in Florida will be certified by Saturday afternoon [after receipt of all absentee ballots on Friday], barring judicial intervention." However, in one of the first indications that Florida election law may cause as many problems as it attempts to solve, Gore supporters pointed out that the very next provision of the election code provided that late results "may be ignored" by the secretary,[96] suggesting (at a minimum) that they did not have to be ignored. In light of this, Warren Christopher called her actions "arbitrary and unreasonable" and said that she "appeared" to be motivated by her position as co-chairperson of Bush's Florida presidential campaign.[97] The Bush campaign characterized her announcement as "an objective decision based on the law of Florida."[98]

To say the least, Harris's announcement posed a serious threat to the Gore undervote strategy. The Palm Beach County recount that had been authorized very early Sunday morning was not even scheduled to begin until Tuesday morning, and the canvassing board estimated that it would take approximately six days to count their 460,000 ballots. Miami-Dade had not yet even made a decision about whether to conduct the 1 percent test recount; a meeting to decide that issue was schedule for Tuesday at 9:30 A.M., seven and a half hours before the secretary of state was insisting that all county votes had to be fully certified. Broward County had hesitated because of the opinion expressed by Roberts that they were not allowed to do manual recounts. If the secretary's position was upheld, then it would be virtually impossible to use manual recounts as a way of determining whether the machine-reported results were the most accurate.

Volusia County, which was proceeding nicely with its recount, had been in court since November 9, asking a judge to prevent Harris from enforcing this deadline in the event that legal recounts were taking place. That lawsuit was now joined by Palm Beach; and in its first official move toward litigation, the Gore campaign also filed a motion to intervene in the case, with Christopher explaining that "the Florida secretary of state has compelled us to appeal to the courts ourselves." To distinguish his lawsuit from Bush's, Christopher said that "we intend to seek a court order not to deny the counting of votes, but rather to allow lawful counting to go to its full completion." This position was consistent with Gore's public statement that same day, in which he expressed the view that "I would not want to win the presidency by a few votes cast in error or interpreted or miscounted, and I don't think Governor Bush does either."[99] As if to prove him wrong, the Bush campaign also filed a motion to intervene, on the side of the secretary of state.

The case was assigned to Leon County Circuit Court judge Terry P. Lewis, a Democrat who was initially appointed to his position by Florida's late Democratic governor Lawton Chiles.[100] During a two-hour hearing on Monday, Judge Lewis questioned how state law could give a county an option to do a hand recount "and you don't give them an opportunity to do it. That seems futile." At the end of the hearing Judge Lewis gave no indication on how he might rule, but he did announce that he would issue his decision the next day.[101]

Also on Monday the Democratic Party filed suit in Palm Beach County Circuit Court to force the county's canvassing board to set aside their strict "detached chad" counting rule in favor of one that also counted ballots with dimpled chads on the grounds that Florida law required the board to base their decision on the intent of the voter; a dimpled chad reflected an intent to vote.[102] On Tuesday the almost forgotten butterfly ballot case ended up in the court of Judge Jorge Labarga, who announced that he would hold a hearing on Friday.[103] Also at this time a little-noticed item appeared in the *New York Times* under the headline "G.O.P Played Role in Absentee Vote." It involved a Republican election official in Seminole County, Sandra Goard, who "allowed Republican workers to camp out in her offices for as long as ten days to make handwritten corrections on [preprinted absentee ballot] applications sent out by the Republican Party" as a way of boosting the Republican absentee ballot vote. A local Democratic lawyer, Harry Jacobs, formally protested Ms. Goard's actions, but the Seminole County election board rejected the protest and formally certified their results. Jacobs was considering filing a lawsuit over the issue.[104]

As promised, on Tuesday morning Judge Lewis delivered his decision. He started by ruling that the statutes required the canvassing boards to certify whatever election returns they had by the established deadline, which was 5:00 P.M. later that day. The statute also said that the secretary "may ignore" late-filed returns, but this meant that she could also choose to accept them;

in other words, the law did not require her to ignore them. Lewis ruled that the only constraint on her choice was that she had to exercise her discretion reasonably, which meant that if Harris was going to reject any late-filed returns she would have to offer a reasonable explanation in support of her decision. If after considering the issue the secretary still rejected the filings, then "an unsuccessful Candidate . . . may file . . . a complaint in Circuit Court contesting the election results" – which was a process that occurred after an election had been certified – since "one of the specific itemized grounds for such a challenge is the 'rejection of a number of legal votes sufficient to change or place in doubt the result of the election.'"[105] The *New York Times* called the decision "a model of common sense and a rebuke to the partisan misreading of Florida statutes by Ms. Harris, who has blurred her twin responsibilities as chief arbiter of the state's election laws and co-chairperson of the Bush campaign in Florida."[106] However, Bush lawyer Barry Richard insisted that the true import of the decision was that the secretary could reject hand recounts as long as she had a reason, and he believed that this meant a quick end to the vote counting in Florida.

Gore's response came through his new lawyer – a lawyer whose presence made it clear to all that the campaign was willing, if necessary, to use a very aggressive litigation strategy to get the votes counted. David Boies had recently received notoriety by leading the government's antitrust prosecution of Microsoft Corporation, and he was widely regarded as one of the country's most experienced and successful litigators. *Time* magazine called him "master of the impossible." In his first statement on behalf of the Gore campaign he expressed hope that "the secretary of state will do the right thing. Now, if [she] arbitrarily refuses to accept the amended returns based on the recount, and violates what this court has ruled is her duty, which is to accept those results unless she has a good reason not to, then we may be back in court."[107]

After the counties submitted their certified tallies at 5:00 P.M. the official Bush lead was 300 votes over Gore. Volusia County beat the clock by five minutes; their final tally showed a net gain of ninety-eight votes for Gore.[108] Broward included in its certification the results from a partial manual recount, which showed a net gain of three votes for Gore, and the next day the board decided to proceed with the manual recount of over 580,000 ballots.[109] The Miami-Dade board finished its 1 percent test recount three hours after the 5:00 P.M. deadline, and after finding only six additional votes for Gore they decided by a 2 to 1 vote to not proceed with a full manual recount.[110] Palm Beach sent the results of the automatic machine recount and then decided to suspend its plans for a manual recount until the state supreme court ruled on whether that count was legally authorized.[111]

THE FIRST CRESCENDO

Over the next few days a country that was racing to keep pace with daily developments increasingly found itself glued to the radio, television, and Internet, waiting to see what would happen during the next hour.[112] The day after Lewis's ruling, Judge Jorge Labarga, a Republican, ruled that Palm Beach County's "detached chad" standard "restricts the canvassing board's ability to determine the intent of the voter" in violation of state law, and he directed the county "to utilize whatever methodology it deems proper to determine the true intention of the voter."[113] This Republican judge had given Gore a legal victory, but the decision was consistent with Florida law and with the decisions of many other courts around the country. Alaskan courts had held that unpunched cards that were nonetheless marked in pen must be counted. The Illinois Supreme Court ruled in 1990 that requiring a chad to be either fully detached or hanging "set too rigid a standard" for determining voter intent, and in a 1996 decision the Massachusetts Supreme Judicial Court held that indentations on ballots were a sign of voter intent.[114]

At 9:00 A.M. on Wednesday November 16, in response to Judge Lewis's decision, Secretary of State Harris petitioned the Florida Supreme Court to order a halt to all manual recounts and to take control over the election process by consolidating all election lawsuits into one state circuit court.[115] When the Florida high court rejected Harris's request, it became the second court (in addition to the federal district court) to refuse to issue an injunction shutting down the hand recounts. The decision was important, and to many minds indicative of the Court's sympathies; at a minimum, this court was not going out of its way to protect the Texas governor's shaky, vulnerable lead. With that lead having shrunk from 1,900 votes to 1,700 to 300, it seemed as though every hour in which counting was allowed to continue brought Gore closer to victory. This decision led Palm Beach to immediately authorize (once again) the recount of the entire county. Canvassing board chairman Judge Charles Burton, who initially voted against a full recount until he could get some legal clarification on whether recounts were acceptable in these circumstances, declared now that "[t]hey have given us that authority, so we intend on proceeding until such time as the recount is concluded."[116]

In addition to its decision to allow recounts to proceed, the Florida Supreme Court also took its first step toward resolving some of the key questions that had been developing. Specifically, it allowed the secretary and the two campaigns to intervene in the case brought by Palm Beach seeking clarification of the disagreement between Harris and Attorney General Butterworth on the basic legality of authorizing hand recounts under these circumstances. The case was *Palm Beach County Canvassing Board v. Harris.*

Also, following up on Judge Lewis's ruling, the secretary of state directed the three counties that were still conducting recounts to explain by 2:00 P.M. on Wednesday why she should accept late returns from them.[117] Not surprisingly, they essentially wrote back that recounts had been authorized out of concern that the machine tabulation was not accurate; some also noted that because of the size of their county the recounts could not be completed before the deadline. However, the secretary's office had already expressed the view that this was not a legitimate basis on which to authorize a recount. Seeing the writing on the wall, the Bush campaign welcomed her demand for an explanation, arguing that Democrats in selected counties were not engaged in "recounting"; rather, "they are reinventing, attempting to reinterpret the results of an election and the intentions of the voters by subjective, not objective means." While it looked as if Harris might be successful in stopping the recounts, other Bush supporters were not taking any chances. For example, Republican House majority whip Tom Delay sent a staff memo to congressional Republicans pointing out that the House and Senate can reject a state's electoral votes if they decide the votes are tainted. "If there are feelings this is being stolen, there will probably be calls for action," said one Republican.[118]

Later that evening, in a speech timed to interrupt the evening newscasts, Al Gore made a public offer to George W. Bush that was an important development in the public relations battle. Shifting away from his focus on selective recounts in specific counties – which arguably was a (convenient) limitation imposed by Florida law – Gore said that he would end all further legal action if the Texas governor agreed to support Gore's call for a careful hand recount of *all* sixty-seven Florida counties. The move represented a culmination of the early post-butterfly strategy to emphasize "counting all the votes" over technical legal challenges to the results; no doubt, it also represented a concern that the existing recounts would soon be legally shut down.[119] It was designed to place the vice president squarely in the middle

★ WHO WON?

of prevailing public opinion (which still favored recounts) and put Bush in the uncomfortable position of rejecting an effort to avoid litigation and find out who actually got the most votes in Florida.

However, just moments after Vice President Gore made his offer for a statewide recount and just six hours after the county canvassing boards submitted their explanations for why they needed more time, the secretary of state ruled that "the reasons given in the requests are insufficient to warrant waiver of the unambiguous filing deadline imposed by the Florida Legislature." She explained this conclusion by stating her belief that the only legitimate reasons for allowing late returns were "proof of voter fraud that affects the outcome of the election," "substantial non-compliance with statutory election procedures," and "extenuating circumstances" beyond the power of election officials, such as power outages.[120] Harris's announcement allowed Bush to reject Gore's offer by saying that he was just following the law. As he put it in his response to the country a few hours later, "This process must have a point of conclusion, a moment when America and the world know who is the next president. . . . Tonight, Florida's chief election official [has] reaffirmed" the deadline set out in Florida law. "The next and final deadline comes Friday at midnight," when absentee ballots were due.[121]

The Gore campaign immediately characterized the secretary's announcement as an abuse of her discretion and a violation of Judge Lewis's order. By going back into Lewis's court it was also obvious that the case would be going to the Florida Supreme Court. Suddenly, there was increased attention on these justices. Former Florida Supreme Court justice Alan Sundberg rejected "out of hand any suggestion that the Florida Supreme Court is either Democrat-oriented or Republican-oriented. I am satisfied to a moral certainty that their party affiliations will not have any effect on the ruling of these cases." However, Republican state senator-elect Ken Pruitt said that he believed the court's decision to allow hand recounts to continue was motivated in part by "the loyalties of Democratic appointees." One Republican attorney from Jacksonville said that the justices were not political, and that they tried "to clearly interpret what the statutes say." Miami-Dade Circuit Court judge Cindy Lederman referred to the court as "a well-respected group of jurists who will follow the law."[122]

Conservative law professor Michael McConnell said, "If I were a betting man, looking at the unanimously Democratic composition of the Florida Supreme Court, I would put my money on a reversal" of Harris's decision to impose the deadline and not accept late returns. He predicted that the composition of the Court "will be the basis for Republican claims that the process is biased." However, he then pointed out that this alone was not a reason for people to call into question the authority or legitimacy of that institution: "Judges are human, and anyone who thinks they are apolitical hasn't much experience with judges. . . . The Florida Supreme Court was properly appointed" and "unless they do something that is blatantly contrary to the law – which is unlikely when the eyes of the world are upon them – their decision should be accepted as legitimate and, barring unforeseen new legal complications, final." He added that "[t]here do not appear to be federal issues, so the U.S. Supreme Court will not become involved."[123]

While William Safire agreed with the prediction that the Florida justices "would probably continue to allow hand re-re-counts to go forward, hoping that Gore would come out ahead," he also expressed his belief that the only way to stop this "would be to go to the U.S. Supreme Court to argue that a manual recount would introduce more human error or possible mischief. . . . The Supreme Court . . . would put its imprimatur on the best way to decide who shall occupy the presidency. And the vast majority of Americans would readily accept the decision."[124] The *Wall Street Journal's* Robert Bartley agreed that "the Supreme Court is the one body with the prestige to lend legitimacy to any decision." By contrast, Jeffrey Rosen, a law professor and legal affairs writer for the *New Republic*, began expressing the first set of concerns about the impact of such an intervention on that institution. "The harsh reality of this battle is that partisanship is unavoidable; it will infect whomever we entrust with decision-making power. Accordingly," he advised, "the best we can do is to confine this power to the partisan officials – and Florida and ultimately in Congress – whom the voters can eventually hold accountable for the outcome. . . . By resisting the urge to intervene, the Supreme Court can preserve its own legitimacy at the very moment when the other two branches of national government will be unmasked before a divided nation as narrowly self-interested." He recognized that this "may not be an inspiring outcome," but he added that "if history is any guide, the alternative is far worse."[125]

However, Judge Lewis was about to prove that partisanship was not always unavoidable. On Friday morning, November 17, Lewis upheld the authority of the secretary of state to ignore late filed returns. He explained that "the purpose and intent of my [earlier] order was to insure that she in fact properly exercised her discretion, rather than automatically reject returns that came in after the statutory deadline. On the limited evidence presented, it appears that the Secretary has exercised her reasoned judgment to determine what relevant factors and criteria should be considered, applied them to the facts and circumstances pertinent to the individual counties involved, and made her decision. My Order requires nothing more."[126] On behalf of the Bush campaign, Jim Baker declared, "the rule of law has prevailed."[127]

Gore lawyers immediately appealed to the Florida Supreme Court. They soon found out that the federal courts were not going to stop them, for now. The seven Republican and five Democratic judges of the Eleventh Circuit announced unanimously that they were denying the Bush request for an emergency injunction to end the hand recounts. "Both the Constitution of the United States and 3 U.S.C. § 5 indicate that states have the primary authority to determine the manner of appointing Presidential Electors and to resolve most controversies concerning the appointment of Electors."[128] While the Bush campaign expressed its disappointment, it also observed that the judges "specifically noted we are free to return to the federal courts to present our constitutional challenges to the selective and subjective manual recount process at an appropriate time in the future."[129]

A few days before Lewis's second decision, many commentators concluded that most of the key decision-makers in this dispute were making decisions that coincided with their predicted political preferences. Harris was the most obvious, but there were also dueling advisory opinions from the Republican director of the Division of Elections, Clay Roberts, and Democratic attorney general Butterworth. A Democratic district court judge, Donald Middlebrooks, ruled against Bush's request for an emergency injunction. When one looked more deeply, however, this simple assumption of pure partisan reasoning was harder to sustain. After all, the opinion of the Democratic federal judge was upheld unanimously by a federal court that included a majority of seven Republicans. Republican state circuit judge Jorge Labarga had authorized a less strict standard for the review of ballots in Palm Beach. And then there was Terry Lewis, whose decision on Friday morning to uphold Harris's discretion was not what one would predict from a partisan.[130]

Was it reasonable to expect a partisan – even a partisan judge – to rise above his or her political preferences? In the middle of this hectic week, the iconoclastic literary and legal theorist Stanley Fish wrote an opinion in the *New York Times* in which he commented on the perception that everyone involved was simply manipulating the language of high principle to promote low politics. While he claimed that "the only principle operating here is that each party thinks its candidate deserves to win and that the fate of the nation hangs in the balance," he also concluded (typically, for Fish) that this was inevitable, even salutary. The moral, he said, is "not that the political landscape is populated by hypocrites who talk the noble language of principle but then go about practicing politics and usual." Instead, the moral is that "practicing politics as usual is what everyone always does and should do."[131]

Later the same day that Lewis refused to practice what Fish considered to be "politics as usual," the Florida Supreme Court accepted jurisdiction over the Gore appeal of that decision and set oral argument for Monday, November 20, 2000.[132] As its final act of the day, it added the following: "In order to maintain the status quo, the Court, on its own motion, enjoins the Respondent, Secretary of State and Respondent, the Elections Canvassing Commission from certifying the results of the November 7, 2000, presidential election, until further order of this Court. It is NOT the intent of this Order to stop the counting and conveying to the Secretary of State the results of absentee ballots or any other ballots."[133]

Those other ballots were due at midnight. Without the Court's intervention the secretary of state would have certified the election results the next morning, for candidate George W. Bush, while hand recounts were still going on.

CHANGING THE RULES?

THE FLORIDA SUPREME COURT, ROUND ONE

The big question is what is the purpose of an election law?
Katherine Harris thinks the purpose of an election law is to allow
her to administer it. The Supreme Court says no, the purpose of the
Florida election statute is to count every vote.
Yale University law professor Akhil Reed Amar[1]

From its denunciation of "hyper-technical reliance upon
statutory provisions" to its fabrication of new statutory deadlines,
out of whole cloth, the court showed contempt for the authority of the
legislature and set the rules for the conduct of elections, which is explicitly
vested in them by Article II of the U.S. Constitution.
University of Utah law professor Michael McConnell[2]

Judges on supreme courts often must face the decision whether to grant a last-minute stay of execution to a condemned prisoner. But no last-minute reprieve in a capital case received the national attention that followed the Florida Supreme Court's decision to spare Al Gore from his approaching midnight hour.

After her legal victory in Judge Terry Lewis's courtroom on the morning of Friday, November 17, Secretary of State Katherine Harris was poised to seal Gore's fate by certifying the results of the Florida election after counting the mostly Republican absentee ballots and ignoring the ongoing manual recounts in Democratic counties. In just eleven days, George W. Bush's lead in Florida had dropped from more than 1,900 votes to just 300 out of almost 6 million cast in the state. There was good reason to think that this lead could not withstand the manual inspection of the undervote in Democratic counties that used punch card ballots. Machines were unable to find votes on thousands and thousands of cards, and it was generally assumed that a manual inspection of those ballots would result in a significant number of new votes – either because the inevitable and salutary process of vote recovery that was associated with the traditional and routine practice of looking at ballots (the Gore position) or because the local partisans who examined the ballots would find some way to create new votes or otherwise manipulate the process to Gore's advantage (the Bush position). Either way, it seemed certain that if those Democratic canvassing commissions looked at enough of those ballots they would find the votes that Gore would need to win.

Because Gore could only win if recounts were allowed, the Republican strategy from the beginning had been to stop any effort at recounts, first by turning to the federal courts in the hopes that they would find a legal reason to stop this practice and then by calling on a political ally in Florida. Secretary of State Harris was just a short few hours from completing her mission and certifying George W. Bush the winner of the Florida election when the justices of the Florida Supreme Court intervened, first by ruling that the recounts could continue and then by enjoining the secretary from certifying the results of the election until after the Court had ruled on the legality of the manual recounts. *Time* magazine likened Gore to "a death-row inmate walking the long green mile – and getting a temporary stay of execution right outside the death chamber." The Court's actions "might be seen as the great turning point for Gore" or "as a final glimmer of false hope."[3]

The decision of the state high court culminated an amazing eleven days in which almost all the legal issues that would persist throughout the dispute were identified and initially debated (if not resolved), including the legality of the butterfly ballot, the circumstances under which counties could authorize manual recounts, the standards for reviewing ballots to determine voter intent, the equal protection and due process challenges to recounts conducted without clear statewide standards, the discrepancy between the seven-day deadline for certifying results and the authority of counties to conduct recounts, and the fairness of Republican election officials allowing Republican Party members to fill in missing voter information from Republican absentee ballot applications. Still, for all the legal wrangling, courts had not been the driving force behind the controversy during this first phase. Local canvassing boards had made almost all of the key decisions regarding whether or not to conduct recounts. Elected state officials dominated the debates about whether these recounts were legal and by when they had to be completed. Judge Lewis tugged a bit at the secretary of state by requiring her to make it clear to everyone that she was the one making the decision to ignore the recounts (and was not merely required by the law to act as she did). But once that was done he deferred to her authority.

The Florida Supreme Court's decision that Friday afternoon, November 17, was the first indication that judges might be prepared to force state officials to pursue particular courses of action. There is nothing necessarily illegitimate about such a development. In fact, we typically expect judges to give orders to state officials if they believe that those officials are not following the rules. For Gore supporters the supreme court's intervention promised to rescue an orderly and proper recount from the clutches of a partisan hack. As they saw it, the arbitrary and willful power of unprincipled politicians would finally be supplanted by the rule of law. The Bush camp did not see it this way. If one assumed that Judge Lewis was correct that state law gave Katherine Harris the discretion to ignore the results of recounts completed after November 14, then a decision of the state justices to prevent her from properly certifying the election would not be the restoration of law but an assault on lawful authority. From this vantage point, the court would be seen more properly as an activist, partisan institution that was prepared to exercise raw power in order to benefit a favored candidate.

For anyone who did not have a stake in the outcome of this dispute these competing characterizations might have seemed much too stark and combative. A dispassionate observer might have suggested that neither of these views made enough room for the possibility that law may be uncertain and that there were many equally plausible ways of evaluating the claims of both sides. This is the sort of relaxed attitude about law that most people have when they hear about controversies that do not affect them personally or professionally; if people think about them at all is usually enough to be reassured that decision-makers are being deliberate and seem to be acting in good faith. But during the second week of November 2000 it was almost impossible to find anyone who could afford such a relaxed attitude about how judges might proceed in the election dispute. The issues had evolved in such a way that it seemed reasonable to assume that the decision of the Florida court on whether to allow recounts to continue would most likely determine who would be the next president of the United States.

The day after the Florida Supreme Court announced its intention to intervene, Bush's lead over Gore widened from 300 to 930 votes. That was the preliminary effect of incorporating the results of absentee ballots into the vote totals.[4] Seemingly overnight those absentee ballots had become a new front in the recount war. The struggle over absentee ballots pitted those cast by military personnel, who were assumed to be more supportive of Bush, against those sent by State Department employees in foreign missions, who were assumed to be Gore supporters. In Tallahassee, Republican lawyer Jason Unger urged the board to accept military ballots, even without proper postmarks, "since they are overseas fighting for their country." In the end, Unger was able to talk twelve counties into ignoring many technical violations of the laws regulating these ballots, and the result was a gain of 176 net votes for Bush. But he urged no such leeway for U.S. diplomats; for example, he successfully challenged two ballots that were apparently sent from U.S. embassy personnel in India to someone in the United States and postmarked in Maryland.[5] Democratic observers, on the other hand, worked hard to make sure that military ballots fully complied with all state laws regulating absentee ballots – and to disqualify those that did not.

No one seemed particularly interested in Republican efforts to scrutinize the ballots of diplomatic personnel, but Republicans knew that a story about Democrats challenging the votes of military personnel was political dynamite. For Republicans, the general category "overseas absentee ballots," which had been selectively challenged by both sides, became simply "military ballots" with the focus on Democratic efforts.[6] Bush forces started spreading the story to reporters in Florida and arranged to have family members of service men whose ballots had been disqualified show up on the morning television talk shows. By the next day Republicans issued a statement from retired Army General H. Norman Schwarzkopf, saying that "it is a very sad day in our country when the men and women of the armed forces [who] are serving abroad and facing danger . . . are denied the right to vote" because of what he called "some technicality out of their control." Other Bush surrogates, including former presidential candidate and war veteran Bob Dole, New York governor George Pataki, and Montana governor Marc Racicot made sure that the story circulated through many news cycles.[7] The story represented a serious blow to the momentum that had developed with the call to "count every vote." The Gore campaign was so concerned about it that the vice president's running mate, Joe Lieberman, made it a point on the Sunday morning news shows to suggest that military absentee ballots should be given every benefit of the doubt.[8]

This battle over absentee ballots would escalate in the coming days.[9] But for the time being, most of the intensifying controversy surrounded the ongoing hand recounts. After the Florida Supreme Court ruled to allow recounts to continue during the appeal of Judge Lewis's ruling, Miami-Dade once again reversed course and authorized a full manual recount,[10] which meant that three counties were now looking to see if undervote inspection would change the outcome of the election. Gore supporters knew that it was imperative to make these counts proceed as quickly as possible and to have them appear to be as orderly as possible. By contrast, it was in the interest of Republicans to have these recounts proceed as slowly as possible and to portray the process as a mess.[11] One Bush adviser said that the "Republican team decided on Saturday to dramatize their criticism of the hand recounts by using evidence from the field." In other words, the essence of the battle was now "a contest between dueling images of chaos and order." It was an image contest that each side said was "at the strategic heart of each side's legal and political objectives."[12]

The Bush campaign instructed Montana governor Marc Racicot to lead the assault by repeating stories of "Bush ballots mixed in with Gore ballots, of ballots used as fans, of exhausted elderly counters dropping piles of ballots on the floor where they were trampled by other counters," all in the hope that "when the American people learn about these things, they're going to ask themselves what in the name of God is going on here." Bags of chad were also brandished before television cameras as more evidence of sloppiness.[13] Republicans accused Democratic officials of dropping ballots and even swallowing chads as a way of destroying evidence that ballots were being mishandled or new votes created.[14] In response Democratic officials charged Republicans with "doing everything possible to impede" a hand recount that would "guarantee that the will of the people will be reflected" in the vote.[15] Republicans attempted to slow down hand counting in Palm Beach, challenging many votes that reporters believed to be clearly punched. In one precinct, 281 of 1,741 ballots were challenged, thus relegating them to a special pile that would have to be reviewed, one by one, by the three-member canvassing commission. In other cases Republicans failed to provide enough counters to assemble counting teams. At one point, Judge Charles Burton told a Republican observer, "I certainly want to give you guys an opportunity to look, but we can't spend twenty minutes on each ballot." In light of these efforts election officials began to express concerns that they may not finish before Thanksgiving.[16]

On the legal front, complaints were still being filed in state circuit, with Republicans looking for a judge who would shut it all down and Democrats trying to force counties to use more generous standards for counting votes.[17] Gore supporters worried that Gore was not picking up enough votes. By the end of Friday, with 122 of 604 precincts counted, Gore had netted thirty-eight new votes, and a day later, with one third of the precincts reporting, Gore had picked up just seventy-nine. Democrats asked circuit judge John Miller to instruct Broward to move off the "two-corner chad" rule and adopt instead a rule that considered dimpled ballots if the ballot as a whole suggested the voters' intent. The judge told Democrats to wait until Monday to hear whether the state's high court had something to say about standards. He added, though, that "if I find that the board isn't counting the pregnant chads and all the other stuff that's supposed to show . . . the intent of the voter, I will tell them to do it all again."[18] In light of that, on Sunday the Broward board voted to adopt the general "voter intent" standard, much to the chagrin of Republicans who charged that "Gore and his attorneys are trying to come up with ways to continue counting until they get the result they want." Given that Broward would become the one place where significant votes were eventually found for Gore, this switch under pressure from this judge turned out to be extremely important.[19]

As people waited for the Florida Supreme Court to take up these issues polls showed that around 61 percent of people said they thought it was more important to "remove all doubt" about the results than to "get matters resolved as soon as possible." When asked whether they thought counting punch card votes by hand was more or less fair than machine counts, opinion was split 43 percent (more fair) to 44 percent (less), although Gore voters thought it was more fair by a margin of 67–20 percent, while Bush supporters thought it was less fair by 72–20 percent. Results also suggested some maneuvering room for the Florida Supreme Court: in one poll, 61 percent considered it acceptable if the Florida vote became final without hand recounts, while a full 71 percent thought it would be acceptable if a court stepped in and ordered the recounts.[20] Mainstream elite opinion reflected these attitudes. The *New York Times* editorialized that the "court in its rulings next week should make clear that manual counts, which are allowed under Florida law, are to be included in the final tally."[21] The news analysis provided by the *Los Angeles Times* said that by accepting the case the

Court provided "a crucial opportunity to gain the one thing that no one in the ballot counting process appears to have so far – broadly accepted legitimacy as a neutral referee." This was important, because it was most likely that this court would be "the last legal word on the balloting question," since "the U.S. Supreme Court repeatedly has said that it has no authority to alter a state Supreme Court's interpretation of its own state's laws," and it would be a "difficult task" to find a federal issue that could be the basis of federal court involvement.[22] In their news analysis, the *Boston Globe* explained that "the true meaning of the court's intervention will be to convey legitimacy on whatever result finally emerges from the deadlocked election in Florida. . . . [C]ourts are where the unreasonable are forced to seek reason," and "this is one of those moments when the nation needs a reasoning branch of government."[23]

Others also began to take steps to prepare public opinion for a judicial resolution of the dispute. Former American Bar Association President Chesterfield Smith of Miami, who argued more than a hundred cases before the Florida high court since 1948, reassured the public that "[t]his is not an ideological court. They will try to decide this case based on the law." Jon I. Mills of the University of Florida's law school predicted that the justices "will not view this as a partisan matter or an ideological issue. They will be writing for history."[24] Even Leonard Garment, former counsel to Richard Nixon, said that while judges may not be perfect, compared with conventional politicians "they are marvels of civic virtue."[25] While he did not vouch for their virtue, Columbia University history professor Alan Brinkley expressed hope that the judges of the Florida Supreme Court would be the most likely institution "to produce a result that would seem more or less fair. The members are, to be sure, appointees of Democratic governors, but despite their recent wrangling with Jeb Bush, my impression is that they have a reputation for impartiality and fairness."[26] By contrast, many Republicans were setting the stage for resistance to an unfavorable ruling. House Majority Leader Dick Armey declared that "I'm not sure I'm willing to say that the presidency of the United States for the next four years should be decided by seven Democrat judges."[27] The *National Review* took a more gloves-off approach. They referred to the Florida Supreme Court as "that murderer's row of liberal activists," and they warned that "a final decision that goes for Gore will be greeted with extreme, and deserved, skepticism." They also noted that there is "a conservative case for inculcating a reverence, even a logically unwarranted reverence, for imperfect but useful institutions. There is no good case for inculcating reverence toward corrupt ones."[28]

While commentators expressed hope or concern, the lawyers for the two campaigns prepared the arguments they would be submitting before the Florida Supreme Court in the case of *Palm Beach County Canvassing Board v. Harris.*

The Gore brief was written primarily by Washington lawyer David Boies and Florida attorney W. Dexter Douglass.[29] They emphasized that in close elections Florida law provided for the use of manual recounts to ensure the most accurate result, with the main object being "to determine the voter's intent" so that the election result reflects the people's expressed views.[30] Citing the Florida Supreme Court's 1917 case *Darby v. State*, the Gore lawyers argued that "the Board must examine each ballot for all evidence of the voter's intent and make its determination based on the totality of circumstances." The brief made particular note of the 1996 Massachusetts case *Delahunt v. Johnston* and especially that court's language that the mere "presence of a discernible impression made by a stylus" is "a clear indication of a voter's intent" even if the chad remains entirely in place on the punch card.[31] However, "instead of seeking to facilitate" the completion of this process "the Secretary of State has chosen repeatedly . . . to try to stop or delay the lawful manual recount of ballots." They claimed that her position would effectively nullify that part of state law that allows for manual recounts and would lead unlawfully to the rejection of "ballots that are conceded to have been validly cast, and that were identified in a properly initiated and conducted recount." This would be "a revolutionary change in Florida law" and would result in the unacceptable conclusion that "she may disregard properly cast votes . . . even if ongoing recounts are in the process of demonstrating that valid ballots were not tabulated *and that the wrong candidate is being certified the winner*" (emphasis in original). Given that this position is clearly mistaken and inconsistent with Florida law and basic democratic principles, "her rejection of these ballots . . . is not entitled to any deference" since it amounts to "an abuse of her discretion" as an election official.

On the central issue of the statutory deadline, though, the lawyers argued that no portion of Florida law "imposes any deadline for the submission of corrected, amended, or supplemental returns deemed necessary by the county canvassing board to ensure that the return submitted accurately and completely reflects the votes counted initially and in any recount." This emphasis on accurate and complete results rather than fixed deadlines was reinforced by the official statutory definition of "the official return of the election" to include "the return printed by the automatic tabulating equipment" plus "write-in, absentee, and manually counted votes."[32] They suggested that the best reading of the deadline plus the recount provisions was "that all manually recounted votes be tabulated and that certification be delayed pending the completion of a manual recount that was requested on a timely basis." This was also the reading that was most consistent with the court's 1988 decision in *Chappell v. Martinez,* which stated that "the electorate's effecting its will through its balloting, not the hypertechnical compliance with statutes, is the object of holding an election." They ended by arguing that there is a weighty national interest "in avoiding uncertainty or confusion regarding the identity of our President-elect," and this meant that the state canvassing commission should certify the election only after "the most accurate vote count possible."

The Bush brief, written primarily by former deputy assistant attorney general Michael A. Carvin, Florida lawyer and former state deputy attorney general Barry Richard, and Washington attorney Benjamin Ginsberg, began with a simple statement of law:[33] "Two statutes control this case. Section 102.111 of the Florida Statutes provides that the Elections Canvassing Commission 'shall ignore' late-filed returns, and Section 102.112 provides that the Commission 'may ignore' late-filed returns. . . . Simply put, [petitioners] ask this Court to revise the statute's plain directive that late-filed returns 'may be ignored' to read instead that the Secretary '*may not* ignore' late-filed returns if the county board is conducting a manual recount." The Gore team's theory "literally rewrites the Florida code." Whatever one feels about the appropriateness of manual recounts, "the legislature has plainly *required* county canvassing boards to complete their work, including any recounts, within seven days of an election" and "just as plainly *requires* the Commission to certify final election results" even when doing so would be "to ignore returns from county canvassing boards that fail to meet their deadline."[34] If the counties had no general obligation to get the job done in time it would be "extraordinarily inequitable" for the legislature to authorize personal fines of $200 per day against county board members, but that provision was also a part of the statutory scheme.[35] Indeed, this statutory language "vividly illustrates that the Florida legislature . . . did not either view manual recounts as essential to accurately determining the vote count or treat the endless pursuit of time-consuming manual recounts as more important than the finality and equal treatment insured by having a uniform deadline."

If recounts could be continued even after the statutory deadline, then for how long could they go on? The Gore lawyers seemed to be requesting an open-ended injunction that would allow recounts indefinitely, but "we must assume that even Petitioners agree that some deadline at some point is appropriate prior to the Inauguration itself." But if that was correct then their request amounted to "asking the Court to substitute a judicially created deadline for the date selected by the legislature," which is a power that the court did not have. Moreover, as a warning to the state court that their word may not be the last one, the lawyers argued that "*federal* law places additional constraints on courts that require them strictly to adhere to the legislature's prescribed manner for conducting an election to choose a state's presidential electors. Under 3 U.S.C. § 5, a State is required to select its electors 'by laws enacted *prior* to' election day," and "no provision of state law in effect prior to the election . . . granted *courts* equitable power to disregard both the deadline and the Secretary's exercise of reasoned discretion." Moreover, the U.S. Constitution in Article II, Section 1 "provides that the *legislatures* of the States will prescribe the manner in which presidential electors are chosen," and it followed that "all actors at the state level – including judges – are bound to respect the choices made by the Florida legislature as to the process of selecting the state's presidential electors." In passing, they briefly added that partial manual recounts in selected counties, with no meaningful standards for determining a vote, might also violate both the equal protection clause and the due process clause of the Fourteenth Amendment of the U.S. Constitution.

In their "answer brief" to the Bush arguments, the Gore lawyers added one surprising element to their submission: they requested that the court draw on its equitable powers under the Florida Constitution to instruct the canvassing boards "to apply the objective intent standard to determine whether to count a ballot." They noted that "different canvassing boards have used different standards in recounting ballots" and that several trial court judges had already been asked to evaluate the legality of various standards. It was obvious that "this issue must ultimately be resolved by this Court" and in light of "the expedited time frame in which the issue must be addressed," it was best that "it be resolved now." Clarifying the proper legal standard would also "ensure that the counties use a proper standard – and a uniform standard – as they conduct the manual recounts now underway." The only possible standard under Florida law, at least since the 1917 case *Darby v. State,* was one in which the entire ballot was reviewed to see if the intent of the voter could be discerned. The brief also underscored that this standard "is part of an extensive and comprehensive body of law, well-established throughout states." The brief highlighted other state case law illustrating this point[36] and also pointed out that even the Texas recount statute signed into law by Governor George Bush allows for a vote to be recorded if "the chad reflects by other means a clearly ascertainable intent of the voter to vote."[37]

At 2:00 P.M. on Monday, November 20, two days after the Bush campaigned hoped that Harris would declare Bush the winner, much of the country witnessed an unprecedented event: live coverage by the major national networks, local affiliates, and cable news stations of oral arguments before a state supreme court.[38] It was the first time that the country would have a chance to hear focused exchanges in the legal issues that were now at the heart of the presidential contest. Rather than hear the usual day-after-day political spinning from both camps, the public would see extended colloquies between judges and lawyers, in a surrounding where respectful and temperate arguments replaced the more familiar cacophony of overheated accusations. It would at least seem as if the election dispute had reached a more dispassionate and impartial forum.

Privately, though, the Bush lawyers had good reasons to be concerned about whether they could expect an open-minded exchange from these justices. That same morning, as Bush attorney Michael Carvin was making final preparations for oral argument, he reportedly received a note from a source close to the Florida Supreme Court indicating that the justices had already composed a draft opinion on the basis of the briefs that had been submitted. They intended to rule for Gore and extend the deadline five days. There was nothing illegal or even unethical about a group of judges making a decision based on written arguments, but in such cases judges do not typically then "go on the nation's television screens and act as if their minds were still open." When Carvin asked Bush overseer James Baker how he should proceed, Baker advised him to "[j]ust stand up there and answer their questions."[39]

At the appointed hour, Chief Justice Charles T. Wells opened the proceeding by noting that "the court is, certainly, aware of the historic nature of this session and is aware that this is a matter of utmost and vital importance to our nation, our state, and our world."[40] Very quickly Wells asked the lawyer for Attorney General Butterworth, Paul Hancock, what his position was "as to the date in December that the Florida's electoral votes would be prejudiced or not counted in the electoral college, if there is not a certification by the secretary . . . ?" It was an extremely revealing question, since it suggested that Wells was already thinking beyond the question of whether the seven-day deadline was fixed toward the date to which it might be extended. It confirmed for Carvin and other Republicans that the case was already decided.[41]

Hancock's answer seemed straightforward at the time, but it would take on great significance later in the saga: "December 12, Your Honor, is my understanding. The electoral college meets on December 18." December 12 was the deadline set in federal law (3 U.S.C. § 5) for states to resolve all disputes over the appointment of presidential electors in order to ensure that the Congress would not attempt to question the legitimacy of their appointment. States could take longer than this date if they wanted and still have their votes counted in the electoral college, but a lingering dispute meant that a state would not be able to take advantage of this congressionally-granted "safe harbor" for their electors. There was nothing in state law that mandated this deadline but at the time it seemed like a safe and reliable date to pick. After all, it was still twenty-two days away, and they had every reason to think that if the justices were favorably inclined toward their position it would not take twenty-two days to get the votes counted.

After brief appearances by representatives from two of the canvassing boards the Gore campaign's star lawyer, David Boies, approached the bench. He began by offering what he hoped would be a persuasive, comprehensive reading of the various Florida statutes governing recounts, deadlines, certifications, and contests. "We believe that if you read all of those sections together, what you have is a requirement of the counties to come forward with their returns seven days after the election. Those returns will then be supplemented by manual recounts, by absentee ballots. And then there will be an official return. And that official return will then be certified. And at that point, we believe, 168, [the] contest [provision], takes place if there's going to be one." Some of the justices were worried that a further delay in certification might prevent a candidate from "contesting" the result in time before the presidential electors had to be chosen. Wells asked Boies: "If the counsel for the attorney general is correct and Dec. 12 is the date by which . . . the certification has to be made for the Electoral College," then does that mean that "all of the controversies and contests in the state have to be finally determined by that date[?]" Boies's answer, at the time, seemed perfectly safe: "I do, Your Honor."

Boies also had to reject any assumption that the seven-day deadline was fixed by the legislature. "The legislature is saying you must get your returns in by seven days, but . . . nothing in that statute says the official returns have to be completed by seven days, [and] the official returns [are] defined in statute to include the result not only of the initial returns but of the manual recounted votes and of the absentee votes that are not included in those first seven days." Justice Harding asked, "What is the time limit, then?" Boies responded: "Well, Your Honor, if I were sitting in your chair, that would be a difficult question for me. . . . If you work backward from how much time you do realistically need for a contest, that amount of time, working back from Dec. 12, could guide the court in determining what was the outer date from the time that the recount had to be completed." Moreover, "the Secretary of State's discretion to the extent that she has any, would be discretion to say, 'I need to have the results by this particular date in order to be sure that the results are included by Dec. 12.'"

In response to Justice Quince's question about whether "any mark made by the voter would be evidence of that voter's intent and should be counted as such?" Boies said, "I think so, Your Honor." Justice Barbara J. Pariente then asked, "Is the uniformity of how these manual recounts are conducted essential to the integrity of the process or also to the constitutionality of the statute?" Boies answered, "Your Honor, I think it is important to the integrity of the process. I think if you had very wide variations, you could raise constitutional problems." However, it was Boies's position that the variations existed only on the margins, since the vast majority of disputed undervote ballots were being treated in precisely the same way. In response to Justice Pariente's inquiry about whether selectively recounting some punch card counties gives them "a greater voice in this election than other counties," Boies initially responded that any candidate could have requested a manual recount if there was a belief that the machine tabulations were not accurate, but then he added that "if you concluded that it was essential to avoid unfairness or some kind of overweighting of one county's vote over another county's vote, this court has within its equitable power to have a statewide recount." With that, Gore's official legal position was now identical to his public offer to support a statewide recount.

The lawyer for the Bush campaign, Michael Carvin, hammered home the inflexibility of the certification deadline and the more appropriate option of raising concerns about undervotes in an election contest rather than during this phase in the process. "May it please the court, as the colloquy today indicates, there is a very clear procedure for resolving all the questions that the justices have asked. And that's set forth in the statute. You set a firm deadline and you make sure that everyone gets their votes in at the same time and if there are any problems in terms of voter tabulations or to the kinds of questions that we've done, you've got to keep to that deadline so you'll have time to do the election contest after that." This deadline should be treated as inflexible because "[t]he legislature has no preference for manual recounts as the most accurate way of determining votes, which is why they make it entirely optional. The only right and duty in the statute is the right of the state officials to have the election returns after seven days. That is a mandatory duty. . . . And they expressly contemplated that all counties, regardless of whether conducting manual recounts, would play by the same rules and get their election returns in on time."

Carvin mentioned in passing that they had complained in federal court "about the ad hoc nature of the way in which ballots are tallied in different counties," but when asked why he was not raising the equal protection argument before the state supreme court, he replied that "there's a much simpler basis for deciding this case than going all the way to the U.S. Constitution," namely, enforcing the mandatory statutory deadline. When Justice Pariente asked him specifically whether "you are asking us to resolve" the claim that the recount "process is inherently flawed and unconstitutional," Carvin replied, "No, Your Honor. I think we should follow the process that's set out in the statute." There were a number of other times when Carvin refused to respond to very specific questions about whether he wanted these justices to address potential flaws in the recount process itself. It is difficult to avoid the conclusion that he simply did not want the Florida justices to resolve any possible flaws that might exist in the manual recounting process. His focus was on stopping recounts by insisting that they were just too late, and if the Florida court did not do that then perhaps these issues could be revisited by a different court. Carvin ended with a thinly veiled warning when he said that "federal courts – federal law will not allow the State of Florida to change the rules of the election, after the election has taken place, to avoid precisely the evil I have been discussing, which is that there will be ad hoc decision-making that could be influenced by subjective or partisan concerns."

After a few more attorneys spoke, Boies got the final word. The justices still wanted clarification on the basis for their "authority to set a [new] deadline [for official certification of the election results]?" Boies responded that the adjustment in the deadline was part of the process of interpreting these conflicting laws. What the court "has to do, is to reconcile the entire statutory scheme, and the statutory scheme, long before there was this election, provided for manual recounts, and this court, I suggest, cannot presume that the legislature meant to provide for these manual recounts and yet to make that an illusory right. . . [T]he counties have said that [if] you will tell us what the standard is and leave us free from interference, we can get this done in a matter of days. . . . [A]nother way of approaching it is to say we will give you the standard to apply. We will tell you to get it done in seven days [and] you would certainly have enough time after that, to complete a contest." With that final suggestion – seven more days of counting before officially certifying the results – the case was submitted, and the justices retired. The proceedings took just under two-and-a-half hours.

The *Los Angeles Times* perceptively noted that the justices "seemed focused much less on whether than on how to include the results from the manual recounts" that Bush was trying to exclude completely. Chief Justice Wells in particular "seemed very concerned about deadlines. But by contrast with Harris and her lawyers, who have stressed the Nov. 14 deadlines in the law, the cutoff date that he focused on was the practical deadline of how long the recounts could go on while still allowing the state to choose its 25 electors by Dec. 12."[42] An editorial in the *Boston Globe* concluded that "the justices of the Florida Supreme Court demonstrated yesterday that, if it comes to a legal battle, theirs is the venue where it should be fought. . . . Their questions were a refreshing contrast to the propaganda barrages of both campaigns over the past 13 days. Their ruling . . . holds the promise of bringing legal order and prompt resolution to the 2000 presidential election."[43] The *Philadelphia Inquirer* echoed the sentiment, saying that "maybe [it] isn't such a terrible thing after all [that] the post-election endgame has fallen into the clutches of the legal system, as opposed to the political one. . . . [The hearing] before the Florida Supreme Court in Tallahassee was a model of civility, decorum and reasonableness. . . ."[44] Writing in the *New York Times*, Professor Steven Gillers of New York University Law School said that "[t]he Supreme Court is now the only state institution able to quell the political paranoia of all but the fiercest partisans and bring this presidential election to a credible close. . . . The court should set a timetable for the resolution of all election challenges before the Electoral College meets on Dec. 18. . . . The court should also provide guidance on issues now before lower courts," such as the standards to be used in evaluating ballots. He added that "because United State's Supreme Court review of these issues is remote, the State Supreme Court's answers to them now will hasten the end of the story."[45]

While the country was transfixed by the oral arguments, other important developments continued to unfold on that Monday. Judge Jorge Labarga, who heard arguments the previous Friday on the Palm Beach butterfly ballot dispute, ruled that he did not have the authority to order a revote. He recognized that there were times when the laws of Florida and other states have been interpreted to allow for this extraordinary remedy,[46] but he noted that none of these cases involved elections for president, and "our forefathers included clear and unambiguous language in the Constitution of the United States which require that presidential 'electors' be elected on the same day throughout the United States."[47] One columnist called the decision "heroic" and suggested that "it underscores why the switch from Florida's political corridors to its courts should be reassuring."[48] Lawyers representing Palm Beach immediately appealed.

In another courtroom, Democratic activist Harry Jacobs won a round in his Seminole County lawsuit against Republican efforts to rehabilitate absentee ballot applications that had missing voter identification numbers. Judge Debra Nelson, a recent appointee of Jeb Bush, rejected Republican efforts to throw out the lawsuit. A hearing on the matter was scheduled to occur in one week on November 27.[49]

In the meantime, the Palm Beach recount was continuing – albeit at a snail's pace and without much headway for Gore. Approximately 104 out of the county's 531 precincts had been counted, with Gore netting a gain of just three votes. Even though Palm Beach was officially using a general "intent of the voter" standard – which theoretically allowed even dimpled chads to be counted if there was general evidence of voter intent – in practice the canvassing commission was not counting dimpled chads, explaining that it was usually "impossible to tell whether the dimples represent a vote, a mistake or a change of heart." Because of Democratic objections, those ballots were set aside in case a judge ordered the board to once again change the standards it was using to determine a valid vote.[50] Moreover, Judge Charles Burton noted that because of frequent objections it was "extremely unlikely" that the job would be completed by Thursday, Thanksgiving Day. The board announced that if they did not finish by Thanksgiving they were planning on taking a break for the holiday starting late Wednesday. Miami-Dade was also moving slowly, with 67 of the 614 precincts counted and an unofficial net gain of 46 votes for Gore. By contrast, Broward was moving more quickly, completing 544 of its 609 precincts and finding Gore an additional 117 votes.[51] This county was hopeful that it could complete its recount before Thanksgiving.

THE DECISION

Just hours before the Florida Supreme Court was to hand down its decision, a useful summary of recent events was provided in an on-line dialogue between Professors Alan Brinkley and Michael McConnell; their exchange also demonstrated the extent of the partisan divide even between scholars of good will. Brinkley said that "everything I see and read suggests that the counting itself is proceeding reasonably smoothly and responsibly. Evidence for that is, among other things, that these counts, directed by Democrats, are not turning up many votes for Gore." The Republicans "are so determined to portray the count as 'chaotic' and unjust, that they are inventing or egregiously exaggerating all sorts of fantastic stories about abuses in the voting." His overall view was that Bush's miniscule lead was based on "an honest, if perhaps incomplete, count," and that Gore had an "equally legitimate claim that ballot irregularities (some of them uncorrectable) almost certainly cost him many thousands of votes in Florida." Noting that "nothing is harder in any walk of life than accepting that there can be two legitimate, opposing positions," he ended by suggestion that it was "up to the court to save both these campaigns from themselves."[52]

McConnell acknowledged that "the court seemed a port of reasonableness in the storm of overheated partisan accusation," at least in the sense that it was "a forum where bombast is replaced by sober recitation of fact and law. But," warned McConnell, "the courts can be masters of illusion – willfulness in the robes of law." He advised that "it is a mistake to think that judges are immune from partisan considerations," but he added that "it is also a mistake to think they are merely politicians." In this case he thought the court was constrained in at least three ways: first, by the language of the statutes, which (he thought) required counties to report election results within seven days and allowed the secretary to ignore late returns; second, by the need to at least appear evenhanded – "probably more of a constraint than the statutory language" since judges, while political, also "have an even stronger desire to be seen as a judge who decides cases dispassionately and fairly, according to the law"; and third, by practicality, in particular the looming deadlines for the selection of presidential electors. McConnell's suggestion for the best way out was for the court to rule that Harris could impose the deadline and ignore late results, but that she could not force the county boards to stop counting, and if those counts reveal that (in the language of the election contest statute) "a number of legal votes sufficient to change or place in doubt the result of the election" had been rejected by Harris then this could "serve as the basis for a contest." He ended by warning that if the Florida court tried to act more boldly "then they deserve all the criticism they will get."[53]

It did not take long to find out how the justices would proceed. At 9:45 P.M. on Tuesday evening, in a dramatic courthouse announcement carried live across the country, the Florida Supreme Court issued its decision in the case of *Palm Beach County Canvassing Board v. Harris*. The justices ruled unanimously that Secretary of State Harris had abused her discretion by not accepting late-filed results; they also ruled that the counties would have until 5:00 P.M. on Sunday, November 26 – five days away, at the end of the Thanksgiving holiday weekend – to turn in the results of manual recounts to Harris, at which point Harris was free to certify the official election results. The decision was exactly what Carvin had been told it would be before oral arguments.

The court began by placing its decision in the larger context of the Florida Supreme Court's election law jurisprudence. "Twenty-five years ago, this Court commented that the will of the people, not a hyper-technical reliance upon statutory provisions, should be our guiding principle in election cases." In the case of *Boardman v. Esteva* (Fla. 1975) the justices wrote that "by refusing to recognize an otherwise valid exercise of the right of a citizen to vote for the sake of sacred, unyielding adherence to statutory scripture, we would in effect nullify that right." They said that their goal today was the same as it was then, "to reach the result that reflects the will of the voters, whatever that might be."[54] Anticipating a concern about the court "rewriting" state legislation, the justices immediately added that "this fundamental principle, and our traditional rules of statutory construction, guide our decision today."

After ruling that counties had the authority to do recounts simple as a "human check on both the malfunction of tabulation equipment and error in failing to accurately count the ballots," they then noted that for large counties "the time frame for conducting a manual recount . . . is in conflict with the time frame for submitting county returns."[55] While the court could have followed the advice of Bush lawyers and resolved the conflict by simply favoring the deadline over the recount, the justices decided instead that it was more proper to give legal effect to all elements of the election law. This was possible because the "mandatory language" telling the secretary of state that she "shall" ignore late returns "conflicts with the permissive language" of the following section that said that she "may" ignore those returns.[56] They used what they called "traditional rules of statutory construction" in including that the "may ignore" language better represented the legislature's intent. For example: (a) the more specific statute was the permissive one; (b) "it also is well-settled that when two statutes are in conflict, the more recently enacted statute controls the older statute"; (c) the statutes should be read in a way that does not "render meaningless or absurd any other statutory provision," and it would be meaningless to assess "fines against members of a dilatory canvassing board in order to force them to get in late returns as soon as possible" unless late returns could be accepted; and (d) "related statutory provisions must be treated as a cohesive whole," which in this case meant that the deadline should be read in light of the fact that manual recounts are also authorized and might take more than the allotted time.

However, in considering "the circumstances under which the Secretary may lawfully ignore returns filed pursuant to" the manual recount provision, the justices said, "it is necessary to examine the interplay between our statutory and constitutional law at both the state and federal levels." In a new section of the opinion (Section VIII) entitled "The Right to Vote," the justices held that existing election laws "must be liberally construed in favor of the citizens' right to vote"[57] so that courts do not "lose sight of the fundamental purpose of election laws," which is "to facilitate and safeguard the right of each voter to express his or her will in the context of our representative democracy." In other words, "technical statutory requirements must not be exalted over the substance of this right." All of this led the court to declare that ignoring returns "is appropriate only if the returns are submitted to the Department so late that their inclusion will compromise the integrity of the electoral process" either by preventing someone from contesting a certification or by precluding Florida voters from participating fully in the federal election process. "To disenfranchise electors in an effort to deter Board members, as the Secretary in the present case proposes, is unreasonable, unnecessary, and violates longstanding law."

The court then quoted from the Illinois Supreme Court case *Pullen v. Mulligan* (Ill. 1990) to make the point that "where the intention of the voter can be ascertained with reasonable certainty from his ballot, that intention will be given effect even though the ballot is not strictly in conformity with the law. . . . To invalidate a ballot which clearly reflects the voter's intent, simply because a machine cannot read it, would subordinate substance to form and promote the means at the expense of the end." Finally, "we conclude that we must invoke the equitable powers of this Court to fashion a remedy that will allow a fair and expeditious resolution of the questions presented here." The justices then ordered Secretary Harris to accept all amended returns up through Sunday, November 26 at 5:00 P.M. In a footnote the court also observed that "at oral argument, we inquired as to whether the presidential candidates were interested in our consideration of a reopening of the opportunity to request recounts in any additional counties. Neither candidate requested such an opportunity."

The court did not give Boies the seven days he was hoping for; just five, with a holiday smack in the middle of the extension. Perhaps more important, the court also did not clarify the other issue that Boies told them was squarely before the court – the proper legal standard for evaluating the ballots for voter intent – at least not beyond the oblique reference to the discussion of voter intent in the excerpt from the Illinois Supreme Court's opinion.

THE REACTION

The Florida Supreme Court's astonishing decision was like a starter's gun triggering at least three simultaneous races: the race to complete (disrupt) the newly revitalized hand recounts, the race to Washington to seek (head off) the Supreme Court's intervention, and the race to legitimate (delegitimate) the Florida Court's decision. There was also a race to the hospital, as Bush running mate Dick Cheney suffered a "mild" heart attack a few hours after the decision was announced.[58]

With the Gore campaign desperately trying to chip away at an unbelievably close 664-vote Bush lead, Gore supporters welcomed the ruling, even though many worried that the court's deadline was less than completely helpful. Boies said, optimistically, that "there is no basis to appeal to the [U.S.] Supreme Court," since that body had repeatedly said that it has no authority to alter a state court's interpretation of state law; in fact, the *Los Angeles Times* reported that even some Bush "campaign insiders privately remain dubious that the federal judiciary will overrule Florida's top court on a matter of state law."[59] The public face of the Bush campaign, however, was strong, insistent, even furious. The measured, diplomatic tone that Jim Baker had struggled to maintain (not always successfully) finally collapsed. He called the ruling "unfair and unacceptable" and suggested that the GOP-run state legislature might have to intervene. He accused the justices of having "pretty well rewritten the Florida electoral code" and insisted that "it is not fair to change the election laws of Florida by judicial fiat after the election has been held."[60] Bush himself accused the state supreme court of "overreaching its authority," adding that "we believe the justices have used the bench to change Florida's election laws and usurp the authority of Florida's election officials."[61] More generally, "within hours of the judicial ruling . . . Republicans launched a full-scale attack on Florida's Supreme Court."[62] The House majority leader, Dick Armey, said, "I don't think the country will accept a clearly partisan decision by a partisan court." House majority whip Tom DeLay called the ruling "a blatant and extraordinary abuse of judicial power. With this decision, a collection of liberal activists has arbitrarily swept away thoughtfully designed statutes to ensure free and fair elections and replaced them with their own political opinion."[63] Missouri Senator Christopher Bond said he was "stunned" by the decision and added that Bush "is being victimized by an opponent who will do anything to win – even after the election is over."[64]

Conservatives were mustering up what some referred to as "impeachment outrage," that visceral commitment to all-out political warfare that characterized the effort to impeach President Bill Clinton just two years earlier. One analyst said simply, "This is impeachment, the sequel." Popular conservative radio talk show host Rush Limbaugh announced that "the whole thing has been rigged and we've known it from the get-go." Grover Nyquist, head of Americans for Tax Reform, accused Gore of "trying to steal the election" by "changing the rules."[65] Conservative columnist George Will charged that "Al Gore's assault on the rule of law, crowned with success by Florida's lawless Supreme Court, has now become a crisis of the American regime. . . . By legislating – by airily rewriting Florida's election law and applying it retroactively to this election – the court has thrown down a gauntlet to the state's legislature."[66]

The Republican rhetoric was so blistering that it became a major topic of debate in the *New York Times*. Anthony Lewis said that the Bush campaign was "playing with fire" and using language that "recalled a dark episode in our recent history" when Southern segregationists vowed to resist the authority of the U.S. Supreme Court after *Brown v. Board of Education*.[67] Bob Herbert charged the Republicans with "coming dangerously close to breaking faith with the system" by stating that they would simply refuse to accept any outcome that flowed out of the decision of the Florida Supreme Court.[68] The *New York Times* claimed that Bush "risks undermining the rule of law and the office he hopes to occupy."[69] New York University law professor Barry Friedman said that by "treating the courts as if they were just one more partisan institution, staffed with political hacks who decide cases consistent with their parties' views," the Republicans along with some sympathetic "legal scholars" who "should know better" are acting in ways that "threaten to undermine respect for the judicial system as a whole." The truth of the matter is that "the Florida Supreme Court's decision was law, in the sense that the opinion relied on standard methods of legal interpretation," and while "reasonable legal minds might differ as to how that conflict should be resolved" the decision as a whole "was an entirely lawyerly undertaking." He ended by suggesting that "we will have done ourselves a disservice if in the interest of solving this short-term problem we attack the long-term integrity and neutrality of the judiciary."[70] Most law professors, however, were sharply split along ideological lines.[71]

While Gore supporters got the chance they were hoping for, it was also becoming clear to them that the vote counters were not as eager to find Gore votes as was hoped. The day after the court's decision, Democratic lawyers went back to Judge Labarga's court in Palm Beach to argue that the canvassing board was disqualifying too many of the dimpled ballots. In addition, the board had accumulated more than 8,000 questionable ballots, and concerns grew that there was insufficient time to review them prior to the court's new deadline.[72] The news was slightly better in Broward County, where new votes were being recovered from the recount at a quick enough pace to be completed in time.[73]

However, it was Miami-Dade that made the next day's headlines. Around 10:00 A.M., the canvassing board announced that in order to meet the court's deadline they would cease the hand recount of all 654,000 ballots and instead focus only on the more than 10,000 "undervote" ballots they had identified. That announcement once again tapped into Republican impeachment outrage, and in protest "a horde of shouting, shoving protestors – many wearing suits and ties – stormed an upper floor of a downtown skyscraper." The crowd, which included staff members of House Republicans who had been flown to Florida to help in the battle, tried to push their way into a computer room, sending police racing to the rescue of the board. Some members of the crowd also jostled the local Democratic chairman and prevented him from leaving the building after they saw him holding a sample ballot. After this episode the board reconvened under police escort, and less than two hours after its initial decision the three board members "abruptly announced they were quitting, citing the lack of time to conduct even a more limited canvass of the" undervotes. The board members denied that they were reacting to crowd pressure; instead, they focused on the deadline and on the perception that they were not engaged in a fair and open process.[74]

It was a stunning setback for the Gore campaign, which barely had time to enjoy the benefits of the Florida Supreme Court decision. Lawyers immediately filed suit to force the board to do the recount, claiming that their decision "flies in the face of an unambiguous, unanimous Supreme Court decision of less than 24 hours ago."[75] However, on Thanksgiving Day, in the case *Gore v. Miami-Dade County Canvassing Board,* the same Democratic justices who apparently went out of their way to assist the vice president unanimously turned him down. The decision was particularly painful because Gore had gained 157 votes in that county before the recount was halted, and by all indications (at the time) there were plenty more where that came from.[76]

The Miami-Dade decision was not the only bad news for the Gore campaign. Not long after that announcement, Judge Labarga ruled that he would not force the Palm Beach Canvassing Board automatically to tally "dimpled" ballots; as long as the board had no per se rule of exclusion and was attempting to interpret each ballot, they were within their authority to be the principal fact-finder with respect to voter intent.[77] At the same time, Republican leaders of the Florida legislature, outraged by the Florida court's decision, took their cue from Jim Baker's statement and began considering a special legislative session "to seat a set of electoral college members who favor Bush, regardless of the vote's outcome." The incoming speaker of the House, Tom Feeney, saying that he was moving "to help resolve the constitutional crisis . . . the court has created," had already prepared a two-page legal analysis arguing that the legislature could appoint its own slate of electors if it appeared as though the voting dispute would not be resolved by December 12.[78] Palm Beach also decided to take Thanksgiving off, and there were concerns about whether it was going to complete its recount. As one Republican spokesman put it, "It appears that there is much to be pleased with."[79] By Thanksgiving, the only good news for Gore was that the Broward County recount was adding to his vote total – a net gain of 225 with approximately 1,700 still to be reviewed by the canvassing commission.[80] Still, that county alone was not going to produce the votes that Gore needed by Sunday to overcome his official 930 vote deficit against Bush.[81]

And, of course, the Bush campaign was heading for the U.S. Supreme Court.[82] By Thursday night the Gore lawyers filed their opposition to the request for Supreme Court review, arguing that it was a "bald attempt to federalize a state court dispute" based on "wild, irresponsible and utterly unsupported allegations concerning the conduct of those recounts."[83] The press focused most on the Bush camp's claims that the selective recounts violated the equal protection and due process clauses of the Fourteenth Amendment. Increasingly, though, people were taking notice of "a third and more novel claim": that the Florida Supreme Court decision violated the state legislature's power under the Constitution to direct the selection of electors. It was an unfamiliar claim; it was not discussed in constitutional law casebooks and it thus was probably never discussed in any law school courses on constitutional law – no surprise, since (as far as anyone could tell) there were no especially interesting Supreme Court cases on the issue. It was uncharted territory, and the idea that the U.S. Supreme Court would jump on such an obscure and undeveloped argument seemed far-fetched.

However, the more that people considered the claim, the more that the Republican's public reaction to the Florida Supreme Court's decision began to make sense as something other than simple anger and frustration. Calling the Florida Supreme Court "lawless" and charging it with "changing the rules" after the election, might not have been mere political hyperbole. Slowly, it was beginning to seem like a predicate for an innovative constitutional argument and a way around the traditional deference that federal courts showed to state courts when state judges interpreted state law.

Some former law clerks to conservative justices indicated that they would not be surprised if the Court took the case. UC Berkeley law professor John C. Yoo, a former law clerk for Justice Clarence Thomas, said that it would be best for the country if the Supreme Court got involved, since "the political process is starting to break down" and the Court "is the only institution that could claim sufficient legitimacy to actually give a decision that would be obeyed without dispute."[84] However, not everyone was so sure. Jeffrey Rosen advised the justices not to enter this political thicket. "By trying to take charge of the electoral dispute, the [Florida] justices may have imagined that they could resolve it. Instead, they may have succeeded only in making it worse. Let's hope the United States Supreme Court resists the temptation to lend a similar helping hand."[85]

3

A SHOT ACROSS THE BOW

THE U.S. SUPREME COURT
ENTERS THE FRAY

★ ★ ★

[It is most important] that the [U.S. Supreme] court do itself no harm.
It easily could if it issued a split decision and the split seemed even in part
to follow political lines. The court's authority would be sorely damaged for
little gain. That authority—the acceptance of the court's decisions as legitimate
and binding even by those who deeply disagree with them—is one of the
great national treasures. We would rather the court punt
than split in this ragged way.
Editorial, *Washington Post*[1]

The days following the Florida Supreme Court's November 21 ruling extending the deadline for submitting the results of manual recounts were a roller coaster ride for the country and the campaigns.[2] What appeared initially to be a decision that could easily set the stage for a Gore vote-counting victory quickly turned into something much more complicated, and much less favorable to Gore. Recounts were set to proceed in three heavily Democratic counties, and then suddenly the road that had been cleared by the Florida justices once again become bumpy, with some lanes becoming fully blocked.

Palm Beach County was not proceeding quickly enough and was being very stingy in its evaluations of disputed ballots.[3] Much more devastating was the unexpected decision of the Miami-Dade Canvassing Commission to end its recount, just hours after deciding to go ahead with an examination of disputed "undercount" ballots and just minutes after Republican demonstrators created a stir outside their meeting. Democrats responded with an announcement that they would contest that decision after the election had been certified; they also requested that the Justice Department investigate whether Republican protestors "managed to create a climate of fear and intimidation."[4] The next day, matters were made even worse for Gore when Nassau County election officials voted to certify the original returns announced on election night rather than the tally derived from the automatic recount, an action that resulted in a net gain of fifty-one votes for Bush. Gore lawyers pledged to contest the results in this county as well.[5] The only good news for Gore came from Broward, which was proceeding with the inspection of disputed ballots and finding a good number of votes. Still, Gore was behind by 930 votes, and by the Friday after Thanksgiving it was clear that he would not be able to make up that number of votes in Broward alone. Even with more help from Palm Beach he would still probably come up short when the 5:00 P.M. Sunday deadline arrived.[6]

In light of all of this, the Bush campaign's decision to appeal to the Supreme Court – which initially seemed like an essential (albeit somewhat desperate) effort at undoing the damage caused by the Florida Court's decision – was starting to be seen as a useful but perhaps unnecessary safety net. Some true believers supported the legal arguments, but most observers thought that it was extremely unlikely that the justices would be able to find either the political incentive or the legal foundation to intervene in this state court's interpretation of its own state laws.[7]

And so it was a surprise to most observers when on Friday, November 24, just one day after Thanksgiving and two days before the recount deadline, the justices of the Supreme Court announced that they were stepping into the fray.[8] As a result of the Bush appeal, the case was given the name *Bush v. Palm Beach County Canvassing Board*. Oral arguments were scheduled for Friday, December 1, in one week.

Interestingly, the justices decided to not focus on the question of "whether the use of arbitrary, standardless, and selective manual recounts that threaten to overturn the results of an election for President of the United States violates the Equal Protection or Due Process Clauses."[9] There had been enough experience with recounts (and enough complaints from Republicans) to make ripe an investigation of the standards that were supposed to be governing the process. It was widely assumed at the time that the justices did not believe that this argument had any legal merit.[10]

Instead, the focus was on Bush's claim that the Florida Supreme Court had not followed the state election statutes. Typically it is up to states to debate whether state courts have correctly interpreted state law. However,

★ A SHOT ACROSS THE BOW

Bush's lawyers pointed out that Article II, Section 1 of the U.S. Constitution gave state *legislatures* the authority to determine the manner by which presidential electors would be appointed, and they claimed that this provision gave the U.S. Supreme Court the authority to review state court interpretations of those state laws that were part of that process. This argument was supplemented by a reference to the federal law that regulates aspects of presidential elections; 3 U.S.C. § 5 was designed to give states some reassurance that Congress would not challenge their presidential electors. The promise was that if states resolved disputes over presidential electors early enough (no later than six days before the Electoral College was scheduled to meet, which in 2000 was December 12) and in accordance with state laws that existed prior to Election Day, then those electors would be moored in what Gore attorney Laurence Tribe referred to as a "safe harbor" and would be counted by the Congress. Of course, from the vantage point of the Gore camp, this is precisely what happened in Florida, given that the existing law allowed for recounts. However, the Bush camp argued that the Florida court ignored those provisions establishing the deadline after which the secretary of state may ignore votes. Thus, the Florida court's decision was not only a mistake of state law but also violation of the federal Constitution and federal law.

In granting the petition for review, the justices specifically instructed the parties to submit briefs only on these arguments. The Court added one additional question for the parties to address: "What would be the consequences of this Court's finding that the decision of the Supreme Court of Florida does not comply with 3 U.S.C. Sec. 5?" It was a question that was on everyone's mind.

THE CERTIFICATION AND THE CONTEST

Bush attorneys reacted to the Supreme Court's announcement with "whoops of delight," believing that it was an ominous sign for Gore and a sign that "we have more cards to play than they do."[11] The initial response of most court watchers was surprise that the justices would intervene in a dispute that had traditionally been considered a matter of state law; those who were surprised often regained their composure by speculating that the justices were merely trying to bestow some legitimacy on the process or trying to "calm the storm."[12] Linda Greenhouse noted that "by seizing a central role for itself," the Court "put on the line its own legitimacy as an institution able to rise above partisan rancor and to serve as a fair and neutral arbiter, the honest broker that many people have found absent from the scene so far." She expressed concern, though, that "a decision split along the court's usual ideological fault lines could be questioned by partisan supporters of Vice President Gore, perhaps damaging the court's credibility and doing little to calm the political tempest."[13] Walter Dellinger, President Clinton's former solicitor general, suggested that this was nothing to worry about, since "the justices are much more concerned about their role in history than the outcome of any particular presidential election," which means that the justices will not "decide this case on a partisan basis."[14] This was consistent with the reassurances that others were giving about how the justices "are usually thought of in ideological or philosophical but not partisan terms," which was important because the "effort to rise above party and politics matters; the perception that courts are nonpartisan, if not nonpolitical, is in some sense the bedrock of their extraordinary authority in this country." On the other hand, there was an abiding concern among many that "this year's election cases could damage that authority."[15] Moreover, at least two conservative legal scholars expressed the belief that the Court would not have taken the case unless it planned on reversing the Florida court, even at the "risk of being tarred as partisan."[16]

After this initial round of commentary, attention quickly turned back to vote counting. The good news for the Gore campaign was that Broward County finished its recount at 11:51 P.M. Saturday night, finding 567 votes for Gore.[17] However, the three-member Palm Beach Canvassing Commission, after having taken a break on Thanksgiving, was now working around the clock, knowing that they had to review three hundred cards an hour (one ballot every twelve seconds) to make the Sunday 5:00 P.M. deadline.[18] With four hundred Republican protesters in the streets, the Palm Beach count turned into a mad dash. Around noon on Sunday they realized they would not finish on time, and so the canvassing board faxed a letter to Harris asking for an extension. Three hours later she responded, predictably, that she could not alter the Supreme Court's deadline. Judge Burton told reporters that "the secretary of state has decided to shut us down." At a little after 4:00 P.M., with a bit less than a thousand ballots still to review, the board decided to keep counting and submit partial returns at five o'clock. The partial returns reported a net Gore gain of approximately 180 votes. This was not bad, but in the final hours the board was rejecting almost every ballot they were reviewing, leading Democrats to estimate that the board's more strict (and then arbitrarily dismissive) standards cost the vice president around eight hundred votes.[19]

At 7:30 P.M., just two and a half hours after the Florida Supreme Court's deadline, the state's elections canvassing commission met before a battery of television cameras to finalize their work. After stating that "it remains my opinion that the proper returns in this election are the returns that were certified by those deadlines," which would be a Bush margin of 930 votes, Secretary Harris announced that Palm Beach's partial manual recount, which showed a gain of 176 votes for Gore, would be rejected as inconsistent with the recount provision of state law, which she interpreted as requiring a full recount. That meant that she would be reverting to the results reported after the first mandatory machine recount – more than two weeks earlier. The results: after one hundred million votes cast nationwide, and almost six million in Florida, George W. Bush had an official lead of 537 votes over Al Gore.

After that figure was announced, Harris uttered the words that the Bush campaign had been waiting to hear since the election nineteen days ago: "On behalf of the state Elections Canvassing Commission and in accordance with the laws of the state of Florida, I hereby declare Gov. George W. Bush the winner of Florida's 25 electoral votes for the president for the United States."[20]

A half-hour earlier, Palm Beach finished its recount.

A few minutes after Harris's announcement, Senator Joe Lieberman, Gore's running mate, addressed a nationally televised audience and called the results "an incomplete and inaccurate count" that left the Gore campaign with no choice but to contest the results in court.[21] Lieberman was followed immediately by Baker, who called on Gore to concede the election; he also reasserted that Bush would "absolutely" go ahead with its U.S. Supreme Court appeal, explaining that "we have no assurance that the other side will stop."[22] Later that night Bush gave a nationally televised speech, saying that "Secretary Cheney and I are honored and humbled to have won the state of Florida, which gives us the needed electoral votes to win the election." Dick Cheney was chosen to head the official transition to a Bush administration.[23] Florida governor Jeb Bush signed the paperwork officially certifying his older brother the winner of Florida's twenty-five Electoral College votes.[24] Some Republicans began referring to his brother as "president-elect." Democrats said that this title was premature.[25]

The following evening, before a prime-time television audience, the vice president explained that for three weeks he had been trying unsuccessfully to get "a single full and accurate count" of the Florida vote. "Two hundred years from now, when future Americans study this presidential election, let them learn that Americans did everything they could to ensure that all citizens who voted had their votes counted."[26] In other words, attorneys for Gore had filed a lawsuit contesting the certified election results. Under a 1999 state law designed to make it easier for courts to examine and correct these results, an election could be successfully contested if one could establish that the vote totals included "a number of illegal votes" or rejected "a number of legal votes sufficient to change or place in doubt the result of the election."[27] The lawyers claimed that this happened in three counties. As for Miami-Dade, they argued that it had a "mandatory obligation" to complete its authorized recount of roughly 10,750 undervote ballots, and if such a review was completed it could result in another six hundred votes for Gore. They also wanted the results from the Miami-Dade partial manual recount be included in the state's final tally, which would give the vice president an additional 160 votes. As for Palm Beach, they asked that the results of their recount be included in the final tally, which would give Gore approximately 215 votes. They also asked for a review of approximately 892 disputed Palm Beach ballots that had been segregated at the request of Democratic observers who believed that they reflected a vote for the vice president. As for Nassau County, they asked the court to include the results of their mechanical recount rather than the county's initial count, which were the results that the secretary relied on and which cost Gore another fifty-one votes. In all, the lawsuit requested a bit more than four hundred additional votes be given to Gore immediately; of course, because that was obviously not enough to win, recounts would also have to begin again – and soon.[28]

Hearings in the case *Gore v. Harris* began Monday, November 27, in the courtroom of Leon County Circuit Court judge N. Sanders Sauls. The campaigns were represented primarily by David Boies and W. Dexter Douglas (for Gore) and Barry Richard and Phil Beck (for Bush). Sauls was a former conservative Democrat who switched to the Republican Party right before Republican Governor Bob Martinez appointed him to the bench in 1989. He was characterized as a "straight shooter" and a "bit of a maverick" who had gotten in trouble with the Florida Supreme Court two years earlier for his activities as the chief judge of the Second Judicial Circuit. (He had been accused of playing favorites and unfairly firing the local court administrator.)[29] More significant, the Gore team had been informed by local lawyers that Sauls was the "worst judge we could have gotten," a conservative whose "social circles were all Bush friends."[30] It became clear early on that Sauls was not going to be overly helpful. On Tuesday, he announced his intention to start the trial on Saturday, December 2 – later than the Gore campaign wanted, given the few days it would take to conduct the trial, plus (if they won) the time it would take to review the ballots, plus the December 12 deadline that once seemed so far away but now was now fast approaching (due to Gore's success in getting the deadline for certification postponed).[31] On Wednesday, Boies was telling Judge Sauls that "we believe the counting has to start right away" on the 13,300 contested Palm Beach and Miami-Dade ballots if Gore would be in a position to benefit from a favorable ruling. When the judge held firm to his timetable, the attorneys asked the Florida high court to order Sauls to start; however, that court turned them down later in the week.[32] Sauls was willing to authorize the moving of 1.1 million ballots to his Tallahassee courthouse, but he did not promise to review them, saying simply that "I have no idea what we're going to do concerning ballots, counting or not counting ballots, [but] we need to have some ballots on hand."[33]

The Gore contest was premised on the assumption that for Gore to win he needed to get a court to authorize manual inspection of undervote or disputed ballots. But a front-page story in many newspapers on Tuesday, November 28, raised the possibility that the vice president may have another judicial route to the White House. The case of *Jacobs v. Seminole County Canvassing Board,* which had been percolating for weeks, was finally drawing significant attention.[34] It involved a challenge by a local Democratic lawyer, officially unaffiliated with the Gore campaign, to the efforts of Republican election officials and party officials to fill in missing voter information on Republican absentee ballots. The supervisor of elections in Seminole County, Sandra Goard, conceded in a deposition that she allowed two Republican party operatives to spend ten days in a back room of her office correcting 4,700 Republican absentee ballot applications so they would not be thrown out. State statutes were purposefully very strict about absentee ballots because of extensive Florida experience with voter fraud, and Goard acknowledged that the law prohibited third parties from filling in information on already signed forms. She also conceded (according to the complaint) that "no one ever was allowed to correct applications in the past, and that her staff assisted the GOP representatives by sorting Republican applications from Democratic applications – something else that had never been done before." Lawyers also determined that "some Democratic ballot applications apparently arrived without some of the required information, but they were thrown out and Democrats were not provided the same opportunity to make them comply" with state law. Suddenly, this lawsuit was now seen as "one of Gore's best shots at winning the White House." It was also seen as the suit that forced a reversal in the "principled" positions of the campaigns, with Democrats arguing that there should be strict enforcement of statutory requirements even if this resulted in ballot disqualification, and Republicans arguing that the rights of the voters to have their votes count was more important than "hyper-technical" compliance with state law.[35]

Also, on Tuesday, November 28, a special committee of the Florida legislature met in preparation for a special legislative session designed to appoint its own slate of electors if these disputes were not resolved by December 12. A number of constitutional scholars were strongly critical of the legislature's actions, pointing out that the Constitution gives state legislatures the authority merely to establish "the manner" by which electors would be chosen and then noting that the Florida legislature established the manner in its election laws – a vote on Election Day. The concern was that any postelection attempt by a legislature to "reclaim" its presumptive "plenary" power and overturn the results of an election could create havoc in future presidential elections, as partisan majorities in statehouses across the country considered whether they should act whenever they were unhappy with the popular vote. Despite these worries, the Florida Republicans were going to do all they could to ensure a Bush victory, and (as always in this dispute) it was easy enough find a law professor with prestigious credentials to vouch for the legitimacy of a particular course of action. A day later, on a strict party-line vote, the committee decided to recommend a special legislative session.[36]

With all that had happened since the previous Friday, the urgency of the review of the Florida Supreme Court's decision to the U.S. Supreme Court had dissipated. Even if the Gore contest made headway, by Friday, the day set for oral arguments in Washington, Gore "will be well into a completely separate legal process" involving not the deadline for certifying an election but rather the standards for contesting a completed certification. The case would not technically be moot, since the delayed certification reduced Bush's lead from 930 to 537, but that difference obviously did not make a difference in determining who received the state's Electoral College votes.[37] Some thought that, at best, the Court's decision "will define the depth of the hole Gore needs to dig out of in the contests."[38] Others thought that, as a way out of the political thicket, the court "will dismiss it as moot as soon as the process has played out,"[39] while still others suggested that "the issue might not be mootness, but ripeness" in the sense that it was not yet clear whether a resolution of this question would matter.[40] The editorial in the *Chicago Tribune* speculated that the Court's most "shrewd" option would be to "simply listen but not rule any time soon" so that "if and when the case no longer matters, the court could dismiss it."[41]

The brief for the Bush campaign was written primarily by Michael Carvin, Barry Richard, Theodore Olson, and Benjamin Ginsberg.[42] The focus of their argument was the claim that because the Florida Supreme Court drew on its "equitable" powers in "altering Florida's methods and timetables for the determination of controversies regarding the appointment of presidential electors" it was acting contrary to Article II, Section 1 of the Constitution and the "requirement" in 3 U.S.C. § 5 that all disputes regarding presidential electors be resolved exclusively by reference to "laws enacted prior to" Election Day. The lawyers pointed out that the section 5 language "was enacted in 1887 as a reaction to the contested Hayes-Tilden election of 1876, a contest marked by naked partisanship, post-election maneuvering and accusations of corruption. In adopting the statutory scheme that emphasizes certainty and clear, pre-set rules to govern disputes, Congress was evidently determined to avoid a similar episode." While under normal circumstances state courts may have some equitable authority to make adjustments in legislatively determined timetables, and while in general state court interpretations of state law should not be second-guessed by federal courts, "[u]nder 3 U.S.C. § 5, however, this Court has an independent obligation to ensure that Florida resolves any controversies over the appointment of electors by reference to the rules enacted by the legislature prior to the election, not *post hoc* standards announced for the first time by courts some two weeks after the election." They cited the largely unknown case of *McPherson v. Blacker* (1892) to make the point that disputes arising out of the appointment of electors are not merely political questions but raise "a judicial question" for federal courts.

In this case the review process was simple enough. Florida statutes say either that the secretary of state "shall ignore" or "may ignore" returned filed after the seven-day deadline, but the Florida court "concluded retroactively that the Elections Canvassing Commission shall *not* and may *not* ignore late-filed returns, but *must* hold the results of a national election open for an additional extended period of time." Thus, "the decision below was not dictated by preexisting law and, in fact, the statutory provisions applicable to resolving disputes over the appointment of electors were expressly overridden. . . . Indeed, it dismissed such provisions as inconvenient '[t]echnical statutory requirements.'"

This was the same basis for arguing that the Florida court had violated Article II, Section 1 of the Constitution. Citing *McPherson* again, they argued that "the Constitution 'leaves it to the legislature *exclusively* to define the method of effecting the object' of appointing electors." This exclusive authority was assaulted both by the Florida court's invocation of its equitable powers and by its reference to "the Florida constitution as '[t]he abiding principle governing all election law in Florida.'" While the provisions of a constitution are "an acceptable source of law for an election of a state official, it cannot suffice with respect to the appointment of presidential electors," presumably because the state's constitution did not reflect the exclusive, unfettered choice of the legislature.

The Gore campaign brief was written primarily by Harvard law professor Laurence H. Tribe, along with Ronald A. Klain, David Boies, Kendall Coffey, Peter J. Rubin, and Kathleen M. Sullivan.[43] If the centerpiece of the Bush argument was the claim that the Florida court changed the rules, the anchor of the Gore brief was the contrary claim that the decision "was an ordinary exercise in statutory interpretation." The entire Bush argument "rests on intemperate and insupportable mischaracterizations of the Florida Supreme Court's decision as usurping the role of the state legislature. In fact, the Florida court played a familiar and quintessentially judicial role: it interpreted Florida law 'us[ing] traditional rule of statutory construction to resolve [statutory] ambiguities." Merely "permitting state courts to interpret their laws – in ways that will, by definition, disappoint one or another litigant – does not violate either 3 U.S.C. § 5 . . . or the federal Constitution." To rule otherwise would amount to an "attack" on the entire judiciary, and unless rebuffed it "would cast a shadow of illegitimacy over much of the indispensable and wholly lawful work of this Court and of state and federal courts throughout the nation." The Gore lawyers even pointed out (in their reply brief) that the other side "fails even to cite the crucial statute" authorizing manual recounts. "Allowing the legislature's manual recount provisions to be given effect is not like changing the rules after the game has been played."[44]

To cover all bases, the Gore lawyers argued that even if the state high court's decision might be seen by some as enacting new law, it would still not violate 3 U.S.C. § 5 since that section of federal law imposed no requirement on the states to do anything; it merely said that if the states resolve disputes in accordance with existing state law those electors will enjoy a "safe harbor." As one analyst put it soon after passage of the act, "Congress does not command the states to provide for a determination of the controversies or contests that may arise concerning the appointment of the electors, does not even declare it to be the duty of the states to do so, but simply holds out an inducement for them so to act."[45] The brief concluded that a determination of noncompliance with 3 U.S.C. § 5 "would not support a reversal of the judgment below"; after all, since "the statute does not require the States to do anything, a failure to meet the standard set out in the statute is not a ground for reversal. At most, the consequence of such a determination by this Court would be to render the safe-harbor provision inapplicable" to the Florida electors. It would then be up to the Congress to decide whether or not those electors would actually be challenged at the time that their votes were counted.

Still, neither this provision of federal law nor Article II of the Constitution was violated by the decision, since the state legislature explicitly gave the Florida Supreme Court the authority to rule on these sorts of cases – thus, a decision by a court is one of the choices made by the state legislature relating to the manner by which presidential electors would be appointed. Bush's lawyers acknowledged that the state legislature could have gone so far as to give the state courts the authority to appoint the electors themselves, and so "surely it may engage in the much less intrusive, and more familiar, role of garden variety statutory interpretation." Of course, they claimed that the Florida court did not merely interpret the law but rather "eviscerated" the state statutes, but this accusation was pure hyperbole. "Indeed, in *McPherson* itself, the state Supreme Court below had measured the statute providing for the appointment of electors for conformity with 'the state constitution and laws,' and this Court concluded that it was 'not authorized to revise the conclusions of the state court on these matters of local law.' This very conclusion is enough to dispose of petitioner's Article II claim."

For all the technical discussions of federal law, at the heart of this dispute was the issue of what counted as a proper interpretation of the law. Every day judges offer interpretations of law that a person could, if properly motivated, characterize as lawless or as inadequately grounded in some legal text. Some might even characterize many Supreme Court decisions this way. Linda Greenhouse of the *New York Times* argued that if the justices were going to find a legal or institutional interest that bisected the partisan divide it could very well be the Court's "stake in rejecting any suggestion that the power of judges 'to say what the law is,' in Chief Justice John Marshall's famous phrase, amounts to 'usurpation.'" She speculated that the Bush view of the Florida Supreme Court as writing new law "may prove a hard sell even for Justice Scalia," who once wrote: "I am not so naive (nor do I think our forebears were) as to be unaware that judges in a real sense 'make' law. But they make it as judges make it, which is to say as though they were 'finding' it – discerning what the law is, rather than decreeing what it is today changed to, or what it will tomorrow be."[46] Greenhouse concluded that "in judging the Florida election dispute, the justices inevitably will be judging themselves."[47] It was a point that would come back dramatically, perhaps unforgettably, during the final act, when the idea would be memorialized by a dissenting justice who believed that an assault on the very idea of judicial authority was precisely the meaning of the Court's efforts.

The day before scheduled oral arguments, the Supreme Court announced that it would be releasing an audiotape of the arguments immediately after the hearing was concluded. It was a clear indication that the justices were mindful of the extraordinary public interest in their participation in this dispute. The cable news channels, along with news radio stations around the country, announced that they would be carrying the broadcast of the oral arguments within minutes of their completion, sometime after 11:30 in the morning on Friday, December 1. Supreme Court scholars had been listening to oral arguments for some time; audio collections of many oral arguments were even available on the Internet.[48] But this would be the first time in history that so many people would be listening to the justices as they put on their public face. People started lining up more than a day early for a chance at one of the few public seats in the Court's chamber.[49]

On the day of the arguments the streets surrounding the Court were jammed with demonstrators and television satellite trucks. It was a sharp contrast to the relative calm inside the building.[50] The courtroom was packed with spectators and dignitaries. In the first row of seats, behind the lawyers, were Republican Senators Orrin Hatch of Utah, Fred Thompson of Tennessee, and former senator Howard Baker. They were seated with Democratic Senators Edward M. Kennedy of Massachusetts, Patrick Leahy of Vermont, and Carl Levin of Michigan. Two of Gore's senior advisers, Warren Christopher and William M. Daley, were also present. Gore's four children were seated one row back. Judge Burton, the chair of the Palm Beach County Canvassing Board, was also in attendance. After all, that board was the named defendant in this action.[51]

Representing the two campaigns were two very experienced veterans of Supreme Court oral arguments – "big guns," as one paper called them: Theodore Olson for Bush and Laurence H. Tribe for Gore.[52] Also participating were Joseph Klock, Jr., the lawyer for the Republican Florida secretary of state, and Paul Hancock, representing the Democratic Florida attorney general.

The argument began promptly at 10:00 A.M. with Olson speaking first.[53] His first sentence charged that the Florida Supreme Court "rewrote Florida legislation," but before he could argue that this violated 3 U.S.C. § 5 Justice Sandra Day O'Connor interrupted and asked: "Isn't Section 5 sort of a safe harbor provision for states" designed to be something that "Congress can look at in resolving such a dispute[?] I just don't quite understand how it would be independently enforceable." This began a line of hostile questioning on the section 5 argument from many of the Court's conservatives, including Anthony Kennedy, Antonin Scalia, and even Chief Justice William H. Rehnquist, who commented that "it seems to me [this section] can just as easily be read as a direction to Congress, saying what we are going to do when these electoral votes are presented to us for counting."

Justice John Paul Stevens then pressed Olson to see if he would acknowledge that there may be some circumstances under which Florida law would require Harris to accept late returns, and it led to a series of staccato exchanges: "Does that mean if there were an act of God that prevented the returns from being filed that she would have discretion either to accept or reject the returns?" Olson: "Yes, I believe – " Stevens: "She would have the discretion?" Olson: "Yes." Stevens: "Would she be compelled in that event to accept the returns?" Olson: "I don't think so. She took the position – " Stevens: "She has the total discretion either to accept or reject?" Olson: "That's – " Stevens: "Is there any circumstance in which she would be compelled to accept a late return?" Olson finally answered no, that "whether it was shall ignore or may ignore, it was not must accept." Stevens: "Under any circumstances it was not must [accept]?" Olson: "No, under no circumstances was it must accept. Now – " Stevens: "Even in an act of God or fraud?" Olson: "I don't believe so, Justice Stevens." Stevens: "Okay." Like most cross examinations, it did not break the witness or force him to admit a mistake, but it led Olson to express an extreme view, and this laid a foundation for later questioning of the lawyer for the secretary of state.

Justice Ruth Bader Ginsburg then said that by focusing on that deadline Olson was "skipping over what I thought was a key piece of the Florida legislation," the recount provision, which allowed a party to request a recount even on the sixth day after an election, and "it would be impossible in a populous county to in one day do what the statute instructs must be done when there's a recount." The Florida court said that "there has to be a reconciliation between this, yes, there can be recounts and, yes, there's a deadline." When Olson responded that the legislature imposed the deadline even with knowledge of the recount provision, Ginsburg replied that while one "can certainly argue" this view "one could also argue what the Florida Supreme Court said, and I do not know of any case where we have impugned a state supreme court the way you are doing in this case. I mean, in case after case we have said that we owe the highest respect to what the state says, state supreme court says, is the state's law." Olson's only response was to reiterate that, in his judgment, the Florida court went too far and rewrote the law.

Stevens jumped back in, saying that in interpreting these competing statutes the Florida judges "relied on four traditional canons of statutory construction." When Olson responded that they merely "recited four canons of statutory construction, Justice Stevens," the justice let out a sound of bemused exasperation, but Olson continued that "it's relatively obvious" that the Florida judges "change[d] the rules."

It might have been predictable that the more liberal members of the Court would challenge Olson's view of the Florida court's opinion, but then Scalia contradicted him, saying "I don't read their opinion that way, Mr. Olson. It seems to me that the portion of their opinion dealing with statutory construction ends with a conclusion that the Secretary has discretion." Olson: "Well, yes, I agree with that up to a point, but then it says that she must accept these returns that are after the deadline." Scalia: "That was not on the basis of any canons of statutory construction. That was on the basis of the state's constitution." Olson: "That's right, but – so there was both going on, and what the court was bound and determined to do was to get to a consequence that the court determined was consistent with the will of the people, irrespective of the statute – ."

Olson did not seem to fully appreciate the significance of Scalia's point, and the rest of the courtroom would not pick up on it for some time. But Scalia's question was the first indication from one of the Court's conservatives about their line of attack, and it was an ingenious way of avoiding a decision that attempted to explain the difference between an acceptable and unacceptable statutory interpretation. The problem with the Florida court's decision was not that it was an unreasonable reading of the statutes; it was that the court's *statutory* interpretation ended with a (reasonable) conclusion that Harris had discretion, but then the court went on and set aside that conclusion after referring to the state *constitution.* If the conservatives could show that the Florida court pitted the state constitution against the legislative scheme, then they could conclude that the state high court undermined the state legislature's Article II authority to control the manner of appointment of presidential electors.

This line of argument also made sense of the conservatives' impatience with Olson's focus on 3 U.S.C. § 5. That federal law simply required the states to resolve conflicts in accordance with state *law* enacted before the election. If the Florida Supreme Court relied both on the state statutes and on the state constitution that would still be relying on preexisting law, since the constitution is part of state law. The provision that would make meaningful Scalia's distinction between the state statutes and the state constitution was Article II, Section 1 of the Constitution, which vests in state *legislatures* the authority to determine the manner of selecting presidential electors. Under this theory, the Florida Supreme Court's decision would not be assailable on any theory that it "changed the law" or "changed the rules of the game"; it would be that the court gave preference to the state constitution over the state statutes, a practice that in normal circumstances was commonplace – even salutary – but that, in these special circumstance, might be unconstitutional if one believed that the U.S. Constitution gives state legislatures the plenary power to choose presidential electors in a manner that violated their own state constitutions.[54]

This would become clearer later in the discussion. For the time being, it receded from attention as Justice David Souter once again picked up on the problem with Olson's Title 3 argument. Souter's problem was that 3 U.S.C. § 5, along with § 15, "has committed the determination of the issues that you raise and the consequences to follow from them to the Congress," and he expressed doubt that "the Federal judiciary [should] be interfering in what seems to be a very carefully thought out scheme for determining what happens if you are right." When Olson said that the statute reflected "Congress' desire to avoid the very controversy, chaos, conflict, which even – " Souter interrupted to say, "Well, but Section 15 assumes that there is controversy and chaos. . . . Section 15 isn't providing for challenges except in situations perhaps exactly like this one. . . . If Congress wanted this Court to get into the issue at this stage, it seems passing strange to me that despite all the elaborateness of Section 15 there wouldn't have been some mention of Federal litigation proceeding in the Section 15 proceeding."

Joseph P. Klock, Jr., was next, representing the Florida secretary of state. Before he could get too far in reiterating how the Florida Supreme Court changed the law, Stevens jumped in, eager to pick up where he had left off with Olson. After Klock reported that Secretary Harris told the canvassing boards that she had the discretion to accept late ballots only in certain cases, such as fraud or acts of God, Stevens asked whether "she would have to exercise her discretion in those conditions," and Klock, in contradiction to Olson, said, "I think she would have to exercise her discretion." Having got what he wanted on this line of questioning Stevens then set another trap. "I understand your position is that [the court's interpretation of Harris's discretion] was entirely new?" Klock: "Yes, sir." Stevens: "I'm just wondering, therefore your submission is that it was not dictated by the constitution or by prior precedent?" Klock: "No, Your Honor."

It was what Stevens wanted to hear: the Florida court did not substitute a case law or constitutional law requirement for the legislative enactment. It was in perfect contradiction to Scalia's line of attack, although most of the lawyers did not yet fully appreciate the significance of the point. But the justices knew, and Rehnquist immediately noticed Klock's "mistake" and attempted to rehabilitate the witness: "I thought you said a moment ago that the court, the Florida court did rely on the Florida Constitution. There's a section of their opinion that's devoted to it."

Klock: "Your Honor, in devising the remedy, they refer to the Florida Constitution, but the issue that we're here on, as I understand it, sir, is whether or not the law changed." He still didn't get it, and Rehnquist was going to have to start spelling it out. Rehnquist: "I think perhaps another statement of the issue is to what extent did the Florida Supreme Court, in construing the statute, rely on more general provisions of the Florida Constitution which they cited in their opinion?" Klock still didn't follow. "I think they did rely, in creating the remedy on the Florida Constitution . . . [but] the issue again is whether or not the law that they articulated on November 21 is different than the law that existed on November 7." This was not helpful for the conservatives. The only basis for striking down the Florida court's opinion simply on the basis of a theory that they "changed the law" was 3 U.S.C. § 5, but the conservatives did not seem completely convinced that this section was judicially enforceable here, and so they wanted to rely on Article II. Scalia: "Your position is so long as it's different, it violates Section 5 and therefore we have a right to step in?" Klock: "Well, Justice Scalia, we have not addressed the Federal issues because, I mean, we're in a situation where you have – " Scalia (interrupting): "Well, this is a Federal court. (Laughter.) What are you here for, if you're not addressing – " Klock: "I understand that, sir. I apologize."

For those listening to the oral arguments up to this point the situation appeared very good for Al Gore. The conservative justices seemed hostile to the notion that 3 U.S.C. § 5 was judicially enforceable, and the more liberal members seemed willing to defer to the judgment of the Florida Supreme Court. There were a few fleeting exchanges in which Justices Scalia and Rehnquist focused on the Florida court's use of the state constitution, but at this point those comments did not congeal into anything that could be considered a line of questioning that was sympathetic to the Bush position.

Next up was Paul F. Hancock, representing Florida attorney general Butterworth. He began with a very important argument designed to undermine the claim that all election-rule decision-making relating to presidential electors had to originate with the Florida legislature. "In implementing the election law, each branch of the Florida government plays a role. For example, the judiciary, or the executive branch of our government has not found itself bound by the technical, hypertechnical requirements of the election law. An example of that is that the, the executive branch has implemented a rule, not a law, but a rule that allows absentee ballots from overseas military voters to be received after the 10 days after the close of the polls. Under the law of the State of Florida [passed by the legislature], all absentee ballots have to be received by the time the polls close on election day." It was an extremely clever rejoinder to the conservatives. After all, if it was wrong for the state high court to rely on the state constitution in determining the election rules, why would it not also be wrong for the state to count absentee votes in accordance with a consent decree that was directly contradicted by state statutes governing absentee ballots? Unfortunately, the argument was quickly sidetracked by Kennedy and O'Connor's concerns about the change in the deadline ("it just does look like a very dramatic change made by the Florida court," said O'Connor), but before long it would become the subject of separate litigation in federal court.

That left Laurence H. Tribe to speak on behalf of Al Gore. Tribe attacked the "popular culture" language that characterized the state high court as having "chang[ed] the rules of the game," saying that this "game is over, and when it's over in a kind of photo finish that leaves people unsure who won, [then] how do you develop . . . greater certainty, and a rather common technique is a recount, sometimes a manual recount, sometimes taking more time would be rather like looking more closely a the film of a photo finish. It's nothing extraordinary. It's not like suddenly moving Heartbreak Hill or adding a mile or subtracting a mile – "

When O'Connor pointed out that the statutory deadline seemed to be very clear, Tribe responded that a rigid deadline "could be a violation of Florida law." Rehnquist saw his chance. "Are you talking about the Florida Constitution?" Tribe: "Well, it might have been a violation – " Rehnquist: "But then you run into the Blacker case," that is, *McPherson v. Blacker.* Tribe did not catch the importance of the point, returning instead to claim that even if there was a change in state law it could not raise a federal issues since

3 U.S.C. § 5 does not impose any particular federal duty on the states. Rehnquist: "It [a federal question] can also arise under the section of the Constitution that was construed in Blacker [Article II]. That's quite independent of 3 U.S.[C.] 5." Tribe returned again to how, in his view, there was no federal question because "3 U.S.C. Section 5 is all carrot and no stick" and Rehnquist shot back, "No. I don't agree with you on that, Mr. Tribe. It seems to me that a Federal question arises if the Florida Supreme Court in its opinion rather clearly says that we are using the Florida Constitution to reach the result we reach in construing the statute. I think Blacker is a strong argument they can't do that."

Tribe had been focusing on Title 3 and now he had to start thinking on his feet.[55] "Well, that they can never avert to their own constitution?. . . Well, what would it be, I wonder, about the circumstances here that would say that in reconciling these provisions [the Florida court did] something federally impermissible." Rehnquist then elaborated his point: "Well, you know, if the Supreme Court of Florida simply said in its opinion, look, these sections of the statute conflict, we've got to under our judicial principles resolve it one way or the other, but – but it doesn't say that. It goes on to say, look, in the light of the Florida Constitution and the general rights conferred there, we are construing it this way."

Tribe caught on: "It seems to me that as a tiebreaker, as a way of shedding light on the provisions that are in conflict, so long as it's not done in a way that conflicts with a Federal mandate, they are not violating any – " But now it was Scalia's turn to outline his argument: "Mr. Tribe, I don't – I don't agree with that. I don't – I don't think that the Florida Supreme Court used the Florida Constitution as a tool of interpretation of this statute." He then reviewed the organization of the state court's opinion, noting that their discussion of the meaning of the statutes concludes by saying that "the county canvassing boards are required to submit their returns to the department by 5 P.M.," after which time the secretary " is permitted to ignore" late returns. "So what the statutory interpretation gives you is a firm termination date of [seven days] and discretion in the secretary. The opinion continues" with a new section on the constitutional right to vote, and the court claims that election laws "are valid only if they impose no 'unreasonable or unnecessary' restraints on the right of suffrage contained in the Constitution. In other words, I read the Florida court's opinion as quite clearly saying . . . our state constitution [the right to vote] trumps that legislative intent [on the firm deadline]. I don't think there is any other way to read it, and that is, that is a real problem, it seems to me, under Article II. . . ." Scalia had just summarized the grounds on which he would be reversing the Florida court's decision.

Tribe started by saying that the Florida legislature had given the high court this authority to review the statutes, but Souter thought that this was not the best defense, and he jumped in to rescue the advocate: "Isn't there another way of looking at what the Florida court did, and that was in effect to apply the statute, the interpretive criterion, that where there is any discretion for interpretation, an unconstitutional result should be avoided," especially under a statute that regulates federal and state elections? Tribe agreed, eventually responding that the Florida court was reconciling conflicting statutory principles, not pitting the statutes against the state constitution. Then Stevens noted that the part of the opinion that Scalia found troubling actually "relies on four things – the Florida Constitution, earlier Florida decisions construing statutes, an Illinois case, and a Federal case, . . . [n]ot just their constitution." Tribe said, "That's right," and then Souter asked, "Is it also true that the . . . [seven-day deadline] cannot stand, not because of the constitution alone but because there are other provisions in the statute that cannot be accommodated with" that deadline? Tribe: "Exactly." Finally, Ginsburg jumped in to complete the argument of the four more liberal members against the conservatives, and – unbeknownst at the time – to outline the only course of action that might bring the liberals and conservatives together, temporarily: "They said that twice, and I think that's critical if you add to that that we read a decision of a state court in the light most favorable to that court and not in the light least favorable. . . . I suppose there would be a possibility for this Court to remand for clarification, but if there's two readings, one that's questionable, one that isn't, all of our decisions suggest that we read the one" that is most favorable to them.

Almost all commentators noted the contrast between the partisan vitriol that had become commonplace and the more technical, focused, esoteric, academic exchanges inside the courtroom. Most noticed that both sides were pushed hard by various justices, and it was also clear that the justices appeared split along ideological lines. Almost no one was willing to make a prediction based on the exchanges, but many expressed concern that the justices would not be able to find that "single voice" that would demonstrate that they had found common ground.[56] A source close to Bush thought that maybe "the Supreme Court will punt, either by saying that it's wrong to inject the court into a political process, or that the certification issues that pertained when Bush filed the case are no longer relevant."[57] Susan Low Bloch of Georgetown University Law Center said that if the court could not reach a consensus it would be best to dismiss the case in order to avoid a politically damaging 5 to 4 decision. "A 5-4 split was clearly developing on the court," said Stephen Gottlieb of Albany Law School, and "the question is, how important do the justices think unanimity is?"[58]

Others, however, noticed both the split and an apparent willingness on the part of the conservatives to press their concerns. Michael McConnell noted that "Justice Scalia and Chief Justice Rehnquist, somewhat unexpectedly, focused on an aspect of the case that had not been emphasized by Bush's lawyers. They interpreted the Florida court opinion as resting on the Florida state constitution," and they seem to think that this was inconsistent with Article II, which "vests authority over the manner of selecting electors in the state legislature, not in the state as a whole. Under that reasoning, the Florida Supreme Court might have violated the U.S. Constitution by complying with the Florida Constitution. Isn't that a strange twist?"[59] Former Supreme Court law clerk Edward Lazarus wrote that the oral arguments "revealed a great deal" about the justices' positions and also "appeared to produce a dramatic shift from the main arguments presented to the court by the parties to a new issue on which the court's decision will turn." He said that it was "a virtual certainty" that the Court would reject the main Bush argument that the Florida court violated 3 U.S.C. § 5, and that they would reject this argument "perhaps unanimously." At the same time, "Justice Antonin Scalia advanced a different reason for striking down" the state high court decision, and that was that the Florida justices violated Article II of the U.S. Constitution "because it invoked the Florida constitution. . . . In other words, the problem with the Florida Supreme Court opinion is not so much that it changed Florida law but that it used the Florida constitution as a kind of trump card to do so." Lazarus said that it was almost certain that Scalia, Rehnquist, and the silent Thomas all favored this view, and that Stevens, Souter, Ginsburg, and Breyer were opposed to it. "All of which means that, as is so often the case with this deeply divided court, the outcome will depend on Justices Sandra Day O'Connor and Anthony Kennedy." Each of them expressed concerns about what the Florida court had done, but they did not "tip their hand" with respect to "Scalia's novel Article II theory. . . . If O'Connor and Kennedy are willing" to follow this theory, then "the court is about to self-inflict a very substantial wound."[60]

Later on the same day as the Court's oral argument, Gore received some bad news from the Florida Supreme Court.[61] The Court ruled on the appeal of Judge Labarga's decision in the "butterfly ballot" case, known as *Fladell v. Palm Beach County Canvassing Board.* In a unanimous per curiam opinion, the justices noted that "a court should not void an election for ballot form defects unless such defects cause the ballot to be in substantial noncompliance with the statutory election requirements . . . [and that] such defects operate to prevent [a] free, fair and open choice." In this case, "we conclude as a matter of law that the Palm Beach County ballot does not constitute substantial noncompliance with statutory requirements," and since this was "the threshold issue" no other aspect of the case need be decided.[62] With that, the case that launched the campaign 2000 election disputes came to an end.

Also on that day, Democrats filed suit in Tallahassee seeking to disqualify nearly 10,000 absentee ballots cast in Martin County on the grounds that the county's Republican supervisor of elections, Peggy S. Robbins, allowed Republican workers to take flawed absentee ballot applications home and correct them but allegedly denied the same opportunity to Democrats.[63] The case, known as *Taylor v. Martin County Canvassing Board,* was similar to the one involving Seminole County that had already been filed, and if successful it would mean a net gain of 2,815 votes for Al Gore.[64] The trial would be held in the familiar courtroom of Judge Terry Lewis.

In another case, a group of Democrats filed suit in Tallahassee that seemingly picked up on Paul Hancock's point in argument before the U.S. Supreme Court. The suit, known as *Harris v. Florida Elections Canvassing Commission,* asked a court to throw out approximately 1,500 overseas absentee votes, mostly from military personnel, on the grounds that they arrived up to ten days after Election Day even though Florida's statutes required absentee ballots to arrive by Election Day.[65] Up until that point few would have imagined that the late-arriving ballots posed any kind of problem, since the ten-day accommodation had been arranged under a consent decree entered into with the federal government.[66] However, Scalia's innovative theory about legislative control cast doubt on whether this practice was acceptable during a presidential election.[67] At risk was every single absentee vote arriving after Election Day yet included in the certified totals – more than enough to erase Bush's margin of victory.

Mostly, though, after the Friday oral arguments at the Supreme Court, the nation's attention turned toward the weekend trial in Judge Sauls's courtroom of Gore's election contest. In a nine-hour session on Saturday, broadcast nationwide, the weighty constitutional issues discussed by the U.S. Supreme Court gave way to a dry discussion of statistics and voting machines. Voting-machine experts and statisticians debated the characteristics and error rates of different voting systems, how "chad buildup" in a Votomatic machine might result in dimpled ballots through no fault of the voter, whether mishandling of voting cards might lead chads to be inadvertently dislodged, the statistics on rates of undervotes in various counties, the standards used in evaluating ballots, and the reasons why Nassau County voting officials reverted back to the results from the original machine tabulation rather than use the results of the automatic recount. After a ten-hour marathon session on Sunday, December 3, Sauls announced that he would have a decision the following day.[68]

On Monday morning there were no signs of anything out of the ordinary happening at the U.S. Supreme Court. The justices took their seats on the bench at 10:00 A.M. and began hearing the day's cases. While there was anticipation for a Court decision, it was not a big surprise that the opinion was not ready yet. The record time in recent years was a four-day turnaround from oral arguments to ruling in the 1971 Pentagon Papers case, which involved an unprecedented federal court injunction preventing a newspaper from publishing a story.[69]

But at 11:45 A.M., without fanfare, an employee of the court's public information office appeared behind the press section in the courtroom with multiple copies of a relatively short document – seven pages. It was a per curiam opinion, an opinion of the Court, meaning that no particular justice's name would be officially associated with its authorship. Amazingly, it was unanimous.

The first three and a half pages reiterated the facts of the case and outlined key aspects of the Florida Supreme Court opinion. The opinion then alluded to Justice Scalia's challenge: "As a general rule, this Court defers to a state court's interpretation of a state statute. But in the case of a law enacted by a state legislature applicable not only to elections to state offices, but also to the selection of Presidential electors, the legislature is not acting solely under the authority given it by the people of the State, but by virtue of a direct grant of authority made under Art. II, § 1, cl. 2, of the United States Constitution," which authorizes state legislatures to determine the manner by which presidential electors will be selected. The Court's concern that was "[t]here are expressions in the opinion of the Supreme Court of Florida that may be read to indicate that it construed the Florida Election Code without regard to the extent to which the Florida Constitution could, consistent with Art. II, § 1, cl. 2, 'circumscribe the legislative power.'" For example, the state court at one point said that "'[t]o the extent that the Legislature may enact laws regulating the electoral process, those laws are valid only if they impose no "'unreasonable or unnecessary'" restraints on the right of suffrage'" guaranteed by the state constitution. Moreover, while the Florida Supreme Court referred in general to 3 U.S.C. §§1–10, it did not specifically address section 5, and "a legislative wish to take advantage of the 'safe harbor' would counsel against any construction of the Election Code that Congress might deem to be a change in the law."

The bottom line result: "After reviewing the opinion of the Florida Supreme Court, we find 'that there is considerable uncertainty as to the precise grounds for the decision,'" and "This is sufficient reason for us to decline at this time to review the federal questions asserted to be present. . . . The judgment of the Supreme Court of Florida is therefore vacated [that is, voided, but not reversed] and the case is remanded [sent back] for further proceedings not inconsistent with this opinion."

There was almost no other way to read this unexpected result than as a strategic finesse designed to prevent the Court from having to suffer the criticism associated with an ideological split. The *New York Times*'s Linda Greenhouse said that the justices' "opaque" approach to the state court decision "papered over, barely, their own differences."[70] The conservatives on the Court got part of what they wanted, which was a unanimous statement of the possible Article II limitations that exist when state courts interpret state statutes involving presidential elections; the conservatives also got a chance to include language in the opinion that pointed out the state court's possible constitutional error (the error that Scalia considered indisputable at oral argument) and they persuaded the other members of the Court to agree to "vacate" the state court's decision, thus erasing (for the time being) its authority as a legal precedent.[71] This all added up to what some called a "shot across the bow" of the Florida court – that is, a shot designed to intimidate the state judges into changing course. It was for these reasons that some commentators considered the Supreme Court's decision to be a partial victory for the Bush campaign.[72]

But there was a lot for Gore to be satisfied with as well. Most important, the U.S. Supreme Court did not rule that the Florida Supreme Court violated the Constitution or federal law. Moreover, the more moderate members of the U.S. Supreme Court, who expressed the belief at oral argument that the Florida Supreme Court's decision was an acceptable interpretation of state statutes and did not contravene any federal law, got a result that (for the time being) placed the fate of the Florida court's decisions back into the hands of the Florida judges. Assuming that these state justices were not intimidated by the shot across the bow, they were now in a position to reassert the legitimacy of their decision. It was for these reasons that some commentators argued that this decision was actually a victory for Gore; in fact, arguably, the justices in Washington had just given the Tallahassee justices a precise roadmap for how to rehabilitate their decision and avoid future problems with the U.S. Supreme Court. Michael Glennon, of the UC Davis School of Law, said that "[t]his is similar to a professor giving a term paper back to a student with instructions on how to write it if you want an A."[73] Kim Lane Scheppele of the University of Pennsylvania said that the decision was "all bark and no bite."[74] This was why the Gore lawyers could also express satisfaction with the result.[75]

It would be the last time during this election dispute that the justices would win the praises of a wide variety of scholars. University of Virginia law professor A. E. Dick Howard called the decision "prudent" and "one of the few ways in which they would come up with a unanimous result." Marci Hamilton, a law professor at Yeshiva University in New York and a former clerk to O'Connor, said it was "masterful," since the justices found "an intellectually respectable way" to address the Florida situation without actually deciding it.[76] University of Chicago law professor Cass R. Sunstein called the modest ruling "a triumph of good sense, and even for the rule of law."[77] Edward Lazarus noted that "the Scalia-led faction had to accept not reversing the Florida Supreme Court, while the more liberal wing had to accept that the Florida ruling would not be allowed to stand, at least not without substantial modification." But more significant was that "this graceful exit from the Florida process is an act of statesmanship that deserves commendation. . . . No doubt the justices will think long and hard before jumping into this divisive political fight again. At least – as the action returns to Florida – so one must hope."[78] As David Savage of the *Los Angeles Times* put it, "if nothing else, Monday's decision may allow the justices in Washington to escape the partisan wars with their legal virtue intact."[79]

But most of the reaction was overshadowed by another event that day. As it turned out, the day's most important judicial decision did not come from the U.S. Supreme Court. Instead, as the world would find out a few hours later, state circuit court judge Sauls had made his decision on the Gore contest of the election certification. The news was not good for the vice president.

4

GORE'S LAST CHANCE

THE FLORIDA SUPREME COURT, ROUND TWO

★ ★ ★

*While our nation's citizens have every right to be concerned,
exasperated, fatigued and even cynical, it is my fervent hope that from
these events they will come to understand, if not appreciate, the role of government's Third Branch in the life of our precious democracy. . . . Inevitably the
pundits will opine that a judge's decision is somehow linked to the political
affiliation of the President that appointed the judge. While we at all levels of
the judiciary have come to expect this observation we continue to regret that
some "think" that is so. It may be true that a judge's judicial philosophy may
reflect, to some degree, the philosophy of the appointing President—not a
surprising circumstance—but to assume some sort of blind, mindless,
knee-jerk response based on the politics of a judge's appointer does us and
the rule of law a grave injustice. More importantly it is just wrong.*

Circuit court judge Stanley F. Birch, dissenting in
Siegel v. Lepore (Eleventh Circuit 2000)

It may be hard to imagine that the U.S. Supreme Court could be upstaged
by a local trial court judge on the day it handed down the first decision in
its history that bore directly on the outcome of a presidential election.[1] But
in the hours after the U.S. Supreme Court's opinion in *Bush v. Palm Beach
County Canvassing Board* it was obvious that the future of the 2000 presidential election was in the hands of Leon County Circuit Court judge N.
Sanders Sauls.

Even if the U.S. Supreme Court had handed down a strong and clear ruling on the issues presented to it, the essential question at the heart of that

case was still the legality of the Florida Supreme Court's extension of the deadline to certify the state's election results. But that extension did not produce the benefits that the Gore campaign had wished for, and in the end George W. Bush was still officially declared the winner of the state's election, albeit by 537 votes rather than the original 930. Under Florida law, however, a certified election result was not the end of the matter; candidates still had a right to contest a certified election if they should show (for example) that that official tally did not include a number of legal votes sufficient to change the outcome of the election. Gore contested the election results precisely on those grounds, arguing that the missed legal votes were the so-called "undervote" ballots that were turned in by voters but not registered by automatic vote-counting machines. The trial of this contest action had begun a week earlier in Judge Sauls's courtroom.

The Gore challenge was an uphill struggle. Even if their legal arguments were successful – an unlikely event, given what Gore lawyers knew about Judge Sauls – the Gore campaign had already learned the hard way that vote counting could be a long, unpredictable, and easily disrupted process, particularly when deadlines were looming. A new set of recounts would run up against an apparent deadline of December 12, the point at which Congress had told the states that their electoral votes would not be challenged so long as they resolved all conflicts over the appointment of electors. More certainly, participants assumed that the dispute had to be resolved by December 18, when the electors were scheduled to meet in their respective state capitols to cast their vote.

By Monday, December 4, time looked as if it may have already run out, especially in light of the original Miami-Dade estimate that it could take ten days to complete a count.[2] Still, they had a chance if Sauls was willing to simply count the undervotes (which numbered in the thousands) rather than all the ballots (more than one million). Gore's lawyers thought they made a good case for this approach.[3] During closing arguments, David Boies pointed out that in the vast majority of election contests in Florida, "courts have counted far fewer than all the votes, sometimes as few as two or three or a dozen or twenty; sometimes several hundred, sometimes several thousand." He noted that even the Bush attorneys acknowledged that the Palm Beach Canvassing Board used standards they considered acceptable when they did their manual recount – Bush's lawyers even called Judge Burton to the stand to make that point – and since those ballots were obviously legal votes that were not included in the certified result the official total should be adjusted so that these additional 215 votes were given to Gore. Also, Gore wanted the court to review Palm Beach's decision on 3,300 ballots that Democratic lawyers believe reflected an intent to vote; it was true that they had already been reviewed by the canvassing board, but Boies thought the law was clear that during a contest judges could resolve controversies over the proper interpretation of those ballots.

Boies thought that it was even more clear that the 9,000 unreviewed Miami-Dade undervote ballots included uncounted legal votes and that it was possible with a manual review to "recover" the intent of the voter on a good number of those ballots (between one-fourth and one-fifth) – "more than enough to make a difference in this race."[4] Boies also said that the Nassau County decision to withdraw the results of the automatic recount and instead report the original election night results was flatly contrary to the statutory requirements, and thus an additional 51 votes should be registered for Gore.[5] The bottom line, from the Gore camp's point of view, was that there should be an immediate adjustment in Gore's favor of 266 votes, plus a first-time manual review of 9,000 Miami-Dade votes that were not counted by machines, plus a judicial review of 3,800 disputed Palm Beach ballots.

The main arguments from Bush's lawyer Barry Richard was that canvassing boards had authority under state law to make decisions about recounts and courts could not second-guess those decisions unless those boards abused their authority; thus, if Miami-Dade decided not to count their ballots or if Palm Beach decided that disputed ballots did not display an intent to vote for a candidate, then that was the end of it, unless those decisions were completely unreasonable. As for the claim that manual recounts were necessary to correct potential problems with somewhat unreliable machines, Richard said that "I don't think that any one of us truly believes that the [Florida] Supreme Court will say that all sixty-four counties that used the Votomatic machine must have a hand recount."[6] But Boies disagreed. "[Mr. Richard says,] 'Maybe there are some people who intended to vote, but it's too late, and that's that.' With respect, Your Honor, the Florida Statutes, and the Florida case law does not permit at this stage saying, we're simply going to ignore the intent of the voter, that it didn't get counted by the machine and that's that. Bad things happen, and this is one of the bad things that happened. But the statute provides a mechanism for dealing with" these problems – an election contest, where one side identifies for a court the ballots they think should be counted. "And the Florida Supreme Court could not have been clearer, I suggest, in the Palm Beach County against Harris decision. . . . They said that it is of paramount importance that every vote be counted if you can discern the voter's intent, and they said that it is so important to permit that to be tested in a contest proceeding, that we are going to set a deadline for the certification. . . . And when the Supreme Court made that ruling, they were not merely accepting what we said. They were accepting what Mr. Richard and Mr. Klock said, because they told the Florida Supreme Court that if there's a problem with this election, Vice President Gore and Senator Lieberman ought to challenge it in the contest phase. . . . And the Florida Supreme Court agreed with that, and they said: We're going to cut off the certification proceeding so we can get to the contest, and that's where we are now."

About five hours after the U.S. Supreme Court handed down its opinion, at around 4:45 P.M., Judge Sauls returned to his courtroom to announce his ruling. Rather than focus on whether the certified result contained legal votes that were not counted or illegal votes that were counted, Sauls announced that in order to contest an election "the plaintiff must show that, but for the irregularity, or inaccuracy claimed, the result of the election would have been different, and he or she would have been the winner." That seemed to be a legal mistake by the judge, and one that was fatal for Gore, since it was unclear how they could prove that the results "would have" been different unless one actually counted the disputed ballots; if that was the legal standard for determining whether to count the ballots, then there was no hope.

As for whether the results of the partial manual recounts that were completed by Miami-Dade and Palm Beach should be added to the official results, Sauls concluded that "there is no authority under Florida law [to certify] an incomplete manual recount [or] to include any returns submitted past the deadline established by the Florida Supreme Court in this election." He said that while there was some evidence of "less than total accuracy" in the punch card voting machines used in Miami-Dade and Palm Beach, "these balloting and counting problems cannot support or effect any recounting necessity . . . absent the establishment of a reasonable probability that the statewide election result would be different, which has not been established in this case." As for the standards used by the Palm Beach board during its manual recount, Sauls found no abuse of discretion and no authority on the part of his court to review those ballots anew. He added that another review of those ballots using a different standard would create a "two-tiered" system in which a "voter in a county where a manual count was conducted, would benefit from having a better chance of having his or her vote actually counted," and this could put the state's election results – and its participation in the Electoral College – in "jeopardy" under both the U.S. Constitution and the Florida Constitution.

After concluding that Nassau County's canvassing board also acted within its discretion when it reverted to its original election-night tally after having rejected the results of the automatic recount and that Miami-Dade acted within its discretion when it called off its recount, he said that because Gore was challenging the results of a statewide election "the plaintiff would necessarily have to place at issue and seek as a remedy with the attendant burden of proof, a review and recount on all ballots, and all of the counties in this state." He ended with the traditional language, "the plaintiff will take nothing by this action."[7]

It was as complete a rejection of the Gore claim as could be imagined. By combining an usually high legal standard for winning an election contest with an "abuse of discretion" standard in evaluating the actions of these counties (rather than the Gore standard requiring merely a showing that "places in doubt the accuracy" of those totals) Sauls made it virtually impossible to call into question the results of a certified election. Sauls even adopted a theory that was considered so outlandish that the Bush attorneys did not strongly advocate it, which was that a contest in a statewide election would have to evaluate alleged irregularities in every county in the state. Moreover, in considering whether the results of the election may have been put in doubt by the evidence presented at trial, Sauls never once even looked at one of the disputed ballots, despite repeated requests by Boies; Sauls agreed with Bush lawyers that he did not have to look at the ballots until it could be demonstrated that the ballots would affect the election outcome – which created a serious chicken-and-egg problem, given that the best evidence of whether the result definitely "would be" different were the ballots.[8]

It was a devastating blow for the Gore team, and privately many suggested that they probably could not recover from it.[9] Many front-page stories in the next day's newspapers had the ruling as the banner headline, along with photos of morose Gore lawyers and jubilant Bush lawyers in Sauls's courtroom reacting to the decision.[10] Former Clinton White House chief of staff Leon D. Panetta said that "we're entering the Hail Mary phase of this election." In public the Democratic Party, including House and Senate leaders, were backing a continued fight, even in the face of new polls suggesting that more than half the country was ready for Gore to concede.[11] Still, the ever-optimistic Boies said that there was still time for "a meaningful opportunity to appeal to the Florida Supreme Court" and "there is still time for those ballots to be counted." Moreover, unlike some of the language used by the Bush team when decisions went against them, Boies did not call into question the integrity of the judge or the willingness of the Gore campaign to abide by court rulings. "We have always said that we will accept the rule of law."[12]

If there was one saving grace for the Gore team it was that Sauls seemed to base his decision on a fundamental legal mistake – and to many commentators, an obvious legal mistake. In justifying his requirement that Gore demonstrate a reasonable probability that the election result would be different but for the alleged improprieties, Judge Saul made reference to a 1982 Florida election case, *Smith v. Tynes,* which was written at a time when Florida's contest statute allowed challengers to win only (in most cases) if they could prove allegations of fraud. But Florida's election law had changed since then; in particular, reforms passed by the legislature in 1999 were specifically designed to allow for challenges whenever a plaintiff could show irregularities that placed "in doubt" the official election results. W. Dexter Douglas, one of Gore's top lawyers, even suggested that the sweeping nature of the ruling could make it easier to appeal, because it would be easier to suggest that Sauls engaged in a "broad misreading of the law."[13] Conservative law professor Michael McConnell also thought that Sauls's ruling was a surprise, particularly "in its unequivocal statement that Gore had not shown 'a reasonable probability' that the election might be changed by a recount. . . . This case did not merit the abrupt dismissal that Judge Sauls gave it."[14]

The Gore legal team filed a notice of appeal in the case even before Sauls stopped speaking, noting that "the issues presented are matters of national importance" and "time is extraordinarily short because of the schedule imposed by the electoral college."[15] The election was now four weeks old, and various Electoral College deadlines were fast approaching. Moreover, the Gore contest was not the only legal issue that was still being worked through in the courts. The U.S. Court of Appeals in the Eleventh Circuit was hearing oral arguments on the following day on the original Bush federal challenge to the recount process in Florida – the first lawsuit to have been filed by one of the campaigns. And in two Tallahassee circuit courtrooms, the "wild card" trials involving absentee ballot applications in Seminole and Martin Counties were ready to begin on Wednesday.

The day after Judge Sauls's ruling, the Eleventh Circuit Court of Appeals in Atlanta heard oral arguments in the cases of *Siegel v. LePore* and *Touchston v. McDermott*, which were the Bush campaign's Fourteenth Amendment challenges to the practice for conducting manual recounts in Florida. The claim was that this practice violated both the equal protection clause of that amendment (by treating votes differently and diluting the votes of people in counties that were not manually recounted) and the due process clause (by allowing recounts to be done without adequate standards for preventing arbitrary decision-making). The same court had previously ruled against issuing an emergency injunction based on these claims, but it withheld final judgment on the matter until arguments could be more fully developed about whether stopping the recounts was necessary to prevent "irreparable harm" to Bush. When oral arguments ended, Chief Judge R. Lanier Anderson said the court was "keenly" aware of the fast approaching deadline for Florida's electors to be selected, but he gave no indication how long it would take for the court to rule in the two cases.[16]

It took one day. On Wednesday, December 6, the twelve justices of the Eleventh Circuit distributed 201 pages explaining their position. The decision was a bit heartening to those looking for some signs of judicial non-partisanship. The judges rejected the Bush claims by a vote of 8 to 4, with the majority made up of five Democratic appointees and three Republican appointees. However, all of the dissenters were Republican appointees, including three of the four judges who had been appointed by former President George Bush.[17]

The eight judges in the bipartisan majority expressed their views in a twenty-nine page per curiam decision.[18] After concluding that federal review of these ongoing state court proceedings was still appropriate,[19] the majority ruled that they did not have to decide the ultimate constitutional issues because the only question was whether it was reasonable for the trial court to decide that continued recounts would not irreparably harm Bush. In deciding that this decision was reasonable, the court noted that Governor Bush was certified the winner in the Florida election and that "the Florida Circuit Court in Leon County . . . has now denied the Vice President's request for resumption of manual recounts." It was possible that additional recounts might occur, but they would be pursuant to a specific court order arising out of the election contest rather than the discretionary practices of county canvassing boards, and thus any possible challenges to those potential recounts would "be a substantially different case, raising different legal issues." As for the Bush claim that there may be irreparable injury if recounts lead to the "broadcasting" of potentially flawed election results (i.e., a Gore victory), the judges in the majority ruled that the recounts at issue here led to no such flawed results, and besides, "we reject the contention that merely counting ballots gives rise to a cognizable injury."

While the majority did not feel compelled to address the underlying constitutional question, Chief Judge Anderson decided that some comments would be useful, particularly in light of the decision of the dissenters to spend 138 pages on them. Given the especially sparse discussion of these central issues in the U.S. Supreme Court's final decision in this controversy, it is worth taking a closer look at this exchange of views.

He started by noting that the U.S. Supreme Court, in *Burdick v. Takushi* (1992), held that "when a state election law provision imposes only reasonable, nondiscriminatory restrictions upon the First and Fourteenth Amendment rights of voters, the State's important regulatory interests are generally sufficient to justify the restrictions." The plaintiff's main equal protection argument was that, because recounts are limited to a few counties, undervote ballots reflecting an intent to vote might be counted in some counties but not others, and this means "there is greater certainty in some counties than in others that every voter's intent is effectuated." But in Anderson's view, this was not an equal protection violation. "Taking this argument to its logical conclusion would lead to the untenable position that the method of casting and counting votes would have to be identical in all states and in every county of each state," since it is part of existing election practices (around the country and in Florida) that some states and counties use manual recounts and others rely only on machines. "No court has held that the mere use of different methods of counting ballots constitutes an equal protection violation." Moreover, the U.S. Supreme Court previously held in *Roudebush v. Hartke* (1972) "that recount procedures are a common and practical means of ensuring fair and accurate election results."

Bush lawyers' "attempt to bolster their treat-every-ballot-alike argument by suggesting that partisan influences have tainted" the process. But "the statute itself provides several safeguards against" these sorts of abuses, including the right of all candidates to request recounts, the existence of judges on canvassing boards, and the requirement that the board's activities "be open to the public." Most notably, there was nothing in this admittedly "sparse record" that suggested that any "actual partisan manipulation or fraud" took place in these recounts. The bottom line was that "Florida has a strong interest in ensuring that the results of an election accurately reflect the intent of its voters" and "a manual recount provision as a supplement to mechanical counting provides a valid method to discern the will of the voters, where doubt is raised as to the validity of a machine count."

Anderson suggested that the court might take a different approach to these equal protection arguments if there were allegations that Florida was depriving citizens of the right to vote or was creating political districts "which arbitrarily and systematically granted a lesser voice to some voters based on their geographic location," as in the famous "one person, one vote" cases of the early 1960s.[20] But "the additional scrutiny of ballots afforded under Florida's manual recount procedures does not weigh the value of votes; it merely verifies the count" in a way that is not intentionally discriminatory and does not systematically enhance or dilute the votes of any identifiable class of voters. In other words, a system that allows humans to double-check the tabulations generated by vote-counting machines does not discriminate against anyone, particularly when there are equal opportunities to request the inspection. As for the due process claim that counties were proceeding in a way that was "arbitrary and rife with irregularities," Anderson concluded that the record "fails to establish that the alleged unreliability or inaccuracy of manual recounting rises to the level of a severe burden on the right to vote."

The dissenters were circuit judges Gerald B. Tjoflat, Stanley F. Birch, Joel F. Dubina, and Ed Carnes. Carnes argued that "the selective manual recounts in some of the Florida counties that use the punch card system of voting violate the equal protection rights of the [similarly situated] voters in the other punch card system counties" who "did not receive the benefit of them." The problem, in his view, was that the law allowed a candidate to rehabilitate votes in preferred counties, such as the three heavily Democratic counties selected by Gore. This ability to focus on some undervotes but not others essentially "dilutes the weight of votes" in a way that is prohibited by the Supreme Court's one-person, one-vote decisions, which also prohibited "states from weighting votes differently based on the voters' place of residence." As for the claim that "there are variations among the counties in election systems and different systems give rise to different error rates," Carnes replied that there is a constitutional difference between "the number of vote errors that occur as a result of local variations in choice of vote systems before an election" and "the selective correction of errors based upon county of residence after the election." Counties will not choose vote-counting systems for the purpose of disadvantaging its citizens; but political parties and candidates do have a motivation to choose counties in ways that are designed to maximize some votes over others. In other words, "the intent behind the two actions is different" – one is a discriminatory intent and the other is not.[21]

Tjoflat's dissent was more strident, opening with the accusation that the Florida Supreme Court "changed the standards for counting votes" and "gave its imprimatur to a scheme" of selective vote-searching by a political party and thus "debased the votes of thousands of Florida voters and denied them the equal protection of the laws."[22] He characterized the manual recounts as a "standardless vote counting scheme" that allowed partisan canvassing boards to use subjective standards to review "improperly marked ballots" for the purpose of determining the "intent" of the voter. This "scheme," which Tjoflat called "the selective dimple model," gave unique and unfair advantages to candidates in statewide elections who trailed an opponent by a small number of votes and who had the same party affiliation as canvassing boards in large urban centers; in effect, this "works to deprive voters of their right to vote based on their county of residence and thereby denies them equal protection of the laws." This is particularly true in this case when the actions of Vice President Gore were designed to inflict injury "upon his opponent's supporters" through "planned vote dilution," which is a behavior that "erodes the democratic process" and is thus "certainly actionable" under the civil rights laws. Gore's public commitment to counting the votes was thus transformed into "unlawful discrimination" against Florida voters.[23]

Birch joined the other dissents but wrote separately to emphasize his special concern about the "lack of standards" in the Florida recount statute. He said that the Florida legislature "abdicated its responsibility to prescribe meaningful guidelines for ensuring that any such manual recount would be conducted fairly, accurately, and uniformly." Birch did not mention the legislature's emphasis on an "intent of the voter" standard, and he did not review the litigation in Florida – in particular, before Judge Labarga – on how best to administer this standard during the manual recounts; he also did not respond to Anderson's claim that there was no evidence in the record of systematic partisan bias. Still, he concluded that the effect of this "is to cause votes to be counted (or not to be counted) based only upon the disparate and unguided subjective opinion of a partisan (two members are elected in partisan voting) canvassing board."

Even more interesting were Birch's comments on the role and reputation of the judiciary as it attempted to resolve this lingering, high-stakes dispute.

"While our nation's citizens have every right to be concerned, exasperated, fatigued and even cynical, it is my fervent hope that from these events they will come to understand, if not appreciate, the role of government's Third Branch in the life of our precious democracy." He explained that the main function of courts "is to provide a forum in which disputes . . . can be decided in an orderly, peaceful manner; and with a high level of confidence in the outcome." Given that this court took less than twenty-four hours to arrive at its decision he felt obliged to acknowledge that "any dispute that has at its core the legitimacy of a presidential election . . . deserves the most careful study, thought and wisdom that we can humanly bring to bear on the issues entrusted to us. Thus, I feel compelled to attest to the fact that my brother and sister judges have embraced this case with a sense of duty, concern, and conscientious hard work that is worthy of the issues before us." For those who might doubt that this was true, based on the swiftness of his court's decision, he explained that "long before the anticipated notices of appeal were filed, formally bringing them to us, we were about the study and review of the legal issues to be resolved. Thus, the reader of our opinions in this case should understand that our time for consideration has been considerably longer than it might appear at first blush."

Then, in a remarkable, albeit plaintive, demonstration of how much pressure this dispute had placed on courts, Birch anticipated that "the pundits will opine that a judge's decision is somehow linked to the political affiliation of the President that appointed the judge." But he insisted that "to assume some sort of blind, mindless, knee-jerk response based on the politics of a judge's appointer does us and the rule of law a grave injustice." It was a defense of good faith justice from a judge who knew how the political divide on the court might have looked to some court-watchers. But if it was a preemptive defense of his fellow dissenters, he did not have to worry. The Gore camp had won this round and had no incentive to attack the integrity of these judges.[24]

LEWIS AND CLARK

On Wednesday, December 6, the Republican state legislature decided to move ahead with a special legislative session to appoint a slate of Bush electors. This step was taken with the approval of Florida governor Jeb Bush, although over the objections of state Democrats, whose legislative leader commented: "Sadly, I have to say that I believe this is orchestrated, and the only thing missing from the proclamation today was the postmark from Austin, Texas." The decision was also made with an eye on developments taking place in a variety of Florida courtrooms – not just the appeal of Judge Sauls's ruling before the undependable state supreme court, but also two new trials that were getting under way in Tallahassee.[25]

The cases, *Jacobs v. Seminole County* and *Taylor v. Martin County,* were widely seen as the new "wild cards" in the election litigation – slightly less promising than the contest appeal to the Florida Supreme Court, but plausible enough to make Republicans worry quite a bit and to capture the attention of the country from Wednesday through Friday.[26] At stake were approximately 25,000 absentee ballots from these two counties, which the plaintiffs claimed were tainted because of allegedly illegal partisan tampering with absentee ballot applications. Because there was no way to tell which of the absentee ballots were among the roughly 4,000 that resulted from this activity, the plaintiffs were asking that all of them be thrown out. Of course, this was considered a long shot, mostly because the remedy of disenfranchising all voters who used absentee ballots seemed draconian and particularly unfair to the innocent voters whose applications and ballots were perfectly in order. On the other hand, the actions taken by election officials and Republican Party workers resulted in the casting of around two thousand Republican ballots that otherwise would not have been cast, and to some it also seemed unfair that Bush's victory was made possible only because of this allegedly illegal activity. Some Gore supporters noted that the Republican willingness to ignore this illegality in favor of counting all the votes was hypocritical in light of their insistence on inflexible adherence to statutory guidelines when it came to recounts and deadlines. Then again, asking that the ballots be thrown out was not exactly consistent with the main Gore message of counting all the votes, and while these lawsuits had not formally been brought by the campaign Gore did express the view that it "doesn't seem fair to me" that the GOP but not Democratic operatives had a chance to correct incomplete applications.[27]

The Martin County case was heading to the courtroom of Judge Terry Lewis, and the Seminole County case was going to be heard before Judge Nikki Ann Clark; thus, "Lewis and Clark" (after the famed early-nineteenth-century explorers) was a useful shorthand for the judges overseeing these virtually identical cases. Republicans were concerned about what these Democratic judges might do, but they were not in a position to challenge the integrity of Judge Lewis, since the Bush team had praised him earlier in the litigation when he upheld Secretary of State Harris's discretion to ignore late-filed returns. However, Clark was another matter. She was an African American woman who had been an aid to the late Democratic governor Lawton Chiles and a former Legal Services lawyer, and this seemed to "petrify" some Republicans.[28] As a result, Bush lawyers had tried to remove her from the case. The best argument they could come up with was that Governor Jeb Bush turned her down for an appeals court spot just a few weeks earlier, and Bush supporters let it be known that they were worried she might be vengeful.[29] To avoid that possibility, Bush attorneys formally asked the judge to disqualify herself, but Judge Clark rejected that motion and an appeals court upheld her decision. As the trial approached, defenders of the judge came forward to combat those accusations and vouch for her integrity.[30] Others suggested that those who called into question the fairness of this African American judge were exploiting racist stereotypes that assumed that whites represented the default standard of fairness and neutrality while blacks always have an agenda. Bush's local Florida lawyers, including Barry Richard, refused to join the attack on Clark, saying later that she was being "erroneously stereotyped" by people from both sides who "don't know her from Adam." It was never mentioned during the dispute that Clark's sister had worked for George W. Bush's father as White House director of media relations.[31]

On Wednesday, December 6, Judge Lewis's case was set to begin at 7:00 A.M., and Clark's, at 8:15 A.M. The fact that these cases were being tried simultaneously in neighboring courtrooms raised the possibility that these judges would strive to coordinate not only the trial schedules (with lawyers running back and forth between the two courtrooms) but also the timing and perhaps even the substance of the decisions, which obviously would give Clark's decision some political cover. The trials were marathon affairs. There was no question that Republican Party officials spent about a half million dollars on a program to send preprinted absentee ballot applications to thousands of Republican voters. These postcards were designed so that voters interested in an absentee ballot would only have to verify the information, sign the cards, and send them in to county election officials. However, a Republican contractor mistakenly printed voters' birth dates in a spot reserved for voter identification numbers. When Seminole County elections supervisor Sandra Goard and Martin County elections supervisor Peggy Robbins received these signed applications, they were prepared to reject them as invalid because of the missing voter identification numbers. However, Republican Party political director Todd Schnick called Goard and secured an agreement that allowed Republican workers to use a back room at the election office to correct 2,126 ballot applications that had not yet been thrown out. They spent about three weeks, unsupervised, filling in the missing information, and this resulted in an additional 1,833 votes from registered Republicans. Republican Party official Tom Hauck worked out a similar deal in Martin County, but in that case party officials were allowed to remove the incomplete applications from the elections office for several days. Hundreds of flawed absentee ballot requests from Democrats were thrown away, and election officials did not give Democratic Party officials the same opportunity to salvage the applications.

The legal basis for these challenges rested on that section of Florida law that required voters to disclose the information on ballot applications[32] and that made it a felony for any unauthorized person to request an absentee ballot on behalf of someone else.[33] There were some questions about whether the statutes actually prohibited others from adding information on applications that were supposed to be provided by the voter, but the Bush lawyers argued the key issue was whether the "will of the voters" was reflected in the election, and if so, then the results of the election should not be set aside "even when there has been substantial noncompliance with the election laws."[34]

In the event that the judges were uncomfortable with the thought of throwing out all absentee ballots the plaintiffs did suggest the option of merely adjusting the certified vote totals so as to eliminate the inappropriate benefit that Bush received from this activity. In the Seminole County case a statistician estimated that the actions of Republican officials resulted in 1,504 votes for Bush; in the Martin County case the estimate was 558 extra votes for Bush.[35] If the judges choose not to toss out all 25,000 absentee ballots then an adjustment in the official results along these lines would be more than enough to erase Bush's official lead of 537 votes.

One day after the trials were completed, in a coordinated release of two separate opinions, both judges ruled that while election supervisors violated the Florida statutes, their actions were not egregious enough to warrant disqualifying the absentee ballots in these two counties. "Despite the irregularities in the request for absentee ballots . . . the election results reflect the full and fair expression of the will of the voters."[36] They placed particular emphasis on the language used by the Florida Supreme Court to open its opinion in *Palm Beach County Canvassing Board v. Harris:* "The right to vote is the right to participate. . . . We must tread carefully on that right or we risk the unnecessary and unjustified muting of the public voice. By refusing to recognize an otherwise valid exercise of the right of a citizen to vote for the sake of sacred, unyielding adherence to statutory scripture, we would in effect nullify that right."[37] There was no sign from the Bush team that they disagreed with this principle as applied in this case. Democratic lawyers were less happy, and they filed notices of appeal even before the announcement of the judgment was complete. They were heading toward a court that had its hands full, for on the days that the Lewis and Clark trials were taking place the Florida Supreme Court had accepted briefs and heard arguments on the Gore appeal of Judge Sauls's ruling on his election contest.

BACK TO THE FLORIDA SUPREME COURT

While noting that the Florida Supreme Court was the Gore campaign's "favorite forum," most legal experts expressed "doubt that the state justices, under the pressure of time and politics, will dramatically intervene once again to revive Gore's fading hopes."[38] As early as Tuesday Bush attorneys were saying "flatly that if the Florida Supreme Court authorizes new recounts, they are prepared to challenge such a decision before the U.S. Supreme Court as an impermissible effort to change the election laws after election day." While so much had been happening in so many courtrooms, it was important to keep in mind that the U.S. Supreme Court's decision had occurred only on Monday, just three days before the Florida Supreme Court's oral argument in *Gore v. Harris*, and Bush officials believed that the decision was best understood "as a shot across the bow, warning the state court not to press too far with actions that can be interpreted as rewriting the rules on the fly." As one Bush attorney put it, "We have this open invitation from the U.S. Supreme Court to appeal."[39] Not surprisingly, the Bush lawyers reminded the Florida justices of this at the end of their brief when they wrote that "the application of counting standards in different counties as well as the occurrence of manual recounts in only selected counties or selective portions of counties violates the equal protection and due process clauses of the U.S. Constitution." Not only was this a warning about another rebuke from the U.S. Supreme Court; it was a demand that the only acceptable way to deal with the problem of undercounted votes was the apparently impossible option of recounting the whole state.[40]

On Thursday, December 7, at 10:03 A.M., the Florida justices once again took a public stage in the election contest, just seventeen days since their previous oral argument. While the stakes were just as high, the justices were keenly aware that they were in a very different circumstance this time around. They were self-conscious about the approaching federal deadlines and the hovering U.S. Supreme Court, and they knew that time was of the essence. Even the structure of the oral arguments reflected this sense of urgency. While during the first round the parties were given a leisurely two and a half hours, this time the whole thing would be completed in a brisk sixty-eight minutes.

Once again the Gore campaign was represented by David Boies. Before Boies could get out one sentence of argument, Chief Justice Charles T. Wells said that he wanted to "start right off" with a concern that he wanted all counsel to address. The Florida statutes did not specifically give the Florida Supreme Court the authority to review a decision of an election contest by a circuit court; the election contest statutes only refer to the circuit courts' jurisdiction to hear the contest, and the only other basis for appellate review would seem to be provisions of the Florida Constitution. Under the U.S. Supreme Court's Article II analysis, did this call into question whether the Florida Supreme Court could hear an election contest in a presidential race? Boies responded that whenever the state legislature passes a law it assumes that the background authority of the state's appellate courts is in place, and it does not have to insert anew into every act the basis for this review authority. This was particularly true for a law that was designed to apply to all state elections, not just nonpresidential elections.

Thus, right off the bat, it was clear that the chief justice had foremost in his mind the U.S. Supreme Court's warning about state legislative control over the process of appointing presidential electors. It also seemed as if he was searching for a reason to not take up the case. However, as it turned out, none of the attorneys was willing to give him this way out – at least not during oral arguments.

Justice Fred Lewis asked why Boies's concern about how the certified results might have missed legal-but-not-yet-inspected undervotes would not require the court to apply any relief "on a statewide" basis? Boies answered that it could not be the law of the state that recounts had to be conducted everywhere, because that would make the current election result defective, since some counties already had their manual recount results included in the certified result. He pointed out what the campaign had know from the beginning: state law instructed candidates to focus their complaints on particular ballots in particular counties, and there was no suggestion in state law that a focused contest should trigger reviews and recounts in places where they were not requested. Still, the issue continued to bother the justices, including those who were predicted to be most sympathetic to his argument. As Justice Barbara J. Pariente put it, "If we're looking for accuracy . . . then why isn't the request made [to count all the undervotes], and why wouldn't it be proper for any court, if they're going to offer any relief, to count the undervotes in all of the counties?"

When Barry Richard stood up for the Bush campaign he was also asked by the chief justice whether the supreme court had the authority to hear this appeal, despite the fact that the legislature did not explicitly provide for this authority specifically in the contest statute. His answer: "Indeed you do, Your Honor." When Harding pressed the point by noting that the statute talked about the circuit court and not the Florida Supreme Court, Richard said that he believed that the circuit court's ruling was subject to the Florida Supreme Court's authority. Justice Harry Lee Anstead wanted to make sure that his court's authority would not later be called into question by the Bush campaign. He asked Richard whether his "bottom line" answer was that the state supreme court could properly hear this case. Richard replied, "[Y]es." Anstead: "And the federal *McPherson* case does not affect that jurisdiction." Richard: "No sir." When Anstead followed up by asking whether the court's authority in this case was the same as its authority to review any election contest case, Richard said: "Precisely, Your Honor. . . . It doesn't make any difference whether we're talking about school teachers and laborers or presidents and kings, the rules are the same."[41]

It would take Richard less than twenty-four hours to take back those answers.

In the meantime, the justices went on to push Richard on the question of whether the contest statute required courts to ascertain whether legal votes had been included in the final tally. Justice Pariente then pointed out that the newly passed contest statute instructed judges to do whatever was necessary to "ensure" that each allegation was investigated, but Richard argued that the only allegation that had to be investigated was whether the local boards abused their discretion. When Boies approached for his final remarks, the chief justice questioned whether there was anything that could be done about the matter at this late date. "We don't have a remedy here that can do that by December 12." Boies disagreed, claiming first that much of the remedy would require simply a legal finding that certain already "recovered" undervotes from Palm Beach and Miami-Dade should be included in the official results and then insisting that the other "ballots can be counted in the time available. Obviously, time is getting very short. We have been trying to get these ballots counted, as the court knows, for many weeks now."

The news analyst for the *New York Times* noted that it appeared as though the justices were searching "desperately for a way out," perhaps by arguing that they lacked jurisdiction in this case.[42] The report in the *Washington Post* was that a court that had previously shown "self-confidence" when approaching the first case "seemed chastened, if not humbled" this time around.[43] The *Chicago Tribune* reported that "the toughest questions appeared to be directed to Gore lawyer David Boies."[44] Even some conservatives thought that Republicans had little to fear. Robert Alt, a conservative legal analyst, noted that the Florida court had spurned Gore several times since its first decision – denying his efforts to force Judge Sauls to start recounts early and turning back an appeal of the infamous "butterfly ballot."[45] On the other hand, it was also noted that some of the justices seemed genuinely troubled by Judge Sauls's approach to the contest, particularly his unwillingness to see whether legal votes were missed. Conservatives also continued to worry that the Florida justices "just want to help Al Gore so badly that the heart overrules their head."[46]

In a last-ditch legal effort to deny Gore even this threadbare hope, the Bush team attempted on Friday morning to submit a "clarification of argument," which rescinded Barry Richard's oft-repeated claim that the justices had the authority to take jurisdiction in the case. Their position now was that the court's only appellate authority was based on the state constitution and under the U.S. Supreme Court's opinion that was not an acceptable legal basis for resolving disputes regarding the selection of presidential electors. Gore's lawyers quickly filed their own response, but it was unnecessary; the Bush clarification would not be accepted. The court must have already decided.[47] As the *Philadelphia Inquirer* put it on Friday morning, "the Bush-Gore electoral war could go either way. It might be almost over. Or it might be on the verge of going nuclear."[48]

It went nuclear. At 4:01 P.M., just a hundred minutes after Lewis and Clark rejected efforts to throw out 25,000 absentee ballots, Florida Supreme Court spokesman Craig Waters approached a podium in front of the court building and announced before throngs of television cameras the decision in the case *Gore v. Harris.* The court ordered recounts of undervotes to begin, not just in the counties selected by Gore, but throughout the entire state. Moreover, the court ordered Bush's official 537 lead trimmed down to 154 votes with the automatic inclusion of full recount results from Palm Beach and partial recount results from Miami-Dade. It was a 4 to 3 decision, with Justices Anstead, Lewis, Pariente, and Quince siding with Gore. Chief Justice Wells and Justices Harding and Shaw dissented.

The four-member majority explained their decision in an unsigned per curiam opinion. After noting that "we have jurisdiction,"[49] they laid out their reasoning. The major premise of the argument was that the Florida contest statute required judges to correct any problems that might be caused when a certified election result that fails to include a sufficient number of legal votes casts doubt on the accuracy of the result; the minor premise was that a ballot was still "legal" in Florida even if it was filled out (or punched) in a way that could not be read by a machine, as long as the intent of the voter could be determined. (In other words, it had never been the law in Florida that a ballot was illegal just because a voter might not have followed the rules by failing to properly mark or punch a ballot.) The result followed from these premises: the trial court erred by not including the 215 net votes for Gore identified by the Palm Beach Canvassing Board (legal votes discovered by an inspection of undervotes), by not including the 168 net votes for Gore identified by Miami-Dade in their partial recount (same), and by refusing to examine the 9,000 Miami-Dade votes that were never manually reviewed (where there was reason to believe that there were recoverable legal votes in that batch). At the same time, in light of this analysis, "the ultimate relief" requires "counting of the legal votes contained within the undervotes in all counties where the undervote has not been subjected to a manual tabulation" just to make sure that all possible legal votes in this statewide election are included in the official tally; this amounted to approximately 42,000 ballots spread out over sixty-six counties. On the other hand, because Palm Beach County already reviewed 3,300 ballots there was no basis for independent judicial review of their decision that there were no legal votes among that batch. Moreover, the justices ruled that Nassau did not make a mistake when it reverted to its election-night totals (after concluding that the machine recount was faulty because a stack of votes was inadvertently left out of that count).

The justices laid out this argument in language that clearly demonstrated their sensitivity to the U.S. Supreme Court's Article II concerns. Their analysis was based exclusively on the text of the contest statute that had been "established by the Legislature," and they approached this task "cognizant of the federal grant of authority derived from the United States Constitution and derived from 3 U.S.C. § 5," which emphasized the importance of resolving election disputes based on "laws enacted prior to" Election Day. In addition to the contest statute, the Florida legislature also mandated that no vote shall be ignored "if there is a clear indication of the intent of the voter" on the ballot, unless it is "impossible to determine the elector's choice";[50] this legislative preference was reiterated in the recount statutes where ballot inspectors are required to determine the voter's intent and not focus on whether voters followed instructions.[51]

Consequently, the justices remanded the case back to the circuit court to "commence the tabulation of the Miami-Dade ballots immediately. . . . Moreover, since time is also of the essence in any statewide relief that the circuit court must consider, any further statewide relief should also be ordered forthwith and simultaneously with the manual tabulation of the Miami-Dade undervotes." The final sentence of the opinion: "In tabulating the ballots and in making a determination of what is a 'legal' vote, the standard to be employed is that established by the Legislature in our Election Code which is that the vote shall be counted as a 'legal' vote if there is a 'clear indication of the intent of the voter.'"

Wells, who during oral argument was obviously skeptical about proceeding any further, started his dissent by making "it clear at the outset . . . that I do not question the good faith or honorable intentions of my colleagues in the majority." But he "could not more strongly disagree" with their decision to reverse the trial court, and he predicted that their decision "cannot withstand the scrutiny which will certainly immediately follow under the United States Constitution." Despite the majority's care to anchor their decision in the Florida statutes, Wells believed that their decision to force new manual recounts "has no foundation in the law of Florida as it existed on November 7," which in his judgment delegated decisions about recounts to election officials subject only to a review of whether they had abused their discretion. He also expressed "a deep and abiding concern that the prolonging of judicial process in this counting contest propels this country and this state into an unprecedented and unnecessary constitutional crisis," especially in light of the widespread belief that the lack of clear legislative standards for reviewing ballots creates "equal protection concerns which will eventually cause the election results in Florida to be stricken by the federal courts or Congress."

Justice Harding, a nominal independent, dissented separately, joined by Justice Shaw, who was widely viewed as one of the most liberal members of the Court. This division made it clear that these judges were not dividing along traditional ideological lines; they were also not obviously influenced by appointment politics, since the one justice on the court who was nominated by Jeb Bush, Peggy A. Quince, voted with the majority. The key pattern in the division was that the dissenters were the most senior members of the court.[52] They believed that Judge Sauls was wrong to use an "abuse of discretion" standard and to require Gore to show a "reasonable probability that the results of the election would have changed," but they nevertheless felt that the Gore team failed to carry "their burden of showing that the number of legal votes rejected by the canvassing boards is sufficient to change or place in doubt the result of this statewide election." Even if they assumed that Gore had met his burden, "the only remedy authorized by law would be a statewide recount of more than 170,000 'no-vote' ballots by December 12," and while it might be theoretically possible to accomplish this it would "come at the expense of accuracy, and it would be difficult to put any faith or credibility in a vote total achieved under such chaotic conditions." They ended with a quote from the legendary football coach Vince Lombardi: "We didn't lose the game, we just ran out of time."

The announcement of the decision sent shockwaves through the country. Some were shocked and jubilant; others, shocked and outraged.[53] Bush representative James A. Baker III called the decision "sad for the nation [and] sad for democracy." House majority whip Tom DeLay was less reserved; in words that echoed President George Bush's reaction to Saddam Hussein's invasion of Kuwait, Delay declared, "This judicial aggression will not stand."[54] The conservative *Weekly Standard* called the decision a "travesty" and expressed hope that "some combination of the Florida legislature, the U.S. Congress, and the U.S. Supreme Court may be able to salvage the lawful result of this election."[55] The chief of staff for the Republican National Committee, Tom Cole, promised "to fight it tooth and nail. . . . It's going to be very hard for Republicans to accept this decision as anything other than liberal, judicial activism gone amok."[56]

Not surprisingly, Gore representative William M. Daley called the decision "a victory for fairness and accountability and our democracy itself."[57] The two Democratic leaders of Congress, Senator Tom Daschle of South Dakota and Representative Richard A. Gephardt of Missouri, released a statement saying that "(w)e are pleased the Florida Supreme Court has ruled in favor of a full, fair, and accurate vote count. Now that the state's highest court has spoken, Americans can finally determine how the citizens of Florida voted on election day, and which candidate truly won the presidency."[58] Democrats also said that this was the only result that would truly determine the will of the people, and efforts to overturn it would be resisted. In referring to the efforts of the Republican-controlled Florida legislature to appoint its own slate, one Democratic official said that "(t)hey're trying to replace the peoples' votes with a partisan Republican vote."[59]

Newspaper editorial writers were also split.[60] Strong support came from the *New York Times*, *Newsday*, the *Philadelphia Daily News*, the *Times Union* of *Albany*, the *Buffalo News* (N.Y.), the *Daily News* of (N.Y.), the *Charlotte Observer* (N.C.), the *News and Observer of Raleigh* (N.C.), and the *Boston Globe*. The *Washington Post* expressed "reservations" about the decision, and there was strong editorial opposition from the *Boston Herald*, the *Dallas Morning News*, the *Salt Lake Tribune*, the *Plain Dealer* of Cleveland, and the *New York Post*, which declared that "whether this attempted hijacking will stand remains to be seen." The *Wall Street Journal's* John Fund advised that "judicial activism – like a high fever – must be broken; it can't be pampered. . . . The federal courts have to act. The U.S. Supreme Court was relatively gentle in its Monday rebuke of the Florida court, giving it an easy way to save face by curbing its judicial activism. Three of the seven Florida justices – the most senior – heeded the message and retreated from their unanimous original ruling. But the Gang of Four apparently don't care."[61]

Many conservatives acted as if they were entitled to a U.S. Supreme Court reversal as the quickest way of shutting down an unacceptable state court. But from a purely legal perspective, it was not obvious that the Florida court's decision violated federal law. Maybe the Florida justices had not learned the political lesson of staying out of this election controversy, but they did seem to learn some legal lessons about how they might insulate their decision from federal review. The majority was very careful to link every element of their opinion to the clear language of the Florida statutory scheme. They also made very specific references to the principles of constitutional law that the U.S. Supreme Court justices emphasized in their decision five days earlier. The justices were also careful to not create any new legal standards in the case; even when it came to addressing the difficult issue of what criteria should be used in evaluating the ballots, the justices limited themselves to the express statutory language of discerning the intent of the voter. Perhaps most important, the justices anticipated the equal protection arguments that had been litigated in the Eleventh Circuit just a few days earlier; they even responded to the main concerns expressed by the Republican dissenters in that case, which was that selected manual recounts unfairly discriminated against voters in other counties who would not obtain the benefit of an attempt to manually rehabilitate their (potentially) uncounted votes.[62]

In addition to the challenge of overturning a carefully written state court opinion, many commentators believed that the Court faced the difficult task of either "shutting down a ballot recount" or "undoing the public results of a recount if Gore takes the lead over the weekend." Shutting down the recount seemed especially unlikely, given that the law only allowed that option if the justices were willing to say that Bush would suffer "irreparable harm" if the hand counts proceeded. Many people assumed that the worst that could happen to Bush is that a recount may, temporarily, put Gore ahead; but even if that problem emerged (which was not a guarantee) it could easily be remedied by a later decision of the Supreme Court invalidating those results and reestablishing the older totals. Moreover, two other federal courts – including a bipartisan majority of the conservative Eleventh Circuit Court of Appeals – had already decided that manual recounts did not represent an irreparable harm to a candidate even if one assumed there may be constitutional problems. Besides, if anyone was faced with irreparable harm it seemed to be Gore, who (apparently) needed the recounts to be completed by Tuesday, just four days away.[63]

The case was remanded back to Judge Sauls's court, but without explanation he recused himself from further proceedings. Under the courthouse's system of rotating assignments the case was then assigned to Judge Nikki Clark, but she was unavailable. The next judge in line was Terry Lewis. Approximately four hours after the high court's ruling, Lewis was overseeing a hearing attended by a now familiar group of Gore and Bush lawyers.[64] Just before midnight, after hearing more than two hours of arguments, Judge Lewis began setting up the process for the state's manual recount.[65] Because the Miami-Dade ballots were already in Leon County, Lewis ordered that the recount of those ballots begin at 8:00 A.M. Saturday morning, with instructions to complete the count by 2:00 P.M. on Sunday. Other counties would inform Lewis of their action plans by late Saturday morning, with the understanding that they too would finish by the same Sunday deadline. To avoid the partisan rancor and disruption that characterized earlier recounts, Lewis ordered that party observers limit themselves to monitoring the process and making written objections; they were not allowed to "make a verbal objection or challenge to any particular ballot determination nor in any way disrupt or interfere with the counting process." If the counting teams could not agree on a ballot, then it would be considered disputed and Lewis would make the final decision. He also suggested that "in the interest of promoting the public's trust and confidence in the objectivity and impartiality of the counting process, the counties are urged – but not required – to enlist the services of its judges where appropriate, in a manner similar to the process outlined above." However, "the method and manner of the count shall be determined by the Canvassing Boards." The standard to be used by everyone in determining whether to count a vote: "if there is a 'clear indication of the intent of the voter' then the vote should be counted. If not, the vote should not be counted."

Judge Lewis added a footnote here: "Some of the parties have requested that I establish specific criteria to utilize in applying this standard. The Florida Supreme Court has been asked at least twice recently to do so and has specifically declined. The only guidance is the language in the statute quoted above." Bush attorney Phil Beck had urged Lewis to be more specific – not because he thought Lewis would change his mind, but (as he said later) because he was hoping that a few U.S. Supreme Court law clerks might be watching the televised proceeding. After the hearing, Beck called Michael Carvin, who was working on the Supreme Court appeal, and told him to make the question of standards a centerpiece of the argument. They were beginning to think that this once-ridiculed argument might now be a winner – either because the problems with the argument were becoming more clear or because the Florida Supreme Court had proceeded in a way that was otherwise airtight and this might be the best argument available to serve up to a pro-Bush Supreme Court majority. At the end of the Lewis hearing, Bush lawyer George Terwilliger ran out of the courtroom so quickly that he bumped into David Boies. "You know what, David?" Terwilliger said. "We just won this case." It was a lot of confidence to place in the Supreme Court.[66]

The hours immediately following the state supreme court's decision were frenzied. But by morning the process had turned into something that looked remarkably smooth and efficient, at least with respect to the counting of the Miami-Dade ballots in Leon County.[67] Judges quietly sorted through hundreds and then thousands of ballots, placing them into labeled shoeboxes. New York Governor George Pataki, a Republican ally of Bush, appeared outside the Leon County Public Library where these recounts were taking place and called the action "nothing but chaos," but reporters said that "inside the library [there] was no sign of chaos." In fact, judges were counting nearly a thousand ballots an hour. At that rate the review of these long-disputed ballots would be completed well before Judge Lewis next-day deadline.[68]

The situation was not quite as smooth everywhere else. While counties with very few (easily segregated) undervotes had it easy, others were facing some challenges. In Santa Rosa County, officials said that they had never segregated the undercounted votes; that would mean manually reviewing more than 50,000 ballots in order to find the votes that the state high court wanted examined more carefully.[69] Duval County, with its all-Republican canvassing commission – and where nearly 42 percent of spoiled ballots (undervotes and overvote) came from predominantly black communities – complained that it was going to have to spend ten hours on Saturday finding the 4,967 undervotes amid their 291,000 ballots. When they faxed their plan of action to Judge Lewis on Saturday morning they made it clear that the county "undertakes the task of counting . . . with grave concerns about the reliability and accuracy of any process for such a recount"; however, they did not elucidate why they feared that they could not reliably conclude whether a ballot reflected the clear intent of the voter. Elections Systems & Software, Inc., a company that builds vote-counting machines, was already delivering special microchips to fifteen Florida counties to help sort out the undervote ballots; other counties learned that their machines could not be programmed to accomplish that and undervotes would have to be segregated from the total vote by hand.[70] Still, while some counties were having trouble getting started, many were moving forward smoothly and systematically, and there was growing confidence among Gore supporters that the leap of faith taken by a bare majority of Florida's high court justices would pay off. For people who believed that, as a matter of principle, these votes should count, the process was important even if Gore did not end up the winner – a distinct possibility, particularly in light of an early Associated Press report that an unofficial tally of all recounts that showed that Gore had netted just sixteen votes statewide.[71]

As the country watched the recounts proceeding on Saturday morning, the Eleventh Circuit Court of Appeals announced that it was refusing the Bush campaign's request for an emergency injunction to stop the recounts. The appeals court, once again divided 8 to 4, disagreed that Bush would suffer "irreparable harm" if the recounts continued. However, in a unanimous vote, the judges ruled that "in order to ensure that the United States Supreme Court has sufficient time to rule" on the Bush appeal, Florida election officials were prohibited from changing "any previously certified results of the presidential election based upon any manual recounts after the existing certification. Nothing in this order should be construed to prevent, obstruct or impede the continuation of the manual recounts that are currently being conducted."[72]

Suddenly, at around 2:45 P.M., the recount efforts faltered. Cable news networks that had been broadcasting the work of the efficient counting teams at the Leon County Public Library were now showing the members of these teams (many of whom were judges) getting up from their folding tables and leaving the building.[73]

The U.S. Supreme Court had just issued an emergency injunction ordering a halt to the hand recounts. Moreover, the previously unanimous Washington justices now found themselves divided right down the middle. The vote to issue the emergency injunction was 5 to 4.

5

THE DAM BREAKS

FIVE JUSTICES PICK A PRESIDENT

★ ★ ★

*[In the long run the decision] will be understood for
what it is: a clearly reasoned judgment rooted in fundamental
law that was also an act of statesmanship of high order.*
Cardozo law professor John O. McGinnis[1]

*[T]he conservatives' decision to reverse a state supreme court's rulings
on matters of state law did not reflect any established conservative position
on any general constitutional question. . . . [T]he troubling question is being
asked among scholars and commentators whether the Court's decision . . .
reflected not ideological division, which is inevitable, but professional
self-interest. . . . We should try to resist this unattractive explanation. . . .
Unfortunately, however, the legal case they offered for crucial
aspects of their decisions was exceptionally weak.*
New York University law professor Ronald Dworkin[2]

When the Bush campaign asked the U.S. Supreme Court to stop a last-ditch effort to recount Florida's ballots they created the first case in U.S. history with the names of two presidential candidates in the title. The election litigation had always been a battle between the vice president and the Texas governor, but now it had officially become *Bush v. Gore.*

In their written argument to the justices, the Bush lawyers reiterated their earlier accusations about how the Florida Supreme Court had changed the law governing election contests, in violation of Article II of the Constitution and 3 U.S.C. § 5.[3] However, in their new opinion, the Florida justices seemed to be extremely careful about focusing on the meaning of the Florida statutes, without reference to other sources of state law that the U.S.

Supreme Court (surprisingly) had declared out of bounds in a presidential election. The Florida majority was so mindful of the need to avoid "creating new law" in a presidential election that it even refused to go beyond the legislative standard of determining "the intent of the voter" when it gave instructions about how the recount was to proceed. The Bush lawyers also reasserted arguments about the arbitrary and discriminatory nature of hand recounts, but the Florida court had also been apparently responsive to these concerns when it rejected the Gore request for selective recounts in favor of a state inspection of undervotes. Finally, to get an emergency injunction, Bush had to demonstrate that he would be "irreparably harmed" if recounts were to continue while awaiting a final decision in the case; however, while Republicans certainly wanted the recounts stopped as soon as possible, there was also a belief among many commentators that any harm to Bush by allowing the recounts go to forward would not be "irreparable" (since the results of a recount could be undone later). Given the impending deadline, the only irreparable harm looming would be the harm to Gore if recounts were stopped.

Despite all these reasons to think that these last recounts would proceed, many Republicans had confidence in the U.S. Supreme Court. As it turned out, this confidence was well placed. Less than twenty-four hours after the Florida Supreme Court announced its decision ordering new recounts, five justices of the U.S. Supreme Court ordered them halted. The Court's declaration was clinical: the application for the stay was granted; briefs on the merits of the case were due in roughly twenty-four hours; oral arguments would be held in less than forty-eight hours, on Monday, December 11 at 11:00 A.M. In a development that confirmed many people's worst fears for the Supreme Court, Justices John Paul Stevens, David Souter, Ruth Bader Ginsburg, and Stephen Breyer dissented from the order. The Court was split right down its ideological fault line, with the most conservative five acting over the objections of their more moderate colleagues.

The dissenters argued that the majority was violating established principles of judicial restraint and had acted in a way that "will inevitably cast a cloud on the legitimacy of the election." Their view was that "counting every legally cast vote cannot constitute irreparable harm." These complaints led Justice Scalia to write a rare public explanation of the majority's thinking. In his concurring opinion Scalia explained that "the issue is not, as the dissent puts it, whether '[c]ounting every legally cast vote ca[n] constitute irreparable harm.' One of the principal issues in the appeal we have accepted is precisely whether the votes that have been ordered to be counted are, under a reasonable interpretation of Florida law, 'legally cast vote[s].'" This was a startling and perplexing statement, since the Bush camp nowhere claimed that so-called "undervotes" were, by definition, not legally cast votes and therefore could not be counted.[4]

Scalia continued by claiming that "the counting of votes that are of questionable legality does in my view threaten irreparable harm to petitioner, and to the country, by casting a cloud upon what he claims to be the legitimacy of his election. Count first, and rule upon legality afterwards, is not a recipe for producing election results that have the public acceptance democratic stability requires." This was as close to an overtly partisan assessment of the conflict as we would officially hear from the Supreme Court. The manual recounts threatened irreparable harm apparently because Bush might lose, and if the Court later determined that Bush should nevertheless win the election the fact that a improper manual count resulted in a temporary Gore victory might undermine public acceptance of Bush's presidency. Whether Gore, or other parts of the country, might have countervailing political interests in allowing a recount to continue, even if the results would later have to be withdrawn, was not evaluated in the short opinion.

Finally, Scalia suggested that "permitting the count to proceed on [an] erroneous basis will prevent an accurate recount from being conducted on a proper basis later, since it is generally agreed that each manual recount produces a degradation of the ballots, which renders a subsequent recount inaccurate." Could it be that the conservatives were stopping a bad recount in order to make possible a good recount? To most people it seemed unlikely, but Scalia wanted to leave the impression that this was a real possibility. The country would find out soon enough whether the conservatives honestly thought that this might happen or whether Scalia was attempting to mute some of the criticisms that were likely to come.

THE REACTION

If this was Scalia's purpose, then it was woefully unsuccessful. When the Florida Supreme Court handed down its decision the day before, Democrats reacted with exuberance and Republicans, with outrage; now it was time for everyone to switch once again.[5] Most people immediately understood that "in issuing an emergency order to halt the recount of Florida's ballots, the U.S. Supreme Court all but cleared the way for Texas Gov. George W. Bush to win the presidency"; at the same time, by dividing down ideological lines "the court simultaneously placed itself at the center of the partisan battling over the election."[6]

Politicians and participants reacted predictably. Gore attorney David Boies heard of the Court's actions over lunch, and he reportedly exclaimed, "What possible irreparable harm could they be talking about?"[7] (When commenting more publicly he noted that Scalia "doesn't want to have the legitimacy of [a potential Bush] presidency undercut by the fact that people will know there were more votes for Vice President Gore," and then added that "we think the right way to look at it is the way the four dissenting justices looked at it: that the legitimacy of any president that's elected is going to be impaired unless the American people understand there has been a full and fair count of all the votes."[8]) Democrats were demoralized, but there was no party effort to call into question the legitimacy of the Court's authority. Senator Patrick Leahy of Vermont, the top Democrat on the Senate Judiciary Committee, made the strongest public comment, bemoaning the fact that the decision "has the appearance of a partisan step."[9] But most elected official followed the lead of House minority leader Richard Gephardt, who insisted that they should "respect the courts. . . . If you don't like a decision, appeal it to a higher court, but don't engage in attack politics against the judicial branch of our great democracy."[10]

Many liberal commentators did not share this sense of restraint and had harsh words for the Court's actions – especially for Scalia's explanation of irreparable harm. Thomas Oliphant said Scalia warped "long-established rules" involving irreparable harm and misstated the facts so that he could play "Big Brother [and] protect us from the cloud that is truth" (that is, the truth of the actual vote result in Florida).[11] Edward Lazarus wrote in the *Washington Post* that the decision "has raised the specter that the conservatives are hellbent on putting Bush in the White House, the law be damned," and following Scalia they have "justified stopping the hand counts because a swing in Gore's direction might undermine the legitimacy of a Bush presidency. While such political concerns may be appropriate to James Baker, the notion of preventing the public from learning that Gore received more votes than Bush has no place in the thinking of a politically neutral court."[12] Jonathan Alter of *Newsweek* called Scalia's opinion "one of the most logically shoddy bits of legal reasoning in recent memory. His opinion works only if the starting point of the argument is that Bush deserves to be the president."[13] Alan Brinkley of Columbia University called Scalia's argument "absurdly feeble" and said that "protecting a candidate's controversial claim of legitimacy does not seem to me to be something the

Supreme Court should be exerting itself to protect."[14] Even some conservative commentators had trouble with Justice Scalia's explanation. Michael McConnell commented sarcastically that the logic of Scalia's theory would be for the Court to "burn all the ballots," since that would be the only way to prevent the possibility of later counts leading people to question the legitimacy of a Bush presidency.[15] Terrance Sandalow said the "balance of harms so unmistakably were on the side of Gore" that the granting of the stay was "incomprehensible," an "unmistakably partisan decision without any foundation in law."[16]

However, other conservatives insisted that the Florida Supreme Court had "thumbed its nose" at the justices, and while "some people will say that the court acted politically," you "have to balance that against restoring political stability to the country."[17] Conservative columnist Charles Krauthammer put it in a more colloquial way: "Amid the chaos, somebody had to play Daddy. Its earlier admonition having been ignored, the Supreme Court eschewed subtlety and bluntly stopped the Florida Supreme Court in its tracks."[18] William Safire said simply, "You cannot spit in the eye of the nation's highest court without suffering consequences. . . . Our political process was almost subverted by a runaway court."[19] According to William Kristol, at stake was nothing less than the end of "judicial tyranny."[20]

Up until Saturday afternoon the U.S. Supreme Court seemed to be one of the few institutions in the country that had avoided the corrupting effects of the election saga. In an instant, though, this all changed. "Now we know," wrote the *New York Times*'s R. W. Apple, Jr. "They are just like the rest of us, split right down the middle, divided into two hostile camps."[21] For the first time in this election dispute, many were suggesting that the Court had already undermined its reputation and authority. Ronald Brownstein of the *Los Angeles Times* noted that the five conservatives "may have set a new standard for swallowing [their] previous convictions" on the importance of defending states against federal intrusion, and did so with reference to an "openly political logic" that was designed to ensure that they would not have to face the prospects of "nullifying a popular vote count that, for the first time, put Gore ahead in Florida."[22] Sanford Levinson of the University of Texas Law School said that "this looks like a group of five, hard-line, right-wing Republicans who are willing to do anything to put their guy in office."[23] University of Southern California law professor Erwin Chemerinsky expressed the view that "its image is tarnished in the eyes of many people. . . . It's seen as another political player." A. E. Dick Howard from the University of Virginia said that "I can't think of an opinion in which the court has come closer to planting an image in the public mind of being partisan," and thus "the Supreme Court may lose some of the sheen which it has in the American mind." Mary Cheh, a law professor at George Washington University, suggested that "the good will and the good faith of the people" toward the Court is "a very fragile thing, so you don't want to lose it." With this decision "the mask has fallen and you can see what's really going on. It's very demoralizing to me."[24] Jack M. Balkin of Yale Law School said that "by attempting to shore up Bush's legitimacy, the U.S. Supreme Court has strongly compromised its own."[25] By Monday morning, the *Washington Post* media critic Howard Kurtz noted that "for the first time in a long time, the Supreme Court is under fierce journalistic attack," with the attention so focused and sustained that there was a question about "whether there is a law professor in America who hasn't been quoted on this story."[26]

Still, while besieged by many journalists and liberal law professors, the Supreme Court did have some political advantages as it moved toward a final resolution of the Bush appeal. Opinion polls showed that the public still had considerable faith in the U.S. Supreme Court's ability to decide the election contest fairly. Nearly three-quarters of those surveyed (73 percent) said they would accept as legitimate a decision by the U.S. Supreme Court that resolved the election controversy once and for all. When asked which institution they would "most trust to make the final decision on the selection of the next president," 61 percent said the Supreme Court, compared with 17 percent for the Congress, 9 percent for the Florida Supreme Court, and 7 percent for the Florida legislature.[27] Then again, the public's confidence in the court's impartiality was decreasing: about 66 percent said they felt confident that the justices would be fair to both sides, down from 76 percent just one week earlier. Thirty-two percent had little confidence in the court, and by a ratio of 2 to 1 those who doubted the court's impartiality said the justices were treating Gore unfairly. Among Democratic voters the doubts about the court's fairness rose in a week from 27 to 46 percent. Not surprisingly, about eight in ten Republicans thought that the Supreme Court would be fair to both sides.[28] All of this suggested that the Court had some political room to maneuver, in the sense of making a decision that would be accepted by most of the country, but if it ruled strongly for Bush it would be using up some of its so-called political capital.

Even more importantly for the Court, over the weekend the Gore campaign made it very clear that they viewed the Supreme Court as the final decision-maker on this election contest, and they would accept as legitimate any decision made by the justices. It was a self-conscious appeal "for national unity, whichever way the court rules." Gore lawyer David Boies said on NBC's *Meet the Press* that a pro-Bush ruling would be "the end of it. . . . Their voice is final." House minority leader Richard Gephardt said that he believed Gore would concede if he lost in the U.S. Supreme Court. (He added, though, that Bush should do the same if the tables were turned.)[29] By contrast, the Bush campaign, knowing that it still held the trump cards of the Republican Florida legislature and the Republican majority in the House of Representatives, refused to commit itself to abide by an adverse Supreme Court ruling.[30] Given the writing on the wall, though, it was more significant to secure Gore's agreement. This ensured that the Court at least would be obeyed if it ruled against Gore. Whether it would be politically damaged by such a decision was another question.

THE ARGUMENTS

In making their new case for why the Florida justices violated Article II of the U.S. Constitution, Bush's side claimed that the election contest statute in Florida was designed to have courts review whether election officials acted within their discretion, not to engage in a brand new review of ballots. They also emphasized that Florida's "arbitrary, selective and standardless manual recounts" violated the equal protection and due process clauses of the U.S. Constitution because it "gives the votes of similarly situated voters different effect based on the happenstance of the county or district in which those voters live." In other words, "where there is a partial punch or stray mark on a ballot, that ballot may be counted as a 'vote' in some counties but not others."[31]

Those who wrote the Gore brief had a harder time, because they knew that five justices already had reason to believe that their case was a lost cause.[32] The most that they could hope for was that at least one of the justices who signed on to stop the recount would think twice about the specter of a pure ideological split down the middle. Their main point was that the Florida court's recount order was based on the Florida legislature's decision to "expressly grant[] the courts extraordinarily broad remedial authority" whenever judges had reason to believe that certified election returns might have announced the wrong winner by missing too many legal votes. Their main response to the equal protection argument was that the Florida Supreme Court anticipated all reasonable concerns when it required a statewide review under a single uniform standard. To go further and declare that the equal protection clause requires all ballots to be treated the same would call into question any variation in state or county voting practices and would thus seemingly require the federal imposition of a nationwide, uniform, mechanical standard for ballot counting. Moreover, recount provisions do "nothing more than place the voters whose votes were not tabulated by the machine on the same footing as those whose votes were so tabulated.[33] Finally, even if there is some allegation of an unacceptable discrepancy among counties, the remedy should not be "to end the counting" and thus "toss out lawfully cast ballots"; "it is, instead, to articulate the proper standard and – as required by state law – to have the counting go forward under that standard." A decision to count "none of the votes would be vote dilution with a vengeance."

The oral argument was held on Monday, December 11, at 11:00 A.M.[34] Theodore Olson once again represented Bush. The Gore legal team, however, decided on a change, going with David Boies rather than Laurence Tribe. In part this reflected the hope that Boies's greater familiarity with the details of the Florida legislative scheme, and the history of the recent litigation, would put him in a better position to defend the decision of the Florida court; but there were also reports that Gore thought that Tribe had been somewhat glib, condescending, and unprepared (on *McPherson*) during the first oral argument.[35] As with the first case, the Court announced that it would release an audio recording of the oral argument as soon as it was over. At a little past 12:30 P.M. much of the country hovered around their televisions, radios, and computers to listen to what all expected would be the final public court proceeding of the election 2000 dispute.

Olson was first.[36] When he began complaining about the Florida justices creating "ad hoc, judicially established procedures" in this election contest Justice Souter interrupted to ask, "Well, aren't ad hoc judicially created procedures the point of Subsection 8 of 168 [the contest statute]? I mean, once we get into the contest phase" that legislation gives to courts "as broad a grant to fashion orders as I can imagine going into a statute." Olson agreed that the Florida court should have read the contest statute in light of all the protest phase provisions regarding the authority of other election officials, and Souter said that "I will grant you for the sake of argument that there would be a sound interpretive theory that in effect would coordinate" the protest and contest phases so that the latter would be read in terms of the former. "But that's a question of Florida Supreme Court statutory construction," and "unless you can convince us" that a reading that separates the contest phase from the protest phase is simply out of "the bounds of legitimate statutory construction, then I don't see how we can find an Article II violation here."

When Justice Kennedy asked about Olson's equal protection argument, Justice Breyer quickly jumped in and asked, if the recounts "were to start up again . . . [w]hat in your opinion would be a fair standard, on the assumption that it starts up missing the 12th deadline but before the 18th?" It was an extremely important and telling question, suggesting the possibility – mentioned toward the end of the Gore brief – that the best way to remedy the equal protection problem would be to set correct standards and start over. Olson had no interest in helping the justices figure out how to restart the process, and he said "I don't know the complete answer to that." But Breyer pushed: "You say the intent of the voter is not good enough. You want substandards. . . . And what in your opinion would be the most commonly used in the 33 states or whatever, or in your opinion, the fairest uniform standard?" Olson said that at minimum, a dimple would not be good enough, "the penetration of the ballot card would be required."

Then Souter jumped in; he and Breyer were obviously very interested in pursuing this line of inquiry. He wanted to know if Olson was going to claim that any effort to now clarify the standard – which may be necessary to solve an equal protection problem – would be an unconstitutional violation of Article II: "the closest we can come now under Florida law is an intent of the voter standard. Is it your position that if any official, judicial or executive, at this point were to purport to lay down a statewide standard which went to a . . . more specific level than intent of the voter, and said, for example, count dimpled chads or don't count dimpled chads. In your judgment would that be a violation of Article II?" Olson said that he didn't think so – an important concession, given the apparent interest of these justices in possibly restarting the recounts under a new standard.

But before Olson could be pulled in too deeply into an argument about how to count the undervote, Scalia jumped in. "It is also part of your case, is it not, that . . . there is no wrong [to be corrected in a contest] when a machine does not count those ballots that it's not supposed to count?" Olson: "That's absolutely correct, Justice Scalia." Scalia: "The voters are instructed to detach the chads entirely, and the machine, as predicted, does not count those chads, where those instructions are not followed, there isn't any wrong." Scalia was referring to the point he made in his concurrence to the stay order that undervotes might not be "legal ballots" that deserved to be examined. Olson: "That's correct. . . . this has been euphemistically referred to as legal votes that haven't been counted," and the Florida scheme considered them no-votes.

Souter jumped in again to challenge this constricted view of what should count as a legal vote in Florida: "But as to the undervotes . . . in which there is arguably some expression of intent on the ballot that the machine didn't pick up, the majority of the Florida Supreme Court says you're wrong. . . . Are you saying here that their interpretation was so far unreasonable in defining legal vote as not to be a judicial act entitled, in effect, to the presumption of reasonable interpretation under Article II?" Olson, after having initially shown a willingness to discuss the counting of undervotes, now embraced Scalia's position: "Yes, that is our contention." Souter: "What is it in the contest provision [of the law] that supports the theory that [a decision to treat these undervotes as legal ballots] was a rogue, illegal judicial act?" Olson started to say that there is no reference to them in the statutes, but Stevens jumped in: "There's no definition [of legal ballot in the statutes]. There's no definition. Doesn't the court have to come up with a definition . . . ?" As Olson tried to tie the question back to the responsibilities of county canvassing commissions, Rehnquist cut him off.

Joseph P. Klock, Jr., was next, once again representing the Florida secretary of state. Souter and Breyer were interested in continuing their argument about what standard might be most appropriate if recounting resumed, but Klock stuck to Scalia's position that improperly marked ballots were not legal ballots. Finally, Breyer asked him if he was to "take [a standard] out of a hat" for purposes of doing a manual recount "would [it] be a basically fair one?" and Klock responded that "If I were to take one out of a hat, Your Honor, if I was a legislature, what I would do is I would hold that you have to punch the chad through the ballot."[37]

With that it was David Boies's turn. After some discussion of the December 12 "safe harbor" deadline (which Boies agreed was a concern of the Florida court) Kennedy asked if "in the contest phase, there must be a uniform standard for counting the ballots?" Boies agreed that "there must be a uniform standard," but he added, "I think there is a uniform standard. The question is whether the uniform standard is too general or not. The standard is whether or not the intent of the voter is reflected by the ballot." Kennedy remarked that this standard was "very general" and allowed for variation from county to county and individual to individual. When Boies said that this is true "on the margin . . . whenever you're interpreting intent," Kennedy said that the difference in this case was "you have something objective" to look at. "You are not just reading a person's mind; you are looking at a piece of paper . . . this is susceptible of a uniform standard. And yet you say it can vary from table to table within the same county." Boies modified Kennedy's phrasing by saying "it is susceptible of a more specific standard" (not a more uniform standard), but he also noted that even in states that attempt to provide more specific standards there is usually a "catch-all" provision in the law that said "look at the intent of the voter."

But then Souter jumped in, picking up on Kennedy's concerns. Souter said that these catch-all provisions existed to handle the special cases when it would make no sense to apply an otherwise objective standard. "I think what's bothering Justice Kennedy, and it's bothering a lot of us here, is we seem to have a situation in which there is a subcategory of ballots in which" all we have are dimples or hanging chads, and in these cases "why shouldn't there be one objective rule for all counties? And if there isn't, why isn't it an equal protection violation?" Boies said that these variations would not constitute an equal protection violation because "there are a lot of times in the law in which there can be those variations, from jury to jury, from public official to public official." But Souter responded, following Kennedy's earlier point, that in those situations variations are tolerated because "we are assuming that there is detail that cannot be captured by an objective rule. . . . [W]hat's bothering Justice Kennedy, Justice Breyer, me" is that there should be a way to interpret these ballots without subjective variation. The "physical characteristics" of the ballots should not be "treated differently from county to county."

Souter seemed to be signaling that he and Breyer had identified a line of argument that might attract the support of one of the Court's conservatives, Justice Kennedy. It was not an implausible gambit. Conservatives were still angry at Kennedy for being a sometimes unreliable fifth vote for conservative decisions, and especially for writing an opinion with Souter and O'Connor in *Planned Parenthood v. Casey* upholding a woman's right to choose abortion in some circumstances. Moreover, in that joint opinion, those three justices said they understood the importance of maintaining the Court's reputation for principled decision-making, especially on issues that threatened to divide the Court in ways that appeared narrowly political. Could Kennedy be having second thoughts about a 5 to 4 Supreme Court decision that simply handed the election to Bush?

While this moment in the oral argument can be frozen and extended in an after-the-fact analysis, it was experienced at the time as just another few fleeting seconds, and it is not reasonable to assume that Souter's question should have lead Boies suddenly to abandon his defense of the fairness of the recount. And so in response to Souter's question about the acceptability of county-by-county differences, Boies insisted that it would only be an equal protection violation if one county was using an objective standard to count all indented ballots as votes and another was using an objective standard to not count indented ballots. However, in this case the standard was the same everywhere.

Souter: "All right, we're going to assume that we do have [unacceptable variations from county to county]. We can't send this thing back for more fact-finding. . . . [W]e've got to make the assumption, I think, at this stage that there may be such variation, and I think we would have a responsibility to tell the Florida courts what to do about it." Things were moving very quickly in the courtroom, and it was not yet clear to all participants how the various elements of Souter's arguments were related; but on reflection, it was clear that Souter had been suggesting from the beginning that he and Breyer wanted an option to send the case back to Florida.

Souter: "On that assumption, what would you tell them do to about it?" In other words, what would be the more appropriate objective standard to use if the case was sent back to the Florida courts?

Boies: "Well. . . ." He paused, four seconds, maybe longer. In a different setting it might have seemed like a calculated dramatic pause. But it was not. Just as Olson and Klock did not want to help Souter and Breyer by giving them a better standard to start the recounts, Boies was not sure he wanted to give a better standard that would call into question the legitimacy of the rules that had been laid down by the Florida justices.

Boies: ". . . I think that's a very hard question." (Laughter.)

Scalia: "You would tell them to count every vote." (Laughter.)

Boies: "I would tell them to count every vote." (Laughter.)

It was a great moment and it captured a lot: Boies's frustration at realizing that he might be losing Souter and Breyer and his uncertainty whether to try again to convince Souter to abandon his concerns; Scalia's willingness at this moment to make a teasing reference to what had been the Gore campaign's mantra since the beginning of the dispute – a mantra that was so simple, so persuasive to so many, yet that seemed to be carrying no water in the Supreme Court; and finally, Boies's reassertion of the basic message in the face of Scalia's confident mocking.[38]

Part of Boies's problem was that he had to be extremely cautious about identifying which standard was most fair, because he knew that Broward and Palm Beach Counties used different versions of the "intent of the voter" standard in their counts (with Broward more willing to count dimpled ballots), and if he picked one as his preferred standard he would leave the impression that the other was illegitimate. In the end he was willing to identify for Souter a standard that was a compromise between specificity and generality: ". . . if you're looking for a standard, . . . the Texas standard, if you wanted to specify something that was specific, it gives you a pretty good standard." He was not necessarily wrong about the advantages of the Texas provision – it instructed vote counters to look for some clear ballot characteristics while also including a catch-all instruction to determine the "intent of the voter" – but given that Democrats had been needling the Bush team about how "intent of the voter" was part of the Texas election code, the answer may have seemed a bit too cute. More important, it did not give Souter the level of specificity that would address the concerns he was raising.

O'Connor, however, was giving no indication that she was curious about new standards; in fact, she wanted to know why the challenge of evaluating ballots could not be handled with reference to the rules "the voters are instructed to follow, for goodness sakes?" meaning the instruction to make sure that the chads are fully removed. "I mean, it couldn't be clearer. I mean, why don't we go to that standard?" Boies reminder her that "in Florida law since 1917, Darby v. State, the Florida Supreme Court has held that where a voter's intent can be discerned, even if they don't do what they're told, that's supposed to be counted." Even in the more recent *Beckstrom* case, voters were told to fill in the whole with a no. 2 pencil, and several thousand did not, but their votes were still counted.[39] Boies wanted to make it hard for the conservatives to sidestep all the hard questions by following Scalia's suggestion and declaring simply that, in Florida, the only legal votes were ones that were free from voter error.

It was near the end of Boies's allotted time, but Souter had one more question. "Mr. Boies, let's assume that at the end of the day, the Leon County, Florida, judge, gets a series of counts from different counties, and they heard those counties have used different standards in making their counts. At that point, in your judgment, is it a violation of the Constitution for the Leon County judge to say, I don't care that there are different standards. As long as they purported to follow the intent of the voter, that's good enough." Rehnquist extended Boies's time by two minutes, and Boies responded: "I do not believe that that would violate the equal protection and due process clauses. That distinction between how they interpret the intent of the voter standard is going to have a lot less effect on how votes are treated than the mere difference in the types of machines that are used. . . . There are five times as many undervotes in punch card ballot counties than in optical ballot counties. . . . [T]hat statistic . . . makes it clear that there's some difference in how votes are being treated county by county. That difference is much greater than the difference in how many votes are recovered. . . . So that the differences of interpretation of the . . . general standard are resulting in far fewer differences among counties than simply the differences in the machines that they have." It was an extremely important point for those interested in the equal protection argument; after all, given the different error rates of Florida's various vote-counting machines, the existing election results were also tainted by county-by-county differences in the counting of votes. From this starting point, the Florida Supreme Court's decision could be seen as the best way, under the circumstances, to correct (or at least mitigate) an existing problem, rather than as a corruption of an otherwise impartial vote count. But this point was late in coming and remained underdeveloped in the oral argument.

Not surprisingly, the reaction to the oral arguments focused on the continuing division among the justices and the likelihood that the "conservative majority" on the Court seemed prepared to support the Bush position. "None of the five justices in the majority hinted at readiness to switch sides and back the Democrat's demand for a final recount of the remaining untabulated ballots in Florida," reported one newspaper.[40] Many took note of Souter's efforts to "entice Kennedy into a compromise decision that would permit recounts to resume in Florida under a new standard."[41] The Supreme Court reporter for the *New York Times*, Linda Greenhouse, led her article by noting that "members of the Supreme Court's liberal bloc labored visibly . . . to fashion a compromise that might resolve the case of *Bush v. Gore* and allow the counting of Florida's presidential votes to resume."[42] However, it was also clear that "none of the conservative justices was lured into a discussion of the standards for recounting ballots."[43]

For a short time another other issue arose that intensified awareness about the partisan stakes of the case. It was revealed that one of Scalia's sons was a partner in Theodore Olson's Washington office and that his other son accepted a position with a Miami-based law firm just one day before one of its lawyers, Barry Richard, received a call to represent Bush's interests in Florida. It was also reported that the wife of Justice Thomas, Virginia Lamp Thomas, was working at a conservative research group, the Heritage Foundation, gathering resumes for appointments in a possible Bush administration. There was even some talk about whether Scalia or Thomas should recuse himself from the case, which might result in a 4 to 4 decision that would have the effect of upholding the Florida court's decision.[44] However, most experts agreed that there was probably no technical violations of the rules or professional norms governing recusal, and it was fairly clear that these particular conservatives had moved beyond the point of being concerned about whether they were being perceived as political.[45]

THE DECISION

In the days and hours before the Supreme Court's decision, judges in other parts of the country worked visibly to clear the stage so that the inevitable announcement from the Washington justices would be the actual finale and not simply another round in a still-ongoing legal struggle.

The principal nemeses of the conservative judges in Washington did their part. On Monday, December 11, the justices of the Florida Supreme Court finally responded to the U.S. Supreme Court's decision "vacating" and "remanding" their first decision in *Palm Beach County Canvassing Board v. Harris.* So much had happened since that case was decided that it almost seemed like ancient history; actually, though, the U.S. Supreme Court's decision ordering them to clarify the case had been handed down just one week earlier. In a per curiam opinion, they insisted that "this Court has at all times been faced with a question of statutory construction of Florida's election laws [and] our examination of that issue has been limited to a determination of legislative intent as informed by the traditional sources and rules of construction we have long accepted as relevant in determining such intent." They took issue with the suggestion that they might have used the right to vote granted in the Florida Constitution as a reason to ignore the statutes; instead, the references to "the right of Florida's citizens to vote and to have elections determined by the will of Florida's voters" were treated "as important policy concerns of the Florida Legislature in enacting Florida's election code." They also clarified that the November 26 date "was not a new 'deadline'" that would be imposed in future elections; it was an attempt to apply "all the provisions of the Code as a consistent whole" in the circumstances of this election. There was only one dissenter, the obviously chastened Chief Justice Wells. He wrote simply: "I dissent from issuing a new decision while the United States Supreme Court has under consideration *Bush v. Gore* . . ., and I do not concur in the reissued opinion."[46]

On Tuesday, December 12, the Florida court also handed down a decision in the just-completed trials on the Seminole and Martin County absentee ballot cases. Republicans had repeatedly characterized that high court as almost fanatical in its willingness to disregard the law in order to promote their partisan agenda, but in *Jacobs v. Seminole County Canvassing Board* the justices unanimously ruled that the ballot applications, while faulty, were nevertheless in substantial compliance with the law; in particular, they included enough information to "establish the qualifications of the applicant." They stressed that they found the actions of the elections supervisor "troubling" and their opinion should not "be read as condoning anything less than strict adherence by election officials to the statutorily mandated election procedures."[47] While some critics claimed that these otherwise activist justices really had no choice given the clarity of the law, others interpreted their actions as another example of how this Court was consistently willing, despite the technical limitations of the election code, to find a reason to count all the votes.[48]

Some federal courts were also clearing the ground for *Bush v. Gore.* Almost lost among the tumult surrounding the U.S. Supreme Court's December 9 injunction was a decision by U.S. district court judge Maurice Paul in the case *Harris v. Florida Elections Canvassing Commission.* At issue in the case was the relevant law of Florida relating to the acceptance of absentee ballots during presidential elections. Florida's statutes required all overseas ballots to arrive by 7:00 P.M. on Election Day. However, at the initiative of the U.S. Justice Department, state officials in the executive branch entered into a consent decree in which the state agreed to accept overseas absentee ballots up through ten days after an election, presumably to give military personnel more time to vote. While in normal circumstances this might be considered an entirely salutary step, the complaint in this case charged that the U.S. Supreme Court's new interpretation of Article II of the Constitution in *Bush v. Palm Beach County Canvassing Board* only allowed state statutory law to govern election rules in presidential elections. Specifically, since the extended ten-day deadline had never been enacted by the Florida legislature, it could not be applied in this election. In other words, if it was unconstitutional for the Florida judiciary to extend a legislative deadline for when counties had to report their votes, it should also be unconstitutional for Florida's executive branch (working with the federal government, which has no authority to decide the manner of appointing presidential electors) to extend a legislative deadline for the receipt of absentee ballots. The upshot of this argument was that all absentee ballots arriving after Election Day should be disqualified. It was stipulated that 1,575 of the overseas absentee votes received after November 7 went for Bush/Cheney and 836, for Gore/Lieberman. If this alleged constitutional mistake was corrected it would result in Gore/Lieberman willing the Florida election by 202 votes.

Judge Paul began his opinion by explaining that the consent decree, which eventually became part of the state's administrative code,[49] "was the product of the state executive branch, the authorized representative of the state in a lawsuit against the state, enacting a measure to bring the state into compliance with a federally ordered mandate in a situation where the state legislature refused to do so." This was a seemingly fatal characterization of the facts, especially since the judge also explicitly found that the state legislature considered but decided against passing a ten-day extension. Nevertheless, Judge Paul concluded that "the fact that this rule has been in effect, without controversy or attempt by the legislature to overrule it, is a recognition by the legislature that they were subject to the Court's authority as expressed through the administrative rule." This was a strange observation. A legislature buckling under to someone else's authority is not an exemplar of having exclusive authority. Nevertheless, the judge held that the legislature's "lack of challenge" meant that the legislature "should not be read to be in conflict with the statute but instead to be engrafted onto it." At a minimum, one might say that the judge in this case, appointed by Ronald Reagan in 1982, was not highly motivated to worry whether the proper amount of respect and deference had been given to the exclusive authority of the legislature to determine the rules in presidential elections. Remarkably, in his discussion of the nature of the state legislature's power to control the appointment of presidential electors, the trial court judge made no mention of the U.S. Supreme Court's *Palm Beach* decision, even though it had been handed down five days earlier and had seemingly established the most relevant precedent imaginable on the specific issue at stake in the case.[50]

The case was immediately appealed to the U.S. Court of Appeals for the Eleventh Circuit. On Monday, December 11, a three-judge panel of that circuit – made up of Judges J. J. Edmondson (appointed by Reagan), Susan Harrell Black (Bush), and Ed Carnes (Bush) – upheld Judge Paul's decision in the case. Ironically, to say the least, they noted that the Florida high court in *Palm Beach County Canvassing Board v. Harris* referred to the ten-day extension in their discussion of various deadlines in the Florida election scheme, and while this opinion "has been vacated," the judges concluded that the court's words are "important and persuasive" on the issue of "how the absentee ballot law has worked" in the state. They added that to throw out these ballots "would be a significant change in the actual election practices of Florida" and would be inconsistent with the preference in Florida law in favor of "counting ballots." Their only discussion of the constitutional issues that were so central to the complaint was the comment that "we have seen nothing and been cited to nothing indicating the Florida's legislature . . . has ever expressed an intent to overrule the Rule."[51]

After these disputes were resolved, the country simply waited to hear from the U.S. Supreme Court. The waiting took the form of a vigil. The experience with the first decision led everyone to realize that the justices would not be making announcements regarding the timetable for the decision. Reporters waited outside the Court all day on Tuesday. During the day, the Florida House of Representatives voted to approve a Bush slate of electors. The state senate was scheduled to act the next day, but some expressed the hope that "the Supreme Court would unilaterally slam dunk this thing so we could all go home."[52] Night fell, and some began to wonder whether the country would need to wait another day, but reporters noticed that the workers in the clerks office did not go home at their usual time, and so maybe it was still worth waiting. Still, the night was getting long. Just before 10:00 P.M. CNN's Larry King warned, "No Supreme Court decision tonight, and ice storm tomorrow." And then he was interrupted.

At 10:00 P.M., exactly five weeks after election night, and on the date when federal law encouraged states to resolve all disputes over the appointment of presidential electors, the U.S. Supreme Court distributed its decision. By the time the pressroom staff passed out copies, the justices had already left the building.[53] Unlike the practice in Florida, no court personnel were there to provide helpful summaries of the decision. Reporters scrambled on live television to figure out what the Court had said. There was a per curiam opinion; but there were also other opinions, many of them, a total of sixty-five pages. Reporters on live television frantically flipped through the pages to find clues. It looked as if four justices were in dissent, but the per curiam opinion also mentioned something about seven justices agreeing that there were equal protection problems. Flipping to the end of the per curiam opinion it said that "the judgment of the Supreme Court of Florida is reversed, and the case is remanded for further proceedings not inconsistent with this opinion." Some reporters thought for the moment that they were sending it back once again to the Florida Supreme Court, and they speculated that maybe that was a good sign for Gore. Others pleaded with their network anchors to be patient, so as to avoid another election night embarrassment of calling the votes for one side only to have to take it back later. Still, the country was waiting for answers. Could the recounts start up again? Was Souter successful in putting together a coalition to do the recounts under a different standard?[54]

No. The five conservatives stood firm in favor of stopping all recounts, and stopping recounts meant a Bush victory.

This was the bottom line result, but there was also a complicated split among the justices about why recounts should or should not be continued.

In a graceless and underdeveloped thirteen-page per curiam opinion that reflected the pressures of time, Rehnquist, O'Connor, Scalia, Kennedy, and Thomas concluded that the recount that was authorized by the Florida Supreme Court violated the equal protection clause. In an attempt to convey their sympathy with those whose votes were not tabulated by the vote-counting machines, they acknowledged that the "closeness of this election, and the multitude of legal challenges which have followed in its wake, have brought into sharp focus a common, if heretofore unnoticed, phenomenon" – the fact that around 2 percent of ballots do not register a vote for president. "After the current counting, it is likely legislative bodies nationwide will examine ways to improve the mechanisms and machinery for voting." However, at this time, the Court was not going to solve that problem by allowing a manual inspection of these undervotes.

The majority's point of departure was the claim that states may not, "by arbitrary and disparate treatment, value one person's vote over that of another" in a manner that "dilutes the weight of a citizen's vote." These justices concluded that "the recount mechanisms implemented in response to the decisions of the Florida Supreme Court do not satisfy the minimum requirement for non-arbitrary treatment of voters necessary to secure a fundamental right." This was because the standard that was used in evaluating ballots – determining the "intent of the voter" – was too general and allowed for too much variation in the treatment of ballots. They agreed that there are times in the law when more general standards might be used without causing equal protection problems (even if they lead to unequal results in similar circumstances), but in this case ballot counters are asked to "interpret the marks or holes or scratches on an inanimate object," a "thing, not a person," and this makes it possible for "the search for intent" to be "confined by specific rules designed to ensure uniform treatment." As examples of nonuniform treatment of ballots, the majority noted that the Florida court's decision mandated the inclusion of partial recounts from Miami-Dade, recount totals from counties that used different standards in evaluating ballots, and totals from one county (Palm Beach) that seemed to switch its counting standard a number of times.

While the majority mentioned the Court's "one person, one vote" districting cases of the early 1960s, it did not explain how the requirement that political districts have roughly the same number of people in them led to this Court's completely innovative rule that in this case there can be no "arbitrary or disparate treatment" of ballots. It was also noteworthy that the justices made it clear that they were not concluding that ballots must always be treated the same in every circumstance. In one of the most controversial passages of the opinion, the majority wrote that "[o]ur consideration is limited to the present circumstances, for the problem of equal protection in election processes generally presents many complexities." The problem, though, was that it was not clear why the concern about unequal treatment was a problem with the recount but not, for example, with the original count, which was based on many different ballot-counting practices throughout the various counties in Florida. The justices considered it important to specify that "the question before the Court is not whether local entities, in the exercise of their expertise, may develop different systems for implementing elections. Instead, we are presented with a situation where a state court with the power to assure uniformity has ordered a statewide recount with minimal procedural safeguards." In theory, though, courts always have "the power to assure uniformity" – for example, by declaring unconstitutional the use of "different systems for implementing elections" – yet traditionally it has been assumed that good faith variation among localities raised no equal protection objections. Without explaining the distinction more carefully one might be led to believe that the main difference between seeing a problem with variations in manual counting and not seeing a problem with the use of different voting systems was that the combination of these statements left the existing Bush victory intact and prevented it from being challenged.

Still, it was not unimaginable that the state could quickly standardize recount standards and provide for appropriate review of decisions. If this was a possibility – at least until Florida courts said otherwise – then why not proceed with that process in this case? Scalia had said in his concurring opinion of the stay order that one advantage of stopping a flawed recount was that it protected fragile ballots so that they might be available for a perfected recount; was now the time to act on that suggestion? The majority thought not. In the only time during this dispute that these justices were willing to defer to the state high court, they wrote that "the Supreme Court of Florida has said that the legislature intended" to take advantage of the federal "safe harbor" provided in 3 U.S.C. § 5, and that statute "requires that any controversy or contest that is designed to lead to a conclusive selection of electors be completed by December 12. That date is upon us, and there is no recount procedure in place under the State Supreme Court's order that comports with minimal constitutional standards. Because it is evident that any recount seeking to meet the December 12 date will be unconstitutional for the reasons we have discussed, we reverse the judgment of the Supreme Court of Florida ordering a recount to proceed."

The five conservatives then informed the world that actually "seven Justices of the Court agree that there are constitutional problems with the recount ordered by the Florida Supreme Court," and they referred to dissenting opinions by Justices Souter and Breyer. The majority reported that these dissenters thought it would be appropriate to remand the case back to the Florida courts so that they might order a constitutionally proper recount, to be completed by the date when the Electoral College was required to vote – December 18. However, the five other Washington justices responded that this option was inconsistent with Florida law, as interpreted by the Florida high court, which required these disputes to be resolved by the end of the day – that is, within two hours.

The justices ended their per curiam opinion by assuring the country that "none are more conscious of the vital limits on judicial authority than are the members of this Court, and none stand more in admiration of the Constitution's design to leave the selection of the President to the people, through their legislatures, and to the political sphere. When contending parties invoke the process of the courts, however, it becomes our unsought responsibility to resolve the federal and constitutional issues the judicial system has been forced to confront." In a case that some would characterize as an exemplar of the fearless and politicized use of Supreme Court power, the bare majority ended its opinion donning the language of a reluctant, duty-bound Court, merely doing its job.

The majority remarked earlier in its opinion that by focusing on the equal protection elements of this case, "it is not necessary to decide whether the Florida Supreme Court had the authority under the legislative scheme for resolving election disputes to define what a legal vote is and to mandate a manual recount implementing that definition." But not all members of the majority agreed that these other issues were unnecessary to decide; in fact, three of the five justices who participated in that per curiam opinion – Chief Justice Rehnquist, Justice Scalia, and Justice Thomas – wanted to decide these issues as well. The chief justice began by noting that deference to state court interpretations of state law is not appropriate in a case involving the appointment of presidential electors, since Article II of the Constitution confers this power "on a particular branch of the State's government," the state legislature. Thus, in their judgment, from now on in U.S. presidential elections, the rule should be that any "significant departure from the legislative scheme for appointing Presidential electors presents a federal constitutional question."

As a way of conveying their depth of feeling about the Florida Supreme Court, these justices likened it to some of the most biased, untrustworthy state courts in U.S. history – the high courts of the segregationist South during the period of resistance to civil rights and desegregation. They noted that in *NAACP v. Alabama ex rel. Patterson* (1958) the U.S. Supreme Court was willing to tell the Alabama Supreme Court that it was misreading its own law in its effort to undermine that organization. In *Bouie v. City of Columbia* (1964), the justices challenged the South Carolina Supreme Court's interpretation of its trespass law as part of a case against sit-in demonstrators. "What we would do in the present case is precisely parallel: Hold that the Florida Supreme Court's interpretation of the Florida election laws impermissibly distorted them beyond what a fair reading required, in violation of Article II."

The language was strong, even incendiary (especially considering the presence on the Florida Supreme Court of two African American judges). And so it raised an important question: what exactly was it about that court's interpretation of the Florida contest statute that was so clearly wrong? For one thing, the Florida court "determined that canvassing boards' decisions regarding whether to recount ballots past the certification deadline . . . are to be reviewed *de novo*"; however, the three conservatives concluded instead that "the election code clearly vests discretion whether to recount in the boards" themselves, which meant that the only acceptable standard for judicial review of their authority is "abuse of discretion," not a separate determination by a judge whether there are reasons to support a recount. "Moreover, the Florida court held that all late vote tallies arriving during the contest period should be automatically included in the certification regardless of the certification deadline," thus "virtually eliminating both the deadline and the Secretary's discretion to disregard recounts that violate it." These justices were not explicit about this, but both of these complaints were based on the assumption that the election contest statute (which mentioned nothing about the authority of canvassing boards or the inflexibility of deadlines) had to be read alongside separate parts of the election code, especially those parts that emphasized the finality of earlier decisions. In their judgment, reading the contest statute as a stand-alone part of the code was essentially the same as changing the law rather than interpreting it. The complaint was an interesting contrast to their position in the first case, in which they accused the Florida justices of changing the law when they attempted to reconcile different parts of the election code.

But there was more. Picking up on Justice Scalia's passing remark in his stay opinion, these justices found that "the court's interpretation of 'legal vote,' and hence its decision to order a contest-period recount, plainly departed from the legislative scheme." In their judgment, Florida statutory law cannot reasonably be thought to *require* the counting of improperly marked ballots. It was a confident conclusion, but (as Boies pointed out at oral argument) it was also seemingly at odds with more than eighty years of Florida case law, dating back at least to *Darby v. State* in 1917 and reasserted as recently as the *Beckstrom* case in 1998. It also seemed inconsistent with the language in the Florida statutes (section 101.5614) that said that "no vote shall be declared invalid or void if there is a clear indication of the intent of the voter" (as well as other parts of the code directing election officials to look for voter intent). Rather than analyze this claim these justices wrote simply that "we will not parse that analysis here, except to note that [this provision of the election code] was . . . entirely irrelevant." More important was the fact that voters were given clear instructions to check their ballots to ensure that the cards were punched "clearly and cleanly." They concluded by expressing the view that the Florida justices went on "a search for elusive – perhaps delusive – certainty as to the exact count of six million votes." The language is strong, but it should have come as no surprise. During oral arguments Justice Scalia mocked the Gore slogan to "count all the votes"; now it was clear that these justices believed that this goal was nothing short of delusional.

Needless to say, the dissenters did not believe that reinspecting undervote ballots was illegal or quixotic. In the first sentences of his dissenting opinion, joined by all four dissenters, Justice Souter emphatically expressed the view that

> The Court should not have reviewed either *Bush v. Palm Beach County Canvassing Bd.* . . . . or this case, and should not have stopped Florida's attempt to recount all undervote ballots . . . by issuing a stay of the Florida Supreme Court's orders during the period of this review. . . . If this Court had allowed the State to follow the course indicated by the opinions of its own Supreme Court, it is entirely possible that there would ultimately

have been no issue requiring our review, and political tension could have worked itself out in the Congress following the procedure provided in 3 U.S.C. § 15. The case being before us, however, its resolution by the majority is another erroneous decision.

With this statement, Souter let it be known that the Supreme Court's initial decision to grant certiorari and hear the first Bush appeal had been supported by only the five conservatives and that these four dissenters were reluctant participants in the Supreme Court's 9 to 0 per curiam opinion. It was clear now, if it had not been before, that the Supreme Court's involvement in the election 2000 dispute, from the beginning, reflected the wishes of only a bare majority of the Court.

The dissenters were now free to explain why they believed that all of this should have been avoided. From Souter's point of view, the issues in this case were remarkably "straightforward," and none "is difficult to describe or to resolve." On the question of whether the Florida Supreme Court "somehow" violated 3 U.S.C. § 5 when it ordered the recount, Souter said that the "issue is not serious. . . . No State is required to conform to § 5" if it cannot resolve all disputes by the specified date, and "the sanction for failing to satisfy the conditions of § 5 is simply loss of what has been called its 'safe harbor.' And even that determination is to be made, if made anywhere, in the Congress."

Picking up on the concurring justices' argument about the Florida court's interpretive mistakes, Souter thought it was enough to note that the actual language of that statute said that a "'rejection of a number of legal votes sufficient to change or place in doubt the result of the election'" could be the basis for overturning a certified election. There was no mention in the statute about deferring to election officials when investigating this question. Moreover, contrary to the position of the concurring justices, Souter noted that state law did not clearly define "legal vote," and this meant that the state supreme court was "required to define it." Florida court did this by looking to another statute dealing with damaged or defective ballots, which says that no vote shall be disregarded "'if there is a clear indication of the intent of the voter as determined by a canvassing board.'" While it was possible for that court to adopt the more constricted definition of legal vote adopted by Rehnquist, Scalia, and Thomas, there was nothing in the statute requiring that approach.

Then, parting company with Justices Stevens and Ginsburg, Souter indicated that the only issue raising "meritorious argument for relief" was the equal protection argument. He believed that the Florida courts may have dealt with the issue on their own "if the state proceedings had not been interrupted, and if not disposed of at the state level it could have been considered by the Congress in any electoral vote dispute." In other words, his view was that even assuming a constitutional problem, there was no legitimate basis for the U.S. Supreme Court to try to solve it. However, given that the state proceedings were "interrupted" and that "time is short," he believed that it would have been sensible for the Court to remand the case back to the Florida courts with instructions to use a standard that would ensure the equal treatment of "identical types of ballots used in identical brands of machines and exhibiting identical physical characteristics." He believed that it was still possible to proceed with the recounts under an improved standard because the electoral votes were not due to be cast for another six days, and "unlike the majority, I see no warrant for this Court to assume that Florida could not possibly comply with this requirement" in this amount of time, especially in light of the fact that "before this Court stayed the effort to do that the courts of Florida were ready to do their best to get that job done."

In a separate dissent, Justice Breyer also began by declaring: "The Court was wrong to take this case. It was wrong to grant a stay." It was wrong because while "the political implications of this case for the country are momentous, [the] federal legal questions presented, with one exception, are insubstantial." In particular, he wanted to emphasize that it was incorrect to claim (as the concurring justices suggest here) that the Court's initial decision in *Bush v. Palm Beach County Canvassing Board* stood for the proposition "that a state court decision that threatens the safe harbor provision of § 5 does so in violation of Article II." While he thought there were legitimate concerns about the differential treatment of identical ballots, he insisted that there was still "no justification for the majority's remedy" of halting the recount entirely. Obviously, the recount could not be completed by December 12, but he thought that standard practice would demand that the Court "permit the Florida Supreme Court to decide whether the recount should resume." Instead, the majority "crafts a remedy out of proportion to the asserted harm" and prevents a more sensible remedy that "would itself redress a problem of unequal treatment of ballots" caused by the disparate rates of ballot disqualifications caused by different vote tabulation equipment in different counties. After all, "in a system that allows counties to use different types of voting systems, voters already arrive at the polls with an unequal chance that their votes will be counted," and "I do not see how the fact that this results from counties' selection of different voting machines rather than a court order makes the outcome any more fair. Nor do I understand why the Florida Supreme Court's recount order, which helps to redress this inequity, must be entirely prohibited based on a deficiency that could easily be remedied."

Breyer then got the heart of his complaint. He noted that while the "selection of the President is of fundamental national importance," that "importance is political, not legal," and "this Court should resist the temptation unnecessarily to resolve tangential legal disputes, where doing so threatens to determine the outcome of the election." He said that the Constitution and federal statutes recognize a role for state judicial proceedings and for the Congress, but nowhere in the law does it provide "for involvement by the United States Supreme Court." He reviewed the legislative history of the Electoral Count Act of 1887 to demonstrate that (in the House committee's report) "the power to determine" the results of controversies over presidential electors "rests with the two Houses, and there is no other constitutional tribunal." This is why the Electoral Count Act laid out a "detailed, comprehensive scheme" by which Congress would work through such disputes. Moreover, the Congress that passed that act was "fully aware of the danger that would arise should it ask judges, unarmed with appropriate legal standards, to resolve a hotly contested Presidential election contest." After all, the writers of the act had recent experience with the participation of five Supreme Court justices in the Electoral Commission that worked to resolve the Hayes-Tilden electoral dispute. Those justices divided along partisan lines, and the one who cast the tie-breaking vote, Joseph P. Bradley, "immediately became the subject of vociferous attacks." Bradley might have thought he was protecting important principles, but they were, in the words of Alexander Bickel, "trivial" to the public and "overwhelmed by all that hung in the balance."[55] The lesson that Congress learned was that "in this highly politicized matter, the appearance of a split decision runs the risk of undermining the public's confidence in the Court itself." That confidence is a "public treasure" that "is a vitally necessary ingredient of any successful effort to protect basic liberty and, indeed, the rule of law itself." Unfortunately, the Court's actions instead "risk a self-inflicted wound – a wound that may harm not just the Court, but the Nation."

The other two justices had even a stronger reason to object to the Court's intervention. Unlike Souter and Breyer, they thought that the Florida recount raised no equal protection concerns. Justice Ginsburg pointed out that the cases referred to by the concurring justices to justify their challenge of the Florida Supreme Court "are embedded in historical contexts [that are] hardly comparable to the situation here" – in particular, "Southern resistance to the civil rights movement." The concurring justices' "casual citation of these cases . . . might lead one to believe they are part of a larger collection of cases in which we said that the Constitution compelled us to train a skeptical eye on a state court's portrayal of state law." But current dispute "involves nothing close to the kind of recalcitrance by a state high court that warrants extraordinary action by this Court. The Florida Supreme Court concluded that counting every legal vote was the overriding concern of the Florida Legislature when it enacted the State's Election Code. The court surely should not be bracketed with state high courts of the Jim Crow South." In normal circumstances, deferring to state courts' interpretations of their own laws "reflects the core of federalism, on which we all agree," even when the justices otherwise debate the proper contours of federal-state relations. "Were the other members of this Court as mindful as they generally are of our system of dual sovereignty, they would affirm the judgment of the Florida Supreme Court." When she ended her opinion, she replaced the customary "I respectfully dissent" with the more perfunctory "I dissent."

The final dissenting opinion came from John Paul Stevens. He began by insisting that Article II of the Constitution did not require the U.S. Supreme Court to parse out the relative balance of legislative versus judicial power in state election disputes. Even in *McPherson v. Blacker* (1892) the Court noted that state power under Article II includes that which is "forbidden or required of the legislative power under state constitutions as they exist." In general, "neither § 5 nor Article II grants federal judges any special authority to substitute their views for those of the state judiciary on matters of state law." As for the equal protection concern, Stevens emphasized that this constitutional provision has never before been used to call into question the traditional practice of manually recounting ballots; moreover, "there is no reason to think that the guidance provided . . . by the 'intent of the voter' standard is any less sufficient" for equal protection purposes "than, for example, the 'beyond a reasonable doubt' standard employed everyday by ordinary citizens in courtrooms across the country." If, however, one still believed that a more objective standard was constitutionally required, then "the appropriate course of action would be to remand to allow more specific procedures for implementing the legislature's uniform general standard to be established." Instead, the majority "effectively orders the disenfranchisement of an unknown number of voters whose ballots reveal their intent – and are therefore legal votes under state law – but were for some reason rejected by ballot-counting machines." The majority justified its decision with reference to the deadline mentioned in 3 U.S.C. § 5 even though that statute includes nothing that prevents states from counting votes long after that deadline. In fact, "in 1960, Hawaii appointed two slates of electors and Congress chose to count the one appointed on January 4, 1961."

For Stevens, it was particularly distressing that some of his colleagues insisted on portraying the Florida Supreme Court as doing something out of the ordinary. The truth, as he saw it, was that "it did what courts do – it decided the case before it in light of the legislature's intent to leave no legally cast vote uncounted." As long as "we assume – as I do – that the members of that court and the judges who would have carried out its mandate are impartial, its decision does not even raise a colorable federal question." By contrast, underlying "petitioners' entire federal assault . . . is an unstated lack of confidence in the impartiality and capacity of the state judges who would make the critical decisions if the vote count were to proceed. Otherwise, their position is wholly without merit. The endorsement of that position by the majority of this Court can only lend credence to the most cynical appraisal of the work of judges throughout the land." It was in this context that Stevens wrote the lines that were the most heavily quoted from among the dissenting opinions:

> It is the confidence in the men and women who administer the judicial system that is the true backbone of the rule of law. Time will one day heal the wound to that confidence that will be inflicted by today's decision. One thing, however, is certain. Although we may never know with complete certainty the identity of the winner of this year's Presidential election, the identity of the loser is perfectly clear. It is the Nation's confidence in the judge as an impartial guardian of the rule of law.

Stevens's language suggested that it was the majority's disdain for the good faith of state judges that would undermine the country's confidence in judges. But even if this sentiment was expressed in good faith and not with ironic intent, it would soon become clear that this overestimated the extent to which the country was willing to take to heart the majority's explanation of its decision. As it turned out, the problem was not so much that the people would feel persuaded by the majority and thus lose confidence in state judges; it was that many people thought (rightly or wrongly) that the five conservatives on the U.S. Supreme Court – through their own actions – were the ones not acting as "impartial guardians of the rule of law." While some might have viewed the majority's actions as reluctantly (and paradoxically) using extraordinary judicial power in order to assault judicial activism and restore faith in the rule of law, many others would instead view the conservatives' decision as exemplary of precisely the problem they claimed to be correcting.

THE REACTION

In the words of one newspaper, "coast to coast, the realization set in that the 2000 election was finally, unbelievably, over. No more sleepless nights with cable TV bloviators; no more suspense around the water cooler. The wounds from the thirty-six-day struggle were still raw, but if there was any common ground, it was a widespread sign of relief that the national shouting match was ending."[56] It was obvious to most that the decision left Gore no options. Within minutes of its release the chair of the Democratic National Committee, Ed Rendell, was on television indicating that Gore would have to concede the election. Democratic senator Robert Torricelli of New Jersey agreed that "the race for the presidency has come to an end." Democratic congressman James P. Moran said simply, "It's checkmate." The Bush camp, knowing that the next move was Gore's, had James Baker issue a simple, short statement saying that they were "very pleased and gratified that seven justices of the United States Supreme Court agreed that there were constitutional problems with the Florida recount ordered by the Florida Supreme Court." After thanking everyone who helped in their effort he said, "This has been a long and arduous process for everyone involved on both sides." Because the hour was late and the opinion of the Court was a bit difficult to decipher, the Gore campaign said simply that it was "reviewing the 5-4 decision issued tonight by the Supreme Court of the United States" and "it will take time to completely analyze" its "complex and lengthy" decision.[57]

Gore's lawyers spent the night looking for an opening, but it was clear by Wednesday morning that there was no room to maneuver.[58] In a short, televised address to the country at 9:00 P.M., Vice President Al Gore offered the concession that the Bush campaign had been hoping for since the early morning hours of November 8. As he put it, "Just moments ago, I spoke with George W. Bush and congratulated him on becoming the forty-third president of the United States, and I promised him that I wouldn't call him back this time." In a speech that was widely praised for its graciousness, he explained that the rule of law was "the source of our democratic liberties," and "I've tried to make it my guide throughout this contest. . . . Now the U.S. Supreme Court has spoken. Let there be no doubt, while I strongly disagree with the court's decision, I accept it." He quoted Stephen Douglas's remarks when he lost the presidency to Abraham Lincoln: "Partisan feeling must yield to patriotism. I'm with you, Mr. President, and God bless you."[59] A few minutes later, Texas Republican governor George W. Bush went before an audience of four hundred supporters inside the chamber of the Texas House of Representatives and, in a televised speech, laid claim to the White House while invoking Abraham Lincoln's words, "Our nation must rise above a house divided."[60]

Gore's concession convinced the Florida legislature that it was no longer necessary to appoint its own slate of electors.[61] It also led Governor Jeb Bush to send to the National Archives a Certificate of the Final Determination of the Contests Concerning the Appointment of Presidential Electors, in which he wrote that the Gore contest to the election results has been "finally determined in favor of Governor George W. Bush and that any further pending contests have been effectively nullified by the United States Supreme Court."[62]

Almost all newspaper accounts of the Court's opinion noted the "historic" or extraordinary nature of the decision, the "deep division" among the justices along ideological lines, O'Connor and Kennedy's decision to break from their conservative colleagues to force a "surprisingly limited" ruling,[63] the willingness of Justices Souter and Breyer to give some credence to the equal protection argument, the dissenters' "angry" characterization of the majority's action as a historic mistake and a "self-inflicted wound," and the bottom line – that the decision "handed the presidential election to George W. Bush." They also freely speculated on whether the decision would undermine the authority of the Court.[64] Many of the same themes were picked up by the foreign press. "The Federal Supreme Court convened court twice to intervene in the general election for the first time ever in US history," wrote on Beijing newspaper. "Americans always flaunt 'the president who is chosen by the people,' but this time the nine great judges of the Supreme Court had to give the final verdict." In taking up this "hot potato," the Court "ended up really burning its own hand." A South Korean newspaper said that Bush was the first president elected by the Court. *Le Monde* (Paris) published an editorial entitled "Judges Govern America" that claimed the Court ruled "on strict party lines."[65]

It did not take long for newspapers to provide a rough first history of the Court's decision-making process of the case. Within hours of the Supreme

Court's oral argument, the five conservatives were apparently united on a decision that would overturn the Florida Supreme Court on the grounds that it had unconstitutionally changed voting rules after Election Day. There was even some reason to hope that the decision might be handed down that evening; the high court's public information office even sent out for Chinese food and prepared for a long night. However, this "clear and simple" rational faded when Justices Kennedy and O'Connor decided to break from the three other conservatives – probably because they were not convinced that the Florida justices had obviously misread the Florida statutes. With that, what was originally designed as the majority opinion quickly became Chief Justice Rehnquist's concurring opinion. This led to a scramble for a rationale that might unite five decisions behind a ruling.[66] According to one report, Justice Kennedy took it upon himself to work on an opinion that focused on the recount standards, but "he has a slow, deliberate style that works against him when under pressure."[67]

Most of the immediate editorial commentary took the language of "self-inflicted wound" as its point of departure and was sharply critical of the Court. Strident criticism came from the *New York Times*, the *Los Angeles Times*, *USA Today*, the New York *Daily News*, the *Honolulu Advertiser*, the *Boston Globe*, the *Atlanta Constitution*, the *Star Tribune* of Minneapolis–St. Paul, the *Denver Post*, the *Capital Times* of Madison, the *Philadelphia Daily News*, and the *New Republic* (which called the decision "Orwellian").[68] More positive reviews came from the *Cincinnati Post*, the *Chicago Tribune*, and the *Wall Street Journal*.[69] There were some scholars who came to the defense of the Court. Pepperdine University law professor Douglas W. Kmiec, an adviser to the Bush legal team, boldly (but unpersuasively) declared that the Court's ruling "was not along partisan or ideological lines" since two of the dissenters also agreed that there were equal protection problems with the recount. More generally, he suggested that "the court's decision is law, not politics. . . . [L]iberal and conservative justices alike protected our cherished democratic tradition with a soundly reasoned *per curiam* voice of restraint."[70] John O. McGinnis said that in the "long run" the decision "will be understood for what it is: a clearly reasoned judgment rooted in fundamental law that was also an act of statesmanship of high order" by a majority that knew it "would be attacked as political partisans . . . in the press and the legal academy."[71] UCLA law professor Daniel Lowenstein called the majority's decision "brilliant" and "a home run" because the decision did not rely "on complicated legalisms or arcane constitutional provisions." Instead, it "zeroed in on the pernicious aspects of what the Florida Supreme

Court had done" – which was to authorize an "inexcusably stacked recount" – and the Washington justices did it in a way that could be "read and understood by any citizen."[72]

But these strong defenses of the majority's arguments were few and far between. University of Utah law professor Michael McConnell, who believed the recounts to be illegal, nevertheless called the decision a "failed attempt at compromise" which gave Bush "a victory on the weakest of all available grounds," since "there is nothing in the Florida court opinion or the state statutes that expresses a preference for [the safe harbor deadline] over completion of a count under state law." He also marveled at "the lack of political judgment" that the decision entailed, particularly the unwillingness of the conservatives to follow Souter and Breyer in supporting a remand back to the Florida court, which was a result that "could have achieved near-unanimity" and "would be vastly reassuring to the American public. . . . Instead, the Supreme Court held that there should be a recount, but there is not time enough to do it. That leaves Bush as president not so much by the will of the electorate, but by default."[73] At least one conservative took an even more forceful stand against the decision. "[T]o any conservative who truly respects federalism, the majority's opinion is hard to respect, and the concurring opinion . . . should be rejected in its entirety," wrote John J. DiIulio, Jr., in the *Weekly Standard*. "Why, suddenly, do intercounty and intra-county differences in election procedures, which are quite common in every state, rise in the Florida case to the level of 'equal protection' problems solvable only by uniform standards (by implication, uniform national standards) and strict scrutiny from federal courts? . . . [And why] does the nation's highest court substitute its own resolution of the ultimate 'political question' for the Constitution's explicit, black-letter reliance on state legislatures and, if need be, the U.S. Congress?" Even though he found the result politically desirable, he felt forced to conclude that "it is bad constitutional law."[74]

However, many of the early defenses offered by conservative commentators focused not so much on the quality of the Court's legal reasoning but on how the majority performed a political service by stopping what was considered to be the illegitimate activism of the Florida Supreme Court – what William Kristol of the *Weekly Standard* called "judicial usurpation"[75] – and by heading of a lingering constitutional crisis that might have caused if competing slates of Florida electors were sent to a Congress where the House was controlled by Republicans and a 50-50 Senate was presided over by Vice President Gore.[76] The most systematic elaboration of this argument came from conservative federal appeals court judge Richard A. Posner in an article published in the *Supreme Court Review*. In order to deny Gore supporters any sense of entitlement he began his discussion with a careful empirical analysis of the election outcome in Florida to make the point that the result was a statistical tie, with any outcome falling within the margin of error of any counting system. He also constructed statistical projections that were designed to show that Gore would not have necessarily benefited from a complete and fair manual recount of the entire state, although he might have benefited from a selective recount of four Democratic counties if all those counties used the generous Broward standard for evaluating ballots.

After making the argument for why Gore's requested remedy may not have given him the victory he wanted, Posner then turned to the Supreme Court's decision. While admitted that the opinion was not "compelling," he thought that this was a case where judges "have a strong intuition about how a case should be decided yet have difficulty matching the intuition to existing doctrine," especially under unreasonable time constraints. He thought that the majority's equal protection rationale was not compelling because "the conduct of elections has been confided to local government," which meant that "ballots are often counted differently in different precincts" and "such differences had not previously been thought to deny equal protection of the laws. . . ." Moreover, if the justices were serious about these constitutional concerns it would portend "an ambitious program of federal judicial intervention in the electoral process . . . without much forethought about the program's scope and administrability."

That said, Posner thought that the Court acted properly to stop the recount, since in his judgment it could not have been completed in an orderly and acceptable fashion even by December 18, and "the infirmity of the process would have assured a rancorous struggle in Congress when a Gore slate . . . was challenged." It was even possible that the dispute could have led to "further proceedings in the Supreme Court," and if the process lingered, then "the speaker of the House or . . . the president pro tem of the Senate . . ., ninety-eight-year-old Strom Thurmond, would have become acting President" until a winner was somehow determined.[77] In light of this, Posner concluded that he could not "see the case for precipitating a political and constitutional crisis merely in order to fuss with a statistical tie that, given the inherent subjectivity involved in hand counting spoiled ballots, can never be untied." It was because "there was a real and disturbing *potential* for disorder and temporary paralysis" that "the Supreme Court's decision was greeted with relief by most of the nation." He acknowledged the dissenters' point that federal law seemed to point to a congressional resolution of these disputes rather than a judicial resolution, but Posner argued (echoing Scalia's concern) that if Republicans in Congress gave Bush a win by setting aside the results of a recount it "would poison [Bush's] tenure in the office." Since this was an inevitable result of a successful recount, "the Supreme Court took the pragmatic route, cut the Gordian knot, and let Bush get on with the transition and with governing."

Give that the major justification for the Court's involvement was political rather than legal, the only problem with the majority's decision was that it was unpersuasive and left an unfortunate impression that the justices were playing "Gotcha!" with the Florida Supreme Court. For a variety of reasons, Posner thought there were legal, political, and tactical advantages for the majority to have relied instead on the Article II violation that they had already warned the Florida justices about, including the advantage of avoiding the troubling equal protection argument by simply ruling that the Florida high court had no statutory authority to order a recount under these circumstances. For those who might think these considerations a bit too Machiavellian, Posner noted that strategic decision-making was also at work among the dissenters – most obviously by Souter and Breyer with their efforts to tempt Kennedy over to their side. He also admonished the more pure at heart that in "a case so politically fraught, a bit of *Realpolitik* affecting only the ground of decision and not the decision itself should be tolerable to anyone who takes a pragmatic approach to adjudication."[78] As for the argument that the Court sacrificed some of its legitimacy to head off this prolonged crisis, Posner responded that "judges unwilling to sacrifice some of their prestige for the greater good of the nation might be thought selfish." Given his own sense that the majority did the country a service, Posner sharply criticized the four dissenters for "accusing the five-Justice majority of having impaired public confidence in the impartiality of the judiciary. Such an accusation, however heartfelt, is what is called fouling one's own nest."[79]

Liberal commentators, however, had strongly different views about whether the "good of the nation" was linked to stopping the recounts or whether the dissenters were the ones who fouled the nest. Many expressed outrage and disbelief at the majority's actions, and in many cases longtime scholars of constitutional law admitted to having experienced an unprecedented loss of faith in the Court as an institution.[80] Herman Schwartz noted that "Supreme Court buffs are sentimentalists" who like to think the justices care about law, but added that this belief "has taken a terrific beating from the United States Supreme Court."[81] Georgetown University law professor Neal Kumar Katyal, who helped prepare legal briefs for the Gore campaign, called the decision "lawless and unprecedented."[82] Vincent Bugliosi minced no words when he said, "with every fiber of my being," that the "stark reality" was that "the institution Americans trust the most to protect its freedoms and principles committed one of the most serious crimes this nation has ever seen – pure and simple, the theft of the presidency."[83] Jeffrey Rosen's essay on the decision was entitled "Disgrace: The Supreme Court Commits Suicide," in which he insisted that the conservatives' "shabby piece of work . . . made it impossible for citizens of the United States to sustain any kind of faith in the rule of law as something other than the self-interested political preferences" of the justices.[84] Mary McGory called it a "travesty,"[85] and Stanford law professor Henry T. Greely declared that the decision "has shattered [my] faith" that the justices' decisions "reflected a considered effort to do the hard work of interpreting the laws."[86]

New York Times columnist Anthony Lewis reported that many law professors were despairing because they would no longer be able to "convince [their] students that the integrity of legal reasoning matters."[87] Columbia University historian Alan Brinkley went even further, calling the decision "the most dismaying and shocking public event of our time. In an era when respect for the political system and the legitimacy of public institutions has already suffered terrible blows, the U.S. Supreme Court has violated all the norms of behavior that the judiciary has carefully created for itself, shattered its own image in the process, and undoubtedly confirmed the unwarranted belief among many Americans that our political system is hopelessly flawed and corrupt. That is not, I suspect, what Chief Justice Rehnquist and his colleagues had hoped history would remember them for."[88] Gary Kamiya of *Salon* remarked contemptuously that "with their rash, divisive decision to dispense with the risky and inconvenient workings of democracy and simply award the presidency to their fellow Republican, five right-wing justices dragged the Supreme Court down to perhaps its most ignominious point since the Dred Scott decision." He noted that the majority "did not suddenly drop its long-standing aversion to meddling in state affairs and rush into Florida to rectify" the inequality of different voting machines with different error rates; this sort of unprincipled intervention "apparently only happens when a fellow Republican needs rescuing," and it suggests that, from the start, the conservatives "secretly regarded the very idea of a recount as suspect, inferior, secondary, an ignoble and unacceptable tainting of the God-given, majestic, sacrosanct first-count results (which just happened to show Bush in a razor-thin lead)."[89] Columbia University law professor

Eben Moglen summarized the view of many law professors when he wrote that "rarely in its history has the Supreme Court put itself so flagrantly in the wrong, not just with partisans who disagree with the substance of its decision, but with thoughtful lawyers regardless of partisan affiliation, and with the American people as a whole."[90]

Among those joining the chorus was the famed liberal constitutional theorist Ronald Dworkin. Like many of his colleagues he opened with an indictment: "The 2000 election has finally ended, but in the worst possible way – not with a national affirmation of democratic principle but by the fiat of the five conservative Supreme Court justices . . . over the fierce objection of the four more liberal justices. . . . The conservatives stopped the democratic process in its tracks, with thousands of votes yet uncounted, first by ordering an unjustified stay of the statewide recount of the Florida vote that was already in progress, and then declaring, in one of the least persuasive Supreme Court opinions that I have ever read, that there was no time left for the recount to continue." He noted that the 5 to 4 decision would not have been surprising or disturbing "if the constitutional issues were ones about which conservatives and liberals disagree as a matter of constitutional principle," such as federalism, individual rights, or equal protection. "But there were no such constitutional issues in this case: the conservatives' decision to reverse a state supreme court's rulings on matters of state law did not reflect any established conservative position on any general constitutional question." This meant that it was "difficult to find a respectable explanation of why all and only the conservatives voted to end the election in this way," and the troubling question on everyone's mind was whether "the decision reflected not ideological division, which is inevitable, but professional self-interest." Dworkin insisted that "[w]e should try to resist this unattractive explanation" since it is "inherently implausible that any – let alone all – of them would stain the Court's reputation for such a sordid reason, and respect for the Court requires that we search for a different and more creditable explanation of their action. Unfortunately, however, the legal case they offered for crucial aspects of their decisions was exceptionally weak."[91]

Critics focused on specifics of the Court's actions that they found particularly outrageous, both in terms of the decision's legal flaws and the sense of dirty politics that some felt was revealed by the opinion.

Catch-22

One of the most common arguments against the Court was that the majority "laid a trap" for the Florida justices by making it impossible for them to avoid the majority's rebuke. In the Supreme Court's first decision it had explicitly warned the Florida Supreme Court against offering any interpretations that went beyond the rules laid out by the state legislature and especially against creating any new rules or procedures; otherwise, the U.S. Supreme Court might consider them in violation of Article II of the U.S. Constitution, which empowered state legislatures to determine the manner of appointing presidential electors. In their opinion in the Gore contest appeal, the Florida justices seemed aware of this warning and thus were careful to limit the recount standard to the one establish by the legislature for the manual review of ballots (the "discernible intent of the voter" standard). However, the majority in *Bush v. Gore,* citing equal protection concerns, complained that the Florida Supreme Court did not establish a set of standards for the recount that were more clear than those set by the legislature. This led critics to charge that the conservatives on the U.S. Supreme Court had placed the Florida court in a classic "Catch-22": if the state justices created a clearer recount standard their actions would have been voided on the grounds that they violated Article II; on the other hand, by not establishing a clearer standard, the Florida court was criticized for having violated the equal protection clause of the Fourteenth Amendment.[92] Critics could not prove that the conservatives would have responded this way, but it was a sign of their suspicions about the justices' political motivations that the Catch-22 complaint was reiterated so frequently.

Deference to the State High Court and the December 12 Deadline
Many also pointed out the irony of the majority's conclusion that recounts could not continue because Florida law was designed to incorporate the December 12 "safe harbor" deadline. It was true that the Florida Supreme Court had been mindful of this date from the beginning. The irony was that this deadline was nowhere mentioned in the Florida statutes, which according to the conservatives on the U.S. Supreme Court was the only legitimate source of Florida law when it came to the selection of presidential electors. Instead, the conservatives relied on statements by the Florida justices in their first decision – the decision that the U.S. Supreme Court had vacated out of concern that it was not obviously based on what the legislature actually wrote. Critics thought it was suspicious that the majority was willing to defer to that court for purposes of stopping a recount but for no other purpose; similarly, in every other instance these judges inquired about whether the Florida court's opinion reflected the language of the statutes (which nowhere mentioned this deadline), but here they did not. At a min-

imum, normal practice would seem to call for the issue of the deadline to be clarified by the state court rather than by the U.S. Supreme Court. Of course, there were obvious political reasons why the conservative majority on the Supreme Court would not want to give the state court another chance to decide whether to continue, but unless the Washington justices were willing to declare that they were putting Florida law into federal receivership (which was essentially the position of the three concurring conservatives), they had an obligation to let the lawful decision-makers make the call.

Moving beyond the deference question to the substance of the deadline argument, critics charged that there was no legal basis for thinking that this election dispute had to be resolved by December 12. Even many conservatives agreed that "this was the least convincing portion of the Court's opinion,"[93] since this "safe harbor" deadline seemed designed more as a guideline for Congress than a firm, judicially enforceable federal mandate. As it turned out, a number of states in the 2000 presidential election waited until after this supposedly deadline before making an official report about their electors to the federal government and they suffered no adverse consequences.

Running Out the Clock

The conservative majority emphasized that there was simply no more time to complete the recount, but many critics charged that the justices themselves were largely responsible for this delay when they refused to address the equal protection argument when it was first raised during the original Bush appeal in *Bush v. Palm Beach County Canvassing Board*. At that time Bush asked the Court to decide "whether the use of arbitrary, standardless and selective manual recounts" violated the Fourteenth Amendment, but the justices pointedly sidestepped that question in order to focus instead on arguments about Article II and 3 U.S.C. § 5. Because the Florida justices had the benefit of knowing the U.S. Supreme Court's position on those questions they were able to fashion a second recount remedy that sidestepped those problems (at least in the minds of six justices); they also had reason to believe (perhaps erroneously) that the U.S. Supreme Court did not consider the equal protection argument to be serious. By delaying consideration of this argument until the last minute the Washington justices prevented the Florida justices from addressing this issue in a timely fashion, and this facilitated the Bush strategy of running out the clock on the recount effort.[94]

Innovative Equal Protection

Not only did the conservatives get to the equal protection argument late in the saga; it was also not clear to everyone that the conservatives had a good faith commitment to the equal protection principles on which they relied. As the *Los Angeles Times* put it, "over the last 15 years, the Supreme Court under Chief Justice William H. Rehnquist has made it nearly impossible to win constitutional claims of unequal treatment" unless one could claim that "government officials were biased and engaged in blatant discrimination." As University of Southern California law professor Erwin Chemerinsky put it, "the Rehnquist court almost never uses equal protection jurisprudence except in striking down affirmative action programs. I can't think of a single instance where Scalia or Thomas has found discrimination against a racial minority or women or the aged or the disabled to be unconstitutional."[95] Harvard law professor Randall Kennedy was particularly outraged that the those conservatives "who have consistently resisted challenges raised by minorities on equal protection grounds . . . embraced that rationale in this instance."[96] In fact, before this presidential election, not one justice on the majority ever expressed a view about equal protection that would lead someone to think that they would have constitutional problems with hand recounts of ballots governed by a general "intent of the voter" standard. It was virtually unimaginable that this innovative application of the equal protection clause would have occurred to them if not for their presumptive political preferences in this case.

There were many reasons why a less motivated decision-maker might have viewed the Florida standard as raising no serious constitutional issue. As Dworkin noted, "a general standard for counting undervotes that may be applied differently in different districts puts no class of voters, in advance, at either an advantage or disadvantage." Of course, while no specific class of voters might be seen as discriminated against, some could complain that counties that used a more generous standard end up recovering votes at a higher rate that counties that were more strict, and this might be seen as "diluting" the power of the votes of the latter counties. For example, many conservatives thought it was unfair for the Florida Supreme Court to allow the official certified result to include ballots from Broward even though other counties (such as Palm Beach) used a stricter standard, since that meant that Broward had a bit more of an impact on the election than was typical (in the sense that other counties were willing to have more of their votes wasted). Setting aside whether the "one person, one vote" precedent required perfect symmetry or only rough equality, it was still not clear why this variation was any more unacceptable than the fact that some counties were more likely to have higher percentages of their votes not counted in the first place because of higher error rates associated with certain ballot tabulation systems. The vote dilution problem seemed to be significantly greater when applied to the differential treatment of how votes were originally counted than when applied to the activity of recovering lost votes under a uniform but general standard of ballot evaluation.

The main alternative to the unpersuasive "vote dilution" rationale was the unprecedented and potentially revolutionary "all ballots must be treated alike" rationale. The problem with this, however, was that it was hard for people to believe that these conservatives (unlike, perhaps, more liberal justices such as Souter or Breyer) actually had a principled commitment to this understanding of equal protection, since it would seem to require judicially imposed uniform national standards for ballot design and ballot-counting machinery.[97]

Forgotten Federalism

The flip side of the concerns about the unprincipled embrace of equal protection arguments was the apparent abandonment of their familiar commitment to federalism and states rights. The point should not be overstated: in other cases the same majority had been willing at times to use federal law and the U.S. Constitution as a basis for striking down certain state practices, particularly when states engaged in race-conscious policymaking such as affirmative action or racial gerrymandering. But these were narrow exceptions to a broader effort to shield traditional state activities from federal supervision – particularly state activities that represented the traditional functions of state governments. Vanderbilt Law School professor Suzanna Sherry was not the only one to note that most of the Court's federalism cases were "jurisprudentially predictable," but in this case it seemed as though "the politics and jurisprudence were in conflict" and "there is really very little way to reconcile this opinion other than that they wanted Bush to win."[98]

Good for This Day and Train Only

When the majority wrote that their consideration of the issues in this case was "limited to the present circumstances" it brought to mind the complaint of Justice Owen Roberts more than fifty years earlier, when he charged his brethren with rendering a decision that was "good for this day and train only."[99] For many critics, while it was bad enough that the majority offered an extraordinarily unpersuasive legal justification for its decision, it was even worse that those justices did not even seem willing to stand behind the principles they were professing. Of course, subsequent events might prove these suspicions wrong, especially if the conservative majority were to go on to develop a robust equal protection jurisprudence that systematically addressed the differential treatment of ballots in U.S. elections. In the meantime, however, the fact that the majority made it a point to say that its discussion on key points may only apply in this special case was more evidence that the commitment to those principles was political rather than principled. As David D. Cole of Georgetown University put it, the majority "created a new right out of whole cloth and made sure it ultimately protected only one person – George Bush."[100]

It should be emphasized that these various arguments represented the complaints of mostly liberal academics. While liberals were arguing that the justices shaped their arguments to match the politics, other observers could have also asked whether the same was happening in the legal academy as well, on both sides of the ideological spectrum. As Judge Richard Posner put it, if one examined "the public comments made by professors of constitutional law during the postelection litigation, it becomes apparent that the academic practice of constitutional law is as political as the judicial practice. Liberal professors who spend their time trying to find a satisfactory rationale for decisions that they like, such as *Roe v. Wade,* made no effort to salvage *Bush v. Gore,* while conservative professors found themselves unaccustomedly supportive of a decision that whatever its merits, which obviously I think not inconsiderable, cannot avoid the label 'activist'. . . ."[101]

THE AFTERMATH

In the weeks after the decision, while much of the country seemed to refocus attention on the more ordinary politics of presidential transition and cabinet appointments, the law professorate stayed busy debating the decision and speculating on its long-term impact. Three leading scholars of election law produced a casebook on the dispute, entitled *When Elections Go Bad,* within weeks of the dispute's resolution.[102] Law professors made last-minute adjustments to their classes, with some wondering what they were going to tell their students about the legal basis of the Supreme Court's decision.[103] Outside the classroom, many law professors felt compelled to take a strong stance against the decision. More than six hundred law professors from across the United States – an impressive and revealing number – lent their names to a full-page ad in the *New York Times* on January 13 to tell the country that, in their professional judgment, "the U.S. Supreme Court used its power to act as political partisans, not judges of a court of law." They accused the court of "suppressing the facts to make the Bush government seem more legitimate" and thus acted "as propagandists, not judges." They ended by declaring: "As teachers whose lives have been dedicated to the rule of law, we protest."[104] One of those who organized the ad, Stanford law professor Margaret Jane Radin, explained that she "was just outraged. I thought the rule of law collapsed and that it was akin to a coup d'etat. It was beyond the pale and went against all legal precedents. It was a naked power grab."[105] Similar language was used by another prominent legal scholar, Bruce Ackerman of Yale Law School, went so far as to call the Supreme Court's actions a "constitutional coup" that "betrayed the nation's trust," even though he was also willing to admit that the "Justices' intervention may be viewed more charitably" if one assumes that continued recounts may have led to competing Bush-Gore slates of electors and a deadlocked Congress. Still, he insisted that even that scenario was not reason enough to justify the Court's intention, and given the illegitimacy of this power grab he called on the U.S. Senate to refuse to approve any Supreme Court nominees by President Bush throughout the Bush presidency, even if that meant leaving seats vacant.[106]

Many who were suspicious or critical of the decision searched out more clues of the majority's bad faith. Some looked for signs that Justice O'Connor might take the benefit of her labors and seek to retire – assuming, in the words of Edward Lazarus, that she was "exhibit A of the internal conflict of interest at the court which drove one of the worst decisions in history"; there was much speculation about whether her decision to hire law clerks for the term beginning October 2001 suggested that this assumption was wrong or that she was simply being especially devious.[107] On the lookout for even better evidence, Harvard Law School professor Alan M. Dershowitz wrote an opinion piece in which he asked "what should a law clerk do if he or she were to have observed any improprieties by justices of the U.S. Supreme Court in relation to the recent election case?" Providing his own answer, he advised that they "would be ethically obliged to come forward and disclose any such improprieties." For example, if any law clerk heard Justice O'Connor discuss how her vote would affect "her retirement plans" then "he or she would be ethically obliged to disclose" such a conversation. For clerks who refused to talk, he warned that "judicial historians will almost certainly discover someday what went on behind the scenes of the high court's result-oriented decision in the election case" and the "tarnished reputations" will apply not only to the justices but to "law clerks who may have known but who remained silent."[108]

While there was a fairly strong consensus among most legal academics and editorial writers that the Supreme Court had done a terrible job and perhaps even undermined its legitimacy, the reaction among the public was more calm and evenly divided.[109] Two days after the decision, when asked if the "Supreme Court has maintained an objective balance" or has "become too political," 43 percent considered the justices objective while 48 percent considered them too political.[110] This was roughly similar to the results of another poll released a few days later, which indicated that 48 percent said they had a "great deal of confidence" in the Court or "quite a lot" of confidence, while 52 percent said they had "some" or "very little" confidence in the Court. These numbers were significantly lower than they had been two weeks earlier, when 57 percent gave the Court high marks and 39 percent expressed low confidence, but the responses were not much different than those had been gathered the previous June in a *USA Today* Poll, and the results made it clear that almost half the country was still willing to express their solid support for the justices. Perhaps more important, 54 percent said that the court did the right thing in stopping the Florida recount, and more than half said the decision was based on an honest interpretation of the law rather than based on partisan politics.[111] Moreover, 62 percent of those polled said they were "relieved" the fight was over. Only about one in three said they felt "cheated" by the outcome, with 18 percent saying they were "angry" about the final result.[112]

Still, all the news was not good for the Court. A Gallup poll released in January 2001 found that the Court's overall approval rating was not that different than it had been in August 2000, before the election controversy. But this overall statistic masked a marked change in the partisan reaction to the Court. Approval of the Supreme Court among Republicans jumped from 60 percent to 80 percent; among Democrats, though, the numbers feel from 70 percent in August to 42 percent in January. Support from independents also fell a bit from 57 to 54 percent.[113] Apparently, what once was a relatively nonpartisan attitude about the Supreme Court among the public at large had become a matter of significant political saliency and division.

In the weeks following the Supreme Court's decision, while President-elect Bush prepared his transition to power, there were lingering reports about ballot-counting and electoral practices in Florida. Of special interest were the efforts by news media to begin reviewing the ballots that the U.S. Supreme Court would not allow to be counted. That activity, which was made possible by Florida's "Government in the Sunshine" laws, began within a week of the high court's final decision.[114] By mid-January 2001, the *Palm Beach Post* had completed its review of the 10,600 "undervote" ballots from Miami-Dade County and found that Bush actually gained six votes over Gore.[115] A few weeks later the *Miami Herald* reported that, using the most generous vote-counting standard (including dimpled chads), Gore "would have netted no more than 49 votes if a manual recount of Miami-Dade had been completed." The implication was that if Katherine Harris had not attempted to block the first set of Gore requested recounts then Bush would have won at the time of the first certification.[116] The *Palm Beach Post* also reported that Gore would have gained 784 votes if the Palm Beach County Canvassing Board – which consistently adopted standards that Democrats considered too strict – used instead a "dimpled chad" standard in evaluating ballots.[117] Not long thereafter, the *Miami Herald* reported that if the U.S. Supreme Court had not blocked the statewide recount of 64,000 undervote ballots, Bush's margin of victory may have actually increased from 537 to 1,665 votes under a generous "intent of the voter" standard. Ironically, if the stricter Bush standard had been used, Gore could have eked out a victory by three votes. If a loose standard was also applied to the undervote in Broward, Palm Beach, and Volusia Counties, (which were excluded from the Florida Supreme Court's order), it would have given Gore a victory by a few hundred votes.[118]

One of the surprises to emerge out of these manual inspections of ballots was that so-called "overvotes," which in theory were caused by a machine dependably tabulating a vote for more than one presidential candidate, often revealed clear indications of a vote for just one candidate. Less than a week after Gore conceded the election, the Orlando *Sun-Sentinel* reported that an inspection of more than six thousand discarded presidential ballots in Republican Lake County (where Bush won by 15 percent) resulted in a recovery of 130 net votes for Al Gore. Because Lake County used an optical scanning technology there were no debates about dimpled or hanging chads; in fact, "in each case, an oval next to [Gore's] name was filled in with a pencil and the voter mistakenly filled in another oval next to a spot reserved for write-in candidates, writing in Gore's name or running mate Joe Lieberman's there as well."[119] Later reports indicated that hand recounts in Orange County would have uncovered "clear presidential votes" in 799 ballots that had not been counted by machines because special pens had not been used, resulting in a net gain of 203 votes for Gore. A review of uncounted ballots in sixteen predominantly Republican counties that used mostly paper ballots found that Gore would have gained 569 votes, or 32 votes more than Bush's certified margin of victory.[120] In many cases this overvote problem was tied directly to a county's wealth and literacy rate. For example, a confusing ballot and unforgiving optical scanners resulted in the overvote rejection of 1 out of every 8 ballots (more than 2,000) in Gadsden, Florida's only county with a black majority; by contrast, wealthy Leon County's use of a more straightforward ballot, combined with aggressive voter education and on-the-spot tabulation machines (that immediately determined whether a ballot was defective so that voters could correct mistakes), led to essentially no overvotes at all in the presidential race.[121]

By late January 2001 there were also reports that the presumably more reliable optical scanning machines were actually less reliable than the problem-plagued punch card Votomatic machines: 5.7 percent of ballots were rejected by the former compared with 3.9 percent in counties that used the punch card system. The *Sun-Sentinel* examined more than 15,000 ballots rejected by the optical scanning machines and found that "on more than 1,700 ballots, the voter's choice for president was clear, but the ballot was rejected nonetheless," while in an additional 5,000 cases voter error "made it impossible to determine the voters' intent." If all ballots exhibiting a clear intent had been reviewed and counted, Al Gore would have benefited from a net gain of 366 votes.[122] Around the same time the *Washington Post* reported that a review of all Florida overvotes showed that "Gore was by far most likely to be selected on invalid overvoted ballots, with his name punched as one of the choices on 46,000 of them" compared with Bush who "was punched on 17,000."[123]

It was also made clear that the central constitutional problem identified by a majority of the U.S. Supreme Court – the lack of consistency in the evaluation of ballots – had been a feature of the Florida election from the beginning, and not simply a feature of the contested recounts. On election night, some counties certified only the votes that machines tallied; but others looked at ballots that had been rejected by the machines but still revealed voters' intent. One of the biggest disparities among the counties related to how election officials evaluated ballots where voters filled in the oval for a presidential candidate but then also wrote that candidate's name in the write-in section. Of fifteen counties reviewed by the press, six had a policy of counting those as legitimate votes while nine others rejected them, either because no one attempted to review them or because canvassing boards decided they should not count. Some counties made sure not to punish voters who appeared to make an inadvertent dot or erased a choice, even going so far as to put white stickers on ballots to cover up spots that workers did not want machines to read; but the practice elsewhere was simply to disregard those ballots.[124] If the recounts were unconstitutional for the reasons stated by the majority in *Bush v. Gore,* then it appeared as though the certified election results suffered from precisely the same problem.

There were a few concrete political responses to these various complaints and reports. A National Commission on Federal Elections, cochaired by former presidents Jimmy Carter and Gerald Ford, announced plans for a series of public hearings to discuss voting reforms.[125] The Florida Governor's Task Force on Election Procedures, Standards, and Technology recommended the use of optical-scanning systems for all future elections, among other reforms.[126] The U.S. Commission on Civil Rights conducted fact-finding hearings into alleged voting irregularities in Florida. They took testimony from African American residents who claimed that they had been intimidated, explored reports that Florida had engaged in a "voter-cleansing" program that was designed to remove felons from the voter rolls but that may have wrongly kept thousands of eligible voters (particularly minority voters) from casting ballots,[127] examined claims that there was an unusually heavy police presence in minority communities on Election Day, and heard from Secretary of State Katherine Harris, who told them that "the integrity of our elections was very important" to her.[128] Civil rights groups also filed a lawsuit claiming that Florida's election system systematically disadvantaged minority voters through poorly designed ballots, antiquated election systems, breakdowns in registration, and the unavailability of assistance in certain precincts.[129]

While liberal critics debated how to transform their outrage into political action – which mostly involved lying in wait in the hope that they could mobilize effectively against Bush's inevitable judicial appointments – Florida Republicans moved quickly and concretely against their now infamous supreme court. Two days after the decision in *Bush v. Gore,* state Republicans began discussing how the more liberal members of the state's high court would be targeted for removal from office the next time they faced voters. Of the four who voted to continue the recounts only one was scheduled to come up in a "merit-retention" election within two years, Justice Harry Lee Anstead. The three justices who voted with him would not be in a similar situation for six more years, since they had sailed through their merit-retention election on Election Day 2000. Also on the ballot in 2002 was Chief Justice Charles Wells, who wrote a passionate dissent against the last recount order. (Also in the minority were Major B. Harding, who was scheduled to face voters in 2004, and Leander J. Shaw, who was set to retire in 2003.)[130] Within a week of the decision, a separate group had been formed, called the Emergency Florida State Supreme Court Project, and it was asking for donations to help oust Anstead, Wells, and Shaw. The solicitation letter characterized the state high court's behavior as "an outrageous, arrogant, power-grab by a left-wing court which is stuck in the liberal 60s."[131] By the end of December, Republican lawmakers, picking up some initiatives that had been initially proposed the previous spring, announced that they were considering changes in the structure of the state's high court, including adding two new seats, creating a separate high court for death penalty appeals, and eliminating certain parts of the court's jurisdiction.[132]

While these plans were unfolding, the existing Florida Supreme Court was quietly finishing its responsibilities in the election litigation. In their response to the U.S. Supreme Court's nominal "remand" of the *Bush v. Gore* case back to the state high court all of the justices agreed that no further relief was possible. All but one (Chief Justice Wells) wrote to express the view that the recount "standard we directed be employed in the manual recount was the standard established by the Legislature in the Florida Election Code" and if that was not adequate then "we conclude that the development of a specific, uniform standard necessary to ensure equal application and to secure the fundamental right to vote throughout the State of Florida should be left to the body we believe best equipped to study and address it, the Legislature." The court's leading liberal, Justice Shaw, who had dissented from the final recount decision, also wrote separately to express his view that the "divisive and confounding" nature of this case "lies not in the partisan nature of the issues but rather in the deeply rooted, and conflicting, legal principles that are involved." While he disagreed with the U.S. Supreme Court's determination that December 12 was a firm deadline under Florida law, he had come to believe, "given the tenor of the opinion in *Bush v. Gore*," that it would not have been possible under any deadline for the Florida court to "have crafted a remedy under these circumstances that would have met the due process, equal protection, and other concerns of the United States Supreme Court." He ended his opinion by saying that he commended "the other justices of this Court, each of whom approached this case with a sworn resolve to be objective, honorable, and fair."[133]

Not long after the Florida Supreme Court finished its work on this dispute, the U.S. Supreme Court cleared its plate of the remaining election litigation. On January 5, 2001, the justices turned down three leftover appeals. One involved hand recounts in various Florida counties, another involved the claim that Texas electors should not be allowed to vote for Bush and Cheney because both were residents of Texas (and the Constitution required that electors vote for at least one person who is not a resident of their state), and the third was the appeal in *Harris v. Florida Elections Canvassing Commission* on the question of whether it violated Article II for Florida officials to accept overseas ballots that arrived in Florida past the statutory deadline of November 7.[134] With this troika of decisions, barely noticed amid the preparations for a new administration, the U.S. Supreme Court's participation in the election 2000 disputes came to an end.

On December 18, 2000, the 538 presidential electors gathered in the fifty state capitals and the District of Columbia to cast their ballots for president. While this process usually proceeds without attention or commentary, there was an unusual amount of interest in the workings of the Electoral College this year, and so cable news networks covered the action in a number of states. Given the closeness of the vote it was understood that a switch by just three electors across the country might create a new crisis, but Gore had previously made it clear that he rejected any effort to benefit from so-called "faithless electors," and there was no expectation that this was a real possibility. In Tallahassee, Florida's twenty-five electors cast their votes for Bush; the ceremony revealed none of the drama or division that had taken place over the thirty-six days after the election, and which had ended just six days earlier. By the end of the day Bush had received the support of 271 electors; Gore received 266 votes.[135] It was the closest margin of victory in the Electoral College since the disputed presidential election of 1876, when another extended contest eventually resulted in Rutherford B. Hayes being given one more electoral vote than the winner of the popular vote, Samuel J. Tilden. Gore's popular vote margin over Bush had risen to 539,897 on the day that the Electoral College met, but those were not the votes that counted.[136]

On January 6, 2001, the day after the U.S. Supreme Court dismissed its last set of election cases, the U.S. Congress met in joint session to open and count the electoral votes for president. The session was presided over by the president of the Senate, Vice President Al Gore. When the ballots from Florida were presented, a dozen members of the Congressional Black Caucus arose, one after the other, objecting to the Florida electors. Under the rules, an objection could not be debated, so only perfunctory statements were made. After each objection the president of the Senate asked whether their objection was in writing and whether a Senator also signed it. But none of the members of the Congressional Black Caucus could get a single senator to join with them in opposition to the Florida result as was required by 3 U.S.C. § 15. In turn, one by one, the objections were set aside. It took almost twenty minutes before Florida's votes were accepted, but in the end they were accepted; that was the law. "We did all we could," said Democratic Representative Alcee L. Hastings from Florida to the presiding officer. "The chair thanks the gentleman," Gore replied with a smile. Vermont Senator Patrick J. Leahy later explained why no senators participated in the objection to the Florida electors: "There is a great deal of frustration that the Supreme Court decided the election by stopping the count in Florida. As much as I disagree with the court's decision, I uphold it as the law of the land and won't object."[137]

In that spirit, at 2:50 P.M., Vice President Gore officially announced that the Texas governor had received a majority of the votes of the Electoral College and would become the forty-third president of the United States. On January 20, 2001, amid controlled demonstrations that did not disrupt the solemnity or ceremony of the occasion, George W. Bush, son of a former president, took the oath of office. As is customary, the oath was administered by the chief justice of the United States.

6

THE POLITICS BEHIND
THE VOTES THAT COUNTED

★ ★ ★

*I plead with you that, whatever you do, don't try to apply the rules
of the political world to this institution; they do not apply. . . . I have yet
to hear any discussion, in nine years, of partisan politics.*
Justice Clarence Thomas[1]

*[The election dispute] tested our constitutional system in ways it
has never been tested before. . . . The Florida state courts, the lower federal
courts and the Supreme Court of the United States became involved in a
way that one hopes will seldom, if ever, be necessary in the future.*
Chief Justice William Rehnquist[2]

It was ironic that the one justice who remained silent during all of the U.S.
Supreme Court's oral arguments in the election dispute became its first public defender. The day after the justices handed down their decision in *Bush
v. Gore* Justice Clarence Thomas held a previously scheduled meeting with a
group of high school students. The meeting was taped and televised by the
cable network C-SPAN, and it received wide notice because the justice used
the event as an opportunity to speak about a timely topic: the role of politics in Supreme Court decision-making. In addition to insisting that "the
rules of the political world . . . do not apply" to the Supreme Court and that
he had never once heard a justice discuss partisan politics in the course of
the Court's deliberations, he also replied to a student's question about what
role a justice's party affiliation played in his or her decisions. "Zero," was the
reply. In fact, he said that when people refer to a justice's political affiliation
in discussing why he or she voted in a particular case it was "like slurring

the process." Later that day, when asked if he agreed with Justice Thomas's remarks, Chief Justice Rehnquist responded, "[A]bsolutely, absolutely."

Thomas was not the only judge involved in these unprecedented cases to insist that conventional politics played no part in the decisions of these courts. Judge Stanley F. Birch of the Eleventh Circuit Court of Appeals made a similar point about those "pundits" who were "just wrong" to assume that judicial decisions in these cases reflect "some sort of blind, mindless, knee-jerk response based on the politics of a judge's appointer." Justice Shaw of the Florida Supreme Court also insisted that the "divisive" nature of the cases reflected "deeply rooted, and conflicting, legal principles" rather that "the partisan nature of the issues." By late January 2001, a few Supreme Court justices made public comments that one court watcher characterized as "damage control." Justice Antonin Scalia attempted to reassure an audience by saying, "Trust me, there was no bitterness at the Court after the decision was made" in *Bush v. Gore*. Two days later Justice Stephen J. Breyer added to the chorus by saying that even in a case as politically charged as this one "it isn't ideology, and it isn't politics" that drives the Court; it is law.[3]

One need not wonder whether the judges doth protest too much to realize that the specter of illegitimate partisan decision-making was in the air. Moreover, not every member of the U.S. Supreme Court who spoke out publicly after the event was as insistent as Thomas, Rehnquist, Scalia, and Breyer that the justices resisted politics and merely followed the law. While she meant her statements to be reassuring, Justice Ruth Bader Ginsburg did express the view that *Bush v. Gore* was an example of "how important – and difficult – it is for judges to do what is legally right, no matter what 'the home crowd' wants," and she agreed with those who thought that "the first instinct of any judge, faced with such a [politically charged] case, would be restraint." Nevertheless, she wanted the country to know that "whatever final judgment awaits Bush v. Gore in the annals of history, I am certain that the good work and good faith of the U.S. federal judiciary as a whole will continue to sustain public confidence at a level never beyond repair."[4] Apparently, in her mind, as in the minds of many, confidence in the good faith of at least some judges was in need of repair in the aftermath of the election 2000 litigation.[5]

In this postelection saga, accusations of partisanship against judges took a while to develop. The first lawsuits on the butterfly ballot were slow to start, and Judge Terry Lewis's initial ruling on whether the secretary of state was allowed to ignore the results of manual recounts was not an obvious victory for either side. But from the moment that the Florida Supreme

Court handed down its first decision extending the deadline for finishing recounts, the charge of unacceptable bias became a mantra of Bush partisans. James Baker led off with an angry complaint about how the Florida justices had changed the rules, and before long Republicans were talking about "a partisan court," "the judges of the Democrats," and a "collection of liberal activists" who replaced the law with "their own political opinion."[6] After the Florida Court's decision ordering a statewide recount, the accusations flew again, with prominent Republicans claiming that the judges "were a bunch of partisan hacks" who do not "care what the law is" and promising that "this judicial aggression will not stand."[7]

Democrats had fewer opportunities to make this accusation. The Florida judiciary was largely (though not exclusively) Democratic, and so Gore supporters had no plausible basis for complaining about political bias when the Florida Supreme Court ruled against them in a number of cases. The Eleventh Circuit Court of Appeal was controlled by Republicans but a majority of that court consistently voted in Gore's favor. The first U.S. Supreme Court decision also provided no opportunity for complaint, since it was unanimous and a bit ambiguous in its implications. However, after the 5 to 4 outcome in *Bush v. Gore,* Democrats finally had their opportunity to decry an "overtly partisan decision" by judges pursuing their "self-interested political preferences" in a way that was "lawless and unprecedented."[8] The hundreds of law professors who sponsored a full-page ad in the *New York Times* denounced the Supreme Court for using "its power to act as political partisans, not judges of a court of law."[9]

It may be tempting to dismiss all of these accusations as sour grapes, with each side simply labeling "partisan" any unhelpful decision made by judges of a different political party.[10] After all, commentators applied the label only to judges with whom they disagreed politically; that is, most Democrats did not think that the Florida Supreme Court was acting partisan and most Republicans thought that the U.S. Supreme Court was motivated by something other than a simple desire to see Bush elected president. Still, the fact that this label is used as political rhetoric does not preclude the possibility that it may also be an accurate way of distinguishing among different kinds of decisions during this election controversy. The trick is to see whether we can make anything more of the idea than is made by partisans interested only in the political benefits of making the accusation.

Essentially, what distinguishes a claim of judicial partisanship is the accusation that judges have offered a bad faith (insincere) interpretation of the law in order to reach a decision that they would not have made otherwise simply because one of the litigants shared their political affiliation. Almost everyone would recognize this as a very serious charge that, if true, should legitimately provoke outrage or worse. Partisan justice may not be a crime, as is bribery, but like bribery it reflects an unacceptable deviation from our normal and reasonable expectations for consistency and impartiality in the decisions of a court of law. However, it is important to emphasize that what makes this behavior a special subset of judicial politics is the combination of legal insincerity and partisan favoritism. Decisions that are legally insincere but motivated by different political considerations – such as intracourt bargaining, institutional legitimacy, or even national security – raise different political questions or concerns; in fact, because some of these considerations are known to be a natural or inevitable part of judicial decision-making, their influence in a case is often not considered ethically questionable.[11] Similarly, a decision that favors a judge's assumed political preferences is not partisan justice if there are reasons to think that the judge would have made the same decision even if the parties were different (for legal or ideological reasons). Admittedly, the question of whether a judge is offering a sincere point of view or a concocted one may be hard to figure out – as the country discovered in the election litigation, the "intent of the voter" (so to speak) is sometimes difficult to discern based on the available evidence, and the standards for evaluating that question may be so subjective that they allow evaluators of different political persuasions to reach different conclusions. Still, as an initial matter, it may possible to agree in principle on what we mean by partisan justice, even if (for the moment) we reserve opinion on what the relevant evidence suggests in this case.

In principle, it may also be possible to identify some considerations that can guide this inquiry. For example, almost all would agree that if a judge votes in a way that is contrary to her or his assumed political preferences, then this is evidence that the decision was influenced by factors other than partisanship. Also, if a judge takes a position that is consistent with her or his assumed political preferences but also receives the support of judges from a different party, then the concerns about partisan justice are mitigated.

More difficult to assess are those times when judges rule in a way that is consistent with their party affiliation without support from the other party – either because the case is never reviewed, or it is only reviewed by judges of the same party, or because judges from the other party disagree with the ruling. However, this alone is not enough to prove partisan decision-making. Disagreements among judges of different political parties occur all the time, for understandable reasons, given what we know about the influence of political ideology on judicial decision-making. In such cases, the question becomes whether the decision seemed to be consistent with the judge's familiar pattern of decision-making or whether it seemed to be an ad hoc deviation from that pattern in order to accommodate the interests of a favored partisan. If there is no prior pattern of decision-making by a judge on the topic, then one can ask whether the judge's decision seemed to be a deviation from generally accepted understandings of the law (assuming such understandings existed). This will not always be easy to determine, since lawyers and judges are often able to construct politically convenient distinctions to justify the selective application of legal rules or principles.[12] Also, if a question is completely unprecedented – in the sense that there are no prior patterns of decisions and there is no governing law – then there is no record of prior consistent behavior from which to deviate, and thus it may not be possible to reach a conclusion one way or the other. Still, the question at least provides some focus for a discussion about how to distinguish acceptable ideological decision-making from unacceptable partisan justice.

All of this means that the most controversial kinds of decisions are those where judges (a) make decisions consistent with their political affiliations that (b) receive no support from judges with different party loyalties and that (c) seem inconsistent with the judges' usual pattern of decision-making or with generally accepted understandings of the existing law. In such cases, the last question would be whether there is any evidence that these judges were motivated by something other than strictly partisan concerns. If there are good reasons to think that they simply did not believe their expressed legal arguments, then are there also good reasons to think that they had other things on their minds besides providing help to a favored candidate?

With these considerations in mind, let me begin a review of the record starting with the judges whose behavior raised the fewest public concerns during the election dispute, and then turn to the competing supreme courts.

ASSESSING PARTISAN JUSTICE BELOW THE HIGH COURTS

The vitriol unleashed against the justices of the state and federal high courts was not leveled at the trial court judges who initially took up these cases, established a record, and made preliminary rulings.[13] This may be because the parties understood that most of these issues would have to be decided at a higher level anyway, and thus it made little sense to spend a lot of time attacking the motives of lower court judges. But it is also true that the overall pattern of decision-making by most of these judges does not fit a theory of partisan motivation.

Many of these judges handed down rulings that were the opposite of what one would predict just on the basis of their partisan background or ideological reputation. For example, after an initial decision that was not an obvious victory for either side, Judge Terry Lewis, a Democrat, ruled that the Republican secretary of state had the authority to disregard the results of manual recounts that came in after the seven-day deadline for counties to report their results.[14] Lewis also ruled against the Democrats in the lawsuit challenging Republican absentee ballots that were allegedly tainted by the efforts of Republican Party officials to fill in missing voter information on absentee ballot applications. It was the same conclusion that had been reached by another Democratic appointee, circuit court judge Nikki Clark, who Republicans were so worried about that they tried to get her dismissed.[15] Earlier, when Republicans tried to get these absentee ballot challenges thrown out, they were turned back by Judge Debra Nelson, a recent appointee of Jeb Bush.[16] Earlier still, at a time when the standards for evaluating chads were thought to be the difference between President Gore and President Bush, Republican state circuit judge Jorge Labarga ruled that Palm Beach's decision to use the strict "detached chad" standard for counting votes violated the requirement in state law to do whatever was necessary to determine the intent of the voter.[17]

There were also some instances of trial judges voting consistently with their political preferences but then receiving support from judges of a different political affiliation. Labarga later ruled against the Democrats when he decided that there could be no revote in Palm Beach County to correct the problems with the butterfly ballot,[18] but this decision was unanimously upheld by the Democratic Florida Supreme Court.[19] Similarly, federal district court judge Donald M. Middlebrooks, a Democrat, ruled against the Bush campaign's early efforts to get an emergency injunction to stop the recounts,[20] but that decision was unanimously upheld by a coalition of seven Republicans and five Democrats on the Eleventh Circuit Court of Appeals.[21]

Two other examples are more open to question. Judge N. Sanders Sauls, appointed by a Republican governor, handed down an aggressive decision against Al Gore in his contest of the certified election, in an opinion that even some conservative commentators considered sloppy on the law and overreaching in its conclusions.[22] Then again, while he did not receive support from a majority of Democrats on the Florida Supreme Court, there were three votes to uphold his decision – two from justices who nevertheless thought that he made a mistake on the law and one, from Chief Justice Wells, that was more generally supportive. It is possible that Sauls and his nominal supporters on the state high court had different motivations: Sauls might have been politically predisposed against the Gore complaint (which is what Gore's lawyers were told)[23] and the Democratic justices might have felt beaten up by the U.S. Supreme Court and besieged by those who were seeking an end to the lingering controversy. But this speculation does not establish a case for judicial partisanship, and in the absence of stronger evidence it is appropriately charitable to assume that there was a plausible legal basis for the decision.

Also, federal district court Judge Maurice Paul, a Republican, ruled against a Democratic challenge to the counting of any absentee ballots that arrived after the deadline set by the state legislature, despite the argument that the U.S. Supreme Court's analysis of the state legislature's plenary authority over presidential elections required enforcement of state statutes over any other source of law.[24] This decision averted an outcome that would have had a catastrophic impact on the Bush campaign; however, unlike a similarly important decision by Judge Labarga, this one never had a chance to receive support from judges of a different political affiliation.[25] At a minimum, one might say that this judge was not as aggressively protective of the legislature's prerogatives as were the conservatives on the U.S. Supreme Court. However, that does not demonstrate inconsistency in Paul's decision-making; after all, even though an arguably contrary precedent was established by the Washington justices five days earlier, it is also true that before election 2000 it was not the practice of federal judges to supervise state court interpretations of state absentee ballot deadlines. While the case might stand as a noteworthy example of how a new constitutional theory was used by Republican judges in two different ways to achieve two pro-Bush results, this is not enough to show that Paul was insincere in his legal conclusions.

A more mixed pattern can be found when we look at the key decisions of the federal court of appeals judges on the Eleventh Circuit. The full court handed down two key decisions during the election dispute:[26] *Touchston v. McDermott*,[27] which unanimously denied Bush's motion for an emergency injunction to stop the recounts, and *Siegel v. LePore*,[28] in which a majority composed of five Democrats and three Republicans again refused to issue an injunction against the recounts, over the dissents of four other Republicans. On the whole this is not evidence of a court driven by judicial partisans. Given that Republican appointees were a majority on the court, it would have been quite possible for them to take steps from the very beginning to call a halt to recount efforts. However, none of the Republicans considered this an appropriate action during the initial request for an emergency injunction. It is true that in both cases the Democratic judges voted for Gore, but in one of those cases they were joined by every Republican judge and in the second case they were joined by almost half of their Republican colleagues. It is possible that the Democratic judges had partisan motivations and the Republican judges thought they were following the law, but there is also no evidence that different motives were at work. When we add to the mix that the prevailing pre-election assumption was that manual recounts raise no serious equal protection concern, then it seems especially appropriate to assume that all of these judges voted on the basis of their best understanding of the law.

The only judges on this court who were not joined by colleagues from the other party were the four dissenting Republicans in *Siegel*. These votes, therefore, are consistent with a theory of partisan decision-making. Obviously, it was no accident that the only judges who thought the recounts should be stopped were Republicans, and so it seems reasonable to conclude that their political sympathies had something to do with their judgment about the legality of these recounts. A sense of partisan eagerness was also evident in the decision of one of the judges (Carnes) to support his position with a detailed empirical critique of Gore's stated reasons for why he selected particular counties for recounts;[29] this material was not part of the record, and as a general rule, appellate judges do not take it upon themselves to build their own personal factual record on which to anchor their analysis. Moreover, unlike Judge Paul, these judges reached a decision that was fairly innovative. The main question, then, is whether it is more reasonable to assume that the equal protection concerns expressed by these judges reflected a good faith interpretation of the law or an interest in concocting any argument that would be helpful to Bush. Here it may be difficult to disentangle good faith judging and political preferences, especially when we consider that we may suddenly develop new good faith opinions about the unfairness of certain processes (previously considered acceptable) only when our political interests are unexpected threatened by those processes (as with selective recounts for some Republicans and variable error rates in vote-counting machines for some Democrats). We may have to hold off a verdict on whether these judges engaged in partisan justice or good faith judging until we see how they apply these same equal protection principles in later cases where the political stakes, and the political beneficiaries, are different.[30]

It should now be more clear why judges on trial courts and intermediate courts of appeal did not come under any public scrutiny or criticism during the election 2000 dispute. In addition to the likelihood that there was simply less political motivation to complain about these judges, we also see that their overall pattern of decision did not provide a good opportunity to make plausible accusations. Moreover, the judges who would have been the best targets of Democratic complaints – the dissenters on the court of appeal – had no impact on the court's actual decision and so were not really worth complaining about.

PARTISAN ASSESSMENTS OF PARTISAN
DECISION-MAKING ON THE FLORIDA SUPREME COURT

The real public debate about judicial partisanship began with the first decision of the Florida Supreme Court. The question of whether this court acted inappropriately may be the central political question in this saga; it is certainly at the heart of the Republican critique about the corrupt use of judicial power during the election 2000 dispute, and it is central to the justification offered by members of the U.S. Supreme Court for their intervention. Unfortunately, it may also be the issue over which the partisan divide will remain the most persistent. Still, it may be possible to get a better perspective on the nature of the complaint.

The Florida high court handed down five decisions that could have determined the outcome of the presidential election:[31] (1) *Palm Beach County Canvassing Board v. Harris*,[32] a unanimous decision requiring the secretary of state to accept the results of hand recounts completed before a court-extended deadline; (2) *Gore v. Miami-Dade County Canvassing Board*,[33] a unanimous decision rejecting a Gore request to order Miami-Dade to resume its recount after the local canvassing board decided it could not meet the court-extended deadline; (3) *Fladell v. Palm Beach County Canvassing Board*,[34] a unanimous decision upholding Judge Labarga's decision on the butterfly ballot and thus rejecting a request for a revote of Palm Beach County; (4) *Gore v. Harris*,[35] a 4 to 3 decision overruling Judge Sauls's decision in the Gore contest and ordering a statewide manual recount of so-called undervote ballots; and (5) *Jacobs v. Seminole County Canvassing Board*,[36] a unanimous decision upholding a lower court ruling that refused to disqualify absentee ballots on the grounds that Republican party officials had added voter information to the ballot applications.

To begin, it is obvious that the justices of the Florida Supreme Court did not consistently vote in favor of Gore whenever they had the opportunity. In fact, these judges voted unanimously against Gore in three of the five cases. There was one case (*Palm Beach*) in which the justices voted unanimously in favor of Gore on an issue that was vital to the continued survival of his campaign, but even then the decision turned out to be much less favorable then was first imagined. The newly created deadline was much shorter than the Gore team requested (so short, in fact, that two of the three counties that were being accommodated could not complete the work and ended up with their votes uncertified) and when given an opportunity to order Miami-Dade to work harder to take advantage of the extended deadline the justices refused; thus, even though Gore received some benefit from the extension (the 567 votes from speedy Broward County), the decision was not as definitively helpful as it might have been. Similarly, in the only other case in which four of the justices voted in favor of Gore (*Gore v. Harris*), the court's decision did not give the Gore campaign the remedy that would have been most favorable to the campaign (recounts in only selected counties). Obviously, as with the first decision, the statewide recount gave Gore a chance that he would not have had otherwise, but it also initiated a process that was much less predictable than would have been preferred by most Democratic partisans.

Thus, the accusations against the court must be refined to suggest a more sophisticated form of judicial partisanship. This is not an unreasonable assumption; we know that judges engage in relatively sophisticated forms of strategic decision-making.[37] The issue, then, is to discern the sophisticated partisan logic behind this pattern. One possibility is that these judges thought it best to show restraint except when matters became crucial to Gore's continued survival. It is true that the two helpful decisions were dramatic in that they each came at a time when Gore looked as if he had exhausted his options, which undoubtedly added to the frustration of Bush partisans (who felt at each time that they were just hours away from victory). However, setting aside the point that these decisions represented, at best, political boosts rather than definitive Gore victories, this "one last chance" theory cannot easily explain why these justices ruled against Gore in the *Jacobs* case, when it was obvious to all that throwing out the absentee ballots really was Gore's last chance (since the U.S. Supreme Court had already called a halt to the statewide recount). A different decision in *Jacobs* would also have had the exemplary benefit of being relatively easy to enforce: rather than try to get more votes for Gore with a unpredictable recount that might not be completed and could be halted by the Supreme Court, a decision to throw out tainted absentee ballots would require merely a court order demanding an adjustment in the certified totals.[38] It is also arguable that the U.S. Supreme Court would have had a more difficult time justifying a decision overturning such a ruling, since applying the technical (and purposefully draconian) requirements of the law regulating absentee ballot applications could hardly be characterized as changing the law and it would seemingly avoid any equal protection complaints associated with the application of vague standards. In sum, for a lawless, activist partisan court, *Jacobs* would seem to be the most tempting case of all.

Another possibility is that the Florida Supreme Court offered as much help as possible in cases in which that help was legally plausible. This would imply that there was no realistic legal option in *Jacobs, Fladell* (revoting Palm Beach County), or *Gore v. Miami-Dade* (forcing the county to restart its recount), but *Palm Beach County* and *Gore v. Harris* provided more opportunities to bend the law toward Gore. However, it should be obvious that this version of the argument is inconsistent with the strong Republican complaint that the Florida justices were willing to disregard clear law to reach their preferred outcome. If there was something about the law in the two pro-Gore cases that made it more plausible for these justices to vote for Gore then those decisions might not be considered completely unreasonable; on the other hand, if the claim is that the justices in those cases completely disregarded the law then there should have been no reason why they did not disregard the law on other occasions when it would have been helpful to Gore.

And this is the point: the legal issues in the two pro-Gore decisions provided more plausible good faith legal grounds for favorable Gore decisions than did the issues raised in the three cases that went against Gore. There was a general consensus of opinion among liberal and conservative law professors alike that the law did not support revoting Palm Beach or throwing out 25,000 absentee ballots. By contrast, opinion was divided (along political lines) on the scope of Secretary of State Harris's discretion to ignore the results of legally authorized recounts and on whether the election contest statute allowed the court to authorize a statewide recount. Obviously, in saying that opinion was divided, I acknowledge that many conservative commentators believed that the Florida justices should have interpreted the law differently in each of these cases. The question relating to partisan justice, however, is not whether the justices agreed with these commentators; it is always possible to make an argument for why a decision should have gone a different way. Instead, the question is whether there is reason to believe that these justices based their decision on something other than a good faith belief about the best interpretation of Florida law. Some conservative law professors may be willing to admit that their more liberal colleagues have such good faith beliefs about one or both of these cases. They certainly know that, with respect to the first case, the supporters of the court's decision considered the statutory scheme to be contradictory and ambiguous rather than crystal clear on the issue of whether the secretary of state had unfettered discretion to ignore results that came in from counties after seven days.[39]

Conservatives might respond that this is an obvious mistake of interpretation given the statutory language that the secretary of state "may ignore" late filed returns; but other parts of the statute allowed counties to authorize recounts, even though those recounts might take longer than seven days to complete in larger counties. Critics claim that rather than balance these competing provisions it would have been more appropriate to keep the deadline inflexible and treat recounts as optional; but setting aside whether that is the only way to interpret these provisions, it is worth noting that the lawyer for Secretary of State Harris (who had no political incentive consciously to misread the statute) admitted to Justice Stevens during the first oral argument that, in his judgment, there were times when the secretary of state could be forced after the seven-day deadline to accept late-filed returns.[40] Thus, with respect to the first case, the debate about the scope of plausible good faith interpretations is actually remarkably narrow, having to do with whether accommodating the results of legally authorized recounts was among those circumstances when courts would be able to force the secretary of state to accept results after this deadline.

Arguably, there is even a strong legal basis for the decision of the majority in *Gore v. Harris.* Just a year earlier, the Florida election code had been rewritten to give judges sweeping new powers to adjust problems that might be caused when certified results were based on a rejection of enough legal votes to cast in doubt the outcome of the election. As a number of the dissenting justices pointed out in *Bush v. Gore,* the language of the contest statute itself was perfectly consistent with every aspect of the Florida court's decision. While it would have been possible (as conservatives claim) to narrow the reach of statute by applying more constricted readings of other parts of the election code, there was nothing implausible about the approach adopted by the Florida majority. In fact, it should be kept in mind that the claim that the Florida court again misread the law in this case was only advanced on the Supreme Court by the three most conservative justices (Rehnquist, Scalia, and Thomas). In other words, even Justices Kennedy and O'Connor refused to associate their names with this analysis. It is possible that they were simply being fastidious about only expressing an opinion on the issues that were absolutely necessary to decide the case. However, unlike the first oral arguments, Justices Kennedy and O'Connor did not show much enthusiasm for this line of argument the second time around.[41] Conservatives may continue to disagree, but the mere fact of disagreement does not seem nearly enough to make a case for bad faith partisan judging.

There is one final reason for thinking that the Florida Supreme Court was ruling in good faith. In addition to the mixed nature of the record (two of five for Gore), the mixed blessings of the two pro-Gore decisions, the decision to uphold the absentee ballots in *Jacobs,* and the (controversial but supportable) legal bases for the decisions in the two pro-Gore cases, we can also tell that the pattern of the court's decisions is consistent with an impartial legal preference for counting votes whenever possible even if strict adherence to legal technicalities would justify not counting them. Bush supporters may have been upset when the court counted votes rather than enforced deadlines, but they did not complain when the justices refused to throw out votes even in the face of tough new statutory prohibitions against tampering with ballot applications. One might complain (as did the three Democratic dissenters) that extending this theme to cover a statewide recount of undervotes was too much too late, but that is a critique of the extent of the majority's enthusiasm for the theme and does not necessarily imply bad faith judging. This is especially important when we recall that this theme had a long-standing place in Florida case law. All seven justices of that court – three of whom voted against Gore four out of five times – reminded the country at the beginning of its first election 2000 opinion that it had ruled twenty-five years earlier in the case of *Boardman v. Esteva* (Fla. 1975) that "by refusing to recognize an otherwise valid exercise of the right of a citizen to vote for the sake of sacred, unyielding adherence to statutory scripture, we would in effect nullify that right." Obviously, this established legal principle did not require the court to give Gore the two uneven victories that he received. But a court that makes a choice to consistently apply a long-established legal principle favoring counting votes over disqualifying votes – even when that principle did not work in favor of their preferred candidate – is not the same as partisan justice. This record is enough to rebut a presumption of judicial realpolitik.

The only two cases that Gore won before the Florida Supreme Court were either vacated or overturned by the U.S. Supreme Court. Without these decisions the record of the Florida litigation would have been a mixed bag, with each campaign winning some cases and losing some, with Democratic and Republican judges voting on all sides of the issue, and with the main court interventions by the state supreme court resulting in a process with an indeterminate outcome. The intervention of the Washington justices was by far the most definitive and one-sided of all the courts – first by overturning a decision that put at risk what would have been a certified 930 vote lead by Bush, then by issuing an emergency order stopping a statewide recount, and finally (and most conclusively) by ordering that no additional vote counting could take place, thus ensuring the Bush victory.

We know from the first few sentences of Justice Souter's dissent in *Bush v. Gore* that the five conservatives were behind every one of these interventions and that the four less conservative justices believed every one to be inappropriate. While the justices cobbled together a unanimous decision in the first case, *Bush v. Palm Beach County Canvassing Board*, there is no doubt that this reflected a strategic attempt by the four less conservative justices to blunt the effects of the majority's decision to vacate the Florida court's opinion by also throwing the case back to the state court; thus, the conservatives cannot claim in any of these cases that their view of the law was shared by others on the Court.[42] Moreover, each of these three interventions was based on different legal issues and conclusions: the enforceability of Article II and 3 U.S.C. § 5 against the Florida Supreme Court's interpretation of state statutes, the existence of irreparable harm to Bush if newly authorized recounts were allowed to go forward during the last appeal, and the equal protection problems associated with the use of an "intent of the voter" standard during a statewide recount of undervotes. The fact that the same group of five justices would reach the same anti-Gore conclusions on three unrelated questions of federal law contributes to suspicions about partisan motivation.

Of course, the other members of the Court chose to vote on the other side of the issue in two of the three cases, and so some may claim that the suspicions of partisanship may fall equally on both sides. But besides the fact that these four justices were willing to vote against Gore in the first case, there were other factors that focus more attention on the conservatives. The very decision to intervene in a presidential election dispute – in what had been traditionally considered a matter reserved to the states under Congressional supervision – was itself a surprising departure from long-accepted practices and assumptions about how such elections would be conducted. It is vital to keep in mind that it was widely believed in the early days of this dispute that the Supreme Court would have no definitive role to play, given the structure of presidential elections under the U.S. Constitution and federal law.[43]

Moreover, this unprecedented intervention was not pursued in order to defend well-established constitutional principles or precedents, such as protecting people against racial discrimination in voting. (Quite the contrary, to say the least.) One of the justifications – that Article II of the Constitution required careful federal supervision of state court interpretations of state law regarding presidential elections – had (in all probability) never previously been theorized or articulated in the history of U.S. constitutional law. The one precedent cited for that proposition, *McPherson v. Blacker,* was completely unfamiliar to the vast majority of constitutional law experts (it was not discussed in any of the leading constitutional law casebooks used in law schools before 2000) and the specific argument about federal supervision of state court interpretations had nothing to do with the issues in that case (which involved the question of whether states were allowed to have presidential electors chosen primarily from congressional districts rather than in one at-large election).[44] Moreover, the specific line of argument developed out of that precedent by the conservative justices in the first case – relating to how state courts could not use state constitutions as a basis for interpreting state statutes governing presidential elections – even took the lawyers by surprise during oral arguments.

The majority's specific equal protection complaint was similarly unprecedented. As Justice Stevens pointed out in his dissenting opinion, the "intent of the voter" standard, which the Court had suddenly declared a violation of the Fourteenth Amendment, was a longstanding part of more than thirty state election statutes. Before election 2000 it had never occurred to anyone that it might raise federal constitutional issues. In fact, differential treatment of ballots seemed to be an inevitable part of the traditional U.S. commitment to state and county-based election processes. It was no surprise that the Bush lawyers initially considered the equal protection argument so weak that they almost abandoned it until they realized that there were not many other lines of attack. It was also no surprise to most commentators when the U.S. Supreme Court initially refused to take up this argument when it was raised in the first appeal.[45] It is noteworthy that the legitimacy of this constitutional argument has even been questioned by leading conservative legal scholars, who worry about the implications of ongoing federal court supervision of all aspects of vote counting.[46]

If the conservatives' intervention was not defensible on the basis of existing constitutional precedents, then was it possible that they were acting in accordance with principles they had consistently espoused in other cases or that they might sincerely hold by virtue of their political ideology (rather than their partisan preferences)? This is hard to believe. Most of the scholars who have expressed some sympathy with the equal protection argument tend to be more liberal and more willing to see the advantages of a uniform national system of voting. While it may not be entirely implausible that the liberal Warren Court might have interpreted equal protection to require uniform methods of vote counting, outside the circumstances of election 2000 it is not plausible to think that the conservatives on the Rehnquist Court would have been motivated to even suggest such a thing.[47] The suspicion that the proffered legal justification did not reflect sincerely held beliefs was reinforced by the majority's statement – immediately after using the argument to kill this particular recount – that "Our consideration is limited to the present circumstances, for the problem of equal protection in election processes generally presents many complexities." The language might have represented an appropriate bit of caution in a case in which the justices did not have the usual amount of time to contemplate the implications of their opinion, but given the ideological dimensions of the principle it is also understandable why critics would interpret this language as designed to limit the reach of an articulated principle that the conservatives used but did not believe in. It also did not help that a similar concern about insincerity arose with the apparent disjuncture between their eagerness to intervene in this case and their strongly held beliefs in other cases about the importance of limiting federal intrusion into traditional state practices. In fact, legal scholars would have to look far and wide for another example of these conservatives questioning state court decisions on state law.

Suspicions about whether the conservatives based their decisions on sincerely held beliefs or ad hoc partisan judgments were also raised in their per curiam opinion when they concluded that December 12 represented a fixed date in state law for the resolution of presidential election disputes. The majority reached this conclusion despite the fact that no such deadline could be found anywhere in the statutes that the conservatives had previously ruled were the only legitimate source of law for Florida during presidential elections. For some reason, on this issue time – and on this issue only – the majority was willing simply to defer to statements by the Florida Supreme Court that the state had intended to take advantage of the so-called "safe harbor" provision of 3 U.S.C. § 5.

Finally, there is good evidence that the conservative had strong political preferences in favor of a Bush victory. Of course, all of the Washington justices had a greater personal interest in the outcome of this case then did any of the state judges, simply by virtue of the president's power to influence the composition (and thus the future direction) of their court through the power of appointment. But there is more specific evidence as well, including Justice Scalia's one-sided discussion of the irreparable harm to Bush's political fortunes when the Court granted the emergency stay, the work being done by Justice Thomas's wife for the Heritage Foundation on behalf of the Bush transition team even before the election was finalized, and the disappointed comments reportedly expressed by Justice O'Connor on election night upon hearing that Gore might have won Florida ("Oh, this is terrible"). There had also been reports that Chief Justice Rehnquist and Justice O'Connor were interested in retiring but, as is typical for modern justices, wanted to wait until a president of their own party had a chance to pick their replacement. By contrast, in terms of partisan motivation, two of the pro-Gore voters (Stevens and Souter) were appointed by Republican presidents, and while it is possible that they may have changed their partisan sympathies as their voting records revealed them to be less conservative (as did other 1970s-era moderate northern Republicans, such as Lowell Weicker), it may also be the case that (for example) George Bush appointee (and New Hampshire native) Justice Souter considers himself a moderate Northern Republican (in the mold of Senators Olympia Snowe or Susan Collins) rather than a pro-Gore Democrat. Many conservative Republicans undoubtedly consider the unexpectedly moderate Souter to be a turncoat and would insist that as far as they are concerned he is essentially a Democrat, but his political sympathies are certainly less obvious than those of the conservative majority. Moreover, while we may never know how the dissenters would have handled the situation had they controlled the Court, in the election 2000 dispute their positions had the protection of precedent in a way that the majority's views did not.

The five justices in the *Bush v. Gore* majority are thus the only judges involved in this election dispute who fall uniquely within the category that is most indicative of partisan justice: they made a decision that was consistent with their political preferences but inconsistent with precedent and inconsistent with what would have been predicted given their views in other cases.[48] Moreover, their decision received no support from any judge with presumably different partisan loyalties. As I will discuss, even some of the Court's defenders agree that the intervention cannot be justified on the grounds of sincerely held legal beliefs. For all of these reasons, it is understandable why many people view the U.S. Supreme Court's actions as exemplars of partisan justice, perhaps even unique in the history of the Court. Certainly the justices did not divide along political lines in the other notorious cases involving the political fortunes of presidency; the Watergate Tapes Case and the Paula Jones lawsuit against Bill Clinton each resulted in bipartisan agreement on the Court. University of Virginia law professor Michael Klarman captured the views of many when he asked rhetorically, "Had all the other facts in the Florida election imbroglio remained the same, but the situation of the two presidential candidates been reversed, does anyone seriously believe that the conservatives Justices would have reached the same result?" Placing the point in larger historical context, he added, "I cannot think of another Supreme Court decision about which one can say with equal confidence that switching the parties to the litigation, and nothing else, would have changed the result." Klarman suggested that the most analogous circumstance might be the Clinton impeachment, where Republicans and Democrats took positions on the standard of what counts as an "impeachable offense" that were directly linked to their partisan commitments. However, he added that the main difference between the Supreme Court's decisions in the election 2000 litigation and the impeachment process – aside from the presumption that an impeachment is understood to be an inherently political process while judicial decision-making typically aspires to something less overtly partisan – is that "the constitutional law of impeachment is highly indeterminate" because of a spare text and sparse precedents while "the constitutional law relevant to adjudicating" the election dispute "was reasonable clear; the majority just did not want to follow it." Thus, "while the Clinton impeachment controversy illustrates partisan preferences dictating the resolution of constitutional indeterminacy, *Bush v. Gore* reveals partisan preferences *trumping* law."[49]

Ironically, suspicions about whether the majority acted on the basis of good faith beliefs about the law are confirmed by some of the Court's strongest defenders, who argue that the actions of these justices are better justified in political terms rather than legal terms. In their view, the main defense against the charge of partisan justice is that the political considerations driving the majority were not strictly partisan considerations. There are two main arguments that fall into this category: the appropriateness of stopping illegitimate judicial activism by the state supreme court and the need to prevent a developing constitutional crisis.

The paradoxical "against judicial activism" argument is premised on the assumption that the majority's outrage over the Florida Supreme Court's actions was based not on their concerns about Bush's political fortunes but instead on a more abstract aversion to courts that do not show enough restraint.[50] However, in order to distinguish this theoretically abstract concern from the specific stakes in this dispute, one would need to make a convincing case that the majority on the Supreme Court would have acted the same way even if Bush was seeking the recounts and Gore was resisting the Florida Supreme Court. This is a reassuringly speculative and untestable basis for a defense. What we do know about what actually happened, however, is that the majority's decision to reach down and take this case – which "startled" the four other justices when they learned of it "shortly before the justices met on the day after Thanksgiving," since they thought it was obvious that "the court would stay away from the Florida election"[51] – was part of a larger mobilization of Republican institutions against the Florida justices: the Republican leaders of the state legislature began exploring whether they could "reclaim" their control over presidential electors by simply appointing a slate of Bush electors (regardless of the outcome of a recount of the vote that the legislature had originally authorized as the way Florida would choose its electors); the Republican leaders of the Congress began exploring their options for rejecting any results that would change the machine-count Bush victory into a manual-recount Gore victory. Immediately before the Florida court reached its decision, a full 71 percent of respondents to one poll thought it would be acceptable if a court stepped in and ordered the recounts.[52]

Despite this, critics of the U.S. Supreme Court should be willing to admit that a reasonable person could conclude that the Florida judges made a legal mistake in the first case. However, there are three reasons why this still did not provide sufficient justification for the Supreme Court's actions during the election crisis. First, the difference of opinion among experts on whether the Florida Supreme Court made a legal mistake in the first case – even if it reflected partisan divisions – was still evidence that the interpretation was not so obviously incorrect that a neutral arbiter should consider it out of bounds. This is another way of saying that a confident partisan viewpoint is not the same as a nonpartisan political judgment about how a general interest was served by the Court's assault on the Florida Supreme Court. Second, and more important, the Florida Supreme Court's decision in *Gore v. Harris* – while just as frustrating to Republicans as its initial decision – was not an obvious example of inappropriate judicial activism even to many conservatives, including Justices O'Connor and Kennedy. In fact, the official justification for the final decision did not rest on a claim about faulty statutory interpretation; instead, it rested on a completely unprecedented theory (about how it was unconstitutional to look for voter intent on recounted ballots) combined with a deference to the state court's interpretation about the December 12 deadline. Thus, the antiactivism argument, which was so powerful for partisans at the front end of the dispute, breaks down well before the Supreme Court's final intervention.

But even assuming that there were legitimate concerns for stopping judicial activism, it does not imply that it was proper for the U.S. Supreme Court to solve that problem. The third and most important reason why the judicial activism complaint is not an adequate nonpartisan political justification for the Court's intervention is that there was a 211-year-old nonjudicial process in place for dealing with the problem. Up until Friday, November 24, 2000 – the day that the U.S. Supreme Court announced it would hear the appeal of the first Florida Supreme Court decision – it was widely understood and accepted that any problems associated with the appointment of presidential electors should be handled by state officials as they saw fit and then reviewed by the U.S. Congress. This practice dated from the beginning of the Republic, and it was the process that was clarified in the Electoral Count Act of 1887, which set timelines for state governments to address and resolve disputes if they wanted to benefit from Congress's "safe harbor" promise of not challenging a state's electors. This was the thrust of Justice Souter's remarks to Theodore Olson at the first oral argument, when he insisted that this act "has committed the determination of the issues that you raise and the consequences to follow from them to the Congress." When Olson responded that Congress passed the statute to avoid "controversy, chaos, conflict," Souter pointed out that "Section 15 assumes that there is controversy and chaos," adding that "if Congress wanted this Court to get involved into the issue at this stage, it seems passing strange to me that despite all the elaborateness of Section 15 there wouldn't have been some mention of Federal litigation proceeding in the Section 15 proceeding."[53] Thus, supporters of the Supreme Court's intervention should have to explain not only why the Florida Supreme Court deserved to be rebuffed but also why the U.S. Supreme Court was the proper institution to address this issue.

This brings us to the second, and potentially more compelling, political justification for the Court's actions. It focuses not on the alleged problem with one institution in need of correction or "adult supervision." Instead, it is premised on an assumption that the political process that might normally have addressed and resolved the election 2000 dispute would have been unable to effectively manage it.

It is not unusual for scholars to suggest that courts occasionally need to step in when the political process breaks down. In the modern era, these sorts of arguments have been used in support of efforts to remove blockages or expand access to the process to those who have been denied such access. This logic, which dates back at least to the Court's famous footnote 4 in the case *United States v. Carolene Products* (1938), was the principal justification for the Court's reapportionment decisions as well as expanded protections for freedom of speech, freedom of assembly, and civil rights – what John Hart Ely classically referred to as the "representation-reinforcement" justification for judicial activism.[54] However, there is nothing in this familiar argument that suggests that the Court should remove an inherently political question from a fully functioning political process if the justices think that the result might just be too messy, controversial, inconvenient, or, well, *political.*

However, this seems to be the essence of this last justification for the Court's intervention in the election dispute. University of Chicago law professor Cass Sunstein referred to the Court's efforts as representing "order without law" – an attempt to impose order on an otherwise disorderly dispute even though there might not have been a legal basis for so doing. While he was critical of the absence of law, he was also willing to give the Court credit for performing a "service" to the nation by resolving the dispute "in a way that carried more simplicity and authority than anything that might have been expected from the United States Congress" and that also possibly "avoided a genuine constitutional crisis." What is the rationale for thinking that there might have been a crisis? Sunstein's explanation went like this. If Gore had won a recount, then state officials would have struggled over whether courts could force the governor to certify a Gore slate. Either way, competing slates would have been sent to Congress. The Republicans in the House would have voted to accept the Bush slate, and the 50-50 Senate, presided over by Al Gore, may have decided otherwise, if everyone stuck to a party-line vote. At that point, 3 U.S.C. § 15 says that if the two Houses disagree on which slate to count then Congress must accept the slate that has been certified by the state's executive. While Jeb Bush had already certified a Bush slate of electors, complications could have arisen if the Florida courts (somehow) successfully ordered the governor to certify a slate of Gore electors. In that case, "the law provides no clear answers" and so "a genuine constitutional crisis may have arisen," one that may not have been settled for some time and not without bitter political feelings.[55] Richard Posner added that "whatever Congress did would have been regarded as the product of raw politics, with no tincture of justice" and "the new President would have been deprived of a transition period in which to organize his Administration and would have taken office against a background of unprecedented bitterness." He explained, not implausibly, that this "is why the Supreme Court's decision was greeted with relief by most of the nation." After all, "Judges unwilling to sacrifice some of their prestige for the greater good of the nation might be thought selfish."[56]

This final political defense only works if one believes that a quick and orderly Bush victory represented "the greater good of the nation." One problem with this claim is obvious: there was no consensus that a continued recount represented a crisis for the country. Of course, Bush partisans often acted as if the harm to Bush was the same as the harm to the country. This was the implication of Justice Scalia's revealing language in his concurring opinion of the Court's emergency injunction, when he wrote that the new recount threatened "irreparable harm to petitioner [Bush], and to the country, by casting a cloud upon what he claims to be the legitimacy of his election." But this view confuses partisan and national interests, and needless to say it did not travel much beyond partisan boundaries. The widespread and vehement response in the mainstream press to the decision in *Bush v. Gore* clearly demonstrated that there was no general perception that shutting down the recount was necessary to avert a crisis. It is true that a majority of the general public exhibited relief after the Court's intervention, but this clearly reflected a weariness with the dispute and a possible fatalism about an eventual Bush victory, rather than an impending sense of constitutional crisis – after all, the day before the Supreme Court's decision more than half (53 percent) of those responding to a poll said they wanted the justices to allow the counting to continue.[57] Moreover, four of the justices on the

Supreme Court also did not believe that an intervention was necessary to avert a crisis, and while one might conclude that these four justices were either naïve or unpatriotic, perhaps a more generous conclusion would be that the specter of a constitutional crisis was more a partisan fantasy than an actual apparition.

What's more, it was not even an especially convincing fantasy. It could not be realistically asserted that ending public weariness or prolonged uncertainty was enough to constitute the greater good of the nation; that would have made the very process laid out in the Electoral Count Act inherently inconsistent with the public welfare, which is preposterous. Instead, the centerpiece of the imagined crisis was the possibility that the procedure laid out in 3 U.S.C. § 15 for resolving disputes would have broken down if the Florida Supreme Court forced Jeb Bush to certify a slate of Gore electors that would then compete against the slate of Bush electors that the Florida governor had already certified. However, under what realistic scenario would Jeb Bush have certified a slate of Gore electors? Under the circumstances it seems highly improbable that he would have done it merely out of respect for the authority of the Florida Supreme Court. It also seems unlikely that he would have buckled under to a threat of contempt, assuming that the Florida justices would have gone that far. Perhaps public opinion would have forced him to sign in the event of a Gore recount victory, but if so then that would have been the best reason to see the process move forward, as the winner of the national popular vote and the new winner of the Florida popular vote had his authorized electors sent to the U.S. Congress by the brother of his opponent. Rather than a crisis that scenario might have been seen as a triumph of democratic politics, even if Congressional Republicans figured out a way to resist accepting those electors.

Even assuming the worst – competing slates of electors being debated by a divided Congress – the situation would have been precisely the sort of high political moment, and hard political decision, that it was designed to be. It would have been serious, but not nearly as serious as the situation in 1876, with the Civil War still fresh in the minds of the battling partisans and old Confederate units prepared to march on Washington to force Tilden's election. There certainly would have been complications, such as the effect of the dispute on presidential transition and the possibility that the House Speaker (or someone else in the order of presidential succession) would have to temporarily take over the presidency if there was no resolution by Inauguration Day. But – and here is the point – this was the constitutional and legal process that was in place, and it would have been out of these considerations that a resolution would have been forged, perhaps (following 1877) as a result of the sort of political deal or compromise that judicial intervention made unnecessary. It would have no more been a crisis than the Clinton impeachment was a crisis – another lingering dispute that tried people's patience, embittered partisans on both sides, weakened the presidency (at least temporarily), and arguably hurt the country (at least in the sense that other political work was delayed). If the U.S. Supreme Court had been controlled by partisan Democrats it may have even been tempted to save the country from the "irreparable harm" of the impeachment saga, perhaps by ruling that the allegations against Clinton did not represent an impeachable offense. Some might respond that there would have been no legitimate legal justification for such an unprecedented and partisan intrusion into an inherently political decision, but that response echoes in the discussion of *Bush v. Gore*.

If the constitutional crisis rationale is not a simple post hoc rationalization of an otherwise inexcusable decision then it mostly represents simple impatience with democratic processes – a preference for quick, clear, imposed solutions over ones that are forged through debate, compromise, or (as was most likely if election 2000 went to Congress) ugly, hardball politics. Sunstein tipped his hand a bit when he noted that if there were uncertainty about which electoral slate was certified by the governor, then a crisis would have occurred because "the law provides no clear answers." But forcing politicians to work through a presidential selection process without the roadmap of a crystal clear legal process is not a crisis; it is democracy, and it has all the disadvantages and advantages of democratic politics, including the ability to force decision-makers to make hard choices and then (if possible) hold them accountable for those decisions. As Michael McConnell put it, even in the very unlikely event that a continued recount would have resulted in a political confrontation in the Congress, "a good case can be made . . . that the Constitution and laws have designated Congress – not the Court – as the final arbiter of such a conflict." If all those representatives engaged in partisan decision-making, then "the nation would have witnessed politicians being politicians, rather than judges being – or appearing to be – politicians."[58] Elizabeth Garrett was right when she wrote that "the lesson is we do not need to be saved *from* politics; instead, the constitutional structure augmented by statutory procedures allows us to be saved *by* politics."[59] There is no other way to ensure political accountability in a decision as important as the election of a president, as the authors of our presidential election process understood.[60]

Finally, the argument that the conservatives were motivated by a desire to save the national from a crisis focuses too much on the endgame and not enough on the overall pattern of decision-making. The truth is that the conservatives had been interested in stopping all recounts from the first moment they asserted themselves the day after Thanksgiving 2000 – at a time when the political concern of Republicans was not a constitutional crisis but a Gore victory made possible by an extended deadline for recounting ballots. In the end, after all the talk of law and high political principle, we are left simply with the raw power of an unrestrained conservative majority intent on making sure that it would decide which votes counted – and which votes would not be counted.

THE OPPORTUNITY TO PICK A PRESIDENT

Even though there is no persuasive legal or political justification for the majority's actions in the election 2000 dispute, it is still possible to sketch out a political explanation for this bold intervention.[61] If Supreme Court justices do not normally act in such an overtly partisan manner, if they are typically concerned about their reputation for impartiality or nonpartisanship, then what was it about the circumstances of election 2000 that made a difference, other than the obvious fact that the justices finally found themselves face-to-face with a historic opportunity to pick a president? Some might think this opportunity was all they needed, but other background political conditions no doubt contributed to the sense that they could safely take advantage of it.

For example, the conservative justices knew that they had a fully mobilized partisan constituency that would vehemently support their intervention. Moreover, Republicans were in control of virtually all of the potential competing political institutions, including the state legislature and executive branch of Florida and the U.S. House of Representatives; they also knew that the Senate and, of course, the presidency would be in Republican hands if the Court was successful in ensuring a Bush victory. This is in sharp contrast to the political context that existed during *United States v. Nixon* (1974), when a Court controlled by a nominal Republican majority[62] became involved only after Republican support for Nixon had started to fade (thus reducing whatever motivation Court Republicans might have otherwise had to come to the defense of their president), and where the Court faced an increasingly determined Democratic Congress, thus making a partisan pro-Nixon decision politically risky. It is also in contrast to the situation in *Clinton v. Jones* (1997), which raised a legal issue (whether presidents can be sued while in office) that did not inspire Democrats to fully mobilize in support of their candidate, perhaps because the full political implications of the decision only became clear in retrospect. Also unlike election 2000, there was a countervailing institutional interest in both the *Nixon* and *Clinton* cases that helped all the justices move beyond any partisan instincts they might have – the routine authority of courts to conduct criminal and civil trials without interference by the president.

The conservative justices therefore knew that an intervention would not be met by any institutional resistance or short-term retribution. In fact, given that their action would help ensure a federal government that would be fully controlled by the Republican Party for the first time in almost half a century, it seemed likely that, if anything, the Court's standing in the other branches (if not among partisan Democrats) would be enhanced, at least temporarily.[63] Even though the intervention might be seen as an assault on the institutional prerogatives of Congress, it was a safe bet that the Republican majority in the House would not complain if they were spared the need themselves to install Bush as president. Also, given the less than enthusiastic support that Gore was receiving from conservative Democrats, it was also possible that some Democratic senators did not completely object to the notion that they might be spared the predicament of having to stand by Gore if the election was thrown into the Congress.

Toward the end of the dispute, the justices also knew that public opinion polls showed that almost three-quarters of those surveyed (73 percent) said they would consider any Supreme Court decision to be legitimate. For reasons possibly having to do with larger changes in the political system relating to the expanded role of courts in U.S. politics, people expressed a preference for judicial resolution over more overtly political processes.[64] The justices could have used this trust to reassure the public about the legitimacy of the unfolding political processes (and thus help make the political option seem even less like a crisis), but apparently there was no motivation for that route. Finally, the conservatives also knew that a pro-Bush result would actually bring an immediate end to the dispute. They knew this, not only because of their political support in other institutions and in public opinion, but because the Gore campaign had made a public pledge just two days before the decision to live with whatever decision the Supreme Court handed down. Unlike other controversial court interventions – on issues such as slavery, the scope of federal power, criminal procedure, abortion, or civil rights – this one would not be a lingering target for groups motivated to mobilize against disagreeable judicial policy-making. In this case, there would be no policy-making as such to try to undo; there would just be a conclusive result along with some lingering resentment among some partisan critics.

Unfortunately for those of us who believe the Supreme Court decisions related to the 2000 election to be the classic exemplars in U.S. history of bad faith justice and contempt of politics, the same reasons that made it politically possible for the conservatives to act also make it unlikely that the decision will have the effect that Justice Breyer worried about in his dissenting opinion in *Bush v. Gore* – the risk that the decision will undermine "the public's confidence in the Court itself" or cause "a self-inflicted wound" that "may harm not just the Court, but the Nation." In this case, many people were generally supportive or relieved, a strong plurality of the country was extremely pleased, and another group was upset. It is not far off the mark to say that the conservatives more or less aligned themselves with the half of the country that was in power with the half of the country that was out of power.[65] This is not a strong starting point for undermining the overall reputation or authority of the Court in the political system. Some liberal activists and many law professors (who are much more liberal than the general population) have an ongoing sense of outrage about the decision, but it is unlikely that the intensity of feeling among rank-and-file Democrats will approach what we saw when, for example, segregationists began mobilizing against *Brown v. Board of Education* or right-to-lifers began mobilizing in response to *Roe v. Wade*. Not surprisingly, when President Bush made his first visit back to Florida in March 2001 there was no sign of angry voters, and planned protest rallies fizzled.[66]

Moreover, those who remain resentful have to face some difficult strategic questions. In particular, they are the most likely to feel tempted into supporting the equal protection rationale of the decision. In a classic example of making political lemonade out of lemons, some have even advocated an effort to build on the decision so as to "create a more robust constitutional examination of voting practices," including "variations in voting machines."[67] If this viewpoint gains liberal adherents, then the political opposition to *Bush v. Gore* may end up divided on the essential question of whether the decision should be condemned or, ironically, praised. A strategic choice to work within the confines of the decision could make it nearly impossible to convince the country that the Court's decision was legally indefensible. However, this sort of litigation strategy might be designed to embarrass the conservative majority into revealing the unprincipled nature of its commitment to equal protection in the 2000 presidential election dispute. It is unclear how much political mileage can be gained by trying to prove that the justices did not really mean what they said; after all, many people already believe that.

The final reason why this is likely to be a relatively harmless self-inflicted wound is that people who are upset about the individual decision in *Bush v. Gore* are not generally opposed to judicial power. There was a time in U.S. history where critics of the U.S. Supreme Court fought the justices by trying to strip away their authority to decide certain kinds of cases. In the early nineteenth century, Southerners who opposed federal judicial supervision of state court decisions repeatedly tried to strip the Court of its jurisdiction to hear appeals from state supreme courts. In the 1950s, members of Congress who were upset with the Court's decisions on domestic security repeatedly attempted to preclude the Court from hearing such cases. Similar measures were introduced after the Warren Court's reapportionment decisions.[68] But over the past forty years, with rare exception, political struggles against the Court have focused more on shaping the direction of judicial decision-making through litigation and appointments rather than power stripping.[69] From the viewpoint of Court critics, the justices on the whole still occasionally hand down decisions they like on important matters such as abortion rights, school prayer, free speech, women's rights, gay rights, and criminal procedure.[70] Even if the overall record of judicial decision-making of the Rehnquist Court is increasingly conservative, there are still incentives for critics to focus on shaping the direction of the Court rather than call into question the very idea of judicial power.[71]

It is possible that *Bush v. Gore* might increase the determination of some groups to change the composition of the Court. Many Democrats pledged no-holds-barred efforts when the issue of judicial appointments arises. Then again, the intensity of feeling among some of the faithful did not lead Senate Democrats to fight hard against George Bush's extremely conservative nominee for attorney general, John Ashcroft, who was eventually sworn into office by his good friend Justice Clarence Thomas. Nevertheless, it seems likely that a Supreme Court vacancy will open up old wounds, and opponents of a possible conservative appointment might wave *Bush v. Gore* like a bloody flag. A few more Senate Democrats may be more willing than would have been the case otherwise to stand up against conservative nominees. Still, we should keep in mind that in light of the recent history of Supreme Court appointments and in light of how closely divided this

Court has been on a range of important issues, there were already good reasons to think that the same groups that are mad about *Bush v. Gore* would also have strongly mobilized around a new appointment even if the Court had stayed out of this dispute. The depth of feeling might be different, but the effect on an already highly charged confirmation process will likely be marginal. If this is correct, then some of the early threats by angry Democrats to retaliate by resisting all appointments to the Supreme Court seems more like a projection of partisan frustration then an accurate assessment of the likely political consequences of the decision. If Democrats are looking for retaliation, they may have to settle for knowing that President Bush may not be able to successfully nominate Justice Scalia to be chief justice when Rehnquist retires. After all, given Scalia's leadership role in the Court's intervention, the perception of a political quid pro quo – chief justice for chief executive – would make such a nomination especially contentious.

Is it possible that this depth of feeling may eventually get translated into a wider societal consensus about the illegitimacy of *Bush v. Gore?* On this point it may be useful to revisit the history of *Brown v. Board of Education.* When the Court decided in 1954 to deploy its power and reputation against the practice of segregation, it was widely criticized as having acted in a way that was lawless and illegitimate. These criticisms came, not just from southern segregationists, but also from the legal community, including the mainstream bar, the Conference of Chief Justices of State Courts, and many elite law professors.[72] In his 1959 foreword to the *Harvard Law Review,* Harvard law professor Henry M. Hart, Jr., complained that the Warren Court "writes opinions which do not explain," and he urged judges to better appreciate "that reason in the life of the law and not just votes for your side." The justices enjoyed some marginal political support in parts of the Eisenhower administration (which had a Justice Department that cared about civil rights and a State Department that was worried about the affect of segregation on Cold War politics)[73] as well as more enthusiastic support from the civil rights movement. Despite that, the complaints of the elite bar about abuse of judicial power were readily translated into hostile political action by Congress, which was upset at the Court for its desegregation efforts and its domestic security decisions. The result was an infamous series of political attacks on the Court that forced the justices to backtrack on some controversial decisions and keep a low profile on others.[74] If one had to bet in the mid- to late-1950s whether the decision in *Brown* would improve or undermine the Court's reputation, all the safe money would have been against the justices.

All of this changed, however, once the country began moving politically in the direction that had been anticipated by the Court in the *Brown* decision. In the words of the late Robert McCloskey, a Court that had lost the traditional support of the business community and earned enemies among white Southerners eventually "acquired some new champions" among "Negroes and Northern liberals of various types." As a result of the 1964 election, conservative antijudicialism "was for the first time being associated with one of the worst popular defeats in electoral history," and President Johnson "helped carry into office an extra contingent of liberal congressmen [and] to decimate the array of those most likely to join an anti-Court movement." The apparent lesson is that while "resistance and retaliation from some quarters may tend to restrict the Court's power, . . . support from other quarters may simultaneously augment it," so in the end the Court's capability and reputation depends largely "on a preponderance of friends over enemies."[75] By the mid-1960s, a case that seemed destined to be an exemplar of illegitimate decision-making was transformed into the modern exemplar of U.S. constitutional law.

Critics of *Bush v. Gore* who are hoping to convince the country that it should share their legitimate disdain have a hard road ahead. In particular, unlike the critics of *Brown,* they do not have aggressive allies in the Congress of the United States, and they do not have entire communities of people willing to engage in massive civil and violent disobedience to challenge the Court. However, because larger political contexts are so central to the Court's overall power and reputation, there are reasons to think that the short-term political legacy of *Bush* may be affected by the outcomes of the elections of 2002 and 2004. If Bush and the Republicans consolidate their power and their electoral support to the point where there are stronger Republican majorities in the Senate after 2002 and a (re)elected President Bush in 2004, then despite the complaints of elite law professors about the legal sloppiness and bad faith of the Court's decision, it is likely that public opinion will continue to look back on the decision with a sense of gratitude. On the other hand, if Democrats are able to mobilize outrage over election 2000 or dissatisfaction with a Bush presidency into political gains in the Senate after 2002 – and especially if Democrats are able to retake the White House in 2004 – then it is possible that the decision in *Bush v. Gore* may be reinterpreted as the illegitimate efforts of determined conservative partisans to steal an election. Of course, at this stage, it is less important to offer predictions than to place on the record what appears to be the sheer contingency of the judgment of history on the meaning of these important events.

Whatever happens in the political realm, the justices' role in election 2000 will no doubt remain a touchstone of academic and legal commentary about the Supreme Court. For some it will be placed within a larger context of cases beginning with *Reynolds v. Sims* and *Baker v. Carr* – part of a more general historical process involving the weakening of the traditional "political questions doctrine" and the expanded application of the equal protection clause to voting rights and democratic processes. At least one scholar has suggested that the case reflects a broader conservative inclination to impose order on democratic politics.[76] Others may see it as another extension of what they consider the general judicialization of politics, associated with the post-1960s Court getting more and more involved in policy issues that had previously been left to legislatures.[77] If this happens then, as Jack Balkin points out, slowly, over time, by a process that has already begun, the arguments that would have appeared "off the wall" to almost any legal scholar before November 2000 will become more familiar;[78] in the words of Mark Tushnet, the decision will be "renormalized."[79] If that happens it would be a disappointing case of revisionism, made possible by an unfortunate professional bias in favor of reconciling court opinions with other court opinions at higher and higher levels of theoretical abstraction. It would distract attention away from what is truly distinctive about the majority's behavior – the unprecedented judicial hubris in taking advantage of a favorable political environment to engage in unacceptable partisan decision-making. As such, the case more properly belongs in what Balkin refers to as the "anticanon," exemplars of judicial mistakes or abuses. Even in the anticanon it should hold a special place – not because it was uniquely evil (plenty of other decisions did much more harm), but because the mistake it represents was not a mistake of constitutional principle but rather the absence of any genuine concern about principle. At a minimum, the case should be remembered as a rare example of low politics within the Marble Temple.

The Supreme Court's decisions in the presidential election dispute are not the only times when the justices have taken advantage of a political context to ignore the law and indulge their political preferences. Consider the case that Chief Justice Rehnquist declared to be "precisely parallel" to what the Court was doing in *Bush v. Gore*. At issue in *Bouie v. City of Columbia* (1964) was a state conviction of civil rights demonstrators who had been involved in a sit-in. They had been allowed to enter Eckerd's Drug Store in Columbia, South Carolina, to shop, but when they attempted to sit at a segregated lunch counter they were asked to leave. When they refused they were arrested and prosecuted under a trespass statute that prohibited "entry on lands of another after notice" that their entry was prohibited. The state supreme court upheld the conviction, explaining that the trespass statute had always been interpreted to cover both prohibited entries and refusals to leave. There was very little precedent for the U.S. Supreme Court to second-guess this sort of state court interpretations of its own criminal laws; however, in this case, the justices reversed the conviction on the grounds that the state court had "unforeseeably and retroactively" changed the meaning of the trespass statute by (essentially) adding a "would not leave" component to a "do not enter" statute. The three dissenters pointed out that no one could reasonably believe that he was invulnerable to a trespass prosecution once he got through the door of a building and thus could stay put even over the objections of the property owner.

The Court's more aggressive posture toward this state court was predicated on the justices' political sympathies for the civil rights movement and their belief that it was appropriate to give these demonstrators as much federal judicial protection as possible. The case is now regarded by many as a flawed Supreme Court precedent on the meaning of due process "notice" requirements in the criminal setting and an extremely unusual example of the Court second-guessing a state court interpretation of state law.[80] Still, most people acknowledge that the political motivation behind the decision was, well, respectable.[81] The justices knew that, after this decision, it would no longer be necessary to use strained legal theories to protect lunch counter sit-in demonstrators; the case was decided right before passage of the Civil Rights Act of 1964, which made it unlawful to discriminate in public accommodations. In other words, they could be fairly confident that this was a decision for this day and train only, a manipulation of the law designed mostly to help out two brave college students whose efforts help set in motion the events that would lead to the passage of the Civil Rights Act.

As a final way of gaining a perspective on the acceptability of the Supreme Court's actions during election 2000, we would all do well to contrast the political motives, and the sense of the greater good, behind this "precisely parallel" case against those that drove the majority in *Bush v. Gore*, and then ask which is the more excusable departure from the normal obligations of good faith judging.

Unlike Al Gore in 2000, Samuel J. Tilden in 1877 never offered his Republican opponent a concession. Democrats called him "President Tilden" throughout Rutherford B. Hayes's term in office. A year after the election, in a speech from the steps of his mansion on Gramercy Park in New York, Tilden called Hayes's victory "the greatest political crime of our history," adding that "the people got robbed . . . of the dearest rights of American citizens. . . . Such a usurpation must never occur again."[82]

Just weeks after the Supreme Court's decision in *Bush v. Gore*, Chief Justice Rehnquist gave a history lecture to the John Carroll Society, a Roman Catholic service organization. His topic was the disputed 1876 presidential election. He noted that during that crisis Hayes and Tilden dispatched lawyers to Florida, and he added jokingly that "there were no early morning flights out of Reagan National Airport to Miami in those days." In particular, though, he wanted to talk about Justice Joseph Bradley, the Republican swing vote on the commission that gave the presidency to Hayes. Rehnquist acknowledged that "the practice of Supreme Court Justices serving on the Electoral Commission raised a question at that time that has recurred since," and he acknowledged that "there are obviously very good reasons for members of the Court to say 'no' when asked." However, he also noted that "the argument on the other side is that there is a national crisis, and only you can avert it. It may be very hard to say 'no.'"[83]

In these comments, Rehnquist seemed to suggest that the Court should be seen as having performed a service to the country by helping to avert a national crisis. There is a vital difference, however, between the position in which Justice Bradley found himself and the Chief Justice's position in 2000. Bradley and his companions, Republicans and Democrats, were asked by both political parties in the Congress to assist in the resolution of an election crisis. By contrast, the chief justice and his conservative companions were effectively told by the Congress in 1887 to stay out; nevertheless, they decided to intervene at the request of one candidate over the objection of the other candidate as well as over those of the other members of the Court.

During debates on the passage of the Electoral Count Act of 1887, Senator Sherman explained why the U.S. Supreme Court was being asked to stay out of this process should it arise again:

> Another plan which has been proposed in the debates at different times and I think also in the constitutional convention, was to allow questions of this kind to be certified at once to the Supreme Court for its decisions in case of a division between the two Houses. If the House should be one way and the Senate the other, then it was proposed to let the case be referred directly to the prompt and summary decision of the Supreme

Court. But there is a feeling in this country that we ought not to mingle our great judicial tribunal with political questions, and therefore this proposition has not met with much favor. It would be a very grave fault indeed and a very serious objection to refer a political question in which the people of the country were aroused, about which their feelings were excited, to this great tribunal, which after all has to sit upon the life and property of all the people of the United States. It would tend to bring that court into public odium of one or the other of the two great parties. Therefore that plan may probably be rejected as an unwise provision. I believe, however, that it is the provision made in other countries.[84]

In light of this, and in light of the partisan nature of the request to intervene, it should have been the easiest thing for our Supreme Court justices to just say no, even if they believed that there were problems with the Florida Supreme Court's decisions. Of course, four justices did say no – not because they were less patriotic than their colleagues, but because they understood that the process set up by the Congress was designed to encourage a state-based system of dispute resolution to be monitored by the Congress. Their willingness to defer to that process exposed how wrong the majority was at the end of *Bush v. Gore* when they declared that they were second to none in their "admiration of the Constitution's design to leave the selection of the President to the people, through their legislatures, and to the political sphere."

Some who are more cynical about judicial power might respond that partisan justice was inevitable under the circumstances. Even before Justice Stevens's lament, they had lost faith in the idea of the judge as an impartial guardian of the rule of law. However, when we look at the record of all the judges who honestly were "forced to confront" legal disputes relating to this presidential election, we see that the judiciary performed much better than these critics might have thought likely. With one stark exception, the record is remarkably consistent with our reasonable expectation that judges, if they so choose, can avoid partisan decision-making, even in the most extraordinary circumstances. Still, that one exception looms large.

As a result the Court has brought itself "into public odium of one or the other of the two great parties." If *Bush v. Gore* was seen by many at the time as providing some quick relief, then perhaps now that we are no longer in the heat of the moment we can reflect more calmly on whether it is best for the country, and the Supreme Court, that this institution be allowed to make decisions that result in the election of a president favored by a five-member majority. However convenient some consider the result, those five votes should not have counted as much as they did, particularly since we know that too many of our justices cannot resist the temptation to engage in unprincipled partisan decision-making.

APPENDIX A

PROVISIONS OF THE U.S. CONSTITUTION
RELATING TO ELECTION 2000 LITIGATION

The U.S. Constitution

ARTICLE II
Section 1

The executive Power shall be vested in a President of the United States of America. He shall hold his Office during the Term of four Years, and, together with the Vice President, chosen for the same Term, be elected, as follows

Each State shall appoint, in such Manner as the Legislature thereof may direct, a Number of Electors, equal to the whole Number of Senators and representatives to which the State may be entitled in the Congress: but no Senator or Representative, or Person holding an Office of Trust or Profit under the United States, shall be appointed an Elector. . . .

The Congress may determine the Time of chusing the Electors, and the Day on which they shall give their Votes; which Day shall be the same throughout the United States.

AMENDMENT XII
(Ratified in 1804)

The Electors shall meet in their respective states and vote by ballot for President and Vice-President, one of whom, at least, shall not be an inhabitant of the same state with themselves; they shall name in their ballots the person voted for as President, and in distinct ballots the person voted for as Vice-President, and they shall make distinct lists of all persons voted for as President, and of all persons voted for as Vice-President, and of the number of votes for each, which lists they shall sign and certify, and transmit sealed to the seat of the government of the United States, directed to the President of the Senate; — The President of the Senate shall, in the presence of the Senate and House of Representatives, open all the certificates and the votes shall then be counted; — The person having the greatest number of votes for President, shall be the President, if such number be a majority of the whole number of Electors appointed; and if no person have such majority, then from the persons having the highest numbers not exceeding three on the list of those voted for as President, the House of Representatives shall choose immediately, by ballot, the President. But in choosing the President, the votes shall be taken by states, the representation from each state having one vote; a quorum for this purpose shall consist of a member or members from two-thirds of the states, and a majority of all the states shall be necessary to a choice. . . .

AMENDMENT XIV
(Ratified in 1868)
Section 1

All persons born or naturalized in the United States, and subject to the jurisdiction thereof, are citizens of the United States and of the State wherein they reside. No State shall make or enforce any law which shall abridge the privileges or immunities of citizens of the United States; nor shall any State deprive any person of life, liberty, or property, without due process of law; nor deny to any person within its jurisdiction the equal protection of the laws.

APPENDIX B
PROVISIONS OF FEDERAL STATUTORY LAW
RELATING TO ELECTION 2000 LITIGATION

United States Code
Title III. The President
Chapter 1: Presidential Elections and Vacancies

§ 1. Time of appointing electors

The electors of President and Vice President shall be appointed, in each State, on the Tuesday next after the first Monday in November, in every fourth year succeeding every election of a President and Vice President.

§ 2. Failure to make choice on prescribed day

Whenever any State has held an election for the purpose of choosing electors, and has failed to make a choice on the day prescribed by law, the electors may be appointed on a subsequent day in such a manner as the legislature of such State may direct.

§ 5. Determination of controversy as to appointment of electors

If any State shall have provided, by laws enacted prior to the day fixed for the appointment of the electors, for its final determination of any controversy or contest concerning the appointment of all or any of the electors of such State, by judicial or other methods or procedures, and such determination shall have been made at least six days before the time fixed for the meeting of the electors, such determination made pursuant to such law so existing on said day, and made at least six days prior to said time of meeting of the electors, shall be conclusive, and shall govern in the counting of the electoral votes as provided in the Constitution, and as hereinafter regulated, so far as the ascertainment of the electors appointed by such State is concerned.

§ 6. Credentials of electors; transmission to Archivist
of the United States and to Congress; public inspection

It shall be the duty of the executive of each State, as soon as practicable after the conclusion of the appointment of the electors in such State by the final ascertainment, under and in pursuance of the laws of such State providing for such ascertainment, to communicate by registered mail under the seal of the State to the

Archivist of the United States a certificate of such ascertainment of the electors appointed, setting forth the names of such electors and the canvass or other ascertainment under the laws of such State of the number of votes given or cast for each person for whose appointment any and all votes have been given or cast; and it shall also thereupon be the duty of the executive of each State to deliver to the electors of such State, on or before the day on which they are required by section 7 of this title to meet, six duplicate-originals of the same certificate under the seal of the State; and if there shall have been any final determination in a State in the manner provided for by law of a controversy or contest concerning the appointment of all or any of the electors of such State, it shall be the duty of the executive of such State, as soon as practicable after such determination, to communicate under the seal of the State to the Archivist of the United States a certificate of such determination in form and manner as the same shall have been made; . . .

§ 7. Meeting and vote of electors

The electors of President and Vice President of each State shall meet and give their votes on the first Monday after the second Wednesday in December next following their appointment at such place in each State as the legislature of such State shall direct.

§ 15. Counting electoral votes in Congress

Congress shall be in session on the sixth day of January succeeding every meeting of the electors. The Senate and House of Representatives shall meet in the Hall of the House of Representatives at the hour of 1 o'clock in the afternoon on that day, and the President of the Senate shall be their presiding officer. Two tellers shall be previously appointed on the part of the Senate and two on the part of the House of Representatives, to whom shall be handed, as they are opened by the President of the Senate, all the certificates and papers purporting to be certificates of the electoral votes, which certificates and papers shall be opened, presented, and acted upon in the alphabetical order of the States, beginning with the letter A; and said tellers, having then read the same in the presence and hearing of the two Houses, shall make a list of the votes as they shall appear from the said certificates; and the votes having been ascertained and counted according to the rules in this subchapter provided, the result of the same shall be delivered to the President of the Senate, who shall thereupon announce the state of the vote, which announcement shall be deemed a sufficient declaration of the persons, if any, elected President and Vice President of the United States, and, together with a list of the votes, be entered on the Journals of the two Houses. Upon such reading of any such certificate or paper, the President of the Senate shall call for objections, if any. Every objection shall be made in writing, and shall state clearly and concisely, and without argument, the ground thereof, and shall be signed by at least one Senator and one Member of the House of Representatives before the same shall be received. When all objections so made to any vote or paper from a State shall have been received and read, the Senate shall thereupon withdraw, and such objections shall be submitted to the Senate for its decision; and the Speaker of the House of Representatives shall, in like manner, submit such objections to the House of Representatives for its decision; and no electoral vote or votes from any State which shall have been regularly given by electors whose appointment has been lawfully certified to according to section 6 of this title from which but one return has been received shall be rejected, but the two Houses concurrently may reject the vote or votes when they agree that such vote or votes have not been so regularly given by electors whose appointment has been so certified. If more than one return or paper purporting to be a return from a State shall have been received by the President of the Senate, those votes, and those only, shall be counted which shall have been regularly given by the electors who are shown by the determination mentioned in section 5 of this title to have been appointed, if the determination in said section provided for shall have been made, or by such successors or substitutes, in case of a vacancy in the board of electors so ascertained, as have been appointed to fill such vacancy in the mode provided by the laws of the State; but in case there shall arise the question which of two or more of such State authorities determining what electors have been appointed, as mentioned in section 5 of this title, is the lawful tribunal of such state, the votes regularly given of those electors, and those only, of such State shall be counted whose title as electors the two Houses, acting separately, shall concurrently decide is supported by the decision of such State so authorized by its law; and in such case of more than one return or paper purporting to be a return from a State, if there shall have been no such determination of the question in the State aforesaid, then those votes, and those only, shall be counted which the two Houses shall concurrently decide were cast by lawful electors appointed in accordance with the laws of the State, unless the two Houses, acting separately, shall concurrently decide such votes not to be the lawful votes of the legally appointed electors of such State. But if the two Houses shall disagree in respect of the counting of such votes, then, and in that case, the votes of the electors whose appointment shall have been certified by the executive of the State, under the seal thereof, shall be counted. When the two Houses have voted, they shall immediately again meet, and the presiding officer shall then announce the decision of the questions submitted. No votes or papers from any other State shall be acted upon until the objections previously made to the votes or papers from any State shall have been finally disposed of.

APPENDIX C

PROVISIONS OF FLORIDA ELECTION LAW RELATING TO THE ELECTION 2000 LITIGATION

The 2000 Florida Statutes
Title IX
Electors and Elections
Chapter 101: Voting Methods and Procedure

§ 101.011. Voting by paper ballot

(1) In counties where paper ballots are used, each elector shall be given a ballot by the inspector. Before delivering the ballot to the elector, one of the inspectors shall write his or her initials or name on the stub attached to the ballot; then the elector shall, without leaving the polling place, retire alone to a booth or compartment provided, and place an "X" mark after the name of the candidate of his or her choice for each office to be filled, and likewise mark an "X" after the answer he or she desires in case of a constitutional amendment or other question submitted to a vote.

§ 101.151. Specifications for general election ballot [paper ballots]

(4) The names of the candidates of the party which received the highest number of votes for Governor in the last election in which a Governor was elected shall be placed first under the heading for each office, together with an appropriate abbreviation of party name; the names of the candidates of the party which received the second highest vote for Governor shall be second under the heading for each office, together with an appropriate abbreviation of the party name.

§ 101.5609. Ballot Requirements [for electronic voting systems]

(2) The ballot information shall, as far as practicable, be in the order of arrangement provided for paper ballots. . . .

§ 101.5614. Canvass of returns

(5) . . . No vote shall be declared invalid or void if there is a clear indication of the intent of the voter as determined by the canvassing board. . . .

(6) If an elector marks more names than there are persons to be elected to an office or if it is impossible to determine the elector's choice, the elector's ballot shall not be

counted for that office, but the ballot shall not be invalidated as to those names which are properly marked. . . .

(8) The return printed by the automatic tabulating equipment, to which has been added the return of write-in, absentee, and manually counted votes, shall constitute the official return of the election. . . .

§ 101.62. Request for absentee ballots

(1)(b) The supervisor may accept a written or telephonic request for an absentee ballot from the elector, or, if directly instructed by the elector, a member of the elector's immediate family, or the elector's legal guardian. . . . The person making the request must disclose: The name of the elector for whom the ballot is requested; the elector's address; the last four digits of the elector's social security number; the registration number on the elector's registration identification card; the requester's name; the requester's address; the requester's social security number and, if available, driver's license number; the requester's relationship to the elector; and the requester's signature (written requests only).

§ 101.67. Safekeeping of mailed ballots; deadline for receiving absentee ballots

(2) All marked absent electors' ballots to be counted must be received by the supervisor by 7 P.M. the day of the election. All ballots received thereafter shall be marked with the time and date of receipt and filed in the supervisor's office. . . .

§ 104.047. Absentee ballots and voting; violations

(2) Except as provided in s. 101.62 or s. 101.655, any person who requests an absentee ballot on behalf of an elector is guilty of a felony of the third degree, . . .

Chapter 102: Conducting Elections and Ascertaining the Results

§ 102.111. Elections Canvassing Commission

(1) Immediately after certification of any election by the county canvassing board, the results shall be forwarded to the Department of State concerning the election of any federal or state officer. The Governor, the Secretary of State, and the Director of the Division of Elections shall be the Elections Canvassing Commission. The Elections Canvassing Commission shall, as soon as the official results are compiled from all counties, certify the returns of the election and determine and declare who has been elected for each office. . . . If the county returns are not received by the Department of State by 5 P.M. of the seventh day following an election, all missing

counties shall be ignored, and the results shown by the returns on file shall be certified.

§ 102.112. Deadline for submission of
county returns to the Department of State; penalties

(1) The county canvassing board or a majority thereof shall file the county returns for the election of a federal or state officer with the Department of State immediately after certification of the election results. Returns must be filed by 5 P.M. on the 7th day following the first primary and general election and by 3 P.M. on the 3rd day following the second primary. If the returns are not received by the department by the time specified, such returns may be ignored and the results on file at that time may be certified by the department.

(2) The department shall fine each board member $200 for each day such returns are late, the fine to be paid only from the board member's personal funds. . . .

§ 102.141. County canvassing boards; duties

(1) The county canvassing board shall be composed of the supervisor of elections; a county court judge, who shall act as chair; and the chair of the board of county commissioners. . . .

(4) If the returns for any office reflect that a candidate was defeated or eliminated by one-half of a percent or less of the votes cast for such office, that a candidate for retention to a judicial office was retained or not retained by one-half of a percent or less of the votes cast on the question of retention, or that a measure appearing on the ballot was approved or rejected by one-half of a percent or less of the votes cast on such measure, the board responsible for certifying the results of the vote on such race or measure shall order a recount of the votes cast with respect to such office or measure. A recount need not be ordered with respect to the returns for any office, however, if the candidate or candidates defeated or eliminated from contention for such office by one-half of a percent or less of the votes cast for such office request in writing that a recount not be made. Each canvassing board responsible for conducting a recount shall examine the counters on the machines or the tabulation of the ballots cast in each precinct in which the office or issue appeared on the ballot and determine whether the returns correctly reflect the votes cast. If there is a discrepancy between the returns and the counters of the machines or the tabulation of the ballots cast, the counters of such machines or the tabulation of the ballots cast shall be presumed correct and such votes shall be canvassed accordingly.

§ 102.166. Protest of election returns; procedure

(1) Any candidate for nomination or election, or any elector qualified to vote in the election related to such candidacy, shall have the right to protest the returns of the election as being erroneous by filing with the appropriate canvassing board a sworn, written protest.

(2) Such protest shall be filed with the canvassing board prior to the time the canvassing board certifies the results for the office being protested or within 5 days after midnight of the date the election is held, whichever occurs later.

(4)(a) Any candidate whose name appeared on the ballot, any political committee that supports or opposes an issue which appeared on the ballot, or any political party whose candidates' names appeared on the ballot may file a written request with the county canvassing board for a manual recount. The written request shall contain a statement of the reason the manual recount is being requested.

(b) Such request must be filed with the canvassing board prior to the time the canvassing board certifies the results for the office being protested or within 72 hours after midnight of the date the election was held, whichever occurs later.

(c) The county canvassing board may authorize a manual recount. If a manual recount is authorized, the county canvassing board shall make a reasonable effort to notify each candidate whose race is being recounted of the time and place of such recount.

(d) The manual recount must include at least three precincts and at least 1 percent of the total votes cast for such candidate or issue. In the event there are less than three precincts involved in the election, all precincts shall be counted. The person who requested the recount shall choose three precincts to be recounted, and, if other precincts are recounted, the county canvassing board shall select the additional precincts.

(5) If the manual recount indicates an error in the vote tabulation which could affect the outcome of the election, the county canvassing board shall:

(a) Correct the error and recount the remaining precincts with the vote tabulation system;

(b) Request the Department of State to verify the tabulation software; or

(c) Manually recount all ballots.

(6) Any manual recount shall be open to the public.

(7) Procedures for a manual recount are as follows:

(a) The county canvassing board shall appoint as many counting teams of at least two electors as is necessary to manually recount the ballots. A counting team must have, when possible, members of at least two political parties. A candidate involved in the race shall not be a member of the counting team.

(b) If a counting team is unable to determine a voter's intent in casting a ballot, the ballot shall be presented to the county canvassing board for it to determine the voter's intent.

§ 102.168. Contest of election

(1) Except as provided in s. 102.171, the certification of election or nomination of any person to office, or of the result on any question submitted by referendum, may be contested in the circuit court by any unsuccessful candidate for such office or nomination thereto or by any elector qualified to vote in the election related to such candidacy, or by any taxpayer, respectively.

(3) The complaint shall set forth the grounds on which the contestant intends to establish his or her right to such office or set aside the result of the election on a submitted referendum. The grounds for contesting an election under this section are: . . .

(c) Receipt of a number of illegal votes or rejection of a number of legal votes sufficient to change or place in doubt the result of the election. . . .

(e) Any other cause or allegation which, if sustained, would show that a person other than the successful candidate was the person duly nominated or elected to the office in question or that the outcome of the election on a question submitted by referendum was contrary to the result declared by the canvassing board or election board. . . .

(8) The circuit judge to whom the contest is presented may fashion such orders as he or she deems necessary to ensure that each allegation in the complaint is investigated, examined, or checked, to prevent or correct any alleged wrong, and to provide any relief appropriate under such circumstances.

APPENDIX D

HIGHLIGHTS OF MAJOR CASES IN THE 2000
PRESIDENTIAL ELECTION DISPUTE

The following cases are mostly listed in the order in which they arose during the election dispute.

Fladell v. Palm Beach County Canvassing Board
  Issue: Was the design of Palm Beach's "butterfly ballot" illegal under state law and did it cause sufficient voter confusion to warrant a revote of the county?
  Decisions: On Nov. 20 Judge Jorge Labarga ruled he had no authority to order a revote in a presidential election. The Florida Supreme Court upheld Labarga's decision on Dec. 1.
  Comment: The case that launched the election 2000 disputes was eventually turned back by both a Republican trial court judge and the Democratic justices of the Florida high court.

Florida Democratic Party v. Palm Beach Canvassing Board
  Issue: Was the Palm Beach Canvassing Board violating state law by refusing to consider "dimpled chads" as possible votes during its manual recount of punch-card ballots?
  Decision: On Nov. 22 Judge Labarga ruled that state law required Palm Beach's Canvassing Board to consider whether the "intent of the voter" could be discerned from ballots with dimpled chads.
  Comment: A Republican judge interprets the state's "intent of the voter" standard in a way that was beneficial to Gore. Judge Labarga rules in a later case that he cannot require the canvassing board to treat dimpled chads as votes, if after reviewing them they decide otherwise.

Siegel v. LePore
Touchston v. McDermott
  Issue: Did the "selective" and "standardless" ongoing manual recounts in Florida violate the due process and equal protection clauses of the Fourteenth Amendment, and if so, did the irreparable harm that might come from these violations justify the granting of an emergency injunction to stop them?

Decision: On Nov. 13, U.S. district court judge Donald Middlebrooks refused to issue an emergency injunction. That decision was upheld by the Eleventh Circuit Court of Appeals on Nov. 17, but they also agreed to hear arguments in the case within a few weeks. On Dec. 6, in an 8 to 4 ruling, the judges on the court of appeal refused to make a decision on the ultimate constitutional issues, but upheld Middlebrooks's decision on the grounds that there was no showing that continued recounts would cause "irreparable harm" to Bush.

Comment: The decision in this case represented a bipartisan coalition of five Democratic appointees and three Republicans; all four of the dissenters were Republicans. While focusing on different issues, the hostility of these dissenters to the recount practices was similar to that which was eventually expressed by the concurring justices in *Bush v. Gore.*

McDermott v. Harris

Issue: Did the Florida secretary of state have the authority to refuse to accept returns from counties engaged in ongoing recounts after a putative Nov. 14 deadline?

Decision: After first ruling that the secretary of state could not simply ignore late returns for no reason, Judge Terry Lewis ruled on Nov. 17 that it was within the Secretary's discretion to refuse to include late-filed returns in the certified results of the election.

Comment: An example of a Democratic judge making a decision that was a serious blow to Gore. The decision also triggered a response from the Florida Supreme Court when the appeal was folded into the following case.

Palm Beach County Canvassing Board v. Harris

Issue: Originally about whether the county had the authority to conduct manual recounts even without evidence of machine error, the case became the vehicle for reviewing Judge Lewis's decision in the *McDermott* case.

Decisions: On Nov. 21, the Florida Supreme Court ruled unanimously that while the secretary of state "may ignore" late-filed returns in certain circumstances, she could not ignore them in this case, when manual recounts had been legally authorized but could not be completed in time and when a delay in receiving the ballots would better accommodate the voting rights of Florida citizens without putting at risk their participation in the Electoral College. The Court ordered the secretary to accept recount results up through 5 P.M. on Nov. 26. The case was appealed to the U.S. Supreme Court (see *Bush v. Palm Beach County Canvassing Board*); that court overturned the case and sent it back to the Florida justices so they could better explain the legal basis for the decision. On Dec. 11, the Florida Supreme Court issued its clarifying opinion, over the dissent of Chief Justice Wells. *Comment:* Many Republicans considered this decision of the Democratic Florida Supreme Court to be lawless and partisan; by contrast, many Democrats considered it an appropriate reconciliation of a poorly written and conflicting election code. In the end, its actual impact on the election 2000 dispute was minimal, since two of the three counties that were hoping for more time to complete their recounts either did not finish in time (Palm Beach) or gave up trying (Miami-Dade).

Bush v. Palm Beach County Canvassing Board

Issue: By ruling against the Florida secretary of state's discretion to ignore county returns after Nov. 14, did the Florida Supreme Court "change the law" of presidential elections in Florida in violation of Article II, Section 1 of the Constitution, which authorizes the Florida legislature to choose the manner of appointing presidential electors, or 3 U.S.C. § 5, which instructs states to resolve election disputes in accordance with the laws that were in place before election day?

Decision: On Dec. 4 the U.S. Supreme Court handed down a 9 to 0 per curiam decision vacating the Florida Supreme Court's decision in *Palm Beach County Canvassing Board v. Harris* and remanding the case back to the Florida justices for a clarification on whether their decision was based exclusively on the Florida statutes or whether it might also be based on elements of Florida law that were not passed by the legislature, such as the Florida Constitution or the court's own "equitable" powers.

Comment: Behind the apparent consensus was a bitterly divided Court. The four justices who would end up dissenting in *Bush v. Gore* went along with vacating the decision on condition that it was also remanded to the state court so that it could have another chance. However, because the decision came more than a week after the secretary of state had certified the election for Bush, it was not immediately clear what would be the effect of the Court's ruling against the Florida court's extension of the certification deadline. This decision was also overshadowed by Judge Sauls's decision in the Gore contest suit, *Gore v. Harris.*

Gore v. Miami-Dade County Canvassing Board

Issue: Was Miami-Dade required to complete a manual recount that it had previously authorized?

Decision: On Nov. 23, the Florida Supreme Court refused to order Miami-Dade to restart its recount.

Comment: An indication two days after the Court's decision in *Palm Beach County* that the Florida justices were not willing to help Gore at every opportunity.

Taylor v. Martin County Canvassing Board
Jacobs v. Seminole County Canvassing Board

Issue: Should absentee ballots in Martin and Seminole Counties be thrown out because county officials allowed Republican Party workers to fill in missing voter information on Republican absentee ballot applications?

Decisions: Taylor was decided by Judge Terry Lewis, and *Jacobs* by Judge Nikki Clark, each of whom ruled on Dec. 8 that despite ballot application irregularities no ballots would be ruled illegal and eliminated from the certified election results. Their decisions were upheld by the Florida Supreme Court on Dec. 12.

Comment: Two Democratic trial court judges and the Florida justices all pass on this opportunity to hand Gore the presidency by eliminating thousands of predominantly Republican absentee ballots.

Harris v. Florida Elections Canvassing Commission

Issue: Did the state's practice (pursuant to a consent decree with the U.S. government) of accepting absentee ballots that arrived after election day violate the Florida statutes and, in the context of a presidential election, also violate Article II, Section 1 of the U.S. Constitution, which gives state legislatures exclusive power to determine the method of choosing presidential electors?

Decisions: On Dec. 9, U.S. district court judge Maurice Paul ruled that the practice was legal despite the statutory language and despite evidence that it took place over the objections of the state legislature. A three-judge panel of the Eleventh Circuit Court of Appeals upheld the ruling two days later.

Comment: Four Republican judges focused much less on the question of whether the legislature's judgment was being thwarted than did the five conservatives on the U.S. Supreme Court in *Bush v. Palm Beach County Canvassing Board.* In both cases the results were helpful to Bush.

Gore v. Harris

Issue: Did the certified election results include a "receipt of a number of illegal votes or rejection of a number of legal votes sufficient to change or place in doubt the result of the election," and if so, should recounts of disputed (or never reviewed) "undervote" ballots begin in Miami-Dade and Palm Beach?

Decisions: On Dec. 4 Judge N. Sanders Sauls ruled against Gore on all aspects of his "contest" of the Florida election results. That decision was appealed to the

Florida Supreme Court, and on Dec. 8, in a 4 to 3 decision, the court ruled that there was sufficient evidence that the certified election results did not include "a number of legal votes sufficient to change or place in doubt" the results of the presidential election. The Florida justices also ruled that the most appropriate remedy was to manually recount all possible missed legal votes, i.e., so-called "undervotes" in the state that had never previously been inspected. This decision was appealed to the U.S. Supreme Court (see *Bush v. Gore*); that court overturned the decision and remanded it back to the Florida court. On Dec. 14, those justices ruled that in light of the U.S. Supreme Court's decision no further relief could be granted. A final opinion was released on Dec. 22.

Comment: It was the second time that the Florida court had attempted to authorize a recount of undervotes, and it resulted in the second intervention of the U.S. Supreme Court.

Bush v. Gore

Issue: Did the Florida Supreme Court violate the Article II, Section 1; 3 U.S.C. § 5; or the Fourteenth Amendment when it authorized a statewide recount of previously uninspected undervote ballots?

Decisions: On Dec. 9, just one day after the Florida court attempted to restart the recounts the five conservatives on the U.S. Supreme Court, over the strong written dissents of the other four justices, issued an emergency injunction halting the effort. On Dec. 12 a deeply divide Court ruled in a per curiam opinion that the recounts that were taking place under the state's general "intent of the voter" standard violated the equal protection clause of the Constitution because the standard made it possible for identical ballots to be treated in different ways by different counters. While this problem could potentially be remedied by having the standard made more clear and starting again, that option was not available because the majority ruled that Florida intended to resolve all election disputes by Dec. 12. Three members of the majority wrote separately to argue that the Florida Supreme Court's decision also "changed the law" in violation of Article II, Section 1 of the U.S. Constitution.

Comment: The next day Al Gore conceded the presidential election to George W. Bush.

NOTES

INTRODUCTION

1. For an overview of election law and examples of judicial decisions, see Issacharoff, Karlan, and Pildes (1998). This is not to say that judges have authority to resolve all election disputes. For example, the U.S. Constitution delegates to the House of Representatives the authority to resolve disputes involving the election of House members. The Florida Legislature, like other state legislatures, had similar authority over the election of its members. However, the existence of these special exceptions makes it clear that the involvement of judges in other election controversies reflects a typical and uncontroversial policy choice rather than an extraordinary occurrence.

2. Because only fifty-four presidential elections have taken place prior to 2000, some might suggest that presidential elections are thrown into court at a rate of once every fifty-five elections. But we should keep in mind that because of the Electoral College every presidential election is actually made up of many separate local decisions. That makes this development even more rare than it might appear when we say that it has happened once every 212 years (although there have been a few times, most notably in 1876 and 1960, when state courts have participated in some aspects of a dispute over presidential electors). In fact, just since 1980 we have had more than three hundred elections for president (held six separate times in each of the fifty states plus the District of Columbia) and only one of them has ended up in the court system. Then again, most elections are not close enough to make judicial battles over a few votes worthwhile.

3. An example of "better" might be the selection of Thomas Jefferson over Aaron Burr when these two candidates tied in 1800 (because of a defect in the original design of the Electoral College that instructed electors to cast two votes for president rather than one vote for president and one for vice president). Some people think an example of "worse" was the decision to pass over Andrew Jackson in favor of John Quincy Adams in 1824, despite Jackson's greater number of popular votes; however, the long-standing view that this represented a "corrupt bargain" between Adams and Henry Clay (rather than an example of representatives voting their constituents' preferences) has recently been challenged (see Jenkins and Sala 1998).

4. There have been other times when questions were raised about the electoral votes of a state but the election was nevertheless concluded since there were enough undisputed electoral votes to determine a winner. For example, in 1873 Congress refused to accept results from Arkansas and Louisiana, mostly because of the disruptive conditions associated with Reconstruction; they also decided not to count Georgia's three votes for Horace Greeley, who had died after the election but before the Electoral College met. Still, this has little effect on Grant's landslide Electoral College victory.

5. The original results were announced by the Republican state canvassing board, which reached its decision after discarding returns it considered fraudulent; this was enough to change a 94-vote lead by Tilden into a 922-vote margin of victory for Hayes. In December, the outgoing Republican governor certified the Hayes electors as duly appointed. A Florida circuit court ruled in January that the Tilden electors were duly elected, and in January the new Democratic governor sent a new certification to the Congress in favor of the Tilden electors.

6. In 2000, Republicans had a narrow majority in the House of Representatives. The Senate was evenly divided, but it was presided over by the vice president of the United States. Until the new administration was elected, this presiding officer was candidate Al Gore, and this gave Democrats control of the Senate for this period.

7. Explaining his decision against Tilden, Justice Miller said that the state court decisions might have been determinative if they had been handed down before the day when the electors cast their votes for president, but since it followed it by a month, it seemed too much like an attempt after the fact to change the results. Justice Clifford responded by noting that the state canvassing board did not announce its pro-Hayes decision until the day that the presidential electors were scheduled to vote, thus making it impossible for a court challenge to have been completed earlier.

8. For more on the election of 1876, see Fairman (1988), Dougherty (1906), Woodward (1951), and Haworth (1906); for a synthesis, see Stoner (2001).

9. 3 U.S.C. § 5. The 1887 act was folded into this statute, which is known as Title III of the U.S. Code (see appendix B).

10. 3 U.S.C. § 15.

11. Before 2000, the only other post–Electoral Count Act controversy over competing slates of electors occurred in 1960, when two slates came in from the new state of Hawaii under the signature of the same governor. The first slate went for the Republican candidate, but the governor sent a second slate right before Congress was scheduled to count the votes, after a court-ordered recount resulted in a razor-thin victory for the Democrats. The presiding officer of the Senate, presidential candidate Richard Nixon, declared that he would count the Democratic slate, and there was no objection from either House of Congress.

12. From *Casablanca* (Warner Bros., 1942).

13. For early arguments against this view of so-called "mechanical jurisprudence," see Pound (1908).

14. Stephenson (1999) documents that the U.S. Supreme Court has been an object of debate in at least one-fifth of all presidential elections. Recently there has been increased attention to judicial elections at the state level. See, for example, the "Justice for Sale" Web site put together by PBS's *Frontline* program, accessible at www.pbs.org/wgbh/pages/frontline/shows/justice/.

15. The leading work in political science on the influence of ideology on Supreme Court decision-making is Segal and Spaeth (1993) (soon to appear in a revised edition). For comprehensive overviews of this literature, focusing on a range of courts, see Baum (1997); Cross (1997); George (1998); Gillman (2001); Pinello (1999); Sisk, Heise, and Morriss (1998); and Songer, Sheehan, and Haire (2000). Most people have not thought much about whether the extent of ideological voting differs depending on what court or what issues one is discussing,

but it may not be too surprising that some studies suggest that the influence of political ideology is most obvious on the U.S. Supreme Court – where the issues tend to be least settled and most controversial – and becomes progressively less observable when we look at state supreme courts, federal courts of appeal, and federal district courts (trial courts), where the issues are (by definition) more routine (Pinello 1999).

16. This approach to the study of judicial politics was known for some time as "political jurisprudence," a label provided by Martin Shapiro (1964, 1984). The classic effort in political science to explain Supreme Court decision-making in terms of the prevailing political consensus in the national government is Dahl (1957); for other examples, see Casper (1976), Clayton (1999), Friedman (1993), Graber (1998), Griffin (1996), Klarman (1996), McCloskey (2000), and Powe (2000).

17. Peretti (1999:133).

18. For a general overview of some of the literature on how the institutional features of Supreme Courts might shape the behavior of the justices, see Clayton and Gillman (1999) and Gillman and Clayton (1999).

19. For an overview of the political background of Supreme Court justices, see Epstein et al. (1996). For a broad survey of the political considerations that have gone into twentieth-century lower federal court appointments, see Goldman (1997). Goldman finds that between 60–73 percent of federal court appointments went to persons who could be labeled party "activists." The concurrent political activities of Supreme Court justices, from the first chief justice John Jay (who was a major foreign policy adviser to George Washington) to Abe Fortas (who was a major foreign policy adviser to Lyndon Johnson), are well known to Supreme Court historians. For another example, see Murphy (1982).

20. On the idea of good faith judging, see Burton (1992). Some political scientists argue that the influence of ideology proves that judges are not basing decisions on the law. But this conclusion is too harsh, since it wrongly assumes that it is possible to force all judges to arrive at the same decisions regardless of their background, experience, or values. For an overview and critique of the political science literature discounting the influence of "law" on judging, see Gillman (2001). One of the leading philosophers of law writing today – who has made a career insisting that judges should always act as if there is always one right answer to hard legal cases – even acknowledges that ideological influences (and thus some variations in the voting patterns of judges) are essential to any sort of honest interpretation of legal materials (see Dworkin 1996:37). This is why judges who defend their commitment to law might also declare "ho-hum" when someone points out that "judges' personal philosophies enter into their decision making" (Wald 1999:236; for another judge's comments, see Edwards 1985).

21. The leading study is by Lloyd (1995), who found that judges were a bit more likely to vote against reapportionment plans that were designed by the opposite party than to vote against a plan drawn up by their own party, but in general were most deferential to so-called nonpartisan plans. Note that while political scientists sometimes use a judge's partisan affiliation as a variable in studies in judicial behavior, in almost every case that variable is treated as a surrogate measure of the influence of political ideology (conservative-liberal effects) rather than as an indication of partisan voting. For example, in a study that found that Supreme Court justices are marginally more likely to support the positions of their appointing president (as represented by the solicitor general) than the positions of a different presi-

dent of the same party, the conclusion reached is not that justices are motivated by a desire to help particular politicians; it is that they are usually more ideologically in sync with their appointing president (in other words, Eisenhower Republicans are different than Reagan Republicans) (see Segal 1990).

22. The practice is known as "strategic retirement." For examples on the Supreme Court, see Atkinson (1999); for the U.S. Courts of Appeal, see Spriggs and Wahlbeck (1995).

23. There are other kinds of political considerations that judges take into account that should be distinguished from partisan decision-making. Judges on high courts often bargain with one another over the language of an opinion (see Maltzman, Spriggs, and Wahlbeck 2000; Murphy 1964). There are also times when judges choose to avoid certain kinds of decisions because they are worried that they might have a negative effect on the judiciary, either by embroiling it in a "political question" or inviting the wrath of another branch of government (see Epstein and Knight 1998; Graber 1995). For examples of the Warren Court's concerns about provoking a hostile congressional response in the late 1950s, see Powe (2000). Constitutional law experts know that the Supreme Court has also created "the political questions doctrine" as a legal basis for avoiding involvement in disputes that the justices think are constitutionally assigned to another branch of government under separation of powers principles (see Strum 1974).

24. See Shapiro (1981); see also Sweet (1999).

25. Schwartz (2000:5, 239). In his recommendations for reform, Schwartz added that "it is especially unwise to require the constitutional court to verify the results of a presidential election in a presidential system" (244).

26. There were Jeffersonian concerns when John Marshall's Court agreed to hear the case of Marbury v. Madison (1803) – which involved a partisan battle over judicial appointments – but despite Marshall's formal assertion of the power of judicial review, these concerns were mitigated when Marshall refused to order the Jeffersonian administration (which would have ignored him anyway) to give the disputed judgeship to the Federalist William Marbury. In the event that Jeffersonians were still nervous about Marshall's use of judicial power he also made it clear in Stuart v. Laird (1803) (through Justice Paterson's opinion) that he would not use the Court to prevent the Jeffersonians from repealing the despised Judiciary Act of 1801. See Graber (1999), O'Fallon (1992); see also United States v. More (1805) and O'Fallon (1993).

27. The "dominant national alliance" language is from Dahl (1957:293); see also Klarman (1996). This alliance with the political agenda of the national center was also central to Marshall's political success with the Jeffersonian Republicans (see Graber 1998). It also helps explain the Taney Court's involvement in the infamous Dred Scott case (Graber 1993; see also Powe 2000).

28. See Thompson (1975:262–63). For more conventional discussions of the rule of law or "legality" as a way of organizing politics, see Fuller (1964) and Shklar (1986). For more on the core concept of "impartial judgment" and the importance of judges offering acceptable justifications for their decisions, see Carter (1998:148–52).

29. Ewick and Silbey (1998:36).

30. See Lind and Tyler (1988).

31. See 28 U.S.C. § 455(a) (2000).

32. Some infamous examples include Justice Samuel Chase's extremely partisan behavior while overseeing trials against Jeffersonian Republicans in the late 1790s (leading to his im-

peachment once the Jeffersonians came to power in 1801) (see Whittington 1999) and Justice John McLean, otherwise known as the "politician on the Supreme Court," who was well known for his presidential ambitions while on the bench from 1830 through the outbreak of the Civil War (see Dougan 1992).

33. McCloskey (2000:12–13).

34. Caldeira and Gibson (1992:660). These authors note that opinion leaders and Court specialists are less likely to give the Court "diffuse support" because they are more likely to condition their support on whether the Court adopts their policy preferences.

35. Hughes (1928:55).

36. Caldeira and Gibson (1992:635–36, 659–60). The authors go on to suggest that the Warren Court's more activist agenda may have cost the Court some diffuse public support. For additional discussions of these issues, see Adamany and Grossman (1983); Caldeira (1986); Daniels (1973); Handberg (1984); Jaros and Roper (1980); Lehne and Reynolds (1978); Mondak (1991); Murphy and Tanenhaus (1968, 1990); Marshall (1989); Tanenhaus and Murphy 1981; Tyler (1990).

37. See Shapiro's (1981) discussion of mediation as central to the maintenance of judicial legitimacy.

38. Pinello (1999) reports that trial court judges are more likely than most other judges to reach the same decisions regardless of their political ideology.

39. On courthouse work groups and communities, see Eisenstein and Jacob (1977) and Nardulli, Eisenstein, and Flemming (1988).

40. See Balbus (1977).

41. The reputations of judges are also aided by the politics of judicial election or appointment, which ensures that most judges reflect the worldviews, and even the biases, of the community at large, which means that their personal reaction to cases is not likely to appear out of the ordinary to a good portion of the people who may be paying attention.

42. In response to an article that suggested that appellate court judges engaged in political decision-making, Judge Patricia Wald pointed out that "a large portion of our cases . . . have no apparent ideology to support or reject at all. . . . For my part, I cannot even imagine having personal feelings about the appropriate regulatory standards for 'retrofitted cell-burners' as opposed to 'wall-fired electric utility boilers'. . . ." (Wald 1999:237).

43. Edwards (1998:1359–60) reports that from 1995 to 1997, the D.C. Circuit had a dissent rate of around 2–3 percent and a dissent rate of 11–13 percent in cases where the court issued an opinion. Only half of these (already rare) dissents followed party-line divisions. "This is, in my view, extremely strong prima facie evidence of consensus among judges about the correct judgment in a given case" (see also Edwards 1985:630). For a different interpretation of this data and of the general phenomenon of dissent, see Revesz (1999:836–38) and Hensley and Johnson (1998). For an overview of research on so-called "easy cases," see Cross (1997:285–287).

44. The data through 1994 can be found in tables 3-1 and 3-4 in Epstein et al. (1996). In 1995, 34 percent of cases were unanimous and 12 percent were decided by one vote; in 1996, 42 percent were unanimous and 17 percent were decided by one vote; in 1997, the numbers were 46 percent and 15 percent, and in 1998, it was 32 percent and 15 percent. Thanks to Jeff Segal for providing the updated figures.

45. See Brown v. Board of Education (1954), Swann v. Charlotte-Mecklenburg Board of Education (1970). One recent study finds that in "politically salient" cases – that is, cases that

people care more about and pay more attention to – the justices are more likely to circulate repeated drafts of an opinion and to work longer on the final product as part of an effort to build stronger majorities (see Maltzman et al. 2000:122; see also Brenner 1990).

46. On the deliberations surrounding Brown v. Board of Education (1954), see Kluger (1976), Powe (2000); for United States v. Nixon (1974), see Woodward and Armstrong (1979).

47. This will be illustrated in the course of the narrative, but for now it is worth noting that the Gore campaign's greater willingness to show respect for judicial authority was mostly due to the fact that courts were his best hope at winning; by contrast, the vote leader Bush knew that litigation was a threat to his nominal victory, unless the point was to get a federal court to stop recount efforts.

48. As the respected authors of an election law casebook on this dispute summarized it, "once the votes are counted, every potential procedural and substantive decision becomes outcome determinative. There are ample reasons to believe that every claim put forward and every decision made will be the product of an attentive eye to the bottom-line result – or at least will be publicly perceived as such" (Issacharoff, Karlan, and Pildes 2001:3). They added that because of this, "this is an area in which courts have been acting and must continue to act with tremendous circumspection" since "the adjudication of claims that will alter the outcomes of high-profile elections threatens significant damage to the integrity of courts." The paradox, though, is that "the failure to provide for a judicial forum threatens to undermine the legitimacy of the political process itself" (3).

49. The previous record was thirty years earlier in the Pentagon Papers case, New York Times v. United States (1971), involving an ongoing injunction preventing a newspaper from publishing a story, in which a ruling was handed down five days after the appeal was granted.

50. Gibson (1983:9).

51. The classic statement on the need to incorporate legal analysis, political analysis, and normative critique comes from Robert McCloskey (1972). He was addressing an earlier generation of political scientists who suggested the separation of these elements of scholarly inquiry: "[There are] those who would confine all evaluation to the historical-technical category [of legal accuracy] and would pronounce it illegitimate even to consider the issues of power or ethics. There are others so dedicated to a value-oriented assessment that they regard legalistic strictures as mere pettifoggery, and probably still others who would prefer to think of the Court purely in terms of its power to govern. It might be sufficient comment on such viewpoints to say that, whatever our preferences, these three different judgment criteria persist in turning up in the debates over judicial behavior; we cannot tame the subject to our own liking, however pleasant this might" (293).

CHAPTER ONE

1. Peter Marks, "High Drama Unfolds on Anchor Desks," *New York Times,* Nov. 8, 2000, B1.

2. *Newsweek,* Nov. 6, 2000.

3. For an example of how political pundits focused on the "trifecta" of Pennsylvania, Michigan, and Florida, see Transcripts, Capital Gang, Nov. 4, 2000, www.cnn.com/TRANSCRIPTS/0011/04/cg.00.html.

4. Katharine Q. Seelye, "Sleep Waits as Al Gore Makes His Final Appeals," *New York Times,* Nov. 8, 2000, B2; Mike Clary, "All Eyes on Florida into the Night," *Los Angeles Times,* Nov. 8, 2000, A1, A23. Unless otherwise noted, all times refer to eastern standard time.

5. Evan Thomas and Michael Isikoff, "The Truth behind the Pillars," *Newsweek,* Dec. 25, 2000, 46–51.

6. For an overview of the mistakes by the media and by the Voter News Service, see Howard Kurtz, "Errors Plagued Night Polling Service," *Washington Post,* Dec. 22, 2000, on-line edition.

7. Mark Z. Barabak, "Candidates Struggle for Bare Margin of Victory," *Los Angeles Times,* Nov. 8, 2000, A21.

8. Josh Getlin and Jeffrey Gettleman, "TV News Badly Embarrassed by Bad Calls," *Los Angeles Times,* Nov. 9, 2000, A1.

9. Not everyone, though. Between 2:00 and 3:00 A.M., the audience for the network news was 225 percent higher than normal. Angie Cannon and Kenneth T. Walsh, "Messier by the Minute," *U.S. News and World Report Online,* filed Nov. 13, 2000, published Nov. 20, 2000, www.usnews.com.

10. Howard Fineman, "Battle Plans," *Newsweek,* Nov. 20, 2000, 13; David Von Drehle, Dan Balz, Ellen Nakashima, and Jo Becker, "Candidates Sensed Defeat – Then Mobilized for Recount," *Washington Post,* Jan. 28, 2001, A1.

11. Kevin Sack and Frank Bruni, "How Gore Stopped Short on His Way to Concede," *New York Times,* Nov. 9, 2000, A1; Richard T. Cooper and James Gerstenzang, "Drama Shifted on Sharp Eye, Cell Phones," *Los Angeles Times,* Nov. 9, 2000, A1. The now-legendary telephone exchange starts with Bush: "You mean to tell me, Mr. Vice President, you're retracting your concession?" Gore: "You don't have to be snippy about it." After Bush said that his brother Jeb had just assured him that Florida was his, Gore responded: "Let me explain something. Your younger brother is not the ultimate authority on this." Bush: "Well, Mr. Vice President, you need to do what you have to do." (Another version of the story replaced "younger brother" with "little brother" and "ultimate authority" with "final arbiter.") *Los Angeles Times,* Nov. 9, 2000, A21. The Florida statute requiring an automatic recount was Fla. Stat. § 102.141(3).

12. "Perspectives," *Newsweek,* Nov. 20, 2000, 9; Getlin and Gettleman, "TV News Badly Embarrassed." News organizations later released reports that were highly critical of their own performance during the controversy, and reforms were promised; Congress also held hearings. David Bauder, "CNN Vote Coverage Called 'Debacle,'" Associated Press, Feb. 2, 2001, dailynews.yahoo.com; Howard Kurtz, "Election Coverage Burned to a Crisp," *Washington Post,* Feb. 15, 2001, C1.

13. David Stout, "Gore's Lead in the Popular Vote Now Exceeds 500,000," *New York Times,* Dec. 30, 2000, on-line edition.

14. Mark Z. Barabak and Mike Clary, "Florida Recount Underway," *Los Angeles Times,* Nov. 9, 2000, A1; David E. Rosenbaum, "Bush Hold Slim Lead over Gore as Florida Recounts," *New York Times,* Nov. 10, 2000, A22.

15. Von Drehle et al., "Candidates Sensed Defeat."

16. For the full text of Bush's statement on the day after the election, see *New York Times,* Nov. 9, 2000, B3.

17. *New York Times,* Nov. 9, 2000, B3.

18. Barabak and Clary, "Florida Recount Underway." On the plane flying into Tallahassee, Gore operatives were briefed on recount procedures by the people who, literally, wrote the book on recounts – Timothy Downs, Chris Sautter, and John Hardin Young, authors of *The Recount Primer* (1994). Von Drehle et al., "Candidates Sensed Defeat."

19. Mike Clary, "Suddenly, the Other Bush Son Is the One in National Spotlight," *Los Angeles Times,* Nov. 10, 2000, A29.

20. Note the material reviewed in the leading law school casebook on the law of democracy in the United States (Issacharoff et al. 1998).

21. Barabak and Clary, "Florida Recount Underway." The NAACP held public hearings on Saturday, Nov. 11, to document general problems with voting in the African American community. See Mark Fineman and Lisa Getter, "Florida's Typical Election Day Is Often a Nightmare," *Los Angeles Times,* Nov. 12, 2000, A1. Later reports suggested that flawed efforts at expunging "felons" from voter rolls may have improperly suppressed black votes. See Gregory Palast, "Florida's Flawed 'Vote-Cleansing' Program," *Salon.com,* Dec. 4, 2000.

22. Near the end of the dispute, a contest to the election was filed alleging civil rights violations, but the lawsuit got nowhere. See Scott Gold, "Black Leaders Sue to Overturn Election," *Los Angeles Times,* Dec. 6, 2000, A24; Brown v. Stafford, Case No. 00-2878, Complaint to Contest Election, Dec. 5, 2000.

23. Ford Fessenden, "Candidates Should Be on the Same Page, Experts Say," *New York Times,* Nov. 10, 2000, A22.

24. Don Van Natta, Jr., and Dana Canedy, "Florida Democrats Say Ballot's Design Hurt Gore," *New York Times,* Nov. 9, 2000, B6; Mark Fineman and Mike Clary, "One Ballot, a Lot of Confusion," *Los Angeles Times,* Nov. 9, 2000, A41.

25. Richard Lacayo, "Eye of the Storm," *Time,* Nov. 20, 2000, 47.

26. By comparison, Buchanan received only 561 votes in Miami-Dade and 789 in Broward County, which both had higher populations than Palm Beach. Even the Buchanan campaign doubted that all those Palm Beach votes were intended for him. See Megan Garvey, "Bay Buchanan Sees Something Peculiar in Palm Beach Voting," *Los Angeles Times,* Nov. 10, 2000, A26. The 19,000 vote "disqualification" was also featured prominently in the banner headline in the *Los Angeles Times* on Nov. 9, 2000.

27. See Fla. Stat. § 101.151(3a)(4); Fla. Stat. § 101.5609(2).

28. Fladell v. Palm Beach County Canvassing Board, filed in the Circuit Court of the Fifteenth Judicial Circuit in and for Palm Beach County on Nov. 8, 2000.

29. On Nov. 13 these cases were consolidated with Fladell v. Palm Beach County Canvassing Board. See In Re: Multiple Cases Involving the 2000 Presidential Election, Administrative Order No. 2.061-11/00, issued by Walter N. Colbath, Jr., Chief Judge.

30. Prominent law professors such as Bruce Ackerman, Ronald Dworkin, and Cass Sunstein joined with celebrities such as Robert DeNiro, Bianca Jagger, Paul Newman, and Rosie O'Donnell to lend their names to a full-page ad in the *New York Times* on November 10; it called for a correction of this mistake either through the creation of a bipartisan electoral commission or by organizing a revote of Palm Beach County.

31. Mark Z. Barabak and Lisa Getter, "Florida Tally Still in Doubt," *Los Angeles Times,* Nov. 10, 2000, A27.

32. Rick Bragg and Dana Canedy, "Agony and Chagrin Over Votes Cast in Error," *New York Times*, Nov. 10, 2000, A1; Mark Fineman, "Where Balloting for Buchanan Surged, Outrage among Voters Who Detest Him," *Los Angeles Times*, Nov. 10, 2000, A1.

33. Stuart Taylor, Jr., "The Legal Road Ahead," *Newsweek*, Nov. 20, 2000, 16B.

34. Palm Beach was not the only county where the Democrats had reason to believe that confused voters may not have accurately conveyed their intentions on the ballot. In Duval County, the ballot listing the presidential candidates also spanned two pages, but not in a butterfly format; voters had to turn the page to see the rest of the candidates. Election officials and official voter instructions told people to "vote every page." For the presidential election this led some 26,000 voters to invalidate their ballots by overvoting. This included almost 9,000 invalidated ballots in African American communities around Jacksonville, which went 10 to 1 for Gore over Bush. Raymond Bonner with Josh Barbanel, "Democrats Rue a Ballot Design in a 2nd County," *New York Times*, Nov. 17, 2000, A1. While the Gore team did not litigate in Duval County, the Reverend Jesse Jackson and the Rainbow Coalition did file an unsuccessful election contest in Duval on Dec. 5, 2000, in the Brown v. Stafford case mentioned above (CV-00-2878).

35. "Statements by Daley and Christopher on Their Findings on the Florida Vote," *New York Times*, Nov. 10, 2000, A27.

36. Richard T. Cooper, "A Different Florida Vote, in Hindsight," *Los Angeles Times*, Dec. 24, 2000, A12; Eric Lichtblau, "Unless Fraud Is Found, Forget Revote, Experts Say," *Los Angeles Times*, Nov. 11, 2000, A15.

37. Don Van Natta, Jr., "Gore Lawyers Focus on Ballot in Palm Beach County," *New York Times*, Nov. 16, 2000, A25.

38. Eric Bailey and Jeffrey L. Rabin, "Election Workers' Nightmare," *Los Angeles Times*, Nov. 10, 2000, A28; Michael A. Hiltzik and Greg Miller, "Fiasco Reveals a Ballot System Full of Holes," *Los Angeles Times*, Nov. 11, 2000, A1. There were also questions about how well the machines aligned the ballots, and whether properly punched holes ended up somewhere other than their intended target. Later reports seemed to confirm this problem in some places. See Amy Driscoll, "Dade Undervotes Support Bush Win," *Miami Herald*, Feb. 26, 2001, on-line edition (reporting 2,058 ballot markings in spaces that had been assigned to no candidate).

39. Mark Z. Barabak and Bob Drogin, "Bush, Gore Camps Dig in as Manual Recount Is to Start," *Los Angeles Times*, Nov. 11, 2000, A1; Jonathan Chait, "Not Equal," *New Republic*, Dec. 25, 2000, 14–15.

40. Fla. Stat. § 102.166 (4)(5).

41. Cooper, "A Different Florida Vote."

42. "Statements by Daley and Christopher on Their Findings on the Florida Vote," *New York Times*, Nov. 10, 2000, A27. It should be noted that Gore's lawyers initially debated whether to push for a hand recount of the entire state. Daley and Christopher dismissed the idea on the grounds that the public would not stand for a recount of six million ballots, that the law required them to focus on problems in selected counties, and that they only needed a few votes. David Von Drehle, Ellen Nakashima, Susan Schmidt, and Ceci Connolly, "In Florida, Drawing the Battle Lines," *Washington Post*, Jan. 29, 2001, A1. In retrospect, the decision to ignore overvotes proved to be a serious mistake. At the time, however, the overvote

problem was mostly associated with the butterfly ballot mistakes (creating votes for Gore and Buchanan) and this problem seemed intractable. There was almost no public discussion of the possibility that an overvote ballot might reveal a clear intent to vote for Gore. Moreover, the successful Bush defense would have been the same either way. Still, Gore's recount specialists believed early on that his strategy was flawed. See Jake Tapper, "And the Winner Was?" *Salon.com*, April 4, 2001.

43. The *Los Angeles Times* picked up on the significance of the case by that Friday. See David G. Savage and Henry Weinstein, "Florida Judges Have Power to Upset Elections," *Los Angeles Times,* Nov. 10, 2000, A1.

44. The major complaint they had about lost votes was tied to the unfortunate decision of the television networks to declare a Gore victory even while polls were open in the Florida Panhandle; but whatever consequences this may have had it was also a problem that was not caused by any legal agent of the State of Florida, and it was not a problem that was going to be resolved by looking more closely at ballots.

45. Cooper, "A Different Florida Vote"; Richard Berke, "2 Strategies, But One Goal," *New York Times,* Nov. 10, 2000, A28; Mark Z. Barabak and Lisa Getter, "Florida Tally Still in Doubt," *Los Angeles Times,* Nov. 10, 2000, A27; Mark Z. Barabak and Bob Drogin, "Bush, Gore Camps Dig In as Manual Recount is to Start," *Los Angeles Times,* Nov. 11, 2000; "Statements by Officials of the Bush Campaign," *New York Times,* Nov. 10, 2000, A26. In this same statement, the Bush campaign's chief strategist, Karl Rove, also returned to the issue of the butterfly ballot, suggesting to reporters that a similar butterfly ballot was used in Cook County, Illinois, the home base of Gore campaign manager Bill Daley. As it turned out, the Cook County ballot was not a butterfly ballot. While it included candidate lists on two separate pages, they were not for the same office, and voters were not directed to punch from a single line of holes in the middle of the page.

46. Editorial, "A Fateful Step toward Court," *New York Times,* Nov. 10, 2000, A30.

47. Editorial, "Let the Votes, Not the Courts, Decide Who Wins," *Detroit Free Press,* Nov. 10, 2000, on-line edition.

48. Laurence H. Tribe, "Let the Courts Decide," *New York Times,* Nov. 12, 2000, on-line edition.

49. R. W. Apple, Jr., "Gore Campaign Vows Court Fight over Vote," *New York Times,* Nov. 10, 2000, A1.

50. Arguments about how the Florida recount laws may not apply to presidential elections or may only apply to individual counties where the margin was closer than one-half of 1 percent, did not seem remotely plausible and were quickly abandoned. Von Drehle et al., "Candidates Sensed Defeat."

51. Mark Z. Barabak and Jeffrey Gettleman, "Bush Builds Lead on Overseas Vote," *Los Angeles Times,* Nov. 19, 2000, A1.

52. Fla. Stat. § 102.166(7).

53. Mireya Navarro, "A Staunch Gore Ally Influences Florida Ballot Fight," *New York Times,* Nov. 15, 2000, A23.

54. Chief Justice Charles T. Shaw was appointed by Chiles in 1994; Justice Leander J. Shaw, Jr., one of two African American justices, was appointed by Graham in 1983; Justice Major B. Harding was appointed by Chiles in 1991; Justice Harry Lee Anstead was appointed

by Chiles in 1994; Justice Barbara J. Pariente was appointed by Chiles in 1997; Justice R. Fred Lewis was appointed by Chiles in 1998; Justice Peggy A. Quince, the first black woman to sit on the court, was nominated first by Chiles but then renominated by Jeb Bush in 1998. See Lisa Getter and Mitchell Landsberg, "Florida Top Court Is in Glare of Spotlight," *Los Angeles Times,* Nov. 16, 2000, A27. *Time* magazine called Harding "the court's only independent"; Quince, "a moderate who leans right"; and Pariente, "unexpectedly moderate" as a judge. "The Florida Supreme Court," *Time,* Nov. 27, 2000, 48–49.

55. Richard Perez-Pena, "Years of G.O.P. Animosity toward Florida's Justices," *New York Times,* Nov. 25, 2000, on-line edition.

56. Issacharoff et al. (2001:7). For example, see Gazma v. Aguirre (5th Cir. 1980) on how federal law must "recognize a distinction between state laws and patterns of state action that systematically deny equality in voting, and episodic events that, despite non-discriminatory laws, may result in the dilution of an individual's vote. . . . [Constitutional law] does not authorize federal courts to be state election monitors." See also Hennings v. Grafton (7th Cir. 1975), Welch v. McKenzie (5th Cir. 1985), and Pettengill v. Putnam County School District (8th Cir. 1973).

57. See appendixes A and B, especially 3 U.S.C. § 5 in appendix B.

58. Michael Cooper, "Florida Official Has Dual Roles in a Maelstrom," *New York Times,* Nov. 14, 2000, A1; Lisa Getter, "Fla. Election Chief Aware of 'Historic' Role," *Los Angeles Times,* Nov. 14, 2000, A18; Mark Fineman, "Harris: Can This Steel Magnolia Take the Heat?" *Los Angeles Times,* Nov. 18, 2000, A1; Tim Padgett, "Woman on the Verge of Certifying," *Time,* Nov. 27, 2000, 42–45.

59. Those nominated by Republican presidents include the following: Stanley F. Birch, Jr. (Bush), Ed Carnes (Bush), Emmett Ripley Cox (Reagan), Joel F. Dubina (Reagan and Bush), J. L. Edmondson (Reagan), and Gerald B. Tjoflat (Nixon and Ford). The Democratic nominees were Chief Judge R. Lanier Anderson III (Carter), Rosemary Barkett (Clinton), Frank M. Hull (Clinton), and Charles R. Wilson (Clinton). Susan Harrell Black was nominated to the district court by Carter and to the circuit court by Bush, and Stanley Marcus was nominated to the district court by Reagan and to the circuit court by Clinton. "Federal Court v. State Court," *Los Angeles Times,* Nov. 16, 2000, A27.

60. David G. Savage and Henry Weinstein, "Harris' Hand-Count Ruling Sets Up Decisive Legal Fight," *Los Angeles Times,* Nov. 16, 2000, A1, A27.

61. One way to measure a justice's ideological inclinations is to look at what percentage of their decisions might be labeled "pro–civil liberties." The latest figures for "percent civil liberties votes" put Rehnquist in the most hostile position (21.8 percent), followed in turn by Thomas (25.7 percent), Scalia (29 percent), O'Connor (35.5 percent), Kennedy (36.9 percent), and then the more liberal justices, Souter (59 percent), Breyer (61.1 percent), Ginsburg (64.4 percent), and Stevens (64.2 percent). This data will be published by Jeffrey Segal and Harold Spaeth in their upcoming revised edition of Segal and Spaeth (1993). Thanks to Jeff Segal for making this prepublication data available to me. For similar data, see Epstein et al. (1996).

62. For background on the pre–New Deal Supreme Court, see Gillman (1993), Cushman (1998).

63. United States v. Lopez (1995).

64. New York v. United States (1992) and Printz v. United States (1997).

65. Alden v. Maine (1999).

66. United States v. Morrison (2000) and Kimel v. Florida Board of Regents (2000).

67. Adarand Constructors v. Pena (1995), Shaw v. Reno (1993), Miller v. Johnson (1995).

68. Cooper, "A Different Florida Vote"; see also Von Drehle et al., "In Florida, Drawing the Battle Lines."

69. Don Van Natta, Jr., "Democrats Tell of Problems at the Polls across Florida," *New York Times,* Nov. 10, 2000, A24.

70. Mark Z. Barabak and Michael Finnegan, "Hand Count Sparks Legal War," *Los Angeles Times,* Nov. 12, 2000, A1, A31

71. For example, see the transcript of the CNN newstalk program *The Capital Gang,* "Which Side Has the Advantage in Historic Election 2000 Showdown?" CNN.com, Nov. 11, 2000. Conservative columnist Robert Novak of the *Chicago Sun-Times* said, "The Gore side has the advantage. And what's why you're seeing some long Republican faces. . . . A heavily Democratic county, if they could get not only a recount, but a hand recount, they could have the inspector say, boy, it looks like there might be an indentation there or maybe somebody made a circle. They would detect the wishes of the voters. Now, you say how can the Republican poll watcher permit that to happen. Well, he'll vote no, but the three-person canvassing commission would say yes." Al Hunt of the *Wall Street Journal* responded: "This is a phony crisis. We're simply trying to find out which candidate got the most votes in the state of Florida. . . . Hand courts are commonplace. I believe they do it in Texas."

72. Evan Thomas, "The Battle after the Bell," *Newsweek,* Nov. 20, 2000, 38.

73. "Election Scrutiny Focused on Palm Beach Ballot," CNN.com, Nov. 10, 2000; R. W. Apple, Jr., "Gore Campaign Vows Court Fight over Vote," *New York Times,* Nov. 10, 2000, A28.

74. Complaint, McDermott v. Harris, filed in the Circuit Court, Second Judicial Circuit, in and for Leon County, Florida, Nov. 9, 2000 (Case No. 00-2700).

75. Nick Anderson, "Hand Recount Judge Is Lauded for Independence," *Los Angeles Times,* Nov. 12, 2000, A30. Among those who vouched for the judge was Joseph P. Klock, Jr., an unknown figure on this date who would have an important role to play later in the saga.

76. Siegel v. LePore, Emergency Motion for a Temporary Restraining Order and Preliminary Injunction and Supporting Memorandum of Law, United States District Court for the Southern District of Florida, Nov. 11, 2000 (Case No. 00-9009), 3, 8. See also their Complaint for Declaratory and Injunctive Relief, United States District Court for the Southern District of Florida, Nov. 11, 2000.

77. Von Drehle et al., "In Florida, Drawing the Battle Lines."

78. Henry Weinstein, "Analysts Call GOP Lawsuit Legally Weak," *Los Angeles Times,* Nov. 13, 2000, A1, A14. There was one legal basis for the Bush lawyers to be a bit hopeful. In an unusual decision five years earlier, known as Roe v. Alabama ("Roe I"), the Eleventh Circuit Court of Appeals ruled (over the dissent of Judge Edmondson) that counting absentee ballots that were invalid under state law would be inconsistent with the Fourteenth Amendment's principle of "one person, one vote" since it "would dilute the votes of those voters who met the requirements [of State law] as well as those voters who actually went to the polls on election day."

79. Weinstein, "Analysts Call GOP Lawsuit Legally Weak."

80. Mike Clary and Meg James, "In Fla. County, It's a Circus Outside, a Matter of 'Chads' Inside," *Los Angeles Times,* Nov. 12, 2000, A29, A31.

81. Von Drehle et al., "In Florida, Drawing the Battle Lines." According to this account, the original "sunshine" test was replaced by a "two-corner" rule. Either way, Democratic lawyers were not happy. These reporters also indicate that the change from the sunshine test to the two-corner test came after Judge Burton had met with a lawyer from the secretary of state's office during a lunch break.

82. "Bush, Gore Supporters Lay Groundwork for Legal Challenges," CNN.com, Nov. 12, 2000.

83. Mark Z. Barabak and Michael Finnegan, "Hand Count Sparks Legal War," *Los Angeles Times,* Nov. 12, 2000, A1; Angie Cannon and Kenneth T. Walsh, "Messier by the Minute," *U.S. News and World Report Online,* Nov. 13, 2000, www.usnews.com.

84. Editorial, "The Bush Lawsuit," *Washington Post,* Nov. 13, 2000, A26.

85. Doyle McManus, "In Any Dispute, Litigation Seems to Be American Way," *Los Angeles Times,* Nov. 12, 2000, A1.

86. E. J. Dionne, Jr., "Suddenly, Bush Likes the Lawyers," *Washington Post,* Nov. 14, 2000, A43.

87. Barabak and Finnegan, "Hand Count Sparks Legal War."

88. Jeff Leeds, "Some in GOP Warn of Peril in Bush Suit," *Los Angeles Times,* Nov. 12, 2000, A33.

89. Weinstein, "Analysts Call GOP Lawsuit Legally Weak." Compare this last comment with William Safire's lament that "Bush lawyers took the federal judicial route to the Democrats' briar patch." "Bush Goes to Court," *New York Times,* Nov. 13, 2000, on-line edition.

90. Kevin Sack, "Judge, Saying He Doesn't Expect to Be Final Arbiter, Won't Stop Hand Recount," *New York Times,* Nov. 14, 2000, A15.

91. Siegel v. LePore (Case No. 00-9009-VCIV-Middlebrooks), Order on Plaintiffs' Emergency Motion for Temporary Restraining Order and Preliminary Injunction, Nov. 13, 2000.

92. Stuart Taylor, Jr., "The Legal Road Ahead," *Newsweek,* Nov. 20, 2000, 16B. The story was filed no later than Nov. 13.

93. Florida Division of Elections, Opinion DE 00-11, Definitions of Errors in Vote Tabulation, Nov. 13, 2000.

94. Florida Attorney General, Advisory Legal Opinion No. AGO 2000-65, Nov. 14, 2000. The cases cited include State ex rel. Smith v. Anderson (Fla. 1890), Darby v. State (Fla. 1917), State ex rel. Nuccio v. Williams (Fla. 1929), and State ex rel. Carpenter v. Barber (Fla. 1940). Conservative law professor Michael McConnell agreed that "Florida law is clear" on the authority of county canvassing boards to use manual recounts to correct errors in machine tabulation, even though he also thought that this process was unfair because "low levels of essentially random error" caused by machines "are more tolerable than selective errors caused by human bias." Michael McConnell, "Dialogues (with Alan Brinkley), *Slate,* Nov. 15, 2000, slate.msn.com.

95. Fla. Stat. § 102.111.

96. Fla. Stat. § 102.112.

97. "Judge to Rule Tuesday Morning on Florida Election Deadline," CNN.com, Nov. 13, 2000.

98. Mark Z. Barabak and Mike Clary, "Vote Fight Hits the Courts," *Los Angeles Times,* Nov. 14, 2000, A1, A20. The next day the *New York Times* editorialized that Harris's decision was "hasty and partisan," a "transparently political effort to curtail the counting of valid votes in Florida" and thus "a twisted exercise of her responsibility as an elected official. . . . The right way to determine the winner in Florida is to complete the manual counting to be certain any ballots that were mistakenly not counted or miscounted by machine are properly tallied." Editorial, "Keeping Counting in Florida," *New York Times,* Nov. 14, 2000, on-line edition.

99. Barabak and Clary, "Vote Fight Hits the Courts"; "Judge to Rule Tuesday Morning on Florida Election Deadline."

100. Michael Finnegan and Stephen Braun, "County Judge Walked Fine Line," *Los Angeles Times,* Nov. 15, 2000, A25.

101. Barabak and Clary, "Vote Fight Hits the Courts."

102. Florida Democratic Party v. Palm Beach County Canvassing Board, Complaint filed in the Circuit Court for the Fifteenth Judicial Circuit in and for Palm Beach County, Nov. 13, 2000. The theory was that, under Fla. Stat. § 102.166(7), the board is required to examine all aspects of the ballot in order to determine voters intent, and a per se rule that only counts a vote if a chad is partially detached will lead some clearly intended votes uncounted.

103. The case had a hard time finding a judge. On Monday, Judge Stephen Rapp, who was scheduled to preside over the lawsuits, recused himself after an attorney claimed he told a lawyer in a courthouse elevator that he had done his part to make sure "the Democrats are run out of the White House." The judge called the allegations "absolutely false" but decided to withdraw from the case anyway. A second judge recused herself because a plaintiff's lawyer had represented her husband in an unrelated matter. A third judge recused himself because he had discussed the case previously with a plaintiff's lawyer. A fourth judge recused himself because two of the plaintiff's attorneys had served as treasurers in his reelection campaign. A fifth judge recused himself by saying his father worked as senior counsel to the attorney general on issues related to the case. Don Van Natta, Jr., "Palm Beach Panel Votes to Proceed on Count," *New York Times,* Nov. 15, 2000, A1. For more on Labarga see Scott Gold and Bob Drogin, "The Judge at the 'Crossroads,'" *Los Angeles Times,* Nov. 23, 2000, A24.

104. Michael Moss with Ford Fessenden, "G.O.P. Played Role in Absentee Vote," *New York Times,* Nov. 14, 2000, A1.

105. McDermott v. Harris, Case No. 00-2700, In the Circuit Court of the Second Judicial Circuit In and For Leon Country, Order Granting in Part and Denying in Part Motion for Temporary Injunction, Nov. 14, 2000.

106. Editorial, "A Breakthrough Ruling in Florida," *New York Times,* Nov. 15, 2000, on-line edition.

107. David Firestone with Clifford J. Levy, "Each Side Wins Enough to Cite a Court Victory," *New York Times,* Nov. 15, 2000, A1, A19; Stephen Labaton, "A Man Who Vanquished Microsoft Takes On G.O.P.," *New York Times,* Nov. 15, 2000, A19; Cathy Booth Thomas, "Master of the Impossible," *Time,* Nov. 27, 2000, 42–43.

108. Somini Sengupta, "Board Wins Furious Race in Bid to Beat the Clock," *New York Times,* Nov. 15, 2000, A18.

109. "A County Reconsiders Hand Count," *New York Times,* Nov. 15, 2000, A18; David Gonzalez and Dana Canedy, "Local Officials and Courts Clear the Way for Recount," *New York Times,* Nov. 16, 2000, A27.

110. Lynette Holloway, "Most-Populous Area Won't Week Recount," *New York Times,* Nov. 15, 2000, A19. The two board members who decided against the full recount were David Leahy, the supervisor for elections who claimed no party affiliation, and Myriam Lehr, a circuit court judge and a professed independent. The one Democrat, Lawrence D. King, voted to pursue the recount.

111. Van Natta, "Palm Beach Panel Votes to Proceed on Count"; Kevin Sack, "Key Recount Waits again for Approval From Court," *New York Times,* Nov. 16, 2000, A27; Timothy Roche, "Punch-Out in Palm Beach," *Time,* Nov. 27, 2000, 44–45.

112. Josh Getlin, "Weary of It All, Maybe, but Nation Talks of Little Else," *Los Angeles Times,* Nov. 16, 2000, A26.

113. Florida Democratic Party v. Palm Beach County Canvassing Board, Declaratory Order, Nov. 15, 2000.

114. Ford Fessenden and Christopher Drew, "Chads Have Their Place in Annals of the Law," *New York Times,* Nov. 16, 2000, A28.

115. Harris v. Circuit Judges, Emergency Petition for Extraordinary Relief, Nov. 15, 2000.

116. "Florida Voting Official's Decision Next on Docket," CNN.com, Nov. 16, 2000.

117. Todd S. Purdum, "Judge Upholds Hand Recounts in Florida," *New York Times,* Nov. 15, 2000, A1; "Statement by Florida Secretary of State," *New York Times,* Nov. 15, 2000, A20.

118. Alison Mitchell, "G.O.P. Begins Jockeying in House on Fate of Election" *New York Times,* Nov. 16, 2000, A25.

119. "Gore's Remarks on Resolving Dispute," *New York Times,* Nov. 15, 2000, A24; David Von Drehle, Jo Becker, Ellen Nakashima, and Lois Romano, "Battle Became War With Time," *Washington Post,* Jan. 30, 2001, A1. For examples of favorable editorial responses, see Editorial, "A Positive Step from Mr. Gore," *New York Times,* Nov. 16, 2000, A30; Bob Herbert, "Running from the Vote," *New York Times,* Nov. 16, 2000, A31.

120. Todd S. Purdum, "Back into Court," *New York Times,* Nov. 16, 2000, A1, A26; "Statement by Florida Election Official," *New York Times,* Nov. 16, 2000, A26.

121. "Bush's Response to Gore Proposal," *New York Times,* Nov. 16, 2000, A24.

122. Lisa Getter and Mitchell Landsberg, "Florida Top Court Is in Glare of Spotlight," *Los Angeles Times,* Nov. 16, 2000, A27; Richard A. Oppel, Jr., "In Florida's State Government, Court Is a Democratic Enclave," *New York Times,* Nov. 17, 2000.

123. Michael McConnell, "Dialogue (with Alan Brinkley)," *Slate,* Nov. 16, 2000, slate.msn.com.

124. William Safire, "Fight to the Finish: Take it to the Supremes," *New York Times,* Nov. 16, 2000, A31.

125. Jeffrey Rosen, "Why the U.S. Supreme Court Would Make Things Worse," *New Republic Online,* Nov. 16, 2000. The history he turned to was the 1876 election dispute, which tainted all involved, including the five members of the Supreme Court who were brought in to provide a thin nonpartisan veneer.

126. McDermott v. Harris, Case No. 00-2700, Order Denying Emergency Motion to Compel Compliance With and For Enforcement of Injunction, Nov. 17, 2000.

127. Mark Z. Barabak and Richard A. Serrano, "Justices Delay Official Tally," *Los Angeles Times,* Nov. 18, 2000, A1, A20.

128. Touchston v. McDermott, No. 00-15985, Order on Emergency Motion for Injunction Pending Appeal, Nov. 17, 2000.

129. "Court Rulings Spell Renewed Life for Recount Efforts," CNN.com, Nov. 17, 2000.

130. Ronald Brownstein, "Official Rulings Mostly Follow Partisan Lines," *Los Angeles Times,* Nov. 15, 2000, A1.

131. Stanley Fish, "The High-Minded Fight over Florida," *New York Times,* Nov. 15, 2000, A31.

132. Palm Beach County Canvassing Board v. Harris, Case No. SC00-2346, Order Accepting Jurisdiction, Setting Oral Argument and Setting Briefing Schedule, Nov. 17, 2000. The court's order also consolidated this case with Volusia County Canvassing Board v. McDermott (SC00-2348) and Florida Democratic Party v. McDermott (SC00-2349).

133. Palm Beach County Canvassing Board v. Harris, Case No. SC00-2346, Stay Order, Nov. 17, 2000.

CHAPTER TWO

1. William Glaberson, "Ruling Is Seen as Affirming Primacy of Will of Voters," *New York Times,* Nov. 22, 2000, on-line edition.

2. Michael McConnell, "Dialogue (with Alan Brinkley)," *Slate,* Nov. 22, 2000, slate.msn.com.

3. Eric Pooley, "Prime-Time Battle," *Time,* Nov. 27, 2000, 33–40, 34.

4. Mark Z. Barabak and Richard A. Serrano, "Justices Delay Official Tally," *Los Angeles Times,* Nov. 18, 2000, A1; Mark Z. Barabak and Jeffrey Gettleman, "Bush Builds Lead on Overseas Vote," *Los Angeles Times,* Nov. 19, 2000, A1.

5. Mitchell Landsberg and Eric Bailey, "Battling Over Absentees, Hand to Hand," *Los Angeles Times,* Nov. 18, 2000, A1, A17; David Von Drehle, Jo Becker, Ellen Nakashima, and Dan Balz, "For Bush Camp, Some Momentum from a Memo," *Washington Post,* Jan. 31, 2001, A1.

6. Jake Tapper, "Did Bush Camp Encourage Military Personnel to Vote after Election Day?" *Salon.com,* Mar. 5, 2001.

7. Von Drehle et al., "For Bush Camp, Some Momentum."

8. David Barstow with Alison Mitchell, "Where Republicans See a 'Mess,' Democrats See 'Smooth,'" *New York Times,* Nov. 21, 2000, on-line edition.

9. Thomas E. Ricks, "Democratic Ballot Challenges Anger Military," *Washington Post,* Nov. 21, 2000, A18.

10. Barabak and Serrano, "Justices Delay Official Tally." The pivotal vote to reverse came from Judge Myriam Lehr, who earlier opposed the recount.

11. The "only one narrative line worth following" is "Bush's attempts . . . to shut down the recounts, and Gore's maneuverings to keep them going at all costs. 'As long as we're counting, it's not over,' says a Gore strategist. A Bush aide puts it this way: 'We're trying to run out the clock . . .'" Pooley, "Prime-Time Battle," 35.

12. Barstow and Mitchell, "Where Republicans."

13. Barstow with Mitchell, "Where Republicans."

14. "Democrat Had Chad Snack, Observer Says," *Los Angeles Times,* Nov. 19, 2000, A25.

15. Barabak and Gettleman, "Bush Builds Lead."

16. Barabak and Serrano, "Justices Delay Official Tally"; Ronald Brownstein, "In This Bitter Fight, the Motto Is: Make Every Ballot Count," *Los Angeles Times,* Nov. 19, 2000, A1.

17. Republican lawyers tried to get Broward County Circuit Court Judge Leonard I. Stafford to stop the recount until they could hold a full trial on its legality and the appropriate procedures, but after seventy minutes of wrangling the judge concluded that the Florida Supreme Court intended for the counts to go on for the time being. Ronald Brownstein, "Democrats Pin Hopes on 'Voter Intent' Ruling," *Los Angeles Times,* Nov. 20, 2000, A1, A14.

18. Geraldine Baum, "Broward Recount Battle Marked by Drama, Comedy," *Los Angeles Times,* Nov. 18, 2000, A16.

19. Brownstein, "Democrats Pin Hopes." *Newsweek* later reported that Boies played a controversial role in Broward's decision to adopt a more lenient standard for evaluating ballots. During the discussions, "Boies himself arrived on the scene in Ft. Lauderdale with a new weapon: an affidavit from a Chicago-area lawyer, Michael Lavelle, describing how a local elections board in Illinois had used the same liberal ballot-counting standard in a case that had been cited by no less an authority than the Florida Supreme Court. Meeting with the Broward County officials, Boies passed the affidavit around like a smoking gun. Only later did it emerge that Lavelle considered his own affidavit to be misleading and had tried to take it back." Gore lawyers eventually corrected the record but by then "Broward had almost finished counting." Evan Thomas and Michael Isikoff, "Settling Old Scores in the Swamp," *Newsweek,* Dec. 18, 2000, 43.

20. The polling data were collected on the PollingReport.com Web site. Throughout this event the candidate's supporters took positions that echoed the views of their favored campaigns. But at this point there was an interesting inversion on the issue of whether this conflict should be handled in state court or federal court: Gore supporters favored federal court by 58–34 percent; Bush supporters favored state courts by 50–40 percent. Undoubtedly this reflected the normal views of these voters on federalism issues; they had not yet updated their thinking in light of the specific strategic environment of Florida.

21. Editorial, "Florida's High Court Steps In," *New York Times,* Nov. 18, 2000, on-line edition.

22. Henry Weinstein and David G. Savage, "Florida Justices May Have Final Word on Ballots," *Los Angeles Times,* Nov. 20, 2000, A1.

23. David M. Shribman, "Crucial Role for the Judiciary," *Boston Globe,* Nov. 20, 2000, on-line edition.

24. Weinstein and Savage, "Florida Justices."

25. Leonard Garment, "Justice Is Not the Issue," *New York Times,* Nov. 19, 2000, on-line edition.

26. Alan Brinkley, "Dialogues (with Michael McConnell)," *Slate,* Nov. 20, 2000, slate.msn.com.

27. Barabak and Serrano, "Justices Delay Official Tally."

28. John J. Miller and Ramesh Ponnuru, "Supreme Mischief," *National Review Online,* Nov. 20, 2000, www.nationalreview.com.

29. The following excerpts are taken from Joint Brief of Petitioners/Appellants Al Gore Jr. and Florida Democratic Party, Palm Beach County Canvassing Board v. Harris, Case No. SC00-2346, submitted Nov. 18, 2000.

30. Fla. Stat. § 102.166 (7)(b).

31. The other state cases mentioned were Pullen v. Mulligan (Ill. 1990) and Hickel v. Thomas (Alaska 1978).

32. Fla. Stat. § 101.5614(8).

33. The following excerpts are taken from Answer Brief of Intervenor/Respondent George W. Bush, Palm Beach County Canvassing Board v. Harris, Case No. SC00-2346, submitted Nov. 18, 2000.

34. Fla. Stat. § 102.111.

35. Fla. Stat. § 102.112(2).

36. Among the cases reviewed: Delahunt v. Johnston (1996) ("a vote should be recorded for a candidate if the chad was not removed but an impression was made on or near it"), Stapleton v. Board of Elections (3d Cir. 1987) ("absent an unequivocal legislative intent to the contrary, we are compelled to uphold the voter's intent to the extent it can be ascertained"), Duffy v. Mortensen (S.D. 1993) (vote should not be excluded because voter's "hand was unsteady or his vision impaired" so long as intent is clear), Hickel v. Thomas (Alaska 1978) (unperforated punch card ballots marked by pen are counted because they reflect voter's intent), Wright v. Gettinger (Ind. 1981) (ballots with partially attached chads counted because they reflect voter's intent).

37. Texas Stat. Title 8 section 127.130(d)(e).

38. Howard Rosenberg, "Florida Airs Some Must-See TV," *Los Angeles Times,* Nov. 21, 2000, A17; Eric Bailey, "A Hot Ticket on a Cold Day in Florida," *Los Angeles Times,* Nov. 21, 2000, A16.

39. David Von Drehle, Jo Becker, Ellen Nakashima, and Lois Romano, "Battle Became War with Time," *Washington Post,* Jan. 30, 2001, A1.

40. The following excerpts from the oral arguments are taken from a transcript of the argument that was made available on line at wfsu.org/gavel2gavel/transcript/00-2346.htm.

41. Von Drehle et al., "Battle Became War with Time."

42. David G. Savage and Henry Weinstein, "Justices Focus on 'How' of Recounts," *Los Angeles Times,* Nov. 21, 2000, A1; Mark Z. Barabak and Richard A. Serrano, "Justices Begin Deliberating," *Los Angeles Times,* Nov. 21, 2000, A1, A18.

43. Editorial, "Rational Justices," *Boston Globe,* Nov. 21, 2000, on-line edition.

44. Editorial, "Justice Behave Better Than Candidate's Camps," *Philadelphia Inquirer,* Nov. 21, 2000, on-line edition.

45. Steven Gillers, "The Court Should Boldly Take Charge," *New York Times,* Nov. 21, 2000, on-line edition. He added that while "one rarely gets to be a judge without a party affiliation," unlike others involved in this dispute "the judges have not been, and could not ethically be, politically active."

46. He cited LaCaze v. Johnson (La. 1974), Beckstrom v. Volusia County Canvassing Board (Fla. 1998), State of North Dakota v. Bakken (N.D. 1983), McCavitt v. Registrars of Voters of Brockton (Mass. 1982).

47. Fladell v. Elections Canvassing Commission, Case No. CL 00-10965 AB, Order on Plaintiffs' Complaint for Declaratory Injunctive and Other Relief Arising From Plaintiffs' Claims of Massive Voter Confusion Resulting From the Use of a "Butterfly" Type Ballot During the Election Held on November 7, 2000, Nov. 20, 2000. Toward the end of his opinion Labarga wrote, "Clearly, a great number of patriotic and deeply concerned citizens of Palm Beach County fear that they may have unwittingly cast their votes for someone other than their candidate. While some may dismiss such concerns without a second thought, this Court is well aware that the right to vote is as precious as life itself to those who have been victimized by the horror of war, to those whose not-too-distant relatives were prohibited from exercising the right to vote simply because of their race or gender, and to those who have risked it all by venturing across an unforgiving sea on makeshift rafts or boats in order to one day exercise the right to vote. However, for over two centuries we have agreed to a constitution and to live by the law." See also Marcy Gordon, "Judge Says No Revote in Palm Beach," Associated Press, Nov. 20, 2000, dailynews.yahoo.com; Scott Gold, "Court Takes Up Call for Palm Beach Revote," *Los Angeles Times,* Nov. 18, 2000, A16; Scott Gold, "With Anguish, Judge Rejects Palm Beach Revote," *Los Angeles Times,* Nov. 21, 2000; A20.

48. Joan Vennochi, "Out of One Florida Court, a Show of Courage," *Boston Globe Online,* Nov. 21, 2000, on-line edition.

49. Mitchell Landsberg, "Judge Upholds Democrat's Lawsuit over Absentee Applications," *Los Angeles Times,* Nov. 21, 2000, A16; "Election Outcome in Florida Supreme Court's Hands," CNN.com, Nov. 21, 2000.

50. Gordon, "Judge Says No"; Barabak and Serrano, "Justices Begin Deliberating." The *Palm Beach Post* later reported that the canvassing commission's refusal to count dimpled chads probably cost Gore almost eight hundred votes. "Palm Beach Count Finds Gore Gain," Associated Press, Mar. 11, 2001, www.nytimes.com.

51. At around this time in Broward County, seventy-year-old elections supervisor Jane Carroll, the only Republican on the county's three-person canvassing commission, suddenly quit her post, explaining that she could not handle the long days and that she was not feeling well. The chief judge of the circuit court appointed Judge Robert Rosenberg to replace her.

52. Alan Brinkley, "Dialogues (with Michael McConnell)," *Slate,* Nov. 21, 2000, slate.msn.com.

53. Michael McConnell, "Dialogues (with Alan Brinkley)," *Slate,* Nov. 21, 2000, slate.msn.com.

54. In support of this statement they also cited Chappell v. Martinez (Fla. 1988) and Beckstrom v. Volusia County Canvassing Board (Fla. 1998).

55. Compare Fla. Stat. § 102.166(4) with §§ 102.111 and 102.112.

56. Compare Fla. Stat. § 102.111 with § 102.112.

57. Citing State ex rel. Carpenter v. Barber (Fla. 1940).

58. Marlene Cimons, "Cheney Suffers a 'Very Slight' Heart Attack," *Los Angeles Times,* Nov. 23, 2000, A1. He was released from the hospital the day after Thanksgiving.

59. Ronald Brownstein, "Gore Must Now Slip through Narrow Window," *Los Angeles Times,* Nov. 22, 2000, A1, A20. The *New York Times* editorialized that the Florida judges "acted in the best interests of the nation" by resolving "conflicting statutory language in favor

of giving the greatest possible say [to voters] in deciding the outcome of the election." Editorial, "The Florida Court Decision," *New York Times,* Nov. 22, 2000, on-line edition.

60. "In Baker's Words . . . ," *Los Angeles Times,* Nov. 22, 2000, A17.

61. Edwin Chen, "Florida High Court 'Overreached' in Ruling, Bush Says," *Los Angeles Times,* Nov. 23, 2000, A22.

62. Henry Weinstein and David Savage, "Judicial Legitimacy May Be the Next Hue and Cry," *Los Angeles Times,* Nov. 22, 2000, A1, A16.

63. Nick Anderson and Janet Hook, "Agitation and Joy Felt on Capitol Hill," *Los Angeles Times,* Nov. 22, 2000, A16.

64. David S. Broder and Matthew Vita, "Bitter Struggle Certain to Escalate," *Washington Post,* Nov. 22, 2000, A1; Janet Hook, "GOP Lawmakers' Rhetoric on Recount Reaches Fever Pitch," *Los Angeles Times,* Nov. 23, 2000, A26.

65. Stephen Braun, "Conservatives Dust Off Impeachment Outrage," *Los Angeles Times,* Nov. 23, 2000, A1.

66. George F. Will, "This Willful Court," *Washington Post,* Nov. 23, 2000, A43.

67. Anthony Lewis, "Playing with Fire," *New York Times,* Nov. 25, 2000, on-line edition.

68. Bob Herbert, "Breaking Faith," *New York Times,* Nov. 23, 2000, on-line edition.

69. Editorial, "Reckless Republican Rhetoric," *New York Times,* Nov. 23, 2000, on-line edition.

70. Barry Friedman, "The Glib Critics of the Courts," *New York Times,* Nov. 24, 2000, on-line edition.

71. Weinstein and Savage, "Judicial Legitimacy May Be the Next Hue and Cry"; Brownstein, "Gore Must Now Slip Through Narrow Window"; William Glaberson, "Ruling Is Seen as Affirming Primacy of Will of Voters," *New York Times,* Nov. 22, 2000, on-line edition; David Von Drehle, "Parties Divide on 'Judicial Activism' Is Nothing New," *Washington Post,* Nov. 23, 2000, A29. A rare exception to this pattern came from Jeffrey Rosen, George Washington University law professor and legal affairs editor for the *New Republic.* He wrote that the Florida Court's decision was "a bold example of judicial activism" and an unwise entry into "a political battle that neither state courts nor the United States Supreme Court can ultimately resolve." He noted that other judges had shown remarkable restraint, from the federal courts that refused to intervene in the recount, to the refusal to order a new election in Palm Beach, to Judge Lewis's decision upholding Harris's authority to ignore late returns. This more cautious approach was justified given the reality that "Republicans in Florida and throughout the United States would never accept a Gore victory won on the basis of a court decision." Jeffrey Rosen, "Florida's Justices Pushed Too Far," *New York Times,* Nov. 23, 2000, on-line edition.

72. Robert Suro and John Mintz, "Standards and Speed Now Crucial," *Washington Post,* Nov. 22, 2000, A1; Scott Gold, "Gore Hopes for Fla. Win Turn to Dimpled Ballots," *Los Angeles Times,* Nov. 22, 2000, A16. Judge Burton, who was overseeing the Palm Beach recount, said that he preferred a stricter standard for counting votes. "If we're going to count it, there has to be clear and convincing evidence that the voter intended to vote." Mark Z. Barabak and Richard A. Serrano, "Court OKs Hand Recounts," *Los Angeles Times,* Nov. 22, 2000, A1, A17.

73. Barabak and Serrano, "Court OKs Hand Recounts"; Serge F. Kovaleski, "Broward County to Review Questionable Ballots," *Washington Post,* Nov. 22, 2000, A28.

74. Mark Z. Barabak and Scott Gold, "Miami-Dade Cancels Recount," *Los Angeles Times,* Nov. 23, 2000, A1; Mike Clary, "Democrats' Hopes Tumbled From Chaos on the 19th Floor," *Los Angeles Times,* Nov. 23, 2000, A1, A28. The board members were Lawrence D. King, a Democratic judge, David Leahy, the county election supervisor with no party affiliation, and Myriam Lehr, who initially sided with Leahy to block a manual recount but then changed her vote. A few days later Leahy reiterated that he considered the Republican group to be "a noisy, peaceful protest." Mike Clary, "Miami-Dade Election Official Denies Being Intimidated," *Los Angeles Times,* Nov. 26, 2000, A17.

75. Barabak and Gold, "Miami-Dade Cancels."

76. Roberto Suro, Jo Becker, and Serge F. Kovaleski, "Florida Supreme Court Rebuffs Gore," *Washington Post,* Nov. 24, 2000, A1.

77. Florida Democratic Party v. Palm Beach County Canvassing Board, Order on Plaintiff's Emergency Motion to Clarify Declaratory Order of November 15, 2000, Case No. CL 00-11078AB, Nov. 22, 2000.

78. Ronald Brownstein, "GOP in Legislature Seeks Way to Give Bush Electoral Votes," *Los Angeles Times,* Nov. 23, 2000, A29; Jo Becker, "GOP Legislators Consider Role in Choosing Electors," *Washington Post,* Nov. 23, 2000, A29.

79. Roberto Suro, "Palm Beach Counting Told to Consider 'Dimple,'" *Washington Post,* Nov. 23, 2000, A28.

80. Suro et al., "Florida Supreme Court Rebuffs." It was during this Thanksgiving Day process of reviewing disputed ballots that an iconic picture was snapped of Broward County Canvassing Board member Judge Robert Rosenberg, a Republican, lifting up his glasses and staring with big eyes at an uplifted ballot.

81. As a hedge against this counting, on Friday, November 24, Republicans asked Leon County Circuit Court Judge L. Ralph Smith to reinstate the absentee ballots of overseas military personnel. The judge gave them little hope, saying that "without any proof that any of these canvassing boards have not complied with the law, the court is very hard-pressed to grant any relief." Michael Cooper, "Bush Lawyers Want Reinstatement of Disqualified Military Ballots," *New York Times,* Nov. 25, 2000, on-line edition. (Cooper observed that "suddenly, the positions of both sides in South Florida were reversed, with the Republicans arguing for leeway in evaluating ballots and the Democrats calling for strict compliance with the rules." Note that it was the Florida Supreme Court's decision to delay final certification that allowed Republicans to raise this issue at this late date.) Before the judge could rule against them, Republicans withdrew the lawsuit, filing them instead in other courtrooms throughout Florida. Michael Cooper, "A Tactical Change in Bush Lawsuit over Military Ballots," *New York Times,* Nov. 26, 2000, on-line edition.

82. Bush v. Palm Beach County Canvassing Board, Petition for a Writ of Certiorari, Nov. 22, 2000.

83. Bush v. Palm Beach County Canvassing Board, No. 00-836, Brief in Opposition of Respondents Al Gore, Jr., and Florida Democratic Party, Nov. 23, 2000. It characterized the "questions presented" as "whether the Florida Supreme Court's interpretation of Florida law presents a substantial federal question for this Court to review or instead a determination reserved to the States?" and "whether the State of Florida's statutorily mandated manual re-

count process, indistinguishable from the laws of other states and reflective of a process that has been applied throughout this country for centuries, violates the U.S. Constitution?"

84. David G. Savage and Henry Weinstein, "Bush Takes His Case to the U.S. Supreme Court," *Los Angeles Times*, Nov. 23, 2000, A24.

85. Rosen, "Florida's Justices."

CHAPTER THREE

1. This followed the U.S. Supreme Court's oral arguments in Bush v. Palm Beach County Canvassing Commission. Editorial, "Politics and the Court," *Washington Post*, Dec. 3, 2000, B6.

2. Ratings for cable news networks continued to be very high. Elizabeth Jensen, "News Networks Seeing Windfall," *Los Angeles Times*, Nov. 25, 2000, A20.

3. Jeffrey Gettleman, "One Dimple, Two Interpretations," *Los Angeles Times*, Nov. 25, 2000, A20.

4. Mark Z. Barabak and Richard A. Serrano, "U.S. High Court Steps into the Fray," *Los Angeles Times*, Nov. 25, 2000, A1, A24.

5. John F. Harris, "High Court to Hear Bush Appeal," *Washington Post*, Nov. 25, 2000, A1; Dana Milbank, "Republican County Decides Recount Doesn't Count," *Washington Post*, Nov. 26, 2000, A9. The elections supervisor, Shirley N. King, explained that 218 were accidentally excluded from the recount.

6. Ronald Brownstein and Janet Hook, "Gore Must Find His Momentum in Palm Beach," *Los Angeles Times*, Nov. 24, 2000, A1, A48.

7. "High Court Intervention Called Unlikely," *Knight Ridder News Service*, Nov. 23, 2000; Rowan Scarborough, "States's Top Court Seen as Voicing Final Word on Vote," *Washington Times*, Nov. 18, 2000, A1.

8. Barabak and Serrano, "U.S. High Court"; William Sherman, "Profs Shocked that Justices Step in Election Mess," *Daily News* [New York], Nov. 25, 2000; David G. Savage and Henry Weinstein, "Justice Dust Off an 1887 Statute for Ballot Battle," *Los Angeles Times*, Nov. 25, 2000, A1, 22; Linda Greenhouse, "U.S. Supreme Court to Hear Florida Recount Case," *New York Times*, Nov. 25, 2000, on-line edition; Charles Lane, "Analysis: The Law," *Washington Post*, Nov. 25, 2000, A1.

9. Bush v. Palm Beach County Canvassing Board, Petition for a Writ of Certiorari, Nov. 22, 2000.

10. In rejecting that argument, the Court was also rejecting the Bush appeal of the Eleventh Circuit's decision in Siegel v. Lepore. Still, since the Supreme Court's rejection of the appeal was made "without prejudice," the case remained alive in the Eleventh Circuit. After the election dispute was over, some of the justices suggested to the *New York Times* that this interpretation was a misunderstanding. They claimed that the equal protection argument was not taken up here because it was scheduled to be fully argued later in the Eleventh Circuit; hence, they denied the federal appeal "without prejudice" and focused instead on the issues that were at the center of the appeal from the Florida Supreme Court. Linda Greenhouse, "Election Case a Test and a Trauma for Justices," *New York Times*, Feb. 20, 2001, on-line edition.

11. Doyle McManus, "Legal Options for Both Candidates Rule Out Hope for Resolution Soon," *Los Angeles Times,* Nov. 25, 2000, A20.

12. Raju Chebium, "Constitutional Scholars Surprised by U.S. Supreme Court Decision to Hear Florida Election Case," CNN.com, Nov. 24, 2000; Andres Viglucci, "Experts Expect State Ruling Will Be Upheld," *Miami Herald,* Nov. 25, 2000, on-line edition; John F. Harris, "High Court to Hear Bush Appeal," *Washington Post,* Nov. 25, 2000, A1; Lyle Denniston, "Duty Moves Supreme Court to Enter Fla. Election Fight," *Baltimore Sun,* Nov. 26, 2000, on-line edition; William Glaberson, "Justices May See Task as Calming the Storm," *New York Times,* Nov. 25, 2000, on-line edition.

13. Linda Greenhouse, "Justices Ready to Walk a Very Fine Legal Line," *New York Times,* Nov. 27, 2000, on-line edition.

14. Charles Lane, "High Court's Credibility, Internal Balance Face Test," *Washington Post,* Nov. 26, 2000, A10.

15. Adam Clymer, "Even When Blind, Justice Feels the Political Winds," *New York Times,* Nov. 26, 2000, on-line edition; David G. Savage and Henry Weinstein, "Role Reversals in Filings with High Court," *Los Angeles Times,* Nov. 28, 2000, A28.

16. Savage and Weinstein, "Justices Dust Off an 1887 Statute"; Glaberson, "Justices May See Task as Calming the Storm"; John Yoo, "The Right Moment for Judicial Power," *New York Times,* Nov. 25, 2000, on-line edition; see also Jeffrey Rosen, "Judge Not: The Supreme Court Puts Itself in Harm's Way," *New Republic Online,* post date Nov. 30, 2000 (issue date Dec. 11, 2000), ww.tnr.com; Jim Hoagland, "The Job before the Justices," *Washington Post,* Nov. 30, 2000, A37.

17. Jeffrey Gettleman and Hector Tobar, "Broward Ballot Stack Down to Sighs," *Los Angeles Times,* Nov. 26, 2000, A1.

18. Mark Z. Barabak and Michael Finnegan, "Florida Recounts Race to Deadline," *Los Angeles Times,* Nov. 26, 2000, A1; Ronald Brownstein, "Final Results Are to Be Certified Today," *Los Angeles Times,* Nov. 26, 2000, A1.

19. Hector Tobar, "A Tempest to the End for Battered Palm Beach," *Los Angeles Times,* Nov. 27, 2000, A1. This figure was later confirmed by one newspaper. "Palm Beach Count Finds Gore Gain," Associated Press, Mar. 11, 2001, *New York Times,* on-line edition.

20. "Excerpts of Harris' Remarks on Florida Vote Certification," *Los Angeles Times,* Nov. 27, 2000, A17.

21. "Text of Lieberman's Statement on Results," *Los Angeles Times,* Nov. 27, 2000, A16.

22. David G. Savage and Henry Weinstein, "U.S. High Court Could Rule, but Will It Matter?" *Los Angeles Times,* Nov. 27, 2000, A15.

23. "Text of Bush's Remarks," *Los Angeles Times,* Nov. 27, 2000, A16. See also Mark Z. Barabak and Richard A. Serrano, "Florida Certifies Bush as Winner; Gore to Challenge Result in Courts," *Los Angeles Times,* Nov. 27, 2000, A1, A17; Ronald Brownstein, "Rivals Down to the Heavy Artillery," *Los Angeles Times,* Nov. 27, 2000, A1, A14; Edwin Chen, "Bush Pledges Unity, Moves to Begin Transition," *Los Angeles Times,* Nov. 27, 2000, A1, A13; Associated Press, "Cheney: It's 'Essential' to Start Transition Process," *Los Angeles Times,* Nov. 28, 2000, A25.

24. Mark Z. Barabak, "Gore Sues over Florida Results: He Asks Public for Patience; Bush Considers Cabinet Picks," *Los Angeles Times,* Nov. 28, 2000, A1, A30; Doyle McManus,

"Both Sides Now Turn to Court of Public Opinion," *Los Angeles Times,* Nov. 28, 2000, A1, A26.

25. Nick Anderson, "Political Title Wave Sweeps U.S. on What to Call Bush," *Los Angeles Times,* Nov. 28, 2000, A23.

26. "Gore: Ignoring Votes Is Ignoring Democracy," *Los Angeles Times,* Nov. 28, 2000, A30.

27. Fla. Stat. § 102.168(3)(c).

28. Gore v. Harris, In the Circuit Court of the Second Judicial Circuit, In and For Leon County, Florida, Civil Division, Case No. 00-2808, Complaint to Contest Election, Nov. 27, 2000. These figures were taken from the complaint and were adjusted as the dispute moved forward. There continued to be a disagreement about whether the Palm Beach number should be 176 or 215 as late as the Florida Supreme Court's decision in Gore v. Harris (2000) (see n. 6). For more on Nassau, see Scott Martelle, "Add Nassau to the List of Problems," *Los Angeles Times,* Nov. 28, 2000, A23.

29. Richard A. Serrano, "Gore's Legal Challenge Gets Underway," *Los Angeles Times,* Nov. 28 2000, A22; Jeffrey Gettleman, "'Straight-Shooter' to Preside Over Florida Case," *Los Angeles Times,* Nov. 28, 2000, A22; Timothy Roche, "The Ball's In Sauls' Court," *Time,* Dec. 11, 2000, 49; David Barstow and Somini Sengupta, "Judge in Case That Gore Lost Had Run-Ins with Justices," *New York Times,* Dec. 7, 2000, on-line edition. This last article reported that Sauls was overturned by appellate courts almost 30 percent of the time.

30. *Newsweek* reported that Boies made the decision early on "to put on a bare-boned, streamlined case before the lower-court judge and hoped that the state Supreme Court would quickly take up the case." Evan Thomas and Michael Isikoff, "Settling Old Scores in the Swamp," *Newsweek,* Dec. 18, 2000, 43.

31. It should be noted that if this compressed period for an election contest did not seem like a bad idea to the Gore campaign when it was first proposed, it was probably because they thought it would be Bush who would be contesting a Gore victory.

32. Gore v. Harris, Case No. SC00-2385, Order in Gore Petition, Dec. 1, 2000.

33. Richard A. Serrano and Scott Gold, "Judges to Have Ballots Brought to Tallahassee Election Trial," *Los Angeles Times,* Nov. 29, 2000, A1; Richard A. Serrano and Michael Finnegan, "Gore Presses Swift Count of Disputed Votes," *Los Angeles Times,* Nov. 30, 2000, A1. When the ballots were shipped up in Ryder rental trucks, anyone in the country who was interested in the 450-mile journey was able to watch the event live on cable news, perhaps wondering what it would look like for the ballots to end up hijacked or scattered across the Florida interstate, blowing in the wind. Michael Finnegan and Massie Ritsch, "A Highway Spectacle, and O.J. Simpson Is There," *Los Angeles Times,* Dec. 1, 2000, A32; Howard Rosenberg, "A Yellow Truck: An Image for the Ages," *Los Angeles Times,* Dec. 1, 2000, A31.

34. Jacobs v. Seminole County Canvassing Board, Case No. 00-2816, Complaint, Nov. 27, 2000.

35. Scott Gold, "A County's Back-Room Goings-On Bring Suit," *Los Angeles Times,* Nov. 28, 2000, A1, A24.

36. Jeffrey Gettleman, "For Florida Legislature, It's Full Speedy Ahead to Name Electors," *Los Angeles Times,* Nov. 29, 2000, A2; Henry Weinstein and David G. Savage, "Legislature's Electoral Power Is a Matter of Debate," *Los Angeles Times,* Nov. 29, 2000, A30; Jo Becker, "Legislators Weigh Role in Choosing Electors," *Washington Post,* Nov. 29, 2000, A23; David

Barstow, "Florida Lawmakers Moving to Bypass Courts for Bush," *New York Times,* Nov. 29, 2000, on-line edition; Scott Gold and Jeffrey Gettleman, "Fla. Lawmakers Battle Over Naming Electors," *Los Angeles Times,* Dec. 1, 2000, A1, A30. The conservative law professors who supported the legislature's plenary authority were Charles Fried, John Yoo, and Einer Elhauge. Bruce Ackerman of Yale University said of this interpretation: "I am just stunned at their dramatic incompetence." Gore's running mate Joe Lieberman said that their action "threatens to put us in a constitutional crisis."

37. Savage and Weinstein, "U.S. High Court Could Rule."

38. Charles Lane, "In Supreme Court, Stakes Seem Lower," *Washington Post,* Nov. 28, 2000, A8. The comment was made by Tony Sutin, dean of the Appalachian School of Law.

39. Savage and Weinstein, "Role Reversals in Filings with High Court"; see also Frank Davies, "Justices Won't Decide Election," *Miami Herald,* Nov. 30, 2000, on-line edition.

40. Lane, "In Supreme Court." The comment was made by Professor Michael Glennon of the UC Davis School of Law.

41. Editorial, "The Supreme Court's Shrewd Option," *Chicago Tribune,* Nov. 29, 2000, on-line edition. See also Frank Davies, "High Court's Historic Case May Be Mostly Symbolic," *Miami Herald,* Dec. 1, 2000, on-line edition.

42. The following summary was taken from Bush v. Palm Beach County Canvassing Board, Case No.00-836, Brief for Petitioner, submitted Nov. 28, 2000. The other lawyers named on the brief are George J. Terwilliger III, Timothy E. Flanigan, Marcos D. Jimenez, Terence P. Ross, Douglas R. Cox, Thomas G. Hungar, Mark A. Perry, John F. Manning, William K. Kelley, and Bradford C. Clark.

43. The following summary is taken from Bush v. Palm Beach County Canvassing Board, Case No. 00-836, Brief of Respondents Al Gore, Jr., and Florida Democratic Party, Nov. 28, 2000. The other names on the brief are Teresa Wynn Roseborough, David I. Adelman, James A. Orr, John J. Fleming, Andrew J. Pincus, Jonathan S. Massey, Neal K. Katyal, and Thomas C. Goldstein.

44. Bush v. Palm Beach County Canvassing Board, Case No. 00-836, Reply Brief for Respondents Al Gore, Jr. and Florida Democratic Party, Nov. 30, 2000.

45. The quoted passage is from Burgess (1888).

46. The case was James Beam Distilling Company v. Georgia (1991).

47. Greenhouse, "Justices Ready to Walk a Very Fine Legal Line."

48. See the on-line U.S. Supreme Court Multimedia Database at oyez.nwu.edu.

49. Mark Z. Barabak and Richard A. Serrano, "Lawyers Spar on High Court Hearing's Eve," *Los Angeles Times,* Dec. 1, 2000, A1, A26; David G. Savage, "To High Court, It Is Also a Counting Game," *Los Angeles Times,* Dec. 1, 2000, A1, A27.

50. Lyle Denniston, "Justices Facing Historic Hearing," *Baltimore Sun,* Dec. 1, 2000, on-line edition.

51. Mary Leonard, "Day of Courtroom Dramas," *Boston Globe,* Dec. 2, 2000, on-line edition.

52. Eric Lichtblau and Robert L. Jackson, "Both Camps Turn to Big Guns for Supreme Court Arguments," *Los Angeles Times,* Nov. 30, 2000, A1, A30.

53. The following is taken from the on-line official court transcript at election2000.stanford.edu/100-836.pdf.

54. This argument had been mentioned by some commentators prior to the oral arguments. See Mark S. Scarberry, "Justices Usurped Legislature's Authority," *Los Angeles Times,* Nov. 23, 2000, B11.

55. At the end of the day, Tribe reportedly told members of the Gore legal team that he was surprised by the prevalence of this line of questioning. John Cloud, "May It Please the Court," *Time,* Dec. 11, 2000, 42–50, 47.

56. David Von Drehle, "Nine Justices But No Single Voice," *Washington Post,* Dec. 2, 2000, A1; Charles Lane, "U.S. High Court Hears Bush Appeal," *Washington Post,* Dec. 2, 2000, A1.

57. Raja Mishra, "Specialists Urge Caution in Predictions," *Boston Globe,* Dec. 2, 2000, on-line edition; Mary Leonard, "Day of Courtroom Dramas," *Boston Globe,* Dec. 2, 2000, on-line edition. See also Lyle Denniston, "Court Audience Left Guessing," *Baltimore Sun,* Dec. 2, 2000, on-line edition.

58. Leonard, "Day of Courtroom Dramas."

59. Michael McConnell, "Dialogues (with Alan Brinkley)," *Slate,* Dec. 4, 2000, slate.msn.com. McConnell noted that a 5 to 4 split on the merits would be very harmful to the Court, and he predicted that the justices would find a way out, either by declaring the case not ripe, or declaring it moot, or saying that it was a political question to be decided by Congress. Floyd Abrams also predicted a dismissal. See Henry Weinstein, "Unanimous Ruling Unlikely Due to Ideological Split," *Los Angeles Times,* Dec. 2, 2000, A1, A21.

60. Edward Lazarus, "The Ways of the High Court," *Washington Post,* Dec. 2, 2000, A25. See also David G. Savage and Henry Weinstein, "Justice Scalia's Novel Legal Theory," *Los Angeles Times,* Dec. 3, 2000, A1, A43. Columbia University law professor Samuel Issacharoff said, "It was a real surprise. An argument that was not put forth by the Bush folks suddenly takes command."

61. Richard A. Serrano and Michael Finnegan, "Gore Is Dealt 2 Key Legal Setbacks in Tallahassee," *Los Angeles Times,* Dec. 2, 2000, A1. The other setback was the refusal to order Sauls to start recounts.

62. Fladell v. Palm Beach County Canvassing Board, Case No. SC00-2373, Dec. 1, 2000.

63. Taylor v. Martin County Canvassing Board, Case No. 00-2850, Complaint, Dec. 1, 2000. See Scott Gold, "Suit Alleges Vote Fraud in Martin County, Fla.," *Los Angeles Times,* Dec. 2, 2000, A20.

64. Of all the absentee ballots, around 6,300 of them voted for Bush, while, 3,479 voted for Gore. Of the 2,132 corrected absentee ballot applications, 1,936 resulted in actual ballots being sent in, and 95 percent of these were for Bush.

65. Harris v. Florida Elections Canvassing Commission, Case No. CV00-2855, Dec. 1, 2000.

66. Consent Decree in United States v. Florida, No. TCA-80-1055 (N.D. Fla. 1982) and Florida's Administrative Code R.1S-2.013 (1998) provided in part: "(7) With respect to the presidential primary and the general election, any absentee ballot cast for a federal office by an overseas elector which is postmarked or signed and dated no later than the date of the Federal election shall be counted if received no later than 10 days from the date of the Federal election so long as such absentee ballot is otherwise proper."

67. Fla. Stat. § 101.67 (2) said that absentee ballots received later than 7:00 P.M. on Election Day shall not be counted.

68. Mark Z. Barabak and Richard A. Serrano, "Gore Asks Judge to Resume Count," *Los Angeles Times,* Dec. 3, 2000, A1; Mark Z. Barabak and Richard A. Serrano, "Ruling on Recount Expected Today," *Los Angeles Times,* Dec. 4, 2000, A1.

69. Cloud, "May It Please the Court."

70. Linda Greenhouse, "U.S. Justices Agree on Need to Clarify Case," *New York Times,* Dec. 5, 2000, on-line edition.

71. It was later reported, according to "a knowledgeable source," that it was Scalia "who forcefully argued that the court's opinion should include an order vacating the Florida Supreme Court's decision" and not merely remanding it for clarification. Bob Woodward and Charles Lane, "Scalia Takes a Leading Role in Case," *Washington Post,* Dec. 11, 2000, A1.

72. David G. Savage, "With Unanimous Compromise, U.S. Justices Leave Little Decided," *Los Angeles Times,* Dec. 5, 2000, A1, A16. Baker's reaction was: "From our standpoint at least, it was a win." Joan Biskupic, "Justices Throw Hot Potato Back to Fla. Court," *USA Today,* Dec. 5, 2000, 4A.

73. Charles Lane, "Justices Return Case to Fla.," *Washington Post,* Dec. 5, 2000, A1; see also Mary Leonard, "Justices Ruling Unanimous, But Not Decisive," *Boston Globe,* Dec. 5, 2000, on-line edition.

74. Emilie Lounsberry, "Justices Decide They Can't Decide," *Philadelphia Inquirer,* Dec. 5, 2000, on-line edition.

75. Laurence Tribe said: "I'm really quite pleased. At various levels this is the best that could have come out of it." Lane, "Justices Return Case."

76. Lane, "Justices Return Case."

77. Cass R. Sunstein, "The Broad Virtue in a Modest Ruling," *New York Times,* Dec. 5, 2000, on-line edition. As the paper pointed out in identifying Sunstein, he was the author of the book *One Case at a Time: Judicial Minimalism on the Supreme Court.*

78. Edward Lazarus, "What the U.S. Supreme Court's Election Decision Means for Bush, for Gore, and for the Court Itself," Findlaw.com, Dec. 5, 2000, writ.news.findlaw.com.

79. David G. Savage, "With Unanimous Compromise, U.S. Justices Leave Little Decided," *Los Angeles Times,* Dec. 5, 2000, A1, A16.

CHAPTER FOUR

1. William Glaberson, "Florida Ruling Dwafts Supreme Court Action," *New York Times,* Dec. 5, 2000, on-line edition.

2. Glaberson, "Florida Ruling."

3. The following is taken from the transcripts of the hearing before Judge Sauls on Sunday, Dec. 3, 2000, in the case Gore v. Harris, Case No. 00-2808.

4. Boies also noted that Miami-Dade had done a preliminary review of the ballots that found 388 additional votes for Gore, and those votes were never included in the state totals. However, he acknowledged that, unlike the case in Palm Beach (where the Bush lawyers

agreed with the standards being used to determine a vote), there was disagreement between the two sides over the criteria used to recover these 388 votes in Miami-Dade. Boies argued that this meant the judge would have to review the ballots himself to see how best to discover the intent of the voter.

5. Boies argued: "Section 102.141 . . . provides that there will be an automatic . . . recount in the event that the election is sufficiently close . . . and if there is a discrepancy between the election returns, and the later tabulation, the machine recount, it is the later tabulation that controls. . . . Now, that doesn't mean it would be impossible to have [another subsequent] tabulation as part of either a protest or a contest [because somebody believes the] statutory recount is wrong. . . . But nobody did that. . . . What they did was the one thing that the statute prohibits them from doing, which is to go back to the election night returns."

6. As for whether votes could be added after the Florida Supreme Court's deadline, Richard said, "We had a major battle before the Florida Supreme Court, and it resolved it, and what it said was: We're going to give you some extra time, but we're going to put a deadline" on the counting, and this court cannot disregard that decision.

7. Transcript of Ruling, Gore v. Harris, Case No. 00-2808, Court Proceedings in the Circuit Court of the Second Judicial Circuit, in and for Leon County, Monday, Dec. 3, 2000.

8. Henry Weinstein, "Last Hope for Gore May Be 1 Word: 'Doubt,'" *Los Angeles Times,* Dec. 5, 2000, A1, A15.

9. The *Wall Street Journal* was so impressed that it immediately (and mistakenly) crowned Judge Sauls one of the "three honest Democrats," alongside Judge Terry Lewis and Charles Burton (who resisted attempts to count dimpled ballots as votes). These were men who "remained judges first, exercising a fidelity to the rule of law," and "when histories of the 2000 presidential election are written" they "will deserve more than honorable mention in a story that has had more than its share of knaves, fools, and blind partisans." John Fund, "Three Honest Democrats," *WSJ.com,* Dec. 5, 2000, www.opinionjournal.com.

10. See, for example, the Dec. 5, 2000, front page of the *Los Angeles Times.*

11. David S. Broder, "Hopes Dim for Gore to Prevail," *Washington Post,* Dec. 5, 2000, A1. The poll was an ABC-*Washington Post* poll, reported in Mark Z. Barabak and Richard A. Serrano, "Rulings Narrow Gore's Options," *Los Angeles Times,* Dec. 5, 2000, A1, A14.

12. Barabak and Serrano, "Rulings Narrow Gore's Options"; Peter Slevin, "State Justices: Last Word?" *Washington Post,* Dec. 5, 2000, A1.

13. Weinstein, "Last Hope for Gore May Be 1 Word," A1, A15.

14. Michael McConnell, "Dialogues (with Alan Brinkley)," *Slate,* Dec. 5, 2000, slate.msn.com.

15. David Firestone, "Gore Loses Florida Recount Case; Puts Last Hope in State High Court," *New York Times,* Dec. 5, 2000, on-line edition; Barabak and Serrano, "Rulings Narrow Gore's Options"; Ronald Brownstein, "As Choices Dwindle, Vice President Will Look to Florida's High Court," *Los Angeles Times,* Dec. 5, 2000, A1, A15.

16. Jean Marbella, "Federal Court Looks Warily at Election Suits," *Baltimore Sun,* Dec. 6, 2000, on-line edition.

17. All of the judges who had been appointed by Democratic presidents voted with the majority in favor of the Gore position – Chief Judge R. Lanier Anderson III (Carter ap-

pointee), Rosemary Barkett (Clinton), Frank M. Hull (Clinton), and Charles R. Wilson (Clinton). Joining them were two judges appointed exclusively by Republicans – Emmett Ripley Cox (Reagan appointee) and J. J. Edmondson (Reagan). The two judges who had been appointed both by Democratic and Republican presidents voted in the majority – Susan Harrell Black (appointed by Carter to the district court and Bush to the circuit court) and Stanley Marcus (appointed by Reagan to the district court and Clinton, to the circuit). The dissenters were Gerald B. Tjoflat (Nixon and Ford), Stanley F. Birch (Bush), Joel F. Dubina (Reagan and Bush), and Ed Carnes (Bush).

18. Siegel v. Lepore, No. 00-15981, Appeal from the United States District Court for the Southern District of Florida, Dec. 6, 2000.

19. The defendants had claimed that the so-called Rooker-Feldman doctrine barred federal courts other than the U.S. Supreme Court from reviewing the final judgments of state courts. See District of Columbia Court of Appeals v. Feldman (1983) and Rooker v. Fidelity Trust Co. (1923). The judges ruled, though, that there was no final state court judgments in this matter. The judges also found that "neither res judicata nor collateral estoppel bars our consideration" of these issues. For an analysis of their discussion of the abstention doctrine, see Issacharoff et al. (2001).

20. See Baker v. Carr (1962) and Reynolds v. Sims (1964).

21. If, for example, the state mandated the types of voter systems used in each county and "deliberately favored urban counties with low-error systems that would keep down the undervote, while sticking rural counties with high-error systems that would increase the undervote [and thereby] reducing their influence in statewide elections," there would be "no doubt that such legislature would be unconstitutional" under the Supreme Court's one-person, one-vote cases.

22. Tjoflat's dissent was formally attached to the companion case, Touchston v. McDermott (Eleventh Cir. 2000).

23. In a bizarre feature of the argument, Tjoflat also argued that this "scheme" violated the "rights of association" of Bush supporters since their collective desire to advance their beliefs were being undermined by a system that inhibited them "from demonstrating their true electoral strength."

24. For an example of coverage of the case, see Edith Stanley, "Bush Loses Appeal of Manual Recount," *Los Angeles Times,* Dec. 7, 2000, A39.

25. Jeffrey Gettleman and David G. Savage, "Florida Legislators Set Special Session," *Los Angeles Times,* Dec. 7, 2000, A1, A42.

26. John Whitesides, "Florida Lawsuits Offer Gore Slim Hope in Election Fight," Reuters, Dec. 6, 2000, dailynews.yahoo.com.

27. Timeline, *U.S. News and World Report,* Dec. 18, 2000, 24.

28. Scott Gold, "Presidential Win Could Turn on Legal Longshot in 2 Fla. Counties," *Los Angeles Times,* Dec. 6, 2000, A1, A25.

29. "Veep's Best Hope?" *Newsweek,* Dec. 11, 2000, 29.

30. Donna Leinand, "Absentee Case Judge Said to Be Fair," *USA Today,* Dec. 6, 2000, 3A.

31. David Von Drehle, Susan Schmidt, James V. Grimaldi, and Jo Becker, "In a Dark Hour, a Last-Minute Reprieve," *Washington Post,* Feb. 2, 2001, A1.

32. Fla. Stat. § 101.62.

33. Fla. Stat. § 104.047.

34. See Taylor v. Martin County Canvassing Board, Case No. 00-2850, Trial Brief of George W. Bush and Richard Cheney, Dec. 6, 2000.

35. Scott Gold, "Absentee Application Fight Hits 2 Courts," *Los Angeles Times,* Dec. 7, 2000, A1; Scott Gold, "Democrats Gain Ground in Absentee Application Case," *Los Angeles Times,* Dec. 8, 2000.

36. Scott Gold, "Judges Let Absentee Votes Stand," *Los Angeles Times,* Dec. 9, 2000, A26.

37. Taylor v. Martin County Canvassing Board, Case No. 00-2850, Final Judgment for Defendants, Dec. 8, 2000.

38. Jeffrey Gettleman and David G. Savage, "Florida Legislators Set Special Session," *Los Angeles Times,* Dec. 7, 2000, A1, A42.

39. Ronald Brownstein, "Gore Faces Two Major Hurdles, Experts Say," *Los Angeles Times,* Dec. 6, 2000, A23.

40. Gore v. Harris, Case No. SC00-2431, Amended Brief of Appellees George W. Bush and Dick Cheney, Dec. 6, 2000.

41. Joseph P. Klock, representing the secretary of state, also affirmed that the supreme court had the authority to review the circuit court's decision.

42. William Glaberson, "Florida Justices' Dilemma – Peek in the Ballot Box or Walk Away?" *New York Times,* Dec. 8, 2000, on-line edition.

43. Charles Lane, "Chastened Justices Rehear Arguments," *Washington Post,* Dec. 8, 2000, A32.

44. James Warren and Monica Davey, "Judgment Day for Gore," *Chicago Tribune,* Dec. 8, 2000, on-line edition.

45. Dick Polman, "What If Ruling Just Opens Another Door?" *Philadelphia Inquirer,* Dec. 8, 2000, on-line edition.

46. Lane, "Chastened Justices"; Warren and Davey, "Judgment Day"; Mark Z. Barabak and Richard A. Serrano, "Florida High Court May Rule Today," *Los Angeles Times,* Dec. 8, 2000, A1, A43.

47. Gore v. Harris, Case No. SC00-2431, Clarification of Argument for Appellees George W. Bush and Dick Cheney, Dec. 8, 2000; see also Reply to Appellees' "Clarification of Argument," filed that same day, and the Court's order unanimously denying the motion to file a clarification of argument.

48. Dick Polman, "What If Ruling Just Opens Another Door?"; Michael Conlon, "Bush Wins Two More Cases on Road to Presidency," Reuters, Dec. 8, 2000, dailynews.yahoo.com; Charles Babington and Peter Slevin, "Judges Deliver Loss to Gore on Absentee Ballots," *Washington Post,* Dec. 8, 2000, on-line edition.

49. In another footnote they remarked about the Bush campaign's "substantial and dramatic change of position after oral argument" in its attempt to submit a clarification of argument. They noted that this argument was also inconsistent with their position in the first case, when Bush lawyer Michael Carvin told the court that the issues in this case were more properly handled in the contest phase.

50. Fla. Stat. § 101.5614(5)–(6).

51. Fla. Stat. § 102.166(7).

52. Jeffrey Gettleman, "A Bench of Independent Minds, 'Supremes' Go Their Own Way," *Los Angeles Times,* Dec. 9, 2000, A33. Earlier in the year, Shaw was so outraged by Florida's use of the electric chair in executions that he took the step of publishing explicit death chamber pictures on the Internet. The pictures graphically depicted the effects of the electric chair on an executed inmate. Adam Cohen of *Time* magazine suggested that the four judges in the majority all considered themselves outsiders. "Quince has spoken publicly about facing racism and sexism in her career: at her first trial as a lawyer, the judge assumed she was the defendant. (And at the first oral argument in this case, when other justices were scrupulously referred to as 'Your Honor,' Quince was at one point addressed as 'Ma'am.') Harry Lee Anstead, who is white, was raised by a single mother in a housing project. R. Fred Lewis, a native of West Virginia, keeps a dish of coal dust on his desk to remind him of his family's coal-mining origins. Barbara J. Pariente, who is Jewish, was raised in an affluent New Jersey suburb by parents who did not attend college." Adam Cohen, "Supreme Contest," *Time,* Dec. 18, 2000, 45.

53. David M. Shribman, "Wrenching Plot Twists in an Endless Drama," *Boston Globe,* Dec. 9, 2000, on-line edition; Kenneth T. Walsh, "Confusion Reigns," *U.S. News and World Report,* Dec. 18, 2000, 21.

54. Janet Hook and Nick Anderson, "Shock, Then Quick Action in Washington," *Los Angeles Times,* Dec. 9, 2000, A1, A27; James Gerstenzang, "Gore Camp Elated by Florida Decision," *Los Angeles Times,* Dec. 9, 2000, A26; Megan Garvey, "Mood Seesaws From Jubilation to Despair at Bush Headquarters," *Los Angeles Times,* Dec. 9, 2000, A27; Frank Bruni, "In the Bush Camp, the Florida Justices' Decision Brings a Sense of Weary Disbelief," *New York Times,* Dec. 9, 2000, www.nytimes.com.

55. Neldon Lund, "Travesty in Tallahassee," *Weekly Standard,* Dec. 9, 2000, www.weeklystandard.com.

56. Richard L. Berke, "Stunned Republicans Vow Fight to End," *New York Times,* Dec. 9, 2000, on-line edition.

57. Mark Z. Barabak and Richard A. Serrano, "Fla. High Court Backs Gore," *Los Angeles Times,* Dec. 9, 2000, A1, A30; Roger Simon, "Hold that Concession," *U.S. News and World Report,* Dec. 18, 2000, 30–31.

58. Tom Bowman and Jay Hancock, "Congress' Reaction Divides on Party Lines," *Baltimore Sun,* Dec. 9, 2000, on-line edition.

59. Berke, "Stunned Republicans." The minority leader of the Florida House of Representatives, Lois Frankel (a friend of Florida Supreme Court Justice Barbara J. Pariente), said she hoped that the manual recounts would be completed before Tuesday, when the House was scheduled to vote on a resolution naming new Florida electors. Marcia Gelbart, "Fla. Democrats Applaud Ruling; GOP Criticizes It," *Philadelphia Inquirer,* Dec. 9, 2000, on-line edition.

60. The following overview is taken from Associated Press, "Editorial Opinion on Fla. Recount," Dec. 9, 2000, dailynews.yahoo.com.

61. John Fund, "Rule of Lawyers: The Federal Courts Must Intervene to Save Us From Political Chaos," *WSJ.com,* Dec. 9, 2000, www.opinionjournal.com.

62. Noah Bierman, "Experts See High Court's Ruling Language as Crafty," *Palm Beach Post,* Dec. 9, 2000, www.gopbi.com/partners/pbpost/epaper/; Kenneth T. Walsh, "Confusion Reigns," *U.S. News and World Report,* Dec. 18, 2000, 24–25.

63. David G. Savage and Henry Weinstein, "Drama Shifts to U.S. High Court, Where Some Tough Options Await," *Los Angeles Times,* Dec. 9, 2000, A1, A30.

64. Scott Martelle, "Case Lands Back in Lap of Well-Respected Judge Lewis," *Los Angeles Times,* Dec. 9, 2000, A27; Scott Gold and Michael Finnegan, "Florida Counties Rush to Recount Unclear Ballots," *Los Angeles Times,* Dec. 9, 2000, A26.

65. These rules were set out in a formal order the following morning. Gore v. Harris, Case No. 00-2808, Order on Remand, Dec. 9, 2000.

66. David Von Drehle, Susan Schmidt, James V. Grimaldi, and Jo Becker, "In a Dark Hour, a Last-Minute Reprieve," *Washington Post,* Feb. 2, 2001, A1.

67. "On television, in the hours before the Supreme Court abruptly pulled the plug, the nation saw a recount process that, while plagued by confusion in some counties, was generally unfolding with order and dispatch." Ronald Brownstein, "In Blocking Vote Count, High Court Shows Which Team It's Rooting For," *Los Angeles Times,* Dec. 11, 2000, A5.

68. Michael Finnegan, "Amid Shouts and Mutters, Judges Start, Stop Recount Inside Tallahassee Library," *Los Angeles Times,* Dec. 10, 2000, A22.

69. Mark Z. Barabak and Richard A. Serrano, "Fla. High Court Backs Gore," *Los Angeles Times,* Dec. 9, 2000, A1, A30.

70. Eric Pooley, "Flipping the Script," *Time,* Dec. 18, 2000, 40; Scott Gold, "Counties Ponder Ballot Logistics," *Los Angeles Times,* Dec. 10, 2000, A22; Jeffrey Gettleman, "In Duval County, Views of Vote Process as Different as Black and White," *Los Angeles Times*, Dec. 10, 2000, A28.

71. Mark Z. Barabak and Richard A. Serrano, "Divided 5-4, U.S. Supreme Court Orders Halt to Florida Recounts," *Los Angeles Times,* Dec. 10, 2000, A1, A28.

72. Siegel v. LePore, 234 F.3d 1218; Touchston v. McDermott, 234 F.3d 1161. Charles Babington, "Little-Noticed Court Decision Held Political Promise for Gore," *Washington Post,* Dec. 11, 2000, A11.

73. Barabak and Serrano, "Divided 5-4."

CHAPTER FIVE

1. John O. McGinnis, "A Just and Wise Action," *New York Post,* Dec. 14, 2000, 41.

2. Ronald Dworkin, "A Badly Flawed Election," *New York Review of Books,* Jan. 11, 2001, on-line edition.

3. Bush v. Gore, Case No. 00 A 504, Emergency Application for a Stay of Enforcement of the Judgment Below Pending the Filing and Disposition of a Petition for a Writ or Certiorari to the Supreme Court of Florida, Dec. 8, 2000.

4. Their brief did note (in two sentences) that Palm Beach voters were instructed to make sure that "there are no chips left hanging on the back of the card," but they did not argue that this instruction meant that cards with hanging chads were not legally cast; instead, they complained about how there was no clear standard for evaluating these legally cast votes. In fact, the Bush lawyers argued that the correct standard for evaluating a punch card ballot required at least a hanging chad, which means it was not their view that whenever a voter cre-

ated a ballot that was not exactly in conformity to voter instructions it should be deemed an illegal ballot and not counted at all.

5. Ronald Brownstein, "For Every Cheer, There's a Jeer From the Other Camp," *Los Angeles Times,* Dec. 10, 2000, A1, A26; James Gerstenzang and Megan Garvey, "When Good News Hits, Remember, There's No Telling What's around the Corner," *Los Angeles Times,* Dec. 10, 2000, A22.

6. David G. Savage and Henry Weinstein, "Did Justices in Word and Deed, Tip Their Hand?" *Los Angeles Times,* Dec. 10, 2000, A1, A23.

7. Eric Pooley, "Flipping the Script," *Time,* Dec. 18, 2000, 34.

8. Brownstein, "For Every Cheer."

9. Mike Dorning, "Decision Casts Court in a 'Partisan Light,'" *Chicago Tribune,* Dec. 10, 2000, on-line edition.

10. Dorning, "Decision Casts Court." Gephardt disagreed with Leahy's comments, saying that "I don't think we get anywhere by impugning the motives of any court in this process." Susan Milligan, "Court Risks Image, Scholars Say," *Boston Globe,* Dec. 11, 2000, on-line edition.

11. Thomas Oliphant, "With Scalia Leading the Way, Supreme Court Commits a Blunder," *Boston Globe,* Dec. 11, 2000, on-line edition.

12. Edward Lazarus, "For the Supremes, a Basic Test of Legitimacy," *Washington Post,* Dec. 11, 2000, A27.

13. Jonathan Alter, "Legitimacy Goes in the Dock," *Newsweek,* Dec. 18, 2000, 47.

14. Alan Brinkley, "Dialogues (with Michael McConnell)," *Slate,* Dec. 11, 2000, slate.msn.com.

15. Savage and Weinstein, "Did Justices," A1, A23. It should be made clear that Michael McConnell, while suspicious of Scalia's argument on irreparable harm, believed that the Florida Supreme Court's decision violated Article II of the U.S. Constitution by changing Florida law and thus deserved to be overturned. Michael McConnell, "Dialogues (with Alan Brinkley)," *Slate,* Dec. 9, 2000, slate.msn.com.

16. Linda Greenhouse, "Collision with Politics Risks Court's Legal Legitimacy," *New York Times,* Dec. 10, 2000, on-line edition.

17. Savage and Weinstein, "Did Justices."

18. Charles Krauthammer, "The Winner in Bush v. Gore?" *Time,* Dec. 18, 2000, 104.

19. William Safire, "Biting the Ballot," *New York Times,* Dec. 11, 2000, on-line edition.

20. William Kristol, "Judicial Tyranny," *Washington Post,* Dec. 10, 2000, B7.

21. R. W. Apple, Jr., "Nation's Fault Line Divides Justices, Too," *New York Times,* Dec. 9, 2000, on-line edition. See also Stuart Taylor, Jr., "The Snippy Supremes," *Newsweek,* Dec. 18, 2000, 35; "Court's Reputation Could Be at Stake," Associated Press, Dec. 10, 2000, www.nytimes.com; Jan Crawford, "Justices, Stepping into the Fray, Risk Lasting Divisions," *Chicago Tribune,* Dec. 10, 2000, on-line edition.

22. Ronald Brownstein, "In Blocking Vote Count, High Court Shows Which Team It's Rooting For," *Los Angeles Times,* Dec. 11, 2000, A5. For a similar criticism of the conservatives' hypocritical abandonment of states rights principles, see Lazarus, "For the Supremes," A27.

23. Robert G. Kaiser, "Slim Majority Raises Fear of Court Partisanship," *Washington Post,* Dec. 10, 2000, A32.

24. "Court's Reputation."

25. Jack M. Balkin, "Supreme Court Compromises Its Legitimacy," *Boston Globe,* Dec. 12, 2000, on-line edition.

26. Howard Kurtz, "For the First Time in a While, High Court Gets Media Drubbing," *Washington Post,* Dec. 11, 2000, on-line edition.

27. Tom Kenworthy, "Americans Worry About Court's Election Role," *USA Today,* Dec. 11, 2000, on-line edition; "Nation Split Over Florida Recount but Trusts U.S. Supreme Court," CNN.com, Dec. 10, 2000.

28. Richard Morin and Claudia Deane, "Slim Majority of Public Wants Count Resumed," *Washington Post,* Dec. 11, 2000, A8. The poll was a *Washington Post*-ABC News survey.

29. "For Gore, It's Likely the Last Stand," MSNBC.com, Dec. 10, 2000; Richard A. Serrano and Richard Alonso-Zaldivar, "Democrats: Gore to Bow Out if Justices Deal a Defeat," *Los Angeles Times,* Dec. 11, 2000, A1. When James Baker appeared on *Meet the Press,* he parroted the point raised by Scalia in his stay opinion: "We're not afraid to let every vote be counted. The issue is, what is every legal vote?"

30. Bob Herbert, "To Any Lengths," *New York Times,* Dec. 11, 2000, on-line edition.

31. Bush v. Gore, Case No. 00-949, Brief for Petitioners, Dec. 10, 2000. The brief was submitted by Theodore B. Olson, Michael Carvin, Barry Richard, Benjamin L. Ginsberg, George J. Terwilliger III, William K. Kelley, John F. Manning, and Bradford R. Clark.

32. Bush v. Gore, Case No. 00-949, Brief of Respondent Albert Gore, Jr., Dec. 10, 2000. The brief was written by Laurence H. Tribe, David Boies, Thomas C. Goldstein, Ronald A. Klain, Kendall Coffey, and Peter J. Rubin.

33. At this point a footnote was inserted to respond to Scalia's suggestion that manual recounts lead to a degradation of the ballots. "This suggestion has scant support in the record, and there is ample evidence to the contrary. . . . More importantly, clearly the question of to what extent recounts of the ballots increase accuracy is a question for the state courts and state election officials under state law, not for this Court to resolve."

34. The Court attracted a considerable number of Bush and Gore protestors. David Stout, "Outside the Courtroom, a Much More Raucous Debate," *New York Times,* Dec. 11, 2000, on-line edition; Ricardo Alonso-Zaldivar and Richard Simon, "Pundits, Political Placards – and a Mule," *Los Angeles Times,* Dec. 12, 2000, A28.

35. David Von Drehle, Peter Slevin, Dan Balz, and James V. Grimaldi, "Anxious Moments in the Final Stretch," *Washington Post,* Feb. 3, 2001, A1.

36. The following was taken from the official transcript, available at election2000.stanford.edu/949trans.pdf.

37. After taking this rather strict but consistent position, Klock went through a bit of a bad period where he twice called justices by the wrong name. Stevens was referred to as "Justice Brennan"; after the laughter, Klock noted, "That's why they tell you not to do that" (refer to a justice by name rather than by "Your Honor"). Souter was referred to as "Justice Breyer," to which Souter responded, "I'm Justice Souter. You've got to cut that out" (more laughter), and Klock said, "I will now give up." Scalia: "Mr. Klock? I'm Scalia." (Laughter.) A very funny moment in the middle of a serious discussion.

38. Some contemporaneous accounts said that it was Souter who made the remark, "You would tell them to count every vote." See Francis X. Clines, "Humor (and Humanity) in Crucial Day at Court," *New York Times,* Dec. 12, 2000, on-line edition; Charles Lane, "Split High Court Grills Bush, Gore Lawyers," *Washington Post,* Dec. 12, 2000, A1; and the transcripts of the oral arguments provided by eMediaMillWorks and published on the *Washington Post*'s Web site. However, conversations with law professors in the courthouse during oral arguments clarify that it was Scalia, and even reporters who initially reported that it was Souter subsequently admitted that they had been mistaken.

39. Boies also displayed his legendary powers of recollection during an exchange with Justice O'Connor, who claimed that the Florida case Boardman v. Esteva held that certified results are presumptively correct and that the Florida Supreme Court "has sort of ignored that Boardman case." Boies responded that the case "relates not to the counting of votes. . . . The Boardman case, the language that you're referring to is at page 268 of the Southern Reporter report of that case. And what is clear from that page and that discussion is it's dealing with the issue of whether or not, because the canvassing board threw away the envelopes from the absentee ballots so they could not be checked, whether that invalidated the absentee ballots."

40. David G. Savage, "Justices Debate Bush vs. Gore," *Los Angeles Times,* Dec. 12, 2000, A1, A27. See also Jan Crawford, "Nation Waits on Supreme Court," *Chicago Tribune,* Dec. 12, 2000, on-line edition. Some took note of Scalia's obvious leadership in the movement to overturn the Florida court and halt the recounts, including his efforts during oral argument to provide Olson with key arguments when he seemed on the defensive. David Von Drehle, "Nine Decisive Votes, Deep Political Peril," *Washington Post,* Dec. 12, 2000, A1 (noting that when Scalia reminded Olson that "it's part of your submission" that "there is no wrong when a machine does not count those ballots that it's not supposed to count," he "sounded almost as if he had joined the Republican team"). In one biting parody of the oral argument, Maureen Dowd depicted Justice Scalia as saying at one point, "Mr. Olson, the legal predicate that seems to have slipped your muddled mind is that recounts are only triggered if there's a problem with the machinery, not in the case of voter error. Come on, Ted, do I have to plead your case for Bush as well as hear it?" Maureen Dowd, "The Bloom Is off the Robe," *New York Times,* Dec. 13, 2000, on-line edition.

41. Henry Weinstein, "Justices Find the Devil Is in the Details," *Los Angeles Times,* Dec. 12, 2000, A1, A29.

42. Linda Greenhouse, "Justices Questions Underline Divide on Whether Hand Recount Can Be Fair," *New York Times,* Dec. 11, 2000, on-line edition; see also Lane, "Split High Court Grills Bush, Gore Lawyers."

43. Savage, "Justices Debate Bush vs. Gore."

44. Greenhouse, "Justices' Questions"; Bob Woodward and Charles Lane, "Scalia Takes a Leading Role in Case," *Washington Post,* Dec. 11, 2000, A1; "Special Session Proceeds as Supreme Court Deliberates," CNN.com, Dec. 12, 2000; Christopher Marquis, "Job of Thomas's Wife Raises Conflict-of-Interest Questions," *New York Times,* Dec. 12, 2000, on-line edition. The federal judge cited 28 U.S.C. § 455, covering disqualification of judges, which requires recusal if a spouse has "an interest that could be substantially affected by the outcome of the proceeding."

45. Robert L. Jackson, "Calls for Recusal of Thomas, Scalia Are Undue, Experts Say," *Los Angeles Times,* Dec. 13, 2000, A25. On the other hand, a federal judge in Nashville from the Sixth Circuit, Gilbert S. Merritt, expressed the view that Thomas should disqualify himself.

46. "State High Court Clarifies Hand Count Ruling," Reuters, Dec. 12, 2000, dailynews.yahoo.com.

47. Justice Shaw recused himself from the case without explanation. In the companion case of Taylor v. Martin County Canvassing Board, the justices simply indicated that their decision in the Jacobs case "controls the outcome" in this case.

48. Scott Gold, "Florida High Court Rejects Absentee Ballot Cases," *Los Angeles Times,* Dec. 13, 2000, A28.

49. Florida Administrative Code § 1S-2.013.

50. The judge mentioned the case in n. 2, but only to make the point that this case was properly before a federal court.

51. Harris v. Florida Elections Canvassing Commission, Case No. 4:00cv453, Order, Dec. 9, 2000; Associated Press, "Court Upholds Military Ballots," Dec. 11, 2000, www.nytimes.com.

52. Jeffrey Gettleman, "Florida House OKs Slate of Electors Beholden to Bush," *Los Angeles Times,* Dec. 13, 2000, A28. The quote was from Jim Horne, a Republican from Orange Park.

53. Linda Greenhouse, "By Single Vote, Justices End Recount, Blocking Gore after 5-Week Struggle," *New York Times,* Dec. 13, 2000.

54. Megan Garvey and Bob Drogin, "On Cold Night, Shedding Light Isn't Easy," *Los Angeles Times,* Dec. 13, 2000, A24.

55. See Bickel (1962:185).

56. Josh Getlin, "It's Finally Over, a Nation Sighs, but Battle Scars May Linger," *Los Angeles Times,* Dec. 14, 2000, A1.

57. David G. Savage and Mark Z. Barabak, "Bush Wins in Supreme Court; Gore is Pressured to Concede," *Los Angeles Times,* Dec. 13, 2000, A1, A25; Doyle McManus and James Gerstenzang, "Gore Silent as Lawyers Grasp for Way to Keep Recount Quest Alive," *Los Angeles Times,* Dec. 13, 2000, A1, A26; Edwin Chen, "Hopes Quietly Rise within Bush Camp," *Los Angeles Times,* Dec. 13, 2000, A1, A29; Nick Anderson and Janet Hook, "To Many on Both Sides of Congress, 'It's Checkmate,'" *Los Angeles Times,* Dec. 13, 2000, A24; "Text of Statements Made by Baker, Daley," *Los Angeles Times,* Dec. 13, 2000, A26.

58. Doyle McManus and Alan C. Miller, "Lawyers Push for Final Appeal, but Gore Passes," *Los Angeles Times,* Dec. 14, 2000, A1, A47. The opening that some lawyers hoped to exploit was to go back to the Florida Supreme Court and ask them if they agreed with the Washington justices that Florida law made December 12 a firm deadline.

59. James Gerstenzang, "'We Are One People': Gore Urges Unity behind Bush," *Los Angeles Times,* Dec. 14, 2000, A46.

60. Edwin Chen and Mark Z. Barabak, "Bush Victorious," *Los Angeles Times,* Dec. 14, 2000, A1.

61. "Fla. Legislature Ends Electors Bid," Associated Press, Dec. 14, 2000, www.nytimes.com.

62. See www.nara.gov/fedreg/elctcoll/2000/certafl.html.

63. Savage and Barabak, "Bush Wins in Supreme Court" ("the majority did not conclude that the hand recounts ordered by the Florida courts were unnecessary or illegal [and] did not rule that the Florida judges had changed the rules after election day"); Charles Lane, "Decision Sharpens the Justices' Divisions," *Washington Post,* Dec. 13, 2000, A1 (the opinion "was also notable for the relative lack of emphasis on" the importance of deferring to the state legislature – "which had seemed to dominate the court's previous discussions of the case – and the relative prominence of the equal protection argument, which the court had only agreed to hear recently when Bush requested a stay over the weekend").

64. Greenhouse, "By Single Vote, Justices End Recount"; Linda Greenhouse, "News Analysis: Another Kind of Bitter Split When Jurisprudence Is Pulled into Politics," *New York Times,* Dec. 13, 2000, on-line edition; Savage and Barabak, "Bush Wins in Supreme Court"; Joan Biskupic, "Ruling Reveals Depth of Divide on the Court; 5-4 Split Puts Justices at Risk of Being Seen as 'Simply Politicians in Black Robes,'" *USA Today,* Dec. 13, 2000, 3A; Lane, "Decision Sharpens"; Michael Tackett, "Divided Court Bars Recount in Major Victory for Bush," *Chicago Tribune,* Dec. 13, 2000, on-line edition; Frank Davies, "Court Couldn't Overcome Bitter Divisions in Crafting Opinion," *Miami Herald,* Dec. 13, 2000, on-line edition; Ann Gearan, "High Court Ruling May Taint Court," Associated Press, Dec. 13, 2000, dailynews.yahoo.com.

65. Dudziak (2001), who cites the following articles from the foreign press: Ren Yujun, "Taking an Inventory after the Curtain Fell on the U.S. General Election," *Renmin Ribao* [Beijing], Dec. 16, 2000, and "Judges Govern America," *Le Monde,* Dec. 14, 2000, translated by the U.S. Foreign Broadcast Information Service (FBIS); and "Dailies Show Concern over Division of Superpower after Election," *ROK Yonhap* [Seoul], Dec. 14, 2000.

66. David G. Savage and Henry Weinstein, "Right to Vote Led Justices to 5-4 Ruling," *Los Angeles Times,* Dec. 14, 2000, A1.

67. Joan Biskupic, "Election Decision Still Splits Court," *USA Today,* Jan. 22, 2001, on-line edition.

68. "Editorials on Supreme Court Ruling," Associated Press, Dec. 13, 2000, www.nytimes.com; Editorial, "The Court Rules for Mr. Bush," *New York Times,* Dec. 13, 2000, on-line edition; Editorial, "Catch-22 Ruling Brings Election Near Messy End," *USA Today,* Dec. 13, 2000, 16A; Editorial, "'Supreme' Court?" *Denver Post,* Dec. 13, 2000, on-line edition; Editorial, "Bush's 5-4 'Victory,'" *Capital Times,* Dec. 13, 2000, on-line edition; Editorial, "Unsafe Harbor," *New Republic Online,* Dec. 14, 2000, www.tnr.com. See also Thomas Friedman, "Medal of Honor," *New York Times,* Dec. 15, 2000, on-line edition ("[Y]ou don't need an inside source to realize that the five conservative justices were acting as the last in a team of Republican Party elders who helped drag Governor Bush across the finish line").

69. Editorial, "A Victory for Equal Protection," *Chicago Tribune,* Dec. 13, 2000, on-line edition; Editorial, "7 to 2, It's Over," *WSJ.com,* Dec. 13, 2000, www.opinionjournal.com; Editorial, "Supreme Irony," *WSJ.com,* Dec. 14, 2000, www.opinionjournal.com.

70. Douglas W. Kmiec, "The Court's Decision Is Law, Not Politics," *Los Angeles Times,* Dec. 14, 2000, B15.

71. John O. McGinnis, "A Just and Wise Action," *New York Post,* Dec. 14, 2000, 41.

72. "A Principled Ruling to Some, a Disaster to Others," *Salon.com,* Dec. 13, 2000.

73. Michael McConnell, "Dialogues (with Alan Brinkley)," *Slate,* Dec. 13, 2000, slate.msn.com. McConnell elaborated on some of these comments in "A Muddled Ruling," *WSJ.com,* Dec. 14, 2000, www.opinionjournal.com.

74. John J. DiIulio, Jr., "Equal Protection Run Amok: Conservatives Will Come to Regret the Court's Rationale for Bush v. Gore," *Weekly Standard,* Dec. 25, 2000.

75. Editorial, "A President by Judicial Fiat," *Weekly Standard,* Dec. 18, 2000, on-line edition. This column, while dated after the U.S. Supreme Court's opinion, was actually written immediately after the Florida high court's decision ordering a new recount.

76. Conservative commentators were not the only ones offering this assessment. Cass Sunstein of the University of Chicago, neither strictly a conservative nor a liberal, also suggested that while the ruling may not "hold up very well," but "as a matter of statesmanship [which quickly resolved a lingering political dispute] it may well be vindicated." Robert G. Kaiser, "Opinion Is Sharply Divided on Ruling's Consequences," *Washington Post,* Dec. 13, 2000, A25.

77. Posner added a footnote here, indicating that he thought a Thurmond presidency unlikely; instead, moving down the line of succession, the office would skip over Secretary of State Madeline Albright, who was not born in the United States, to the secretary of the treasury, Lawrence Summers.

78. Posner acknowledged that his preferred option of relying on Article II rather than the equal protection clause was "not compelled by case law, legislative history, or constitutional language," but he added that it was also not blocked by these considerations. Posner should be credited for making explicit the sorts of political calculations that judges often must engage in, but it is also appropriate to keep in mind that a "pragmatic" mindset does not instruct a judge how to assess a strategic context, and so one should not confuse Posner's assessment with the proper pragmatic resolution. It is likely, in fact, that almost all of the justices believed there were pragmatic components to their positions.

79. Posner (2001). For similar discussions of this political rationale, see Sunstein (2001) and Dennis J. Hutchinson, "Law and Politics in the Supreme Court," *Chicago Tribune,* Dec. 17, 2000, 21.

80. Warren Richey, "Fairly or Not, Court Takes on Political Hue," *Christian Science Monitor,* Dec. 14, 2000, on-line edition.

81. Herman Schwartz, "The God That Failed," *Nation,* Jan. 1, 2001, www.thenation.com.

82. Neal Kumar Katyal, "Politics over Principle," *Washington Post,* Dec. 14, 2000, A35.

83. Vincent Bugliosi, "None Dare Call It Treason," *Nation,* Feb. 5, 2001, 11–19.

84. Jeffrey Rosen, "Disgrace: The Supreme Court Commits Suicide," *New Republic Online,* Dec. 14, 2000, www.tnr.com.

85. Mary McGory, "Supreme Travesty of Justice," *Washington Post,* Dec. 14, 2000, A3.

86. Henry T. Greely, "Court's Intervention Break the Faith," *San Jose Mercury News,* Dec. 15, 2000, on-line edition.

87. Anthony Lewis, "A Failure of Reason," *New York Times,* Dec. 16, 2000, on-line edition.

88. Alan Brinkley, "Dialogues (with Michael McConnell)," *Slate,* Dec. 13, 2000, slate.msn.com.

89. Gary Kamiya, "Supreme Court to Democracy: Drop Dead," *Salon.com,* Dec. 14, 2000.

90. Eben Moglen, "Now, History Will Judge Them," MSNBC.com, Jan. 1, 2001.

91. Ronald Dworkin, "A Badly Flawed Election," *New York Review of Books,* Jan. 11, 2001, www.nybooks.com/nyrev/. Charles Fried of the Harvard Law School, who had written the amicus brief of the state legislature, responded to Dworkin's critique by suggesting that the Court did not really divide neatly down ideological lines, since O'Connor and Kennedy sometimes hand down liberal decisions in other cases (such as in upholding abortion rights in *Casey*). However, an occasional deviation from an otherwise clear pattern of ideological voting, even over an important issue like abortion, is not enough to undermine obvious generalizations about the prevailing political divisions on the Court. Fried also claimed that a decision to allow the recounts to continue would have inevitably led to more legal challenges and new complaints to the Supreme Court, and he asked whether "such a continuation of the legal proceedings, inevitably leading to an indeterminate outcome, [would] really have been a more satisfactory course?" Following Posner, he added that the election was "in effect a tie," which meant that recounts would give us "different results" but "no greater accuracy," and thus the country was faced with "a freakish situation beyond the capacity of any [institution] to resolve to everyone's satisfaction." Dworkin responded by calling "unfortunate" Fried's apparent view that "it does not really matter whether the Supreme Court's decision was defensible because the election was so close anyway that it might as well have been Bush. . . . Fried insists that it is beyond 'our present capacity' to achieve a more accurate vote tabulation. But the careful unofficial recounts now being conducted separately by the *Miami Herald* and by a group of other prestigious newspapers, which Fried declares a foolish exercise, will presumably show that his surprising pessimism is unfounded." Charles Fried and Ronald Dworkin, "'A Badly Flawed Election': An Exchange," *New York Review of Books,* Feb. 22, 2001, 8–10.

92. In his defense of the U.S. Supreme Court, Posner argued that the Catch-22 argument was unsound because creating a clearer standard would not be considered a "change" in the law, since "there is a difference between changing the meaning of a statute and filling in empty spaces in the statute." However, even if he was certain in his mind that it would have been appropriate for the Florida justices to clarify the standard, it also does not seem unreasonable to assume that the Florida justices considered the Washington justices highly motivated to catch them in the mistake against which they warned them.

93. Fried, "'A Badly Flawed Election'"; Michael McConnell expressed the same view.

94. Michael C. Dorf, "Supreme Court Pulled a Bait and Switch," *Los Angeles Times,* Dec. 14, 2000, B15.

95. David G. Savage and Henry Weinstein, "High Court in Awkward Spot Over Equal Protection Ruling," *Los Angeles Times,* Dec. 16, 2000, on-line edition.

96. Savage and Weinstein, "Right to Vote," A1.

97. James V. Grimaldi and Roberto Suro, "Risky Bush Legal Strategy Paid Off," *Washington Post,* Dec. 17, 2000, A32.

98. Greenhouse, "News Analysis: Another Kind of Bitter Split." Michael Greve, while acknowledging that "partisan considerations influenced . . . the justices' rulings," nevertheless thought that the positions of the justices reflected their typical commitment to either "constitutional federalism" or "cooperative federalism." "The *Real* Division in the Court," *Weekly Standard,* Dec. 25, 2000.

99. Smith v. Allwright (1944) (Roberts, J., dissenting).

100. David G. Savage and Henry Weinstein, "Right to Vote Led Justices to 5-4 Ruling," *Los Angeles Times,* Dec. 14, 2000, A1.

101. Posner (2001).

102. See Issacharoff et al. (2001).

103. David Abel, "Bush v. Gore Case Compels Scholars to Alter Courses at US Law Schools," *Boston Globe,* Feb. 3, 2001, on-line edition.

104. William Glaberson, "Court Battle for Presidency Rages On in Legal Circles," *New York Times,* Feb. 1, 2001, on-line edition. The ad was paid for by the liberal People for the American Way Foundation; it also informed readers that if they wanted to make contributions so that they ad could be republished they should contact Law Professors for the Rule of Law at lawprofs@the-rule-of-law.com. A Web site was also created and a listserv was set up to encourage dialogue on "what's next" for those who wanted to protest the decision. Charles Fried, a Harvard law professor who was solicitor general in the Reagan administration, called the advertisement a "preposterous" declaration by people "in the grip of partisan excitement."

105. Abel, "Bush v. Gore Case Compels Scholars to Alter Courses."

106. Ackerman (2001).

107. Charles Lane, "Watch Is on for Signs O'Connor Will Retire," *Washington Post,* Feb. 5, 2001, A17.

108. Alan M. Dershowitz, "Justice May Be Blind, But It's Not Deaf," *Los Angeles Times,* Dec. 28, 2000, B13.

109. Caryn James, "An Apocalyptic Attitude Gripped the TV Commentators, Not Their Viewers," *New York Times,* Dec. 17, 2000, on-line edition.

110. "NBC Poll Takes American's Pulse," MSNBC.com, Dec. 14, 2000.

111. Janet Elder, "Poll Shows Americans Divided over Election, Indicating That Bush Must Build Public Support," *New York Times,* Dec. 18, 2000, on-line edition (reporting on a CBS News poll).

112. Richard Benedetto, "It's Time to Move On, People Say Americans Relieved Fight Is Finally Over," *USA Today,* Dec. 18, 2000, on-line edition (reporting on a *USA Today*/CNN/Gallup Poll). When President Bush made his first visit back to Florida in March 2001 there was almost no evidence of an angry voter backlash. Local Democrats, disappointed at low turnout for protest rallies, nevertheless insisted that "Republicans are in for a shock if they think voters don't remain agitated." Charles Babington, *Washington Post,* Mar. 13, 2001, on-line edition.

113. Wendy Simmons, "Election Controversy Apparently Drove Partisan Wedge into Attitudes towards Supreme Court," Gallup.com, Jan. 16, 2001, www.gallup.com/poll/releases/pr010116.asp.

114. "Fla. Ballots Homeward Bound, Unofficial Count Starts," Reuters, Dec. 18, 2000, dailynews.yahoo.com; Mike Clary, "Broward County Ballots Get Another Once-Over," *Los Angeles Times,* Dec. 19, 2000, on-line edition.

115. "Newspaper Shows Bush Gaining Votes," Associated Press, Jan. 14, 2001, www.nytimes.com. The paper reported that 7,600 votes had no mark at all, and around 2,200 votes had cleanly punched holes in spots dedicated to none of the candidates.

116. Amy Driscoll, "Dade Undervotes Support Bush Win," *Miami Herald,* Feb. 26, 2001, on-line edition. They reported that there were no marks for president on 4,892 ballots and 2,058 bore markings in spaces that had been assigned to no candidate. The claim that Bush would have won is based on this arithmetic: after the absentee ballot votes Bush's lead was 930; Gore received 567 votes from Broward, 174 from Palm Beach, and 49 from Miami-Dade, for a total of 790. That would have left Bush in the lead by 140 votes.

117. "Palm Beach Count Finds Gore Gain," Associated Press, Mar. 11, 2001, on-line edition. More specifically, it was reported that Bush would have gained 14 votes if hanging chads undervotes were counted; Gore would have gained 25 votes if the board counted all ballots where one could see light through a pinhole; and 784 votes if it counted all dimpled chads

118. Jake Tapper, "And the Winner Was?" *Salon.com,* April 4, 2001.

119. David Damron, Ramsey Campbell, and Roger Roy, "Gore Would Have Gained Votes," *Sun-Sentinel,* Dec. 19, 2000, on-line edition. This total did not include hundreds of other questionable ballots in which intent could be discerned in other ways, for example, by noticing that a voter attempted one of the marks on the ballot or wrote next to one mark a note such as "wrong one" or "mistake."

120. "Ballot Review Shows Gore Stood To Gain," *Sun-Sentinel,* Feb. 11, 2001, on-line edition.

121. Bob Drogin, "2 Florida Counties Show Election Day Inequities," *Los Angeles Times,* Mar. 12, 2001, A1. In Leon County there was a total of only 154 uncounted ballots out of 103,418; nearly all the uncounted ballots were from people who intentionally abstained in the presidential race. The final tally in Dadsden: 9,735 votes for Gore, 4,767 for Bush, and 2,085 uncounted ballots.

122. John Maines, Sean Cavanagh, and Megan O'Matz, "Florida 2000: The Lost Vote," *Sun-Sentinel,* Jan. 28, 2001, on-line edition.

123. Dan Keating, "Fla. 'Overvotes' Hit Democrats the Hardest: Gore 3 Times as Likely To Be Listed on Tossed Ballots," *Washington Post,* Jan. 27, 2001, A1. The article also confirmed that Gore was disproportionately affected by the "butterfly ballot"; overvotes in Palm Beach that included Gore's name plus one other person listed near him voted 10 to 1 for the Democrat in the U.S. Senate race.

124. Debbie Salamone Wickham and Harry Wessel, "Ballot Counting Standards Vary Among Counties," *Sun-Sentinel,* Jan. 27, 2001, on-line edition.

125. JoAnne Allen, "Election Reform Panel Tackles Voting Problems," Reuters, Mar. 2, 2001, dailynews.yahoo.com.

126. Sue Anne Pressley, "Election Panel Calls for Changes in Fla.," *Washington Post,* Feb. 24, 2001, A10.

127. The story was first reported in early December. See Gregory Palast, "Florida's Flawed 'Vote-Cleansing' Program," *Salon.com,* Dec. 4, 2000.

128. Sue Anne Pressley, "Civil Rights Commission Looking into Florida Vote Irregularities," *Washington Post,* Jan. 11, 2001, on-line edition; Sue Anne Pressley, "Harris's Election Stance Assailed," *Washington Post,* Jan. 13, 2001, A1. Harris insisted that she did the best she could with the resources available to ensure a fair election. Commissioner Victoria Wilson accused her and other state officials of being "on a merry-go-round of denial."

129. Dana Canedy, "Rights Panel Begins Inquiry Into Florida's Voting System," *New York Times*, Jan. 12, 2001, on-line edition.

130. "Florida Justice Anstead Scutinized," Associated Press, Dec. 14, 2000, on-line edition.

131. Dexter Filkins, "Republican Group Seeks to Unseat Three Justices," *New York Times*, Dec. 20, 2000, on-line edition.

132. David Firestone, "After Recount Battle, More Storms Lie Ahead for Florida Court," *New York Times*, Dec. 23, 2000, on-line edition.

133. Gore v. Harris, No. SC00-2431, Dec. 22, 2000.

134. "High Court Bars 2 Fla. Vote Count Appeals," Associated Press, Jan. 6, 2000, www.washingtonpost.com.

135. Charles Babington, "It's Official: Bush Wins Electoral College," *Washington Post*, Dec. 18, 2000, on-line edition. The only moment that was a bit out of the ordinary came when one of the electors from the District of Columbia, Barbara Lett Simmons, temporarily withheld her vote to call attention to the district's lack of voting members in Congress.

136. John Heilprin, "105.4 Million Voters Cast Ballots," Associated Press, Dec. 18, 2000, dailynews.yahoo.com.

137. Edward Walsh and Juliet Eilperin, "Gore Presides as Congress Tallies Bush Votes," *Washington Post*, Jan. 7, 2001, A1.

CHAPTER SIX

1. These remarks were made to a group of high school students the day after *Bush v. Gore* was decided. Neil A. Lewis, "Justice Thomas Speaks Out on a Timely Topic, Several of Them, in Fact," *New York Times*, Dec. 14, 2000, on-line edition.

2. Irvin Molotsky, "In Year-End Report, Rehnquist Renews His Call to Raise the Salaries of Federal Judges," *New York Times*, Jan. 1, 2001, on-line edition.

3. Tony Mauro, "After 'Bush v. Gore,' Supremes Do Damage Control," Law.com, Feb. 12, 2001.

4. Charles Lane, "Ginsburg Critical on Bush v. Gore," *Washington Post*, Feb. 3, 2001, A2; David G. Savage, "Ginsburg Rebukes Justices for Intervening in Fla. Vote," *Los Angeles Times*, Feb. 3, 2001, A10. The reference to what the "home crowd" wants purposefully echoed a 1980 speech by Chief Justice Rehnquist, when he explained the obligations of a good judge: "He or she must strive constantly to do what is legally right, all the more so when the result is not what the one Congress, the president or the 'home crowd' wants."

5. Justices Kennedy and Thomas also briefly defended themselves before a House appropriations subcommittee, with the former saying that "[W]e will be judged not by what we say after the fact in order to embellish our opinions or detract from what some of our colleagues say, [but] by what we put in our appellate reports." He added, "Over time you build up a deposit, a reservoir, a storehouse of trust. When we make a difficult decision in many areas – and this was not the most difficult decision the Court has made – for many of us, you draw down on that capital of trust. . . . Sometimes it is easy, so it seems, to enhance your prestige by not exercising your responsibility, but that's not been the tradition of our court." "Justices Defend Handling of Florida Election Case," CNN.com, Mar. 29, 2001.

6. Nick Anderson and Janet Hook, "Agitation and Joy Felt on Capitol Hill," *Los Angeles Times,* Nov. 22, 2000, A16.

7. Frank Bruni, "In the Bush Camp, the Florida Justices' Decision Brings a Sense of Weary Disbelief," *New York Times,* Dec. 9, 2000, on-line edition; Edward Walsh and Juliet Eilperin, "Ruling Angers GOP, Heartens Democrats," *Washington Post,* December 9, 2000, A16. In addition to the responses reviewed in the previous chapters, see Cross (2001).

8. Robert G. Kaiser, "Slim Majority Raises Fear of Court Partisanship," *Washington Post,* December 10, 2000, A32; Jeffrey Rosen, "Disgrace: The Supreme Court Commits Suicide," *New Republic Online,* Dec. 14, 2000, www.tnr.com; Neal Kumar Katyal, "Politics over Principle," *Washington Post,* December 14, 2000, A3.

9. William Glaberson, "Court Battle for Presidency Rages On in Legal Circles," *New York Times,* Feb. 1, 2001, on-line edition.

10. Cross (2001) cites Thomas Friedman's comments at a time when Republicans seemed to be changing their characterizations of Florida courts depending on whether they were winning or losing. "Every Florida official, judge and canvassing board has been given a choice: Either rule for Governor Bush or be labeled as illegitimate. When the Florida Supreme Court ruled in favor of Mr. Bush that Miami-Dade County did not have to hand recount, Republicans praised that court for acting responsibly, and when the same court ruled in Al Gore's favor, it was branded as a Democratic rubber stamp." Thomas L. Friedman, "Jeklyll and Hyde," *New York Times,* Nov. 28, 2000, A31.

11. See Epstein and Knight (1998), Maltzman et al. (2000), Murphy (1964). For example, there is evidence that Chief Justice John Marshall offered an insincere interpretation of a congressional lottery statute in order to avoid a conflict with the Virginia Supreme Court (Graber 1995). We also know that Justice Stanley Reed disagreed with the decision in Brown v. Board of Education, but he chose to not write a dissent because he was convinced by Chief Justice Warren that it would not be in the best interests of the country (Kluger 1976).

12. Carter (1998) emphasizes this point in his terrific discussion of "fact freedom" – the ability of a judge to hone in on the special facts about a new case to make it appear either the same as or completely different than a prior case.

13. The analysis in this section of the voting records of these various courts builds on an early analysis of the evidence by Cross (2001).

14. McDermott v. Harris, Case No. 00-2700, Order Denying Emergency Motion to Compel Compliance With and For Enforcement of Injunction, Nov. 17, 2000.

15. Taylor v. Martin County Canvassing Board, Case No. 00-2850, Final Judgment for Defendants, Dec. 8, 2000.

16. Mitchell Landsberg, "Judge Upholds Democrat's Lawsuit over Absentee Applications," *Los Angeles Times,* Nov. 21, 2000, A16.

17. Florida Democratic Party v. Palm Beach County Canvassing Board, Declaratory Order, Nov. 15, 2000.

18. Fladell v. Elections Canvassing Commission, Case No. CL 00-10965 AB, Order (Plaintiffs' Complaint for Declaratory Injunctive and Other Relief Arising From Plainti/ Claims of Massive Voter Confusion Resulting From the Use of a "Butterfly" Type Bal During the Election Held on November 7, 2000, Nov. 20, 2000.

19. Fladell v. Palm Beach County Canvassing Board, Case No. SC00-2373, Dec. 1, 20

20. Siegel v. LePore (Case No. 00-9009-VCIV-MIDDLEBROOKS), Order On Plaintiffs' Emergency Motion for Temporary Restraining Order and Preliminary Injunction, Nov. 13, 2000.

21. Touchston v. McDermott, No. 00-15985, Order on Emergency Motion for Injunction Pending Appeal, Nov. 17, 2000.

22. Transcript of Ruling, Gore v. Harris, Case No. 00-2808, Court Proceedings in the Circuit Court of the Second Judicial Circuit, in and for Leon County, Monday, Dec. 3, 2000.

23. Evan Thomas and Michael Isikoff, "Settling Old Scores in the Swamp," *Newsweek,* Dec. 18, 2000, 43.

24. Harris v. Florida Elections Canvassing Commission, Case No. 4:00cv453, Order, Dec. 9, 2000.

25. Paul was upheld by three Republican appointees on the Eleventh Circuit.

26. Not included in this review is the decision of a three-judge panel of the court (all Republicans) upholding Judge Paul's ruling on counting absentee ballots that came in after the statutory deadline, nor the unanimous decision on Dec. 9, 2000, which simply prevented the Florida Elections Canvassing Commission from changing the certified election results until the U.S. Supreme Court could rule on the Bush appeal of the restarted recounts.

27. No. 00-15985, Nov. 17, 2000.

28. No. 00-15981, Dec. 6, 2000. Essentially the same decision was handed down this day in Touchston v. McDermott, and these two cases are treated as one decision for purposes of this review.

29. Carnes argued that the Democratic Party did not choose these three counties because they had the highest rate of undervotes (and thus represented the places where machine errors were most serious) or because there were more senior citizens and minority voters in these districts. "Instead, the defining characteristic of the 3 punch card counties chosen to undertake a manual recount is that they are the 3 most populous counties in the state, all of which gave the Party's Presidential nominee a higher percentage of the vote than his opponent."

30. Then again, even a partisan may think it is worth it to stand by a principle that was designed to help a Republican become president even if it means that one also uses it to help a few Democratic city attorneys get elected in future cases.

31. Not included in this list is the reiteration on remand of its decision in Palm Beach County Canvassing Board v. Harris, which included a dissent from Chief Justice Wells. In addition to merely reiterating its earlier decision, the case also could have little impact on the outcome of the election, since the issue of the deadline for the original certification was essentially moot by that time.

32. Nos. SC00-2346, 2348, and 2349, Nov. 21, 2000.

33. No. 00-2370, Nov. 23, 2000.

34. No. SC00-2373, Dec. 1, 2000.

35. No. SC00-2431, Dec. 8, 2000.

36. Nos. SC00-2447 and 2448, Dec. 12, 2000.

37. See Murphy (1964), Epstein and Knight (1998).

38. Such a decision would have required some cooperation from the secretary of state and the governor, but these officials would also have to cooperate in certifying the results of a recount.

39. Note especially Scheppele's (2001) review of the various "infelicities" of the Florida election code, which she claims amounted to an actual failure of law.

40. Klock said that Secretary of State Harris believed she could only accept late ballots when there were allegations of fraud or disruptions caused by acts of God. Stevens asked whether "she would have to exercise her discretion in those conditions," and Klock (contradicting Olson's theory of complete discretion after the seven-day deadline) said, "I think she would have to exercise her discretion" and accept late ballots in these cases.

41. At one point, Kennedy and O'Connor reiterated their initial concern about how that court had previously changed the deadline, with Kennedy asking whether it would have been a "new law" if the legislature adjusted the deadline and O'Connor adding, "in the context of selection of presidential electors, isn't there a big red flag up there, 'Watch Out'?" The only other exchange on this issue came toward the end, when O'Connor wanted to know why the state should not just ignore votes when voters fail to follow voting instructions ("for goodness sakes?"). Boies said that the law in Florida for at least eighty-three years was that "where a voter's intent can be discerned, even if they don't do what they're told, that's supposed to be counted" (citing Darby v. State and the more recent Beckstrom v. Volusia County Canvassing Board).

42. While some still claim that Justices Souter and Breyer shared the majority's view that the last recount was marred by equal protection violations, it must be reemphasized that they did not consider these problems justiciable under these circumstances, and their *dissent* made it clear that the Court had no business using that argument as a basis for intervening.

43. As conservative law professor Michael McConnell put it early on in the process while explaining why the issue would stop at the Florida Supreme Court, "there does not appear to be federal issues, so the U.S. Supreme Court will not become involved." "Dialogue (with Alan Brinkley)," *Slate,* Nov. 16, 2000, slate.msn.com.

44. The main complaint was that this process only allowed voters to have an influence over two of the state's twelve electors (one from their congressional district plus one of two selected from "floterial" districts). The gist of the Supreme Court's holding was that this decision was up to states; moreover, since state legislatures were free to prevent their citizens from voting for any of the electors, it was no problem allowing them to vote for only two.

45. Some of the justices who spoke to Linda Greenhouse claim that this initial decision was misunderstood; they say that the issue was not taken up in the first case because it was scheduled to be fully argued later in the Eleventh Circuit; hence, they denied the federal appeal "without prejudice" and focused instead on the issues that were at the center of the appeal from the Florida Supreme Court. But there are good reasons to reject this ingenuous version. The issues that were the focus of the appeal – the meaning of 3 U.S.C. § 5 and the Article II challenge to the state high court's decision – were not any more fully developed than the equal protection argument; in fact, the equal protection argument had been addressed much more than had these statutes during the oral argument before the Florida Supreme Court (at least in the sense that the Florida justices repeatedly asked Bush lawyer

Michael Carvin about it; he consistently said that the state justices should not focus on the issue). Moreover, events were moving very quickly; in particular, when the Supreme Court took the appeal a few days after the Florida Supreme Court decision, it was still possible to think that Gore was going to win the recount and be certified the winner; therefore, when the five justices took the case, they were preparing to rule on whether a Gore victory violated federal law. Given this situation it makes little sense that they believed it would be a good idea for them to focus just on a few aspects of that question and then revisit the equal protection element of the challenge at some later date. It is much more reasonable to think that the five conservatives did not initially believe that equal protection was a plausible basis on which to void a Gore victory. Linda Greenhouse, "Election Case a Test and a Trauma for Justices," *New York Times,* Feb. 20, 2001, on-line edition.

46. See Epstein (2001) (calling the equal protection argument "a confused nonstarter at best, which deserves much of the scorn that has been heaped upon it"); Posner (2001) ("such differences had not previously been thought to deny equal protection of the laws and if they are now to do so this portends an ambitious program of federal judicial intervention in the electoral process, a program the Supreme Court seems, given the haste with which it acted, to have undertaken without much forethought about the program's scope and administrability"); and Robert Bork's comment that the majority opinion "might be debatable" (Maureen Dowd, "Black and White," *New York Times,* Feb. 14, 2001, A31). For an atypical conservative defense, see McConnell (2001) ("why not require every state to adopt a uniform vote counting system?").

47. As Sunstein (2001) put it, imagine that "in 1998, a candidate for statewide office – say, the position of attorney general – lost after a manual recount, and brought a constitutional challenge on equal protection grounds, claiming that county standards for counting votes were unjustifiably variable. Is there any chance that the disappointed candidate would succeed in federal court? In all likelihood the constitutional objection would fail; in most courts, it would not even be taken seriously."

48. Two of the leading political scientists who study judicial behavior predicted back in 1993 that "if a case on the outcome of a presidential election should reach the Supreme Court [then] the Court's decision might well turn on the personal preferences of the justices" (Segal and Spaeth 1993:70). This may be the most prophetic, nonbanal prediction ever made by researchers studying judicial politics, and these researchers deserve enormous credit. It should be pointed out, though, that their view is a bit inconsistent with their general model, which focuses on the influence of a consistent political *ideology* or set of policy preferences on Supreme Court decision-making, not on the influence of ad hoc partisan judgments. For example, in a freedom of speech case involving Republican speakers, it is still assumed that more liberal judges will favor the free speech position; it is also predicted that conservatives would be more likely to strike down limits on campaign spending even if the litigant was the Democratic Party. Segal and Spaeth finesse this issue by using the phrase "political preferences" in their prediction rather than the more typical way they express their position, which is to talk about personal *policy* preferences or ideological influences. While there are good reasons why all commentators understood that the conservatives' political preference would be for Bush, there is also some irony in the possibility that if the conservatives would have rejected the equal protection argument, Spaeth and Segal may have been able to say that this,

too, was consistent with voting their conservative attitudes, and thus making the theory in this case unfalsifiable. Also, Segal and Spaeth may have trouble explaining, from a purely attitudinal perspective, why the three concurring justices signed onto a per curiam opinion whose logic suggested a liberal reading of the equal protection clause when they could have reached the same result by sticking with their Article II argument; if attitudinalists judges are concerned about policy, they should have concurred in the reversal and thus prevented the equal protection policy from obtaining a majority. Finally, attitudinalism has troubling explaining why the four Bush v. Gore dissenters voted with the majority in Bush v. Palm Beach County Canvassing Board. All of these behaviors require considerations of other aspects of judicial politics besides those emphasized by attitudinalists.

49. Klarman (2001). Note that Klarman's comment was about "switching" the parties, not substituting the parties. We can all think of cases where the Court might have voted differently if completely different people were involved.

50. Strauss (2001).

51. Greenhouse, "Election Case a Test and a Trauma for Justices."

52. ABC News/*Washington Post* Poll, Nov. 16, 2000.

53. It is because Souter thought that presidential election controversies were to be handled exclusively by state officials and the U.S. Congress that he disagreed with the majority in Bush v. Gore that any alleged equal protection violation – even if well-founded – justified Supreme Court intervention. This is why it is wrong for conservatives to claim that seven Supreme Court justices agreed that there were justiciable equal protection issues in this controversy.

54. Ely (1980). In footnote 4, the Court expressed doubts about whether it should defer to laws or other practices that restrict "those political processes which can ordinarily be expected to bring about repeal of undesirable legislation" or that tend "seriously to curtail the operation of those political processes ordinarily to be relied on."

55. Sunstein (2001); see also Dennis J. Hutchinson, "Law and Politics in the Supreme Court," *Chicago Tribune,* Dec. 17, 2000, 21.

56. Posner (2001).

57. Morin and Deane, "Slim Majority of Public," A8. The poll was a *Washington Post-ABC News* survey.

58. McConnell (2001).

59. Garrett (2001). Emphasis added.

60. It is interesting to note that within the last decade, these same justices who shortchanged the presidential election process have also ushered in an era of extraordinary skepticism of congressional politics. In particular, the justices have forbidden the Congress from interpreting Fourteenth Amendment rights more broadly than the Court, and the conservative majority has repeatedly rejected legislative findings by the Congress designed to justify laws such as the Gun-Free School Zones Act, the Age Discrimination in Employment Act, the Violence Against Women Act, and most recently, the Americans with Disabilities Act. See City of Boerne v. Flores (1997), United States v. Lopez (1995), Kimel v. Florida Board of Regents (2000), United States v. Morrison (2000), and University of Alabama v. Garrett (2001). The pattern has been pronounced enough that Linda Greenhouse of the *New York Times* has suggested that Congress has become a "target" of these conservative justices. Robert Post, a law professor at UC Berkeley, has said that "the court is acting as if Congress

is just a bad lower court" in need of correction by justices who are better able to make decisions about these matters. "The High Court's Target: Congress," *New York Times*, Feb. 25, 2001, on-line edition.

61. For an example of a social choice analysis of the pattern of majority, concurring, and dissenting opinions in Bush v. Gore, see Abramowicz and Stearns (2001).

62. The Court that decided that case included six Republican appointees and three Democrats. Rehnquist, a Nixon appointee, was on the Court but recused himself from the case. The other Republicans on the Court were Lewis Powell (Nixon appointee), Harry Blackmun (Nixon), Chief Justice Warren Burger (Nixon), Potter Stewart (Eisenhower), and the liberal William Brennan (Eisenhower). The three Democratic appointees were Thurgood Marshall (Johnson), Byron White (Kennedy), and William Douglas (Roosevelt).

63. See Balkin (2001) ("if the Court's 'political capital' is judged by whether politicians are well or ill disposed toward the Supreme Court, then the Supreme Court may well have *increased* its political capital in the short term by halting the recounts"; the author thanked Sandy Levinson for suggesting the point).

64. Tom Kenworthy, "Americans Worry about Court's Election Role," *USA Today*, Dec. 11, 2000, on-line edition; "Nation Split over Florida Recount But Trusts U.S. Supreme Court," CNN.com, Dec. 10, 2000.

65. Klarman (2001) distinguishes eight relevant factors that impact on the Court's reputation or support in the political system: the amount of support or opposition for the Court's decisions; the intensity of that support or opposition; the relative power of the affected constituencies; the level of confidence that a decision will be implemented (rather than evaded or nullified); the lingering nature of the issues involved in the decision; changes in public opinion about a decision; the ability of the Court to modulate the results of a decision in later cases; and whether controversial rulings come in bunches or are scattered among less troubling decisions.

66. Charles Babington, *Washington Post*, March 13, 2001, on-line edition.

67. Sam Issacharoff, "The Court in the Crossfire," *New York Times*, Dec. 14, 2000, on-line edition; see also Editorial, "Supreme Court Fault Lines," *New York Times*, Dec. 14, 2000, on-line edition ("the opinion offered at least a hope that the court might someday apply the same concerns more broadly in elections to insure equal voting rights").

68. Powe (2000).

69. See Silverstein (1994).

70. See Planned Parenthood v. Casey (1992), Lee v. Weisman (1992), Santa Fe Independent School District v. Doe (2000), Texas v. Johnson (1989), United States v. Virginia (1996), Romer v. Evans (1996), and United States v. Dickerson (2000).

71. Not all progressive law professors agree; see Tushnet (1999).

72. See White (1957), Bloch (1959), Davis (1959), *American Bar Association* (1958, 1959); Conference of Chief Justices (1958). Prominent criticisms from elite law professors include Bickel and Wellington (1957), Hand (1958), Hart (1959), Griswold (1960), and (most famously) Wechsler (1959). For a contemporaneous overview of these criticisms, see Lewis (1961). For more recent overviews, see Powe (2000) and Rosenberg (2000).

73. See Dudziak (2000).

74. See Murphy (1962), Pritchett (1961), McCloskey (1972), and Powe (2000).

75. McCloskey (1972:307–8, 351–60).

76. Pildes (2001).

77. Consider Yoo (2001): "Many in legal academia welcomed *Planned Parenthood v. Casey* when it first appeared. I would hazard a guess that many of these same supporters of *Casey* have not rushed to embrace *Bush v. Gore*. Yet, *Casey* contained the seeds – the claims to judicial supremacy, the aggrandized notions of the Court's role in American society – that would blossom in *Bush*. Indeed, one can even view the emergence of the per curiam opinion – clearly the work of Justices Kennedy and O'Connor – as evidence of an ultimately failed effort to rebuild the coalition that had produced the unprecedented *Casey* plurality. As in *Casey*, in *Bush* the Court sought to end a national debate that it feared was tearing the country apart."

78. Balkin (2001): "I don't doubt that very bright conservative legal scholars will be able to rewrite Bush v. Gore to make it make sense. That project, I expect, is already well under way. . . . The more powerful and influential the people who are willing to make a legal argument, the more quickly it moves from the positively loony to the positively thinkable, and ultimately to something entirely consistent with 'good legal craft.'" With enough time and effort, these decisions are no longer seen as "off the wall. They *are* the wall."

79. Tushnet (2001).

80. See Low, Jeffries, and Bonnie (1986:100).

81. See Klarman (2001 and 1991), Powe (2000:227–28), Lewis (1963), and Paulsen (1964).

82. Robert G. Kaiser, "1876's Parallels Hold No Comfort," *Washington Post,* Dec. 17, 2000, A34; "Who Won the 1876 Election?" www.msys.net/cress/ballots2/1876_who.htm (first published in *Buttons and Ballots* 9 [spring 1997]).

83. Charles Lane, "Rehnquist: Court Can Prevent a Crisis," *Washington Post,* Jan. 19, 2001, A24. The speech was given on January 7.

84. 17 Cong. Rec. 817–18 (1886)(Sen. Sherman).

SELECTED BIBLIOGRAPHY

Abramowicz, Michael, and Maxwell L. Stearns. 2001. Beyond Counting Votes: The Political Economy of Bush v. Gore. George Mason University School of Law, Law and Economics Research Papers Series no. 01–09. papers.ssrn.com.

Ackerman, Bruce. 2001. The Court Packs Itself. *The American Prospect*, on-line edition. Feb. 12, 2001. www.prospect.org.

Adamany, David W., and Joel B. Grossman. 1983. Support for the Supreme Court as a National Policymaker. *Law and Policy Quarterly* 5:405–37.

American Bar Association. 1958. Editorial: Controversy about the Judiciary. *American Bar Association Journal* 44:1070.

———. 1959. Editorial: The Right to Criticize. *American Bar Association Journal* 45:262.

Atkinson, David N. 1999. *Leaving the Bench: Supreme Court Justices at the End.* Lawrence: University Press of Kansas.

Balbus, Isaac D. 1977. *The Dialectics of Legal Repression: Black Rebels before the American Courts.* New Brunswick, N.J.: Transaction Books.

Balkin, Jack M. 2001. Bush v. Gore and the Boundary between Law and Politics. *Yale Law Journal.* Forthcoming.

Baum, Lawrence. 1997. *The Puzzle of Judicial Behavior.* Ann Arbor: University of Michigan Press.

Bickel, Alexander. 1962. *The Least Dangerous Branch: The Supreme Court at the Bar of Politics.* Indianapolis: Bobbs-Merrill.

Bickel, Alexander M., and Harry M. Wellington. 1957. Legislative Purpose and the Judicial Process: The Lincoln Mills Case. *Harvard Law Review* 71:1–39.

Bloch, Charles J. 1959. The School Segregation Cases: A Legal Error That Should Be Corrected. *American Bar Association Journal* 45:27–30, 97–99.

Brenner, Saul. 1990. Measuring Policy Leadership on the U.S. Supreme Court: A Focus on Majority Opinion Authorship. In *Studies in U.S. Supreme Court Behavior.* Edited by Harold J. Spaeth and Saul Brenner, 136–48. New York: Garland.

Breyer, Stephen G. 1998. The Work of the Supreme Court. *Bulletin of the American Academy of Arts and Science* 52 (Sept.–Oct.): 47–58.

Burgess, John W. 1888. The Law of the Electoral Count. *Political Science Quarterly* 3:633–53.

Burton, Steven J. 1992. *Judging in Good Faith.* Cambridge: Cambridge University Press.

Caldeira, Gregory A. 1986. Neither the Purse nor the Sword: The Dynamics of Public Confidence in the United States Supreme Court. *American Political Science Review* 80:1209–26.

Caldeira, Gregory A., and James L. Gibson. 1992. The Etiology of Public Support for the Supreme Court. *American Journal of Political Science* 36:635–64.

Carter, Lief H. 1998. *Reason in Law.* 5th edition. New York: Longman.

Casper, Jonathan D. 1976. The Supreme Court and National Policymaking. *American Political Science Review* 70:50–63.

Clayton, Cornell. 1999. Law, Politics, and the Rehnquist Court: Structural Influences on Supreme Court Decision Making. In *The Supreme Court in American Politics: New Institutionalist Interpretations.* Edited by Howard Gillman and Cornell Clayton. Lawrence: University Press of Kansas.

Clayton, Cornell, and Howard Gillman, eds. 1999. *Supreme Court Decision-Making: New Institutionalist Approaches.* Chicago: University of Chicago Press.

Conference of Chief Justices. 1958. Re: The Supreme Court of the United States: Report and Resolution of the Conference of Chief Justices. *Georgia Bar Journal* 21:139.

Cushman, Barry. 1998. *Rethinking the New Deal Court: The Structure of a Constitutional Revolution.* New York: Oxford University Press.

Cross, Frank B. 2001. "The Courts and Partisan Politics." Unpublished manuscript.

————. 1997. Political Science and the New Legal Realism: A Case of Unfortunate Interdisciplinary Ignorance. *Northwestern University Law Review* 92:251–326.

Dahl, Robert. 1957. Decision-Making in a Democracy: The Supreme Court as a National Policymaker. *Journal of Public Law* 6:279–95.

Daniels, William. 1973. The Supreme Court and Its Publics. *Albany Law Review* 37:632–61.

Davis, Charles H. 1959. Constitutional Law: The States and the Supreme Court. *American Bar Association Journal* 45:233–36, 311–12.

Dougan, Michael B. 1992. John McLean. In *The Oxford Companion to the Supreme Court of the United States.* Edited by Kermit L. Hall, 539–40. New York: Oxford University Press.

Dougherty, J. Hampden. 1906. *The Electoral System of the United States.* New York: Putnam.

Dudziak, Mary L. 2001. "The Whole World Is Watching This US Farce": Images of American Democracy in Election 2000. Unpublished manuscript.

————. 2000. *Cold War Civil Rights: Race and the Image of American Democracy.* Princeton, N.J.: Princeton University Press.

Dworkin, Ronald. 1996. *Freedom's Law: The Moral Reading of the American Constitution.* Cambridge: Harvard University Press.

Easton, David. 1975. A Re-Assessment of the Concept of Political Support. *British Journal of Political Science* 5:435–57.

Edwards, Harry T. 1998. Collegiality and Decision Making on the D.C. Circuit. *Virginia Law Review* 84:1335–70.

————. 1985. Public Misperceptions Concerning the "Politics" of Judging: Dispelling Some Myths about the D.C. Circuit. *University of Colorado Law Review* 56:619–46.

Eisenstein, James, and Herbert Jacob. 1977. *Felony Justice: An Organizational Analysis of Criminal Cases.* Boston: Little, Brown.

Ely, John Hart. 1980. *Democracy and Distrust.* Cambridge: Harvard University Press.

Epstein, Lee, and Jack Knight. 1998. *The Choices Justices Make.* Washington, D.C.: Congressional Quarterly.

Epstein, Lee, Jeffrey A. Segal, Harold J. Spaeth, and Thomas G. Walker. 1996. *The Supreme Court Compendium: Data, Decisions and Developments.* 2d edition. Washington, D.C.: Congressional Quarterly.

Epstein, Richard. 2001. "In Such Manner as the Legislature Shall Direct": The Outcome in *Bush v. Gore* Defended. In *The Vote: Bush, Gore, and the Supreme Court.* Edited by Cass R. Sunstein and Richard A. Epstein. Chicago: University of Chicago Press.

Ewick, Patricia, and Susan S. Silbey. 1998. *The Common Place of Law: Stories from Everyday Life.* Chicago: University of Chicago Press.

Fairman, Charles. 1988. *Five Justices and the Electoral Commission of 1877.* History of the Supreme Court of the United States, vol. 7, supplement. New York: Macmillan.

Friedman, Barry. 1993. Dialogue and Judicial Review. *Michigan Law Review* 91:577–682.

Fuller, Lon L. 1964. *The Morality of Law.* New Haven: Yale University Press.

Garrett, Elizabeth. 2001. Leaving the Decision to Congress. In *The Vote: Bush, Gore, and the Supreme Court.* Edited by Cass R. Sunstein and Richard A. Epstein. Chicago: University of Chicago Press.

George, Tracey E. 1998. Development a Positive Theory of Decisionmaking on U.S. Courts of Appeals. *Ohio State Law Journal* 58:1635–96.

Gibson, James L. 1989. Understandings of Justice: Institutional Legitimacy, Procedural Justice, and Political Tolerance. *Law and Society Review* 23:469–96.

———. 1983. From Simplicity to Complexity: The Development of Theory in the Study of Judicial Behavior. *Political Behavior* 5:7–49.

Gillman, Howard. 2001. What's Law Got to Do with It? Judicial Behavioralists Test the "Legal Model" of Judicial Decision Making. *Law and Social Inquiry.* Forthcoming.

———. 1993. *The Constitution Besieged: The Rise and Demise of Lochner Era Police Powers Jurisprudence.* Durham, N.C.: Duke University Press.

Gillman, Howard, and Cornell Clayton, eds. 1999. *The Supreme Court in American Politics: New Institutionalist Interpretations.* Lawrence: University Press of Kansas.

Goldman, Sheldon. 1997. *Picking Federal Judges: Lower Court Selection from Roosevelt through Reagan.* New Haven: Yale University Press.

Graber, Mark A. 1999. The Problematic Establishment of Judicial Review. In *The Supreme Court in American Politics: New Institutionalist Interpretations.* Edited by Howard Gillman and Cornell Clayton. Lawrence: University Press of Kansas.

———. 1998. Federalist or Friends of Adams: The Marshall Court and Party Politics. *Studies in American Political Development* 12:229–66.

———. 1995. The Passive-Aggressive Virtues: Cohens v. Virginia and the Problematic Establishment of Judicial Power. *Constitutional Commentary* 12:67–92.

———. 1993. The Non-Majoritarian Difficulty: Legislative Deference to the Judiciary. *Studies in American Political Development* 7:35–73.

Griffin, Stephen M. 1996. *American Constitutionalism: From Theory to Politics.* Princeton: Princeton University Press.

Griswold, Erwin M. 1960. The Supreme Court 1959 Term—Foreword: Of Time and Attitudes—Professor Hart and Judge Arnold. *Harvard Law Review* 74:81–94.

Hand, Learned. 1958. *The Bill of Rights.* Cambridge: Harvard University Press.

Handberg, Roger. 1984. Public Opinion and the United States Supreme Court, 1935–1981. *International Social Science Review* 59:3–13.

Hart, Henry M., Jr. 1959. The Supreme Court 1958 Term—Foreword: The Time Chart of the Justices. *Harvard Law Review* 73:84–125.

Haworth, Paul L. 1906. *The Hayes-Tilden Election.* Cleveland: Burrows Brothers.

Hensley, Thomas R., and Scott P. Johnson. 1998. Unanimity on the Rehnquist Court. *Akron Law Review* 31:387–408.

Hughes, Charles Evans. 1928. *The Supreme Court of the United States. Its Foundation, Methods, and Achievement: An Interpretation.* New York: Columbia University Press.

Issacharoff, Samuel, Pamela S. Karlan, and Richard H. Pildes. 2001. *When Elections Go Bad: The Law of Democracy and the 2000 Presidential Election.* Westbury, N.Y.: Foundation.

———. 1998. *The Law of Democracy: Legal Structure of the Political Process.* Westbury, N.Y.: Foundation.

Jaros, Dean, and Robert Roper. 1980. The Supreme Court, Myth, Diffuse Support, Specific Support, and Legitimacy. *American Politics Quarterly* 8:85–105.

Jenkins, Jeffrey A., and Brian R. Sala. 1998. A Spatial Theory of Voting and the Presidential Election of 1824. *American Journal of Political Science* 42:1157–1179.

Klarman, Michael J. 2001. *Bush v. Gore* through the Lens of Constitutional History. *California Law Review.* Forthcoming.

———. 1996. Rethinking the Civil Rights and Civil Liberties Revolutions. *Virginia Law Review* 82:1–67.

———. 1991. An Interpretive History of Modern Equal Protection. *Michigan Law Review* 90:213–318.

Kluger, Richard. 1976. *Simple Justice: A History of Brown v. Board of Education and Black America's Struggle for Equality.* New York: Knopf.

Lehne, Richard, and John Reynolds. 1978. The Impact of Judicial Activism on Public Opinion. *American Journal of Political Science* 22:896–904.

Lewis, Anthony. 1961. The Supreme Court and Its Critics. *Minnesota Law Review* 45:305–32.

Lewis, Thomas P. 1963. The Sit-in Cases: Great Expectations. *Supreme Court Review* 1963:101–51.

Lind, Allan E., and Tom R. Tyler. 1988. *The Social Psychology of Procedural Justice.* New York: Plenum.

Lloyd, Randall D. 1995. Separating Partisanship from Party in Judicial Research: Reapportionment in the U.S. District Courts. *American Political Science Review* 89:413–20.

Low, Peter W., John Calvin Jeffries, Jr., and Richard J. Bonnie. 1986. *Criminal Law: Cases and Materials.* 2d edition. Mineola, N.Y.: Foundation.

Maltzman, Forrest, James F. Spriggs II, and Paul J. Wahlbeck. 2000. *Crafting Law on the Supreme Court: The Collegial Game.* Cambridge: Cambridge University Press.

Marshall, Thomas. 1989. *Public Opinion and the Supreme Court.* New York: Longman.

Mason, Alpheus Thomas. 1956. *Harlan Fiske Stone: Pillar of the Law.* New York: Viking.

McCloskey, Robert G. 2000. *The American Supreme Court.* 3d edition, revised by Sanford Levinson. Chicago: University of Chicago Press.

———. 1972. *The Modern Supreme Court.* Cambridge: Harvard University Press.

McConnell, Michael W. 2001. Two-and-a-Half Cheers for *Bush v. Gore.* In *The Vote: Bush, Gore, and the Supreme Court.* Edited by Cass R. Sunstein and Richard A. Epstein. Chicago: University of Chicago Press.

Mondak, Jeffrey J. 1990. Perceived Legitimacy of Supreme Court Decisions: Three Functions of Source Credibility. *Political Behavior* 12:363–84.

———. 1991. Substantive and Procedural Aspects of Supreme Court Decisions as Determinants of Institutional Approval. *American Politics Quarterly* 19:174–88.

Murphy, Bruce Allen. 1982. *The Brandeis/Frankfurter Connection: The Secret Political Activities of Two Supreme Court Justices.* New York: Oxford University Press.

Murphy, Walter F. 1964. *Elements of Judicial Strategy.* Chicago: University of Chicago Press.

———. 1962. *Congress and the Court: A Case Study in the American Political Process.* Chicago: University of Chicago Press.

Murphy, Walter F., and Joseph Tanenhaus. 1968. Public Opinion and the United States Supreme Court: A Preliminary Mapping of Some Prerequisites for Court Legitimation of Regime Changes. *Law and Society Review* 2:357–82.

———. 1990. Publicity, Public Opinion, and the Court. *Northwestern University Law Review* 84:985–1023.

Nardulli, Peter F., James Eisenstein, and Roy B. Flemming. 1988. *The Tenor of Justice: Criminal Courts and the Guilty Plea Process.* Urbana: University of Illinois Press.

O'Fallon, James M. 1993. The Case of Benjamin More: A Lost Episode in the Struggle over the Repeal of the 1801 Judiciary Act. *Law and History Review* 11:43–57.

———. 1992. "Marbury." *Stanford Law Review* 44:219–60.

Paulsen, Monrad G. 1964. The Sit-in Cases of 1964: "But Answer Came There None." *Supreme Court Review* 1964:137–70.

Peretti, Terri Jennings. 1999. *In Defense of a Political Court.* Princeton, N.J.: Princeton University Press.

Peter, Ryan M. 1996. Counsels, Councils and Lunch: Preventing Abuse of the Power to Appoint Independent Counsels. *University of Pennsylvania Law Review* 144:2537–.

Pildes, Richard H. 2001. Law, Order, and Democracy. *University of Chicago Law Review.* Forthcoming.

Pinello, Daniel R. 1999. Linking Party to Judicial Ideology in American Courts: A Meta-Analysis. *Justice System Journal* 20:219–54.

Posner, Richard A. 2001. Florida 2000: A Legal and Statistical Analysis of the Election Deadlock and the Ensuing Litigation. *Supreme Court Review.* Forthcoming.

Pound, Roscoe. 1908. Mechanical Jurisprudence. *Columbia Law Review* 8:605–23.

Powe, Lucas A., Jr. 2000. *The Warren Court and American Politics.* Cambridge: Harvard University Press.

Pritchett, C. Herman. 1961. *Congress versus the Supreme Court, 1957–1960.* Minneapolis: University of Minnesota Press.

Revesz, Richard L. 1999. Ideology, Collegiality, and the D.C. Circuit: A Reply to Chief Judge Harry T. Edwards. *Virginia Law Review* 85:805–51.

Rosenberg, Gerald N. 2000. Mythmaker, Mythmaker, Make Me a Myth: Brown and the Creation of American Ideology. Unpublished manuscript.

Scheppele, Kim Lane. 2001. When the Law Doesn't Count: The 2000 Election and the Failure of the Rule of Law. *University of Pennsylvania Law Review.* Forthcoming.

Schwartz, Herman. 2000. *The Struggle for Constitutional Justice in Post-Communist Europe.* Chicago: University of Chicago Press.

Segal, Jeffrey A. 1990. Supreme Court Support for the Solicitor General: The Effect of Presidential Appointments. *Western Political Quarterly* 43:137–52.

Segal, Jeffrey A., and Harold J. Spaeth. 1993. *The Supreme Court and the Attitudinal Model.* New York: Cambridge University Press.

Shapiro, Martin. 1984. Recent Developments in Political Jurisprudence. *Western Political Quarterly* 36:541–48.

———. 1981. *Courts: A Comparative and Political Analysis.* Chicago: University of Chicago Press.

———. 1964. *Law and Politics in the Supreme Court: New Approaches to Political Jurisprudence.* New York: Free Press.

Shklar, Judith N. 1986. *Legalism: Law, Moralism, and Political Trials.* Cambridge: Harvard University Press.

Silverstein, Mark. 1994. *Judicious Choices: The New Politics of Supreme Court Confirmations.* New York: Norton.

Sisk, Gregory C., Michael Heise, and Andrew P. Morriss. 1998. Charting the Influences on the Judicial Mind: An Empirical Study of Judicial Reasoning. *New York University Law Review* 73:1377–1500.

Songer, Donald R., Reginald S. Sheehan, and Susan B. Haire. 2000. *Continuity and Change on the United States Court of Appeals.* Ann Arbor: University of Michigan Press.

Spriggs, James F., and Paul J. Wahlbeck. 1995. Calling It Quits: Strategic Retirement on the Federal Courts of Appeals, 1893–1991. *Political Research Quarterly* 48:573–97.

Stephenson, Donald Grier, Jr. 1999. *Campaigns and the Court: The U.S. Supreme Court in Presidential Elections.* New York: Columbia University Press.

Stoner, James R., Jr. 2001. Two Elections, Two Constitutionalisms. Unpublished manuscript.

Strauss, David A. 2001. *Bush v. Gore*: What Were They Thinking? In *The Vote: Bush, Gore, and the Supreme Court.* Edited by Cass R. Sunstein and Richard A. Epstein. Chicago: University of Chicago Press.

Strum, Philippa. 1974. *The Supreme Court and "Political Questions": A Study in Judicial Evasion.* Birmingham: University of Alabama Press.

Sunstein, Cass R. 2001. Order without Law. In *The Vote: Bush, Gore, and the Supreme Court.* Edited by Cass R. Sunstein and Richard A. Epstein. Chicago: University of Chicago Press.

Sweet, Alec Stone. 1999. Judicialization and the Construction of Governance. *Comparative Political Studies* 32:147–84.

Tanenhaus, Joseph, and Walter F. Murphy. 1981. Patterns of Public Support for the Supreme Court: A Panel Study. *Journal of Politics* 43:24–39.

Thompson, E. P. 1975. *Whigs and Hunters: The Origins of the Black Act.* New York: Pantheon.

Tushnet, Mark. 2001. Renormalizing Bush v. Gore. Unpublished manuscript.

———. 1999. *Taking the Constitution away from the Courts.* Princeton: Princeton University Press.

Tyler, Tom R. 1990. *Why People Follow the Law: Procedural Justice, Legitimacy, and Compliance.* New Haven: Yale University Press.

Wald, Patricia M. 1999. A Response to Tiller and Cross. *Columbia Law Review* 99:235–61.

Wechsler, Herbert. 1959. Toward Neutral Principles of Constitutional Law. *Harvard Law Review* 73:1–35.

White, Thomas Raeburn. 1957. Construing the Constitution: The New "Sociological" Approach. *American Bar Association Journal* 43:1085–88, 1152–55.

Whittington, Keith E. 1999. *Constitutional Construction: Divided Powers and Constitutional Meaning*. Cambridge: Harvard University Press.

Woodward, Bob, and Scott Armstrong. 1979. *The Brethren: Inside the Supreme Court*. New York: Simon and Schuster.

Woodward, C. Vann. 1951. *Reunion and Reaction: The Compromise of 1877 and the End of Reconstruction*. Boston: Little, Brown.

Yoo, John. 2001. Legitimately Criticizing the Court's Critical Legitimacy. *University of Chicago Law Review*. Forthcoming.

TABLE OF CASES

The following are the full citations for the federal and state appellate cases referred to in the text. Citations to other court filings and lower court decisions can be found in the endnotes.

U.S. Courts of Appeal Cases

Florida Supreme Court Cases

INDEX

decision making in ordinary circumstances, 6–10
good faith judging on part of, 7, 12
impeachment of, 8
as partisan activists, 7
political capital of, 10, 270n. 65
and political consensus, 6
political pressures, 7–8, 10, 200
political sympathies vs. legal decisions,
32–33, 268n. 48
presidential appointments and, 6, 12
value-voting of, 6–7
judicial activism. *See also* Article II of the
U.S. Constitution; judicial partisanship
accusations of, against Florida Supreme
Court, 5, 68–70, 71–72, 81–83,
117–18, 180–84
accusations of, against U.S. Supreme
Court, 5, 151–63, 185–206
judicial authority, election disputes and,
223n. 1
judicial bad faith, accusations of, 12, 72,
198. *See also* judicial partisanship
judicial ideology
in *Bush v. Gore,* 123
effect of, on judges, 7, 55, 173, 175–76,
225n. 20, 261n. 91
and Florida Supreme Court, 55
in *Harris v. Gore* decision, 116
and political ideology, 32–33, 123, 152
judicial impartiality
as basis of rule of law, 8
Birch's comments on, 106, 173
of dissenting judges, 205–6
and Florida Supreme Court, 180–84
Lewis ruling on late returns and, 46–47
relation of, to political capital, 10
and public confidence, 9
Rehnquist's comments on, 173
Thomas's comments on, 172
judicial partisanship
accusations of, in *Bush v. Gore,* 123,
125–28, 153, 154–56, 174–75, 185–206

assessement of, regarding Florida
Supreme Court, 180–84
assessment of, regarding lower court
judges, 176–80
assessment of, regarding U.S. Supreme
Court, 151–63, 185–206
commentators' consensus on, 47, 174
connection of, to appointing president,
225n. 21
and early opinion about U.S. Supreme
Court, 76, 186
Eleventh Circuit Court pattern of,
178–80
in *Gore v. Harris,* 51
in *Harris v. Florida Elections Canvassing
Commission,* 139
and insincere legal interpretation,
174–75
law school professors and, 163–64
New Republic article on, 46
press comments on, 126–28, 152
and Scalia concurring opinion, 124–25
in *Siegel v. LePore,* 179
Tjoflat's accusation of, 106
judicial politics, 225n. 16. *See also* judicial
ideology; judicial partisanship
in ordinary circumstances, 6–10
and challenges of election 2000, 10–12
Judiciary Act of 1801, 226n. 26

Kamiya, Gary, 157
Karlan, Pamela, 36
Katyal, Neal Kumar, 157
Kennedy, Anthony M., 184
conservatism of, 32
defense of decision by, 265n. 5
on Florida Supreme Court reading of
law, 184
percentage civil liberties votes of, 233n.
61
per curiam opinion of, 141
questions during oral arguments by,
131, 132, 267n. 41
and writing of opinion, 153